# The Spirit of Allah

# The
# Spirit of
# Allah

## Amir Taheri

**Hutchinson**
London Melbourne Auckland Johannesburg

*In the name of Allah,*
*the Merciful,*
*the Compassionate*

# Contents

*Appendices*

*Maps*

# Illustrations

# *Chronology*

1902   Ruhollah is born in Khomein

1903   Sayyed Mostafa, Ruhollah's father, dies in a brawl

1906   Mozaffareddin Shah promulgates a constitution in which mullahs are given power of veto on all legislation

1910–11   Struggle between the constitutional government and the despotic Mohammad-Ali Shah, who is eventually deposed. Hojat al-Islam Shaikh Fazlollah Nuri, the standard bearer of fundamentalist mullahs, is hanged in Tehran

1918–19   Foreign troops occupying Iran leave the country. Ruhollah moves to Arak and attends a theological seminary. Then follows Shaikh Abdul-Karim to Qom where he settles

1921   A coup d'état is led by Sayyed Ziaeddin and Reza Khan

1922–26   Reza Khan achieves supreme power. He arranges his own election as the King of Kings, founding the Pahlavi dynasty

1927–40   Reza Shah pursues his secularization campaign; revolts by mullahs are brutally suppressed and the central government imposes its authority throughout the country; the wearing of the veil is prohibited and mullahs are forced to shave and wear a kepi instead of the traditional turban

1941–   British and Soviet troops invade and occupy Iran. Reza Shah is forced to abdicate and goes into exile; his son Mohammad-Reza is sworn in as Shah

1942    Khomeini publishes the first edition of his *Kashf al-Asrar* (*Key to the Secrets*)

1949    Grand Ayatollah Borujerdi leads an extended seminar on the political role of the clergy. Ruhollah is present and sides with the activist faction

1951    Premier Haj-Ali Razmara is assassinated by a member of the Fedayeen of Islam organization. Mossadeq takes over as Premier and the Shah gives the royal assent to a bill nationalizing Iran's oil industry. Relations are severed with Britain and the Royal Navy imposes an embargo on Iran's oil exports

1952–    Mossadeq and the Shah are locked in a struggle for power. Ayatollah Kashani sides with Mossadeq at first but later abandons him for the Shah. Khomeini is active alongside Kashani

1953–54    The Communist Tudeh Party flexes its muscles. The Shah–Mossadeq rivalry comes to a head. The Shah leaves the country, but is returned after an army coup organized with US and British support

1955    A new oil agreement is concluded with major British, American and French companies. SAVAK comes into being and Communists are hunted down. A 600-strong network of pro-Soviet officers is uncovered within the armed forces

1959    The Shah and US President Eisenhower sign a military agreement which the Shah interprets as an American guarantee for his own regime

1960    Borujerdi opposes a moderate law on land reform and is supported by other mullahs. The Shah gives in by asking the government to annul the act. Khomeini publishes the first edition of his *Towzih al-Masayel* (*Explication of Problems*) and begins to be known as an ayatollah

1961–62    Bazaari elements opposed to the Shah establish contact with Khomeini. Borujerdi's death leads to a struggle for succession and Ayatollah Hakim Tabataba'i emerges as victor. Khomeini assumes the title of Grand Ayatollah

1963    Khomeini launches his campaign against the Shah and the latter's reform projects aimed at distribution of land among peasants, emancipation of women and the opening of local government posts to non-Muslims. Khomeini is arrested and taken to Tehran. This leads to mass riots in Tehran and several other cities. Many are killed shouting: 'Hail to Khomeini'.

1964    Khomeini is released from prison but kept under house arrest in Tehran. He is eventually allowed to return to Qom where he resumes his attacks on the government. He singles out for criticism a law extending diplomatic immunity to American military personnel in Iran. He is arrested and forced into exile in Turkey

1965    Premier Hassan-Ali Mansur is assassinated on the orders of Khomeini's aides in Tehran. Amir Abbas Hoveyda takes over as Prime Minister

1966    Khomeini quarrels with the Turkish authorities over their refusal to allow him to wear his religious dress and obtains permission to leave for Iraq after several months of residence in Izmir, Ankara, Istanbul and Bursa. He settles in the holy city of Najaf

1967    The Muslim world is shaken by the defeat of the Arabs by Israel. Ayatollah Mohammad-Baqer Sadr meets Khomeini and suggests an Islamic struggle against the Jewish state

1968    Khomeini resumes his seminary and attracts new students; his circle grows thanks to his radicalism

1969–71    Khomeini makes repeated calls on Iranians to rise against the Shah but is ignored. He particularly denounces the twenty-fifth centenary celebration of the Persian Empire. His aides in Tehran expand their organization and create secret cells in a number of cities

1972–76    Khomeini's lectures attract more and more students in Najaf. Anti-Shah students come to visit him from Europe and the United States. He publishes the first edition of his *Valayat-e-Faqih* (*The Regency of the*

*Theologian*). A more polemical version is also published under the title of *Hokumat-e-Eslami* (*Islamic Government*) and is an attack on the theories of Grand Ayatollah Kho'i

1977    Yazdi advises Khomeini to intensify his anti-Shah campaign, claiming that the new US Administration of President Jimmy Carter wants the Shah to go. Khomeini issues an edict 'deposing' the Shah. The Shah and Carter exchange state visits

1978    The daily *Ettelaat* in Tehran publishes a fake letter insulting Khomeini. There are riots in Qom and, later, in Tabriz and a dozen other cities. Hundreds are killed in clashes with the security forces. Khomeini calls for the overthrow of the Shah and is expelled from Iraq. He goes to France and continues his attacks on the Shah as the tide of revolution sweeps everything in its path

1979    Khomeini returns from exile two weeks after the Shah leaves Iran and is greeted by millions. Bakhtiar's Cabinet disintegrates and the revolution is victorious. In a referendum, the people approve the formation of an Islamic Republic. The American Embassy in Tehran is raided and occupied by revolutionary students who seize the diplomats there hostage. Hundreds of former officials are executed

1980–   Executions continue. The coalition formed under Khomeini begins to suffer serious divisions. Iraq invades Iran and scores major early victories. Bani-Sadr is elected President but a general election gives control of Parliament to his rival Beheshti. An abortive attempt by a US task force to free the hostages fails in the Tabas desert making the future of the captives look bleak. But secret talks between Beheshti and Carter, through special emissaries, lead to a final accord on the release of the hostages

1981    The American hostages are released twenty minutes after Reagan is sworn in as the new President of the United States. The struggle between Bani-Sadr and Beheshti comes to a head. Khomeini backs Beheshti, who emerges victorious. Bani-Sadr concludes an alliance with the Mujahedeen who launch an armed insurrection and, later, murder over two thousand mullahs and top officials, including Beheshti. Bani-Sadr is deposed as President, flees to France and joins the opposition to Khomeini. Iran scores victories in the war with Iraq and Khorramshahr is liberated

1982–83    The new wave of repression, begun in the previous year, is intensified and between 5000 and 10,000 people, mostly supporters of the Mujahedeen, are executed. The number of political prisoners tops 40,000

Grand Ayatollah Shariatmadari is accused of involvement in a plot to kill Khomeini and is 'defrocked'. Ghotbzadeh is executed on a similar charge. Iranian forces carry the war into Iraqi territory but soon run out of steam. The mullahs consolidate their hold on power and purge their former allies in the fight against the Shah.

The top leaders of the pro-Soviet Tudeh Party are arrested and charged with high treason. Thousands of militants patrol the streets of major cities to impose 'Islamic' rules of dress and behaviour

1984–85    Khomeini is reported in poor health and orders a session of the Assembly of Experts which has the constitutional duty of choosing his successor. A tentative agreement is reached on Ayatollah Montazeri but deep divisions remain. The war continues in stalemate after reaching new depths of horror with the Iraqis' use of chemical weapons against Iran's child soldiers. The mullahs are deeply divided on almost all aspects of economic and foreign policy. Khomeini announces the 'annulment' of all laws passed before the revolution. But the decision is quietly forgotten and most of the old laws are applied in the absence of agreement on new ones. Khomeini orders an intensification of efforts to 'export' the Islamic Revolution, first to other Muslim countries and, later, to the whole world. Khomeini's thirty-page testament is deposited in a safe at the Islamic Majlis (Parliament) in Tehran with orders for it to be published within hours of his death.

1986–87    Grand Ayatollah Shariatmadari dies in Tehran
after Khomeini refuses to allow him to travel abroad
to seek medical treatment. Khomeini vetoes several
plans aimed at ending the Iran–Iraq war and vows to
press on with the conflict until an Islamic republic is
installed in Baghdad. Montazeri is officially declared
heir to the ayatollah but is immediately challenged
by both radical and conservative mullahs. Large
numbers of Montazeri's supporters and relatives are
arrested and charged with 'treason'. The leadership
in Tehran is shaken by revelations concerning
secret deals between senior mullahs and the United
States and the supply to Iran of arms from Israel.
Iranian forces score major victories against Iraq but
fail to capture the city of Basra. Khomeini's
appearances in public become less and less frequent
as his health continues to decline.

# Introduction

# *In Search of the Imam*

*O*ne autumn day in 1977 two reporters on the staff of the
Iranian newspaper I edited invited me to hear a cassette
which they took to be a 'master coup' by SAVAK, the Shah's
notorious secret police. The cassette was simply marked 'A Reli-
gious Sermon'. It began with a solemn voice[1] which introduced the
speaker in the following terms: 'The Supreme Guide of the
Islamic Nations, the Smasher of Idols, the One who Humbles
Satan, the Glorious Upholder of the Faith, the Sole Hope of the
Downtrodden, the Exalted Chief, the Vicar of Islam and of
Muslims, the Regent of the Hidden Imam, His Holiness Grand
Ayatollah Haj Sayyed Ruhollah Mussavi Khomeini, May Allah
Grant Him Eternal Life.'

The sermon that followed did indeed sound like a SAVAK
fabrication designed to discredit the Shah's most vociferous critic.
Its theme was the alleged collusion between the Shah and 'the Jews
and the Cross-worshippers' first to 'humiliate and then to
eliminate' Islam in Iran. The Shah, the preacher's voice continued, was 'plotting to make Muslims accept the rule of the
foreign enemies of Islam,' and had even commissioned a portrait
of Imam Ali, the fourth Caliph, which showed the Commander of
the Faithful with blue eyes and a blond beard.

When we listened to the tape, we all agreed that it was the work
of an actor imitating a *rowzeh-khan* (a preacher). How could
Khomeini ignore the real economic and political issues of the
country and make this direct appeal to the basest sentiments of
fanaticism among the illiterate masses? Khomeini was, in his own
way, an intellectual, we argued. He would not antagonize the intelligentsia by taking a deliberately obscurantist line.

The sermon, however, was genuine. It struck the very note of anger it had been aimed at. It frightened the 'little people' of Iran's sprawling, ill-equipped cities. Khomeini told them that not only were they being cheated of a decent life in this world, but by remaining silent witnesses to 'the crimes of the Shah against the Prophet and his descendants' they were now risking the loss of the next. The Shah had tried to teach the 'little people' how to live and had failed. Khomeini set out to teach them how to die and quickly succeeded. The astonished intelligentsia, opposed to the Shah for different reasons, at first waited and watched as the revolutionary storm, stirred by Khomeini, gathered force. Then they too joined the legions of 'the downtrodden' that the exiled Ayatollah brought onto the streets of Tehran.

In only a few months Khomeini was the undisputed leader of an unusual revolution. And on 11 February 1979 this frail-looking octogenarian, who had been chased out of his home and forced to leave the country fifteen years earlier, became the new ruler of Iran. But even then few Iranians knew much about Khomeini. They had observed the shape of his face in the full moon and thanked Allah for the blessing. They had listened to his passionate messages broadcast by the Persian service of the BBC from London. They had killed and died for him, as he had asked. And yet they hardly knew their new 'Imam'.

In 1968, when preparing a series of articles on the power struggle among the Grand Ayatollahs following the death of Grand Ayatollah Hakim in Iraq, I had made some inquiries about Khomeini among the mullahs in the holy cities of Qom and Mashhad. Almost to a man they dismissed him as an idealist who had condemned himself to life-long exile as a result of his uncontrollable passion. In Iran in those days the makers of history had to be recruited from among sober cynics; there was no room for passionate zealots like Khomeini.

In 1977 I resumed my inquiries about Khomeini both in Iran and Iraq with a view, which must now seem utterly naive, to help bring about a reconciliation between him and the Shah. Once Khomeini had seized control of Iran, my journalistic curiosity concerning his life and thoughts immediately became a moral necessity. I had to get to know this almost total stranger who had captured the imagination of my compatriots with his discourse and who was now changing beyond recognition the Iran I had grown to love above everything else. Over the next six years I put together the many pieces of a huge jigsaw, and at times my task was a mixture of detective work and social archaeology. Khomeini was the quintessential mullah, but he had nevertheless adopted Shaikh Abu-Sa'id's method of living so as to leave no personal trace behind. 'Your vanity is a barking dog,' the shaikh teaches. 'Silence it so that no one knows about your passage through this narrow alley which is life.'

The Ayatollah had always shunned inquiries into his private life and disliked talking about himself. Although he had no intention of passing through the narrow alley of life unnoticed, he made every effort to keep the barking dog silent. Even the cult of personality created around him failed to penetrate his inner life. On exceptional occasions he reminisced about his early life. Talking to members of the Iranian national soccer squad in 1979, for example, he recalled his own 'brief and undistinguished career' as a back in Khomein's football team in 1916. And his son, Sayyed Ahmad, was on two occasions authorized to talk about the Imam's life 'just as a man'. He related how the Imam had admonished him for killing the flies which made life 'unpleasant' in the holy city of Najaf. Even the flies had to be seen as creatures of Allah, and respected. And yet this same Imam had not interrupted his prayers when informed that his favourite daughter Sa'ideh, aged only seven, had died. And in 1980 he thanked Allah for having granted 'martyrdom' to his old and trusted friend Ayatollah Mohammad-Baqer Sadr in Iraq.[2]

Piecing together the Imam's jigsaw meant reading and pondering his countless speeches and interviews, as well as his books, which are not easy to digest. But most of all it meant interviewing people who for one reason or another had known the Imam at different stages of his long life. Almost everyone cooperated. It is thanks to their help that this book was made possible.

This book is the story of one man and his revolution. The Islamic Revolution was the first major political cataclysm in history to take place almost entirely in front of television cameras. The world watched in astonishment and dismay as millions of bearded men and women in *chadors*, electrified by religious passion, swarmed onto the streets of Tehran to end the world's oldest monarchy and chase away the world's longest reigning monarch. I witnessed the revolution right from its earliest moment. I did not join or support it. For I did not see the logic of passionate collective acts which, if committed by individuals, are considered reprehensible if not downright criminal. As far as I was concerned, like war, the revolution was a tragedy under any circumstances. A just war is difficult to define; a just revolution even more so. Nevertheless I did not oppose the revolution either; for in 1978–79 there seemed to be no opposing camp. I became a witness, like the 'observer' who, in so many Persian paintings, looks upon scenes of festivity or carnage. I saw the first revolutionary ladies in *chadors* gathering at street corners in Tehran and called them 'the ravens'. They reminded me of Hitchcock's *The Birds*, and their numbers multiplied even faster. Throughout much of the revolution I was in almost daily contact with both the revolutionary organizations and the authorities. On a single day I could meet half a dozen ayatollahs and almost as many generals across the de facto dividing line that was established in Tehran from October 1978 onwards. I also witnessed the Shah's rapid physical and moral decline. Consumed by cancer and often under sedation, the 'King of Kings' came to resemble a ghost in his sad winter palace.

This was a difficult revolution to gauge. In form and style it bore some resemblance to the French Revolution. But it rejected the French Revolution's trinity of values: liberty, equality and fraternity. Unlike the French Revolution, which advocated liberty as an absolute value, even, perhaps especially, against the Almighty, the Islamic Revolution was to end liberties taken with divine law and to restore men to their bondage with Allah. The Islamic Revolution also rejected the notion that men of all creeds could be equals and brothers. Women can never be treated as equal under Islam and non-believers can never enjoy the same rights as believers. The very concept of human rights was 'a Judeo-Christian invention' and inadmissible in Islam.[3] No, this was not a liberal 'bourgeois' revolution. Nor yet was it a confirmation of the Leninist theories of revolution and the state. The Islamic Revolution was not the violent expression of class struggle; it united under its banner both rich and poor. It did not aim to create a golden future but promised a return to a golden past.

During the past seven years many attempts have been made to minimize the role of Khomeini in conceiving and then realizing his design for an Islamic revolution and an Islamic state. Some students have desperately tried to portray the revolution as a movement for democratization in a society long atrophied by tyranny. To sustain such an analysis they have been obliged to present the role of Khomeini as merely secondary. For the Imam has no qualms about announcing that lesser mortals have no right to legislate their own affairs and that democracy can only lead to 'prostitution' [*sic*].

Others who have tried to study the Islamic Revolution in 'historical materialist' terms have also had to push Khomeini into the background.

Both liberal and Marxist historians have begrudged Khomeini his success in leading a revolution that bears his unmistakable personal imprint. And other chroniclers of the Islamic Revolution have failed to pay adequate attention to the Imam's role simply because they know so little about him. So they concentrate on telling and retelling events recorded on thousands of hours of video and in millions of newspaper words. But in this book I have tried to put the focus on Khomeini himself.

The success of the Imam in leading a religious revolution to victory in the twentieth century is a rare achievement. But his success in creating the world's first and only theocratic state since the fall of the Dalai Lama in Tibet is surely unique. The Imam's revolution is the only example of a successful Muslim revolt against a Western or Western-style system of government. He has succeeded where the Mahdi in Sudan, Imam Shamel in the Caucasus, Shaikh Hassan in Somalia and Imam Ghalib in Oman failed.

The story of Khomeini and his revolution is, of course, also the story of contemporary Iran. Khomeini is the quintessential, I am even tempted to say the inevitable, product of Iranian society. He does not describe his revolution as Iranian but as Islamic, and insists that Iran is only the first 'piece of land' where the rule of Allah is re-established. But Iran is not just any 'piece of land'. Khomeini inherited the world's fifteenth largest country in size, ranking twenty-fourth in population and thirteenth in gross national product. He also inherited foreign currency reserves of nearly £15,000 million, plus an oil industry earning £60 million a day. The Shah left behind the world's sixth largest army with the biggest arsenal of modern weapons in the whole of Asia. That army surrendered to Khomeini, who arrived from Paris with Eshraqi's steel nail-clipper the only weapon carried by his entourage. But the same army and its stockpiles of arms and spare parts helped the Imam withstand an Iraqi attack and threaten the closure of the Persian Gulf to international shipping.

But Iran in the past eighty-five years or so, the life span of the Imam, has also been an extremely unruly nation. In that period it has been ruled by two dynasties and six kings before the establishment of the Islamic Republic. Of the six kings of Iran in the period under study, one was assassinated and another died a broken man under the pressure of a constitutional revolution. All the other four were either forced to abdicate or were dethroned. Every one of them died in exile. Not a single one is even buried in Iran today. Of the forty-two Prime Ministers Iran has had in the same period, ten have been assassinated or executed and more than a dozen forced to flee into exile. In this century alone Iran has been invaded by Russian, British, Ottoman and Iraqi armies more than a dozen times, and has been completely occupied by foreign forces in both world wars, despite a declaration of neutrality on both occasions. In the past eighty years Iran has also experienced two revolutions, two coups d'état, a full scale civil war and two dozen major tribal uprisings. The first six years of the Imam's own rule were not quiet either, and there is no reason to believe that the established pattern of Iranian life through centuries has been irrevocably altered with the advent of divine stability. Iran, an old country, is a young nation, and it still has tremendous reserves of energy which can both build and destroy.

The Air France chartered Jumbo which brought the Imam home in 1979 was a political Noah's Ark. In it were politicians of every ilk, bursting with ideas and burning with ambition. Within two years of his historic journey the Imam had destroyed them all. Some were executed, others imprisoned or exiled. Those who just managed to escape with their lives and freedom have contentedly slipped into the historical footnotes reserved for them. Some of them we shall meet in our search for the Imam.

Finally, any story of the Imam and his revolution would be incomplete without reference to the Islamic Republic's far reaching plans to stir revolution throughout the Muslim world, from Indonesia to Morocco. The objective of the Imam, who considers all existing governments in Muslim countries to be illegitimate, is the creation of a single universal Islamic state which can emerge as a world power capable of standing up to the two 'satanic superpowers' of the day: the United States and the Soviet Union. If necessary, the Imam's Enteharis (kamikazes) are prepared to take the holy war into the heart of the 'satanic superpowers'. The Imam, whose many titles include 'He Who Broke the Trinity of Corruption',[4] was in 1985 still confident that his brand of Islam was on the verge of universal victory. But that is a story still to be told.

# 1

# *The Forgotten Oasis*

But let me turn to that beloved one who has been torn away from us; he who has many caravans of hearts accompanying him everywhere. Both High and Low praise his name, his memory, his words, his warm and combative spirit, his will of iron, his resilience, his courage, his vision, his boiling faith. . . . Yes, I mean the soul of all souls, the hero of all heroes, the light of the eyes and the beloved of the Iranian Nation, our esteemed and exalted Master His Holiness the Grand Ayatollah Khomeini. May Allah maintain his shadow. He is a Gift of Allah to our century, to our age. He is the living manifestation of the promise of the Holy Qur'an that Allah shall always dispatch one who is to smash His enemies and bring the wayward back to the Right Path.

Ayatollah Morteza Motahari

Oh, Khomeini! Thou art the Idol of fatherless thugs;
Thou art the Dracula of the Age –
Thirstier for blood than Attila and Genghis
Thy wine is the blood of our nation;
The henna for thy beard is the gore of the young slain.

Piruz Khaefi

Khomeini is a generalist, a kind of philosopher king who means to end corruption and then withdraw to his school at the holy city of Qom.

CIA Memo

*I* n the spring of 1979 Ayatollah Ruhollah Khomeini, then still living in the holy city of Qom where he had taken up residence after his triumphant return and brief stay in Tehran, received a fifty-man delegation from his native town Khomein. The visitors had brought with them a great jar of rosewater and basketfuls of pomegranates – practically all that Khomein had to offer. They also brought with them an invitation from the people of Khomein for the Ayatollah to visit that remote oasis on the fringes of the Iranian desert which he had left, never to return, over half a century earlier. Khomein wanted to honour its most, if not its sole, famous son. The town's main street, single square and only secondary school had already been renamed after the Ayatollah, whose name replaced that of the fallen Pahlavi Shah.

'Visit your own people, O smasher of idols,' the visitors' leader pleaded with the Ayatollah, who, as was his habit, sat on the floor with his eyes firmly fixed on his feet.

The visitors' leader continued, 'Thou art the Spirit of Allah, the Wise Master of Islam, the breath of eternal life on our smothered land. Wilt thou consent to bestow on the people of Khomein the honour and the glory of becoming dust under thy feet?'

The Ayatollah's reply was quick and sharp. 'No,' he said, still watching his toes. 'There will be no visit.'

According to some of those present, many of the visiting Khomeinis were clearly offended. For they loved and honoured their native soil, a land of almost undrinkable salty water and resolutely unyielding fields. But the Ayatollah's answer was characteristic. A few months earlier, on his historic Air France flight to Tehran from Paris, ending sixteen years of exile, the octogenarian doctor of theology had been asked a similar question by an unsuspecting French reporter.

'How does your holiness feel on his return home from such a long exile?' the Frenchman had demanded.[1]

'Nothing,' Khomeini had replied, ending the interview.

For Khomeini any attachment to a town, a country or any geographical entity is considered sinful, meriting expulsion to the lowest recesses of Gehenna. One should only love Allah, and absolutely no one and nothing but Him. Patriotism and nationalism are simply other names for *sherk*, or the belief that Allah should merely share one's love and affection with others. One cannot love even parents, children or friends and still claim to be a true Muslim. It is sufficient to love Allah and trust Him to extend to others who merit to be loved all the affection they deserve.

It had taken the Ayatollah a life of three generations to rid himself of the temptation to love anyone or anything but Allah, the One and the Only True God. In his earlier days, Ruhollah had known moments of great weakness. On occasions he had stood on the edge of the precipice of earthly attachment. He had learned, with how much courage and at the price of how much suffering we shall see, to hold back and to continue grasping the *habl al-mateen* (the firm rope) of faith.

.. No, he could not and would not visit Khomein. Why should he? True, he had been born there and spent his early years there. His father and mother were both buried in Khomein where his ancestral house, a shapeless edifice of mud and brick, had withstood the ravages of the harsh climate of the Iranian plateau. He might even remember the solitary plane tree on the outskirts of the humble town that had often provided him with shade on hot, dusty afternoons when he returned from work in his uncle's modest barley fields. Or he may have remembered the town's semi-derelict and often deserted mosque, a brick building built round a courtyard, at the centre of which stood a rectangular pond of green, stagnant water. The mosque's dome had lost many of its turquoise-blue tiles and the only form of life it supported often consisted of half a dozen old lean pigeons which had built themselves a nest on the mud-covered roof of the main prayer chamber. On Thursday evenings the mosque would be visited by the poor, the desperate and the forgotten ones of this world. Women would tie pieces of cloth to the long-dead tree standing by the pond. Some would weep, others would pray. And on Fridays half a dozen men, mostly old, would gather for communal prayers and recall the glorious days of Islam when every mosque throughout the universe of the Muhammedans had been filled with proud and eager believers, enjoying the pleasure of comradeship in the service of the Only God.

The Ayatollah may have remembered the skinny goats and sheep which, for want of adequate fodder, roamed the dusty streets of Khomein in search of anything that could be nibbled at – from discarded watermelon skins to pieces of cardboard and old newspapers. For several months, while working for his uncle, Ruhollah himself had been in charge of a small flock of sheep and goats, the main part of the family's wealth.

Khomein is one of those Iranian oasis towns that are often described as *akhar-e-khat* (literally, the end of the line). No one with any alternative home would choose to live here. Towns like

Khomein are, in fact, little more than big villages with a bazaar where local peasants exchange their produce for a limited range of necessities and inexpensive luxuries. The official census completed in 1978 showed that Khomein and its adjacent villages had a total population of around 25,000. But the old town itself boasted no more than 3000 souls. Featureless and unattractive, Khomein is hardly ever mentioned in the long history of Persia. The name itself is a curious mixture of *khom*, which in Persian means a jar, and the Arabic grammatical form designating duality. Thus Khomein means the Two Jars. The name originated in the seventh century when one of the Arab armies then embarked on the conquest of Iran camped at the site of the town for a few weeks. The army, commanded by Abu-Ubaidah al-Jarrah, was pursuing a Persian resistance force led by one of the daughters of Yazdegerd, the last Shahanshah (King of Kings) of the defeated Sassanid dynasty. There, according to accounts which mix history with legend as is often the case in the East, al-Jarrah set up two huge jars: one was filled with the juice of the desert's sweet and sour pomegranates, the other offered the thirsty soldiers of Islam a spirit distilled from local grain and perfumed with the essence of a wild plant. The spirit, known as *arak*, was still being produced in 1979 when the Ayatollah's return brought to an end a tradition some thirty centuries old. To the Arab soldiers who had arrived there after months of bitter fighting in the cold mountain regions of the Iranian plateau, Khomein, a mere station on their route to the larger cities of the northeast, must have appeared like an image of paradise on earth. They were, however, never to return, as one by one the greener and more prosperous parts of Persia fell to the Arab advance. Once they had reached Isfahan, Yazd or Kashan, the thought of returning to Khomein would have stirred little joy in their hearts.

During the 1820s the unloved town did, nevertheless, achieve some importance as a regional centre under a local khan known as Yussef Kamara'i. The Qajar state, having just suffered a number of crushing defeats at the hands of the Russians in the Caucasus and Central Asia, was too weak to contend with fissiparous forces active throughout the vast kingdom. In every town of a certain size a new ruling coalition emerged, consisting of tribal chiefs, landlords, the leading bazaar merchants and, inevitably, several mullahs. The demand of mullahs to participate in the new ruling structures springing up throughout the country was the strongest since the early days of the Safavid dynasty in the sixteenth century.

Yussef Khan, like other feudal lords of the day, needed his own doctors of theology but, unable to compete with the wealthier chieftains of the larger and more prosperous cities of central Iran, he could not attract to his modest court any of the prestigious mullahs of Isfahan, Qom, Rey or Mashhad. He had to venture farther afield and look for his mullahs in Mesopotamia.

To take part in a pilgrimage to the holy cities of Mesopotamia, especially Najaf where Ali Ibn Abi-Taleb, the fourth Caliph and the first Imam of duodecimal Shi'ism (see chapter 10) is buried, and Karbala, site of the mausoleum of Hussein, the third Imam, is an honour every Shi'ite strives after. According to Shi'ite tradition, a single pilgrimage to Najaf and Karbala is equal to 70,000 pilgrimages to Mecca, which is, nevertheless, Islam's holiest city. Yussef Khan's ambition was to make the pilgrimage at least seven times. For, also according to Shi'ite tradition, any man travelling to Najaf and Karbala seven times to pay homage to the two Imams will be assured of a place in paradise regardless of the sins he may have committed during his life. Yussef did not achieve his ambition for he died shortly after his fourth pilgrimage to Mesopotamia. It was on his last trip that he brought back with him a young mullah known as Sayyed Ahmad. Sayyed Ahmad was to become Ruhollah's grandfather.

The title of *sayyed*, meaning 'gentleman' in Arabic, is, in its more specific application, reserved for those who claim direct descent from the Prophet Muhammed. To distinguish themselves from the lesser mortals, the sayyeds used to wear a green belt, the colour of the House of Hashem, the Prophet's own 'chosen clan'. The practice continued until Reza Shah, the founder of the Pahlavi dynasty, abolished traditional clothes in the 1920s. The sayyeds who chose to become mullahs had another means of distinguishing themselves from the non-sayyeds in the same profession. In addition to the traditional green belt, they also wore black turbans. Non-sayyeds among mullahs wore white or, in certain instances, cream turbans.

The sayyeds are known as Ahl-e-Bayt or the People of the House, and are marked out for special honours and privileges. No believer is allowed to sit down to a meal unless he has first made sure that not a single sayyed living within seven streets of him is hungry.

Some traditions even attribute medicinal properties to the sweat and saliva of sayyeds. And Ayatollah Khomeini, in his magnum opus *Tawzih al-Masayel* (*Explication of Problems*), writes that sayyed women reach menopause ten years later than non-sayyeds.

One becomes a sayyed only by direct inheritance from one's father. But having a sayyed (or *sayyedeh*, the feminine form of the Arabic word) as one's mother is not without advantages. Children born of sayyed women become *mirzas* or 'those who are princely born' and are thus eligible for a number of distinctions and advantages. And from noon until midnight every Thursday they are considered full sayyeds, their prayers carrying the same weight as the full descendants of the Prophet.

But how does one find out whether or not one is a sayyed? This is a very difficult task indeed. The civilization of Islam, both in Iran and in the rest of the Middle East, has had little regard for the science of record keeping. Until the 1920s Iran did not have a single public record office. Apart from a thousand or so families who were able to produce private genealogical records, no one's memory reached back far beyond their great-grandfather's time. The country's numerous experiences of foreign occupation and countless civil wars over fourteen centuries meant that whole families were wiped out without a trace, to be replaced by new and equally transient ruling clans. Thus the status of sayyeds seldom depended on the possession of actual, verifiable records. The easiest way for a claimant was simply to introduce oneself boldly as a sayyed. In some cases, the trick worked. In others it led to death for the pretenders. Those who falsely claim to be sayyeds become *mahdur ad-damm* (those whose blood must be shed). There is no need to put them on trial or arrange for their punishment through public authorities. It is simply incumbent on every true believer to carry out the sentence. Throughout the ages the charge that a family claiming descent from the Prophet was, in fact, guilty of imposture remained a deadly weapon in clan and tribal feuds.

Among the sayyeds themselves some are more equal than others. At the tip of the pyramid are the Tabataba'is whose name indicates that they are descendants of the Prophet on both sides. Next come the Husseini sayyeds, those who can directly trace their ancestry to Hussein, the third Imam. Following them in order of merit are the Razavi sayyeds, the descendants of Ali Ibn Mussa, the eighth Imam, whose golden-domed mausoleum in Mashhad is Iran's holiest shrine. Hassani sayyeds, who claim descent from the second Imam, Hassan, are but a handful. Imam Hassan does not enjoy the same popularity as his brother Hussein because of the peace he negotiated with Muawyyah who became Caliph in Damascus and is considered a usurper by the Shi'ites. But the most numerous of all sayyeds are the Mussavis, descendants of Mussa Ibn Jaafar, the seventh Imam. There are no accurate statistics showing a clear breakdown of the various categories of sayyeds and their relative numerical strength. But it would be safe to say that the Mussavis account for some 70 per cent of all sayyeds in Iran.

Khomeini himself is a Mussavi sayyed. Other Mussavis in the 'republic' he created in Iran in 1979 include the President, the Prime Minister, the Chief Justice, the Deputy Speaker of the Islamic Majlis (Parliament) and scores of ministers, under-secretaries, governors-general, ambassadors, members of parliament and directors of state-owned corporations.

The reason for the Mussavi sayyeds' numerical superiority is that their common ancestor Imam Mussa Ibn Jaafar achieved a feat unique among the twelve Imams. He lived to a ripe old age whilst most of the others were either poisoned by intriguing caliphs or murdered by fanatics who did not approve of their reading of the Qur'an, Islam's Holy Book. Imam Mussa, although he served a long prison term, had enough time to travel widely both in Mesopotamia and in Iran. Allowed under Islamic law to have four full wives, the Imam also made use of the additional facility offered by the Shi'ite tradition of *mut'aah* or temporary wives. Under this rule a man can take as many concubines as he can treat with honour and justice in accordance with a fully spelled-out contract which can cover a single hour or ninety-nine years. The offspring of a concubine do not enjoy the rights reserved for children of full wives, but they, nevertheless, can bear their father's name and, if he is a sayyed, also use his title. Imam Mussa is known to have married a large number of women during his frequent travels. He did not, perhaps, reach the record of his illustrious ancestor Imam Hassan, who at one point boasted no fewer than fifty-three concubines. But Imam Mussa's lifelong and temporary marriages proved more fruitful. Estimates of the offspring he left behind vary between 135 and 750.

Sayyed Ahmad, Khomeini's grandfather, was, therefore, one Mussavi sayyed among many when he came to settle in Khomein around 1840. But, as a mullah, he had a number of advantages as well as some handicaps. The main advantage he offered was his erudite learning, acquired at Najaf which, in those days, was the only place where Shi'ite theology was still seriously taught. He therefore set up a small theological school of his own to ensure that the ruling coalition had a continuing supply of mullahs. His greatest handicap was his ignorance of the Persian language and literature. His command of the language was adequate for day-to-day needs, but the more complex and exciting universe of Persian poetry and philosophy was closed to him at first, until years of patient study provided him with the necessary keys.

Sayyed Ahmad's family came from the city of Neyshabur, in northeastern Iran. But by the time Sayyed Ahmad arrived in Khomein there was nothing left of the family in Khorassan's city of turquoise. The entire clan had left Neyshabur in the eighteenth century during the brief conquest of India by Nader Shah Afshar. Part of the clan had settled in the Punjab where it seems to have disappeared without trace. A second branch of the family moved north to Kashmir where, according to Shaikh Ali Tehrani, for a long time a close companion of Ruhollah, they still live in a village in the Indian part of the divided state.

Sayyed Ahmad's father had, for mysterious reasons, chosen two different sets of names for himself. To the pupils in the small theological school he had set up in Kashmir he was known as Sayyed Mohammad-Hussein Neyshaburi. But when, probably around 1780, he published a handwritten edition of his one and only contribution to Shi'ite theology, he chose to describe himself as Mir Hamed Hindi, meaning 'the Indian'. Sayyed Mohammad-Hussein, born in Kashmir, died there shortly after having dispatched his eldest son, Sayyed Ahmad, to Najaf to study.

Sayyed Mohammad-Hussein's book, written in rather hesitant Arabic with an admixture of Hindi and Kashmiri words no reader of Arabic would understand, is called *Abaqat al-Anvar* (*Chalices of Light*). Once settled in Khomein, Sayyed Ahmad tried to revise and publish the book, but he abandoned the project in sheer frustration. A carefully pruned edition was published in Qom in 1979 shortly after Khomeini's seizure of power in Tehran. But it was later withdrawn with the promise that the 'authentic version' would soon be published after approval by Ayatollah Khomeini.

*Abaqat al-Anvar* consists of a series of violent attacks on the Sunnis, or 'traditional' Muslims, who form some 85 per cent of the world's Islamic population. It describes them as *koffar al-harbi* (pagans waging war on true believers), and thus fit to be put to the sword. Sayyed Mohammad-Hussein's violent prose and vitriolic style anticipate the writings of his great-grandson, Ruhollah. Sayyed Mohammad-Hussein poses the explosive question Ruhollah put in 1978 when he unfurled the banner of revolt against the Shah: 'Should we, who are prepared to die for Allah, not be equally prepared to kill for him?'

Sayyed Mohammad-Hussein also set up another family tradition – that of using a variety of names at different times. It was, therefore, not surprising that Sayyed Ahmad was, at times, referred to as Mostafavi, meaning 'descendant of the Chosen One' (i.e. the Prophet), although his patron and future father-in-law Yussef Khan preferred to call him Aghay-e-Najafi (the Master from Najaf). Sayyed Ahmad's marriage to Yussef Khan's daughter, Saffiyeh, benefited both men. The mullah from Najaf forged a link with the town's wealthiest and most influential family, with the prospect of becoming a substantial landowner after the old khan's departure for paradise. Yussef Khan, for his part, could now be sure that his blood would mix with that of the Prophet, ensuring everlasting honour and distinction for his offspring.

The family's peace and prosperity proved far more fragile than Yussef Khan had imagined. Under Nassereddin Shah, the central government re-established its authority, smashing many local ruling oligarchies. In the meantime, Khomein relapsed into insignificance. The family had to sell some of their land, while other once fertile fields were left untended to be swallowed up by the ever-hungry desert. By the time Ruhollah's father, Mostafa, was married, at the age of nineteen, the family had already been reduced to the status of sharecroppers. Mostafa had completed his Qur'anic studies with his father, but he could not earn a living as a mullah. The new rich of the region had their own mullahs, and the poor, now hit by heavy taxation by central government, could not maintain more than a few full-time clerics. Mostafa was the second of five children. On Sayyed Ahmad's death the family's remaining land was divided up into still smaller plots, with the eldest son, Ruhollah's uncle, receiving the lion's share. Although people performed their duty of helping feed the sayyed as much as possible, the family was often left without adequate food. The family, now numbering over thirty, including wives, husbands and children, all lived in the mud-brick house where Ruhollah was to be born. The house, slowly crumbling, still stands, or rather leans against neighbouring houses. There is only one storey, consisting of eleven rooms built around a muddy square, at the centre of which is a shallow pond and two ancient, tired-looking trees. Only the main room, known as the *mehman-khaneh* (literally, the guest house), has two large windows. The other rooms are windowless and, when their wooden double doors are fully shut, they are plunged into almost complete darkness. All the rooms have wind towers, mud-brick conduits for any fresh breeze that may blow in hot summers. There is only one – 'Turkish' – toilet, a tiny windowless room built over a sewage well and alive with all manner of creepy-crawlies. By 1978 the house, like others in Khomein, had both electricity and piped water. But that was only a recent innovation, one of the fruits of the 'satanic' Shah's oil-propelled development projects. In its ugly austerity, the house lacks the poetry that gives warmth to traditional Persian houses. Here, we are faced with a temporary abode, a chance dormitory on the roadside rather than a real home. Until 1965 the house was referred to by the local people as Khaneh-e-Hendi, or 'House of the Indians'. But later, Khomeini's brother turned part of it into a garage for his small trucking company and converted the rest into a dormitory for his drivers. As a result, the house became known as Garaj-e-Hendi, or Indian Garage. But it changed its name a third time late in 1978 during the revolution, when the ramshackle edifice was renamed Khaneh-e-Agha, or House of the Master.

But this was much later. Long before that, probably some time in 1887, Sayyed Mostafa, having managed to save enough for a dower, sought and was granted the hand of a local landlord's daughter. The marriage was arranged by the two would-be mothers-in-law. Sayyed Mostafa's chief asset at the time was his claim to sayyedhood. But Sadiqeh, the future mother of the future revolutionary, brought with her not only a dowry, consisting of some tribal rugs, items of clothing and pots and pans, but also the right to a plot of land, so that Mostafa could start to farm for himself. Mostafa was just nineteen. He had stayed a bachelor a shade too long, for Shi'ite tradition requires that a man take a wife, or wives, as soon as he turns sixteen. Sadiqeh was nine years old, exactly the right age for a girl to marry, according to tradition.

No two beings could have been so unlike one another, according to their first son, Morteza, who was born in 1890 or 1891 and is still living in the holy city of Qom. Mostafa was an intense, short-tempered man who would explode at the slightest provocation. He was dour-faced, frugal and hard-working. But he was also unforgiving, and, as a result, he had very few friends. He used his self-imposed solitude as a shield against a world he considered corrupt and corrupting. Morteza, the first fruit of Mostafa's happy marriage, was followed by two daughters, respectively named Gohar al-Sadat (Jewel of the Sayyeds) and Fakhr al-Sadat (Honour of the Sayyeds). Then came two boys who died in their first year. And in 1902, probably on 9 November, Ruhollah was born. Ruhollah did not know his father. For Sayyed Mostafa was killed before the new baby was six months old. When Mostafa died, his young wife, then twenty-four, was once again pregnant. The child, born some seven months after his father's death, was named Sayyed Mohammad-Badreddin. Ruhollah was already staying with his aunt when his father died. There was no room in the paternal house, and the baby had been sent to her. A professional nurse, who served as a surrogate mother for babies in exchange for food and lodging, looked after Ruhollah.

Like most other topics concerning the Khomeini family, Sayyed Mostafa's death has provided the substance of many a legend since the Ayatollah's victory over the Shah. One such, still current in a number of official biographies in Iran and at times quoted by foreign writers, claims that Sayyed Mostafa was a revolutionary who fought against Reza Shah, the founder of the Pahlavi dynasty, before being murdered by the Shah's agents. Some biographies even suggest that Mostafa's murder had been planned by the British, who 'brought their lackey to the Persian throne'. These claims are totally false and solely aimed at creating a Khomeini-versus-Pahlavi mythology. Reza Khan, as he was then known, seized power in a coup d'état in 1921 when he was forty years old, no less than nineteen years after Sayyed Mostafa's death. It was not until 1925, when a docile Parliament declared him Shahanshah, that Reza chose Pahlavi as his surname.

According to Sayyed Morteza, his father was murdered after a row with two bailiffs acting on behalf of an absentee landlord. Morteza does not describe the quarrel, but refers vaguely to 'my father's refusal of an unjust sharing of the crops'. But it is almost certain that the argument arose over the thorny subject of *khums* (literally, one fifth), the Shi'ite principle that 20 per cent of all earned income must be allocated to the sayyeds. The bailiffs, as was usual in those days, may have calculated Mostafa's share of the crops as part of his *khums* entitlement, thus reducing his total claim. They may also have refused to pay him any *khums* at all, reserving it for sayyeds of their own choice. The choice of recipients for *khums* was one of the landlords' most powerful weapons in dealing with abrasive sayyeds. Few people actually dared refuse to pay, so strong was the belief that the curse of the sayyeds could amount to eternal damnation. As a result many sayyeds could live off *khums*. But Mostafa was not one of them. Local tradition still remembers him as a do-gooder who spent almost all of his *khums* revenue on helping the poor and the needy. Few people actually liked the unsmiling sayyed, but almost everyone respected him.

Mostafa's death, more likely the result of an accident rather than a deliberate plot by absentee landlords to do away with a trouble-maker, was to affect Ruhollah's life profoundly and immediately. Evil tongues began to wag. Mostafa, they said, was murdered because his latest child, Ruhollah, was *bad-qadam* (ill-omened). This was in accordance with a deep-rooted tradition in which new-born babies are held to be responsible for the family's good fortune or unexpected suffering. A child who is *khosh-qadam* (good-omened) becomes the subject of veneration. Relatives come to touch him in the hope of benefiting from his supposed good luck. Girls of marriageable age are given pieces of the lucky child's clothes as charms to hasten a keenly desired betrothal. The mother of a *khosh-qadam* is treated with unusual deference even by the other wives of her husband who are usually jealous of her. But the reverse operates for mothers of children who are *bad-qadam*.

The surest sign of a *bad-qadam* is, of course, the fact of being born shortly before a major disaster, usually a death, in the family. And for this Ruhollah qualified eminently. The mere fact of his father's death would have been enough to turn Ruhollah into a child of ill omen, but because his father had been so young, and his death so violent, this made matters even worse. Women gathered on the mud-covered roof of the ancestral home to gossip about the *bad-qadam*. Again and again they went over the circumstances of Sayyed Mostafa's death and noted the strange fact that the poor man had been stabbed six times, one for each month of Ruhollah's age. The undeserved hostility that Ruhollah had provoked was so intense that his mother left him with his aunt, Roqiyyah, who agreed to look after the child as long as necessary. In the event that meant until Ruhollah was sixteen. The unloved orphan never returned to his mother's embrace, and her visits, at first once or twice a week, became rarer and rarer after Mohammad was born. In a natural transfer of affection, Ruhollah came to consider his aunt as his true mother. He continued to respect his mother until her death some fifteen years later, but no mother-and-son relationship was ever fully formed between them.

Years later the select group of faithful followers who saw him as not only a guide but a prophet were able to put the early circumstances of Ruhollah's life to good use. They recalled that the Prophet Muhammed had also been an orphan raised by his aunt and uncle. Was that a mere coincidence, they asked. Or was it that the Almighty was inviting those who wished to see to come forward and recognize the true 'mission' of Ruhollah? The very name chosen for the orphan has also been interpreted as meaning more than it says. Ruhollah means 'the spirit or the soul of Allah'. It is an extremely rare name, which was occasionally used by Iranian Jews who, even until a generation ago, took Muslim names to avoid persecution and violence. In choosing Islamic names they often preferred those that ended with the word Allah: Fath-Allah (Allah's Victory) or even Abdullah (Allah's Slave). Ruhollah, which is in fact written Ruh-Allah, but pronounced with an 'o' instead of an 'a' in the second syllable, is not one of those popular names that come easily to mind when an Iranian family is seeking a name for a new baby. Religious Iranians, that is to say the vast majority, even in the early days of this century, preferred names such as Mohammad, after the Prophet, or Ali, the name of the first Imam, or Hossein, the martyred third Imam. Sayyed Mostafa's choice of the name Ruhollah was unusual. To some Muslims the use of Ruhollah as a first name is sacrilegious. In Persian literature, it is only Jesus Christ, accepted under Islam as a prophet though not the Son of God, who is often described as Ruhollah or 'the Spirit of God'. To the Ayatollah's most ardent admirers, the choice was dictated to Mostafa by Allah himself.

Living with a prosperous aunt and a jovial uncle old enough to be his grandfather, Ruhollah was markedly better off than his brothers and sisters who still lived in one of the large, windowless rooms of their ancestral home. It was their mother's good humour, patience and generosity that made life not only bearable but even pleasant at times. Of all the children, only Ruhollah had inherited Mostafa's short temper and intolerance. Morteza, the eldest, took after Sadiqeh, and missed no opportunity for a bit of gaiety in their grey and grim life, regulated by so many religious strictures as to be virtually unlivable. It was generally assumed in the family that Morteza would go on to become a theologian and succeed his grandfather as a Shi'ite doctor. But Morteza, although he eventually did attend theological courses, was a very reluctant future mullah. Years later, he confessed that he had hoped to become a merchant travelling between East and West. Eventually, however, he became a notary public and continued to practise until 1982. The two daughters would, of course, have no careers as such other than being married off at the age of nine and settling down to a life of motherhood. Lacking anything resembling wealth, their only asset was their lineage.

Looks mattered little, for, like all maidens in that remote desert oasis, they would find husbands through intricate family negotiations and arrangements which almost totally ignored the female physique. So long as a girl was not blind, lame, hunch-backed or ravaged by smallpox (and there were many such), the negotiators did not even mention looks. Such talk was considered a satanic deviation by many traditionalists. In any case, nine-year-old brides could hardly be considered as fully grown women. What mattered most to a girl's family was to find her a husband before she began menstruating. In many of his works Khomeini himself strongly recommends pre-menstruation marriage as 'a divine blessing'. 'Do your best to ensure that your daughters do not see their first blood in your house,' he writes in *Tawzih al-Masayel*, addressing the pious.

What was not discussed in those days was Ruhollah's future career. Mohammad, the youngest of the family, was intended to be the manager of the family's modest farm, but he became a lawyer and was the only one of the three brothers to refuse to wear a turban. The matter of Ruhollah's future was left to Aunt Roqiyyah and her ailing husband Yahya. Both wanted him to become a hakim. The term *hakim* is practically untranslatable for it describes the kind of generalist for which there is no equivalent in English. A hakim is many things in one: he is a doctor of theology, a philosopher, a physician, a lawyer, a poet and, if and when the opportunity arises, a governor of men. But even a future hakim had to begin by learning the holy Qur'an by heart.

Ruhollah's Qur'anic education began shortly after he had completed his fourth birthday. He attended a local *maktab* where a mullah taught the Arabic alphabet to virtual toddlers. *Maktab* is an Arabic word and literally means 'the place of writing'. In the early twentieth century, and until modern schools were set up by the central government from the 1920s onwards, the *maktab* provided practically the only education available to children below the age of sixteen. There were no precise rules concerning the creation and management of *maktabs*. Anybody could set one up and enrol pupils. But most teachers tended to be mullahs, tur-baned masters of theology. Since it was sacrilege even to think of learning anything before a full study of the Qur'an, only those who had a claim to theological knowledge would be accepted by the community as *maktabdar* (schoolmasters). The *maktabs* were financed not only by the parents of the children who attended the classes but also through religious endowments and gifts, in both cash and kind, from the pious. At best, the *maktabs* catered for the education of some 10 per cent of the boys and less than 5 per cent of girls. Needless to say, there were no mixed *maktabs*, although the same *maktabdar* could teach boys and girls on different days. *Maktab* education for girls usually lasted four years (between the ages of five and nine), but boys could stay on until they were sixteen. The first two years at *maktab* were devoted to the learning of the alphabet, calligraphy and the building up of a small but vital Qur'anic vocabulary. The children would then tackle the Si-Pareh (literally, the Thirty Pieces). This is a selection of the Holy Book's thirty shortest suras (psalms) which can most easily be learned by heart. These suras were read, chanted and copied out again and again for two years until they were inscribed on the young minds for ever. This was the only important part of the *maktab* education to be kept in the modern educational system that took shape in Iran between 1925 and 1979. The choice of the thirty suras, obviously determined by their length, had a side effect that cannot have been intended. Most of them belong to the Makki (Meccite) suras and are thus distinct from those 'descended' during the Prophet's years in Medina. In Mecca, Muhammed had been a passionate but powerless preacher of an explosive faith. The suras of Mecca are like sharp but short volcanic eruptions. They warn, cajole, entreat, but rarely threaten. The Medina suras, on the other hand, 'descended' when the Prophet had become the head of a small but expanding and expansionist state. Muslim children, whether attending the old *maktabs* or the modern primary and secondary schools, first learn about their faith through suras that emphasize Allah's boundless mercy. It is in these suras that Islam comes closest to the Christian concept of grace. Only a few Muslims go on to study the Medina suras, in which Allah appears as the Avenger and the Rectifier by Fire, as closely as the suras of Mecca. As a result, whereas the ordinary Muslim feels closest to a warmer, more generous and forgiving vision of Islam, the theologians prefer the sterner vision and see Muhammedanism as a set of strict rules set down by Allah for ever. The first vision emphasizes the possibility, indeed the attainability, of salvation even for the most sinful, provided they sincerely repent, while the second focuses attention on the horrors of damnation. One vision is all hope and optimism, the other marked with profound pessimism.

There were no formal examinations at *maktabs*, although frequent tests were made in which the pupils showed their progress in calligraphy, the recitation of the Holy Book and the meaning of key Qur'anic phrases. Once the *maktabdar* felt that his pupils were sufficiently advanced, he would take them on to the realm of *amthal va hekam* or proverbs and epigrams. The study of the Qur'an would continue. But from the third or fourth years onwards the pupils would also begin reading parts of Shi'ite basic texts. Some of the more outward-looking *maktabdar* also taught their pupils the rudiments of arithmetic and algebra, which has always been an extremely popular science in Persia. Some Persian literary texts, always carefully chosen for their relevance to religious piety and ethics, completed the *maktab* education in later years. Also covered were basic courses in history — always written and taught in such a way as to 'prove' the superiority of Islam — geography and, last but not least, *shari'a* (religious law and practice).

Very few children stayed on at *maktab* beyond the age of twelve. Many died before reaching such an age. Mortality among children aged twelve or under was around 200 per 1000 even in 1960, long after the last of the *maktabs* had disappeared. Also, at a time when life expectancy was around thirty years, most Iranian children could expect to become orphans before turning twelve. Most *maktab* children had to abandon their studies either because they lost their father or had to help run the family farm, shop or handicraft business.

Ruhollah and his younger brother were orphans long before they attended their first *maktab*. But both were fortunate enough to stay on until they were sixteen. Ruhollah was, by all accounts, the more diligent scholar. By the time he had passed his sixth birthday he had learned the whole of the Qur'an by heart and was already developing his talents as a polemicist. His progress was promising enough to encourage his aunt, who was to die shortly before Ruhollah set off for Arak, to set aside a small sum to finance the future Ayatollah's further education.

# 2

# *The Narrow Path*

This world is but a passage; it is not a world in which we ought to live. This [world] is but a way, it is the Narrow Path. . . . What is called Life in this world is not Life but Death. True Life is that offered only in the Hereafter. . . . We are here, in this low, earthly Life, only to perform the duties Allah has set for us to perform. We may, because of our ignorance, consider these duties to be onerous; but these are, verily, the best example of the Almighty's generosity [towards us]. . . . No one becomes a true human being without first crossing the Narrow Path.

Ayatollah Khomeini in an address commemorating the seventh
day of his son Mostafa's death in Najaf, Iraq

*R*uhollah had just turned sixteen when his *maktab* teacher, Sayyed Abol-Hassan, told him that there was nothing more he could learn in Khomein. 'I have taught you all the things that I know, except one,' the old *maktabdar* told the adolescent scholar. 'And that one thing you must go and seek elsewhere. You must become a *talabeh*.' *Talabeh*, translated literally, means 'seeker'. In the more restricted sense of the past two centuries it has come to mean a student of theology, one who aspires to become a mullah.

Sayyed Abol-Hassan's reference to the one thing he had not taught young Ruhollah reflected a long-established tradition in Persian scholarship, literature and art. Since only Allah is capable of perfect creation, no man should even try to rival His work. For centuries Persian scientists have died keeping at least part of their knowledge to themselves, thus escaping the charge that they were trying to appear as if they knew everything. Persian architects and artisans who designed and built so many beautiful mosques in Iran, the Indian subcontinent and Mesopotamia always made sure that at least one deliberate error was made in both plan and execution. That error may be as small as an odd tile that breaks the harmony of an abstract pattern on a mosque wall. But it would be sufficient to demonstrate man's humility even at the highest level of artistic achievement. Even today, the gifted weavers who produce Persia's exquisite carpets and rugs weave a deliberate error into every delicate composition they create.

It was natural for Ruhollah to become a *talabeh*. He belonged to an old and established family of mullahs and his elder brother, Morteza, had just continued the ancestral tradition by spending several years as a 'seeker' in the holy city of Najaf, in Mesopotamia, which was then the main centre of Shi'ite theological studies in the world. Ruhollah, too, would have liked to travel to Najaf but was prevented from doing so because of developments beyond his control. In 1915 the Allies had invaded and occupied parts of Iran. The central government, fragile and still not fully recovered from the ravages of the civil war four years earlier, had all but collapsed. Iran's huge spaces and rugged mountains were difficult to control at the best of times. The demise of the central government complicated matters further.

Brigands began to appear everywhere, making travel dangerous. Local chieftains were quick to regain their autonomy, reducing the vast Iranian mosaic to a sum of conflicting parts. The Arab revolt, engineered and led by the British adventurer and mystic Colonel T. E. Lawrence, unleashed a process that eventually led to the collapse of the Ottoman Empire. In that process, the British seized control of Mesopotamia, severing its links with Iran for a number of years.

The Shi'ites, the majority of the population in southern Mesopotamia, had always secretly desired the collapse of the Ottoman state which, headed by a Sunni Turk who called himself Caliph of All Muslims, symbolized the very essence of satanic deviation from true Islam as they perceived it. At the start of the war, therefore, the Shi'ite leaders in Najaf tacitly endorsed the Allied cause. But when Iran herself was invaded by the Allies, the holy men of Najaf changed their minds and saw the British and their Arab Sunni allies as the new enemies of the faith.

By the time Ruhollah was preparing to leave Khomein, the war was already drawing to a close. But it was still difficult to reach

Mesopotamia over land. The only way would have been a sea voyage from Bushehr on the Persian Gulf to Basra up the Shatt al-Arab. But both Basra and Bushehr were under British control and Ruhollah would have needed their written permission for the journey. That would have meant negotiating with the infidel from a position of weakness and was thus totally inadmissible.

Ruhollah began making inquiries about alternative places of study. There were theological schools in various Indian cities, notably Aligarh where an Islamic movement of reform was in full swing. But, once again, permission for travelling to India had to come from the British.

Inside Iran itself there were more than a dozen theological seminaries, the most renowned at the holy city of Mashhad, with the southern capital of Shiraz also boasting an old tradition of Islamic scholarship at the Shah-e-Cheragh (King of Light) school. The holy city of Qom was at that time little more than a place of pilgrimage and was not distinguished as a centre of Shi'ite learning. Ruhollah's choice was finally narrowed down to the capital, Tehran, and the orchard city of Arak. In Tehran two octogenarian ayatollahs who were reputed to be 'liberals' taught a diminishing number of seekers. The two ayatollahs, Behbehani and Tabataba'i, were both considered too political.

There is no evidence to show that young Ruhollah had already formed any political opinions. But it is possible to speculate that, coming from a remote and backward oasis, he would have found the strict traditional interpretation of Shi'ism more familiar and, therefore, more reassuring. Such an interpretation was being offered at Arak by Ayatollah Shaikh Mohsen Araki who had moved there from Tehran where he had fought against the newly created constitutional government.

Ruhollah finally decided to go to Arak late in 1918, but his departure was once again delayed for several months because of his aunt's death. A few weeks later, Ruhollah's mother also died, thus obliging him to stay in Khomein for another forty days of mourning. By the time he eventually left Khomein he could afford not to look back. The last two persons he may have had some affection for back in Khomein had perished. His relations with his two sisters had always been cordial but cool. As for his two brothers, Morteza and Mohammad, he felt little emotion for them. Morteza was a mild-mannered, almost jovial young man who was already married and trying to improve his material life. Morteza did not consider happiness to be a state of sin as did

Ruhollah. Both Morteza and Mohammad were sociable and genuinely enjoyed the company of people. Ruhollah was the opposite. He seemed to be happy only when left alone in his room, and would spend long hours walking in the desert and praying. To the sycophants who have composed his official biographies since his triumph, Ruhollah's strolls in the desert appear as so many rendezvous with angels dispatched from heaven to communicate with the young man. More plausibly, Ruhollah enjoyed the silence of the desert and the majesty of the vast open spaces punctuated only by camel caravans on the horizon. Ruhollah had begun writing poetry when only ten and by the time he was getting ready to travel to Arak he had composed scores of *ghazals* (sonnets) and *qasidahs* (odes). He must have seen the desert as a constant source of inspiration.

The choice of Ayatollah Araki as his future teacher was to prove a key factor in determining Ruhollah's future views on Islam, politics and life in general. The Shi'ite priesthood was still recovering from the effects of a bitter and bloody feud more protracted than any it had experienced in centuries. The mullahs were, broadly speaking, divided into two camps: the *mashruteh* (constitutionalists) and the *mashru'eh* (theocrats). The split had occurred in 1906 when a coalition of bazaar merchants, Western-oriented intellectuals and big landowners staged a series of demonstrations in Tehran calling for the creation of an Edalat-Khaneh (House of Justice). The desire for reform was reinforced by general dissatisfaction with a weak and corrupt government that was manifestly unable to prevent Iran from becoming a virtual colony in which the two superpowers of the day, Britain and Czarist Russia, had spheres of influence. The Tehrani middle class had not yet forgotten or forgiven the loss of the Caucasus to the Russians which had been completed in 1824. They also resented the British military presence in parts of southern Iran. As the protest movement spread to other provinces, the leading mullahs endorsed it. The Qajar monarch, Mozaffareddin Shah, old, sick and vacillating as he was, proved incapable of stemming the tide of popular discontent. In what may now appear as a dress rehearsal for the Islamic Revolution of 1978–79, the Shah was quickly isolated and left with no choice except to capitulate. Mozaffareddin did just that and signed a decree allowing the election of a House of Justice. At the time he almost certainly did not realize what had been asked of him and what he had finally granted his people. The leaders of the victorious movement, which had already been given the title of Constitutional Revolution,[1] were equally uncertain about their precise demands and what Mozaffareddin had agreed to let them have. The Western-oriented intellectuals, led by Sayyed Hassan Taqizadeh, a mullah who had cast away his turban in favour of a European hat, wanted little short of a parliamentary system that would turn Iran into a constitutional monarchy. Such eminently Western concepts as national sovereignty, the separation of Church and State and individual human rights were introduced as the foundations of a new political and social system. The middle classes loved these new ideas and saw in them a recipe for their own political ascendancy at the expense of the landlords and the mullahs. The first Majlis (literally meaning 'the sitting-place' but used to describe a parliament) was dominated by middle-class deputies, mainly from the bazaar. Its task was to draw up a constitution, something then unheard of in the Islamic world. This meant that the Qur'an would no longer be considered as the one and only constitution of an Islamic state. The constitutionalists were, in effect, plotting the creation of a European-style nation-state in Iran, which was anathematic to Shi'ite theologians. The very notion that elected representatives of the people could gather together and legislate on all matters smacked of heresy as far as the mullahs were concerned. For, according to them, every single law a Muslim would ever need until the end of time is already in existence either in the Holy Book or in the Hadith, the traditions attributed to the Prophet. Mortals cannot legislate. Their sole task is to carry out the laws that already exist. And mullahs are there to make sure that this is the case.

Some of the mullahs, notably the two ayatollahs of Tehran, Tabataba'i and Behbehani, believed they could live with the strange new system proposed by the constitutionalists. They were, at least, prepared to give it a try. They were further reassured, so far as preventing any major deviation from basic Islamic laws was concerned, by a clause included in the draft constitution providing for a panel of five high-ranking mullahs to vet every item of legislation and, if not satisfied, veto it.

Other mullahs, however, considered all compromise impossible. Islam could not be treated as a mere part of life; the reverse was true: life was but a part of Islam. The idea of civil courts acting independently of the mullahs was also unacceptable to the *mashru'eh* mullahs. Since only divine laws were valid, their application could not be entrusted to laymen.

But there were more fundamental objections to the constitution. Strictly speaking, Islam cannot recognize the equality of all human beings. There are no such things as basic human rights, in the Western sense of the term, within the Islamic world view. A strict hierarchy of individual and collective worth is observed. Islam rejects any hierarchy of human worth based on such notions as race, nationality and class. Hitler's National Socialism, based on the cult of the supposedly superior Aryan man, would have been impossible in Islam. Equally impossible is the system of apartheid as practised in South Africa with the support of the main body of the Dutch Reformed Church. But Islam, firmly rejecting the very notion of equality, is capable of developing its own apartheid system. Here, human beings are first divided on the basis of sex. Men and women cannot have exactly the same rights under Islam. Muslim scholars have written countless volumes trying to prove that the inequality of men and women under Islam does not necessarily harm the material and spiritual interests of the latter. This may be so and it is not our purpose to discuss the issue here. All that need be emphasized is that a constitution stating that men and women are equals and must, therefore, enjoy equal rights and opportunities cannot be acceptable to Islam.

Islam further divides human beings into two groups: the Muslims and the non-Muslims. All male Muslims are equal and enjoy the same individual and collective rights and prerogatives. Non-Muslims living in a society where Muslims form the majority and control the state, however, are treated separately. All non-Muslims must pay *jezieh* (head tax) to the Islamic government, in accordance with Qur'anic law. (The practice, however, has been abandoned in the Muslim world since the nineteenth century.) Among the non-Muslims, the Ahl-e-Kitab (People of the Book) form the highest echelon of society. Considered as 'believers', Christians, Jews and Zoroastrians are treated with special deference, although never treated as equals. Even among the People of the Book women are treated as rather less equal than men so far as Islamic law and tradition are concerned. Muslims are allowed to take as wives or concubines maidens or widows from among the People of the Book. Such women automatically become Muslims. But no Muslim woman is allowed to marry a Christian, a Jew or a Zoroastrian without first converting her future spouse to Islam.

Slaves form yet another category in the Islamic sociological system. Muslim slaves are, of course, superior to non-Muslim ones. And, in both cases, women are, once again, considered to be rather less equal in the eyes of Islamic jurisprudence. Slavery has been officially abolished in all Muslim states. The last to do so was Mauritania, which took the brave step in 1980 but still has an estimated 250,000 slaves (some 10 per cent of the population). Throughout the nineteenth century the abolition of slavery was strongly resisted by Islamic theologians as a direct violation of divine laws.

The next category, in descending order of human worth, is reserved for the *koffar* (the unbelievers) who must be converted to Islam, by force if necessary, and who enjoy virtually no rights. Buddhists, Sikhs, Hindus and followers of numerous other faiths are all considered to be unbelievers since they are not mentioned in the Qur'an. In practice, the treatment of religious minorities, including those considered to be 'unbelievers', compares favourably with the record set by other civilizations, notably the Christian, during the past twelve centuries or so. But the fact remains that Islamic doctrine cannot accept even what Islamic practice has established throughout the ages. According to Ayatollah Khomeini, one of the Shah's 'most despicable sins' was the fact that Iran was one of the original group of nations that drafted and approved the Universal Declaration of Human Rights after the Second World War. In 1906 the constitutionalists had committed a similar sin by taking as their model the French Revolution's charter of human rights. Had they succeeded in imposing that model, as the *mashru'eh* mullahs feared, the road would have been paved for the secularization of the Iranian state.

The *mashru'eh* mullahs had other fundamental objections to the constitutional system that was being proposed. They could not allow Western-style taxation to replace *zakat* (a percentage of income donated for the benefit of the poor) and *khums*, the tax paid to the mullahs in general and the sayyeds in particular. Another dangerous idea advanced by the constitutionalists was that of creating a state-run system of education in which religious instruction would form but part of an extended syllabus.

Leading the clerical opponents of the constitutional system was Shaikh Fazlollah Nuri, an obscurantist par excellence who had spent years studying the universe of the jin. Although not a sayyed and wearing a white turban as a result, he had earned the title of Hojat al-Islam va al-Moslemeen (the Vicar of Islam and Muslims) from his numerous pupils and followers. The shaikh had moved to Tehran from Najaf at the turn of the century partly to keep an eye on the estimated three hundred villages left to him on his father's death in 1898. Although an accomplished Islamic jurist and a very shrewd businessman, Shaikh Fazlollah was strangely ignorant of the contemporary political ideologies that were attracting a growing number of Iranians, including many mullahs. He hated anything that might loosen the hold of religion on Iranian minds. His original enthusiastic support for the anti-Shah movement had been caused by a deep misunderstanding. The shaikh had thought that the constitutionalists were demanding a re-Islamicization of Iran by curbing the power of the Shah and increasing that of the mullahs. His one-track mind and vitriolic jeremiads, issued with exceptional gusto to audiences of poor illiterate peasants and shopkeepers, earned him the nickname of Gav-e-Mojassam (the Perfect Ass) from the constitutionalist leaders. His obscurantism was so deep that most of his peers saw him as a man from the farthest recesses of a dark past. Shaikh Fazlollah's only distinguished supporter among the mullahs was Ayatollah Shaikh Mohsen Araki who was to become Ruhollah's teacher in 1918.

Having failed to prevent the establishment of a constitutional system, Shaikh Fazlollah sided with rebellious princelings and aristocrats supported by Russia. It was on their behalf that he declared jihad (holy war) against the constitutional government, announcing that all members of the new parliament and government were *koffar al-harbi* (warlike pagans) and thus their blood ought to be shed by the faithful. The declaration sealed his fate. Arrested while delivering one of his incendiary sermons, the mullah was tried by an Islamic court with a single judge, set up in direct violation of the new constitution. The judge, Ayatollah Zanjani, also acted as prosecutor and found Shaikh Fazlollah guilty of treason, warring on Allah and spreading corruption on earth – all Qur'anic concepts. The rebellious shaikh was duly sentenced to death and hanged at the Tup-Khaneh (Cannon House) Square in central Tehran. A crowd of several thousands had gathered to watch the hanging long before sunrise. A festive atmosphere had been created by constitutionalist musicians singing and playing revolutionary songs. Sweets and fruits were distributed among the spectators. Here and there in the vast square people gathered around dancing bears and playful monkeys while awaiting the real spectacle.

Hojat al-Islam Nuri had just turned seventy-one when he was hanged. He refused to be blindfolded and, throwing his captors off-guard for a few minutes, managed to make one final sermon before the noose was fixed around his neck. In the sermon he claimed that the constitutional system was designed to destroy Islam. 'Either this system must go or Islam will perish,' he shouted amid boos and catcalls. No one could have guessed at the time that Shaikh Fazlollah's last jeremiad would provide the central theme of another revolution nearly seventy years later.

To most people present at Tup-Khaneh that strange morning the hanging of Shaikh Fazlollah appeared as a just punishment for a man who had cooperated with the hated Qajar despots and their Russian protectors. The Hojat al-Islam had also provoked popular hatred because of his opposition to the very idea of reforms that could improve the lot of the poor. But even then the crowd that had watched the hanging had not been unanimous. Some spectators had fought hard to control their tears. One of them was Shaikh Mohsen Araki.[2]

Deeply aggrieved by the execution of his friend and ally, Shaikh Mohsen could no longer bear the thought of living in the capital. To him Shaikh Fazlollah's execution was as grave a crime against Islam as Imam Hussein's martyrdom on the bank of the river Euphrates nearly thirteen centuries previously. The most disastrous immediate effect of the execution was that it split the Shi'ite clergy as they had never been split for centuries. One ayatollah had sentenced another to death by hanging. That would have been unthinkable only a year before it happened. All the major religious leaders had approved the hanging either by remaining silent or by even issuing *fitwas*, or religious edicts, describing Shaikh Fazlollah as Mufsed fel-Ardh (Corrupter on Earth) and therefore punishable by death. Worse still, Shaikh Fazlollah was posthumously dispossessed of his vast estate by governmental decree, setting a very dangerous precedent.

The *mashru'eh* party appeared utterly and irrevocably defeated when Shaikh Mohsen resumed his theological classes in Arak in the spring of 1914. He had hoped to organize a counterattack by the mullahs still convinced that Iran's gradual drift towards a Western system of government would, one day, loosen and finally destroy Islam's hold on society. But Shaikh Mohsen lacked his mourned friend's courage and charisma and soon settled down to a quiet life of teaching, preaching and also producing some of the region's finest grapes. Thus, when Ruhollah finally arrived in Arak and joined the diminishing ranks of the seekers around the shaikh, he quickly realized that he would have to look elsewhere in search of a guide and master.

After brief attendance at a number of other circles of study, Ruhollah eventually joined the group of seekers gathered around one Shaikh Abdul-Karim Ha'eri. A native of the desert city of Yazd, which is known as Dar al-Iman (House of the Faith), Shaikh Abdul-Karim had solid credentials as a teacher and defender of Shi'ite theology. But he realized that the schism caused by Shaikh Fazlollah's revolt and subsequent execution would, if not quickly patched up, discredit the mullahs and further erode their authority as defenders of the faith. He preached reconciliation, pointing out that the upsurge in reformist ideas throughout Iran and the widening constituency for Westernization was making it increasingly difficult for mullahs to follow the late Shaikh Fazlollah in resisting all change and progress.

The schism had left the highest echelon of the Shi'ite clergy in disarray. Collectively known as the *ulama* (literally, the scientists), the mullahs produce in each generation one or more outstanding personalities who are described as *a'alam* (he who knows more than his peers). By 1920 the death of Mullah Mohammad Kazem of Khorassan had removed from the scene the last credible pretender to the distinction. It was Shaikh Abdul-Karim's ambition to bridge the void. To do so he first had to leave Arak, a pleasant town of orchards, vineyards and sweet springs but lacking any special religious or political significance. Shaikh Abdul-Karim had to move to a major urban centre. Tehran, the capital, was automatically excluded because it was the seat of a constitutional government considered to be un-Islamic if not outright anti-Islamic. The only remaining choice was the holy city of Qom, a hundred miles south of Tehran. Dominated by the golden dome of the shrine of Fatima Ma'assoumah (Fatima the Chaste One), sister of Imam Reza, the mud-brick town of Qom was then little more than a place of occasional pilgrimage for devout Shi'ites. Its inhospitable climate, sour water and bigoted populace were so unappealing that even the desert caravans made a point of avoiding it.

Shaikh Abdul-Karim might have chosen Mashhad, the beautiful garden city whose fruit orchards, sweet-water springs and mild climate had made it appear as an image of paradise on earth to Imam Reza, the eighth Imam. But Mashhad already had its fair share of eminent theologians. There, Shaikh Abdul-Karim would have been a small fish in a big pond, something all mullahs try to avoid to the best of their abilities. It was with a select number of his pupils that the shaikh first discussed the idea of moving to Qom in order to create a new centre that would rival those of Mesopotamia and Khorassan. Ruhollah was among them. He enthusiastically supported the idea. He had just turned eighteen and was also tired of Arak. The town had at first held a kind of fascination for him, for it had been in Arak that his father's murderers had been tried and then released without punishment nearly seventeen years earlier. He had heard about that mockery of justice from his mother and others on numerous occasions. And when in Arak he could not have avoided passing by the Ta'aminat (police) building where the two bailiffs accused of Sayyed Mostafa's murder had been briefly held. Ruhollah never spoke about the father he had never known. But in later years he was to describe orphans as 'Allah's own children' and to make of their protection and care 'a most sacred duty'. In a patriarchal society in which one's whole life is structured around the head of the family, losing one's father is always the greatest of tragedies. Whether or not Ruhollah ever harboured any thoughts of revenge is unknown. But avenging those who have been wronged was to become a central theme in all his deliberations and subsequent political discourse. It is more than a coincidence that his favourite among Allah's 999 appellations, as recorded in the Holy Book, has always been al-Montaqem (the Avenger).

Young Ruhollah, however, was neither unduly bitter nor totally without charm. At a height of 1.76 metres (5ft 9ins) he was fairly tall by the Iranian standards of his day. He was slim, but heavily boned, and he looked like a potential athlete. He was already sporting a beard which he kept clean and trim with great care. Unlike most *talabeh* of his generation, he avoided the use of henna. Even in his old age he refused to use henna, so popular among the Shi'ite clergy, for dyeing his beard. His face had regular, almost feminine features, and was dominated by a pair of penetrating eyes. Ruhollah's deep black eyes have been described by more than one intimate as 'fathomless oceans'. It was as if all the hope and despair of youth and all the conflicts in heaven and on earth which occupied his restless mind were reflected in those two mesmerizing eyes.

A hard-working student and an enthusiastic polemicist, Ruhollah won his master's special esteem within a few months. His rise within the circle of seekers was meteoric. It usually takes the most attentive of seekers at least a year before being honoured by being permitted to call on the master at his home. Ruhollah achieved that distinction much earlier. And before his first year with Shaikh Abdul-Karim was over he became the master's personal companion and scribe. Ruhollah's less than perfect handwriting hardly recommended him for the last function, especially at a time when calligraphy was still considered to be one of the highest forms of art in Iran. He was assigned the duty, none the less, thanks to his trustworthiness and obvious devotion to Shaikh Abdul-Karim. In spite of a big age difference (Shaikh Abdul-Karim was sixty, Ruhollah eighteen), the two men quickly grew fond of each other. This type of friendship was not unusual between master and pupil in traditional Iran. But it is also possible that Ruhollah developed deeper filial feelings towards the shaikh. Many years later, when mourning the death of his master, Ruhollah was to speak of the shaikh as 'a true father and guide to all his pupils'. Several of the sonnets Ruhollah wrote in those early days were dedicated to the master theologian who was to put Qom back on the map of Shi'ite scholarship.

Shaikh Abdul-Karim arrived in Qom in the spring of 1920 and purchased a large mud-brick house near the shrine of Fatima. His plan was to give the holy city a complete theological school. At that time Qom produced little more than low-ranking mullahs who could only perform at popular mourning ceremonies and were not allowed to arbitrate in major religious disputes. Many of them could not even read properly and had learned parts of the Qur'an by rote without knowing their meaning. The emergence of a new theological circle was greeted with quiet hostility by the mass of the mullahs in the holy city. They feared even the slightest change in the deadly routine of their derelict town. They were content with the status quo. They occupied the tip of a social pyramid the base of which consisted of an army of fortunetellers, temporary wives, coolies, beggars and, last but not least, gravediggers and undertakers – since the holy city was and remains a favourite burial place for the faithful from all over Iran. Some of the leading bazaar merchants, however, supported Shaikh Abdul-Karim's scheme, recognizing its potential for turning their town into the religious capital of Shi'ism. Their financial support enabled Shaikh Abdul-Karim to begin work without having to sell some of his land at Yazd, as he had originally planned.

By the time Ruhollah arrived in Qom the town's sweltering summer had already begun. Life in Qom in summer can best be understood by those who have worked near a blast furnace. A constant sensation of suffocation combined with unquenchable thirst is only partly forgotten when one is attacked by swarms of flies.

The water, even today, not only tastes almost bitter but has the peculiar quality of promoting even greater thirst. Qom is built on the site of what had been a huge salt lake many millions of years ago. All that remains of the lake now is a salty patch of water known as Howze-e-Soltan (the Sultan's Pond) not far from the holy city. Passing through layer after layer of salt, Qom's water, drawn from a string of deep wells, tastes totally repulsive to those unaccustomed to it. But in those days the town's unpleasant features did not end there. Qom at that time, and until 1950, was served by open sewers which channelled every house's refuse into the town's narrow streets and alleys. As a result the whole town looked and smelled like a gigantic lavatory. The obnoxious smell covered the whole town like an invisible cloud. When a new road was being built in 1948 the truck drivers insisted that it should bypass Qom so that they would not have to suffer the deadly odour. The inhabitants, however, were used to the smell, which formed a basic part of their environment. It is difficult to imagine why anyone who was not a native of the holy city or who did not seek a miracle from Fatima the Chaste would want to live in Qom. Even in the 1950s, at a time when Qom was already established as a great religious centre and had been largely reconstructed on the orders of the Shah, life there could be described as anything but pleasant. It seemed that the entire population consisted of the blind, the lame, the hunchbacked, the sick and the mentally infirm who had been brought there from all over the country in the hope of being cured by the saint. There was an almost equal number of beggars to those who were begged from. The austere town, in which there were no cinemas or any other place of entertainment, lived its public life within the vast courtyard of Fatima's shrine and its surrounding narrow, winding alleys. There, one would be continuously accosted by professional beggars and turbaned miracle workers who promised to cure every ailment. One could also hardly avoid the many hundreds of women of all ages who offered their services as *seeghah* (temporary wife) in exchange for either food and lodging for the duration of the 'contract' or a modest sum of money. One could also find an abundant supply of *mohalels*. These are men who specialize in marrying divorcees for a single night. The marriage becomes necessary when a woman, having been divorced three times by the same husband, is asked, once again, to return to the family fold. Islam rules that a woman who has been divorced three times by a man becomes *haram* (forbidden) to him. It is therefore, necessary for the woman to marry another man and divorce him before she can remarry her original husband. This complicated arrangement has led to the creation of a curious profession: that of one-night husbands. It was in Qom, and still is today, that the faithful would find all the *mohalels* they needed.

Enjoying hardly any agricultural production of significance, Qom relied for its income on pilgrimage as well as a small amount of light industry. Chief among these industries was pottery, which continued to give Qom a certain reputation as a centre of Persian handicrafts. The designs, shapes and patterns remained unchanged for generations in a city where fear of change was widespread even among those classes of society which might have been expected to desire a reordering of the universe. Qom was probably the most conservative of all Iranian cities. That it was to become the capital of the Islamic revolution was in those hot summer days of 1920 unknown to Ruhollah, who was to become the architect of that revolution. Qom's other major source of income was its export of large quantities of *sowhan*, a kind of sweet made of caramelized sugar, pistachio and saffron. *Sowhan* is a great Persian favourite and the fact that it is made in Qom, the one Persian city where good taste and art seem excluded by definition, is considered a miracle in itself.

Shaikh Abdul-Karim's circle, at first consisting of only eight seekers, was soon established despite attempts by local mullahs to discourage the newcomers. The circle was a tiny island in a hostile sea, and but for Shaikh Abdul-Karim's dedication and determination, as well as the tenacity of his original disciples, might have been quickly sucked into the ocean of ignorance, prejudice and fear that surrounded it. Within a few months of its establishment the new circle had attracted nearly a hundred seekers and was already beginning to conquer if not the affection at least the respect of the grim holy city.

# 3

# *How Easy to Become a Mullah*

Those who oppose the mullahs oppose Islam itself; eliminate the mullahs and Islam shall disappear in fifty years. It is only the mullahs who can bring the people into the streets and make them die for Islam — begging to have their blood shed for Islam.

Ayatollah Khomeini

Ruhollah and the few other seekers who had gathered around Shaikh Abdul-Karim hoped to complete a course of studies that would entitle them to be called mullahs. The term *mullah*[1] is a corruption of the Arabic word *mawla*, which means both 'vicar' and 'guardian'. In Persian, however, it has acquired two entirely different, if not conflicting, meanings. A mullah can either be a learned man and thus the word is used as a term of deference and respect, or it can be employed as a term of abuse. In the second case a mullah is a living symbol of bigotry and fanaticism. Thus when one speaks of Mullah Hadi Sabzevari, the eminent Shi'ite scholar and saint, one is clearly using the title to indicate distinction. But when Ayatollah Khomeini's opponents refer to him as the Mullah, or when the British in Somalia spoke of the Mad Mullah, it is obvious that no honour was given or received.

Ironically, the same duality of meaning applies to the term *akhund*, an alternative name for a mullah. This is a corruption of *agha-khandeh*, a Turkish–Persian composite noun, the literal meaning of which is 'named an agha'. In the Seljuk and subsequent Turkic states set up in parts of Iran an agha was a middle-ranking military-cum-civilian official. In the sixteenth century, when the mullahs were gradually introduced into Iranian society by the Safavids, it became necessary to fit them into some category or other within an already hierarchical society. Thus they became *agha-khandeh*, later *akhund*, which meant they had the same rank as an agha so far as landownership and claim to honour and respect were concerned. They represented a new caste of state functionaries and thus were given their own niche within the Safavid social edifice. Later, however, the term lost almost all its original meaning. At first, the emergence of a number of great saintly scholars gave the newly coined word an aura of sanctity. The title of *akhund*, used for Mullah Mohammad Kazem of Khorassan for example, indicated great erudition. During the eighteenth century the word travelled far and wide and even reached Bengal where it was further corrupted to become *khundegar*, once again denoting great learning and wisdom. During the past century or so, however, and especially since the Constitutional Revolution of 1906, *akhund* has acquired a pejorative meaning. It can even mean 'one who has shut his mind to all new ideas'. It is interesting to note that the mullahs themselves, including Ayatollah Khomeini, make use of the alternative meanings of both *mullah* and *akhund*.[2]

Islam was originally meant to be the first major religion to have no priests. Even today the vast majority of Muslims, the Sunnis, are, at least theoretically, supposed to cater for their religious needs without the services of professional holy men. Shi'ism, however, is firmly based on the assumption that the mass of the people are unable to distinguish right from wrong and need to be constantly shepherded through a sinful world. The vast majority of the people consists of men and women who without guidance would fall easy prey to Satan and his agents who are legion on this earth. The mullahs must be such guides; the unlearned people must imitate the learned ones in every domain of private and public life. The principle of *taqleed*, which, translated literally, means 'imitation', is central to Shi'ite theology.

The task performed by a mullah is called *ijtihad*. The Arabic term is explained by Ayatollah Khomeini, basing himself on earlier texts, as meaning to suffer and to strive to the limit of one's abilities. In Islamic theology it refers to the investment of effort in seeking the rules and the laws of the faith from the available sources as well as through the use of reason.[3] Thus *ijtihad* is the exact opposite of *taqleed*, which Khomeini describes as following someone else's view without personal investigation.[4] The small minority of people who are capable of *ijtihad* are called *mustanbat* (he who is capable of deduction) or *mujtahid* (he who can offer guidance). A *mujtahid* is, therefore, responsible for his every act since it is he who decides how each religious stricture should be interpreted and implemented.

To become a *mujtahid* is no easy task and one cannot claim the title simply by completing a specific course of studies and obtaining a recognized degree or certificate. It is a state of being that can only be described as an existential fact. Khomeini, once again basing himself on earlier texts, lists 'the prerequisites' of *ijtihad* as follows:

1. Learning Arabic sciences [*sic*] to the required degree
2. Learning secular terms and the language of the people to whom the Qur'an is addressed and distinguishing between secular concepts and the nuances of science and reason
3. Learning the science of logic
4. Knowing the major issues of theology needed to understand [religious] jurisprudence
5. Sufficient familiarity with the Science of Men[5] to be able to check the authenticity of traditions
6. Familiarity and intimacy with the Qur'an and tradition, which are the most important [factors] in deduction
7. Acquiring skill in deduction so that the power to deduce becomes [the student's] second nature
8. Research into epigrams, narratives, especially of the preceding [guides] so that one does not go against popularly held [views] and consensus
9. Analysing edicts and traditions of the Sunnis, especially where these are contradictory. This [practice] may help in a [better] understanding of the rules
10. Employing maximum effort and all [one's] power in making deductions from the rules

A *mujtahid* does not automatically become a religious guide. The attainment of *ijtihad* is a goal for which all (male) believers could and should strive. A perfect society is one in which the majority of the (male) population has attained that elevated status.

Khomeini's ten-point curriculum for the training of the *mujtahid* is based, almost word for word, on the programme suggested by Shaikh Abdul-Karim for the circle he established in Qom. The shaikh's ambition was to turn his expanding group into a fully fledged *madrasseh* or school. At that time there were only two badly organized *madrasseh* in Qom. Both served as hostels for poor bright boys from the countryside seeking to improve their social status and economic prospects by becoming mullahs. The stipends offered, with the help of merchants and income from Fatima's estate, did not amount to much, but it allowed the novices to live and pray for better times while spending their days debating the ideas of saints long buried. The presence of several theological schools in any town gives it the distinction of being a *howzeh-e-elmieh*, which, translated literally, means a scientific sphere. According to Shi'ite tradition it is only theology that can be described as 'science'. Thus theologians are collectively known as the *ulama* (scientists). The assumption is that the only thing that matters is man's salvation, his life in the hereafter, and that only the ways and means of securing this can be considered worthy of being called science. The sole compromise made by the mullahs on this important point during the past 150 years has been their acceptance of the fact that other subjects such as physics, chemistry and mathematics can also be considered to be scientific. Accordingly, these subjects are often grouped together under the term *ulum-e-jadid* or new sciences.

Qualifying as a *mujtahid* does not automatically entitle one to issue *fitwas* or religious edicts. All that a *mujtahid* can do is decide his own course of conduct and choose how to cope with new problems that arise as life goes on. It is only when a *mujtahid* becomes a *marja-e-taqleed* (source of imitation) that he is entitled to issue edicts and call on the faithful to obey his 'recommendations'. Ayatollah Khomeini, once again repeating Shaikh Abdul-Karim almost word for word, sets five conditions for the *marja*: he should be *a'alem*, that is, one who is a master of theological sciences; he should be *mujtahid*; he should be *'adel*, or one who acts with justice; he should be chaste and pious; and, finally, he should not be acquisitive or domineering.

The *madrasseh* also function as free seminaries. There is practically no age limit for attendance at a *madrasseh*, and in many of them one can find adolescents sitting next to septuagenarian seekers. The technique of instruction most frequently used is based on argument and counter-argument. The master throws out an argument and invites the disciples to debate it. He intervenes every now and then, either to put the debate back on the right track or to inject new elements into the discussion. There are no fixed lengths for periods of study − Islamic theology is compared with an ocean from which everyone can take as much water as he needs.

Seen from the outside, the *madrasseh* appears to be an eminently democratic institution in which the pursuit of knowledge has been liberated from hierarchical and bureaucratic constraints. The model, copied from the schools of ancient Athens as described by Islamic scholars such as Abu-Ali Sina (Avicena) and Farabi, has enchanted a number of Western scholars over the years, and especially since Khomeini's Islamic Revolution. Some have even seen in the *madrasseh* a possible answer to some of the problems of contemporary schools in the West. A closer examination of the *madrasseh*, however, leads to other conclusions. The atmosphere of liberty within which the *madrasseh* is supposed to function appears, when looked at more closely, to be little more than a theatrical convention. The purpose of the *madrasseh* is not to foster freedom of thought or to encourage a spirit of inquiry. On the contrary, the central goal of the Shi'ite theological school has been and remains to this day the preservation of a fixed and unalterable view of existence.

Continuing Iran's ancient Manichean traditions, Shi'ism opposes *fikr* (thought) and *zikr* (reassertion). *Fikr* is admissible only so long as it is aimed at focusing attention on the grandeur and majesty of the Creator and the wisdom of his prophets and imams. Beyond that, *fikr* becomes a deadly sin, a sure step towards the precipice. The word *fikri* (literally, thinking) has come to mean mentally deranged in Shi'ite vocabulary. The perfect state of being is one in which a person has absolutely no thoughts, that is to say, no doubts. Shi'ism has special prayers or incantations for every single hour of the day and for every day of the year. The idea is to keep people's minds constantly occupied with prayers and repetition of special formulas so as to leave absolutely no time for independent thinking. The free debate, starting with the argument introduced by the master, may appear as exciting as a dramatic play, the denouement of which is unknown. But once the denouement and conclusion are known much of the excitement evaporates. The *madrasseh* debate always ends with a reference to the Hadith or the sayings of the Imams and their associates. A quotation, no matter how controversial it may be, is always sufficient to close the debate.

The Shi'ite pedagogic system is based on the belief that every conceivable question has already been answered in the Holy Book, the Hadith and the Akhbar (literally, news, but meaning 'accounts of sayings and deeds of the Imams'). The aim of study is to learn the truth, and the truth is already contained in the Qur'an. What matters is the *batin* or the inner existence of things and not their *zahir* (appearance). Islam is the truth, the rest of existence is merely facts. In any confrontation between truth and fact it is obvious that the former takes precedence over the latter.[6] The *madrasseh* seeks its perfect society, its Utopia, in the distant past, more precisely in the thirteen years during which the Prophet ruled the fledgling Islamic state of Medina and Mecca. It is not interested in the present except to keep the people's faith intact. As for the future, that is the realm of the unknowable. For centuries now the attitude of the *madrasseh* towards the real problems of a changing society has been merely reactive. It has been forced to adopt a stand only under the pressure of events. Believing that change can only lead to a further degradation of society, the *madrasseh* has acted as a powerful voice for conservatism. During some 150 years of attempts by Iran to bring herself into the contemporary world it has resisted all reforms. In its role as guardian of the status quo the *madrasseh* has been a natural ally of the ruling class, despite occasional conflicts with the government of the day.

At the time Ruhollah was beginning his studies in Qom under Shaikh Abdul-Karim, the *madrasseh* was passing through an exceptionally quiet phase. The central government, still recovering from the shock of the First World War during which Iran had been invaded and partly occupied by Czarist, British and Ottoman troops, could not extend its writ beyond the outer gates of Tehran. In the Caspian province of Gilan, a populist movement, led by one Mirza Kuchak Khan, a mullah turned guerrilla chief, had established the so-called Republic of the Jungle, mixing parts of Islam's egalitarian message with revolutionary slogans borrowed from the Bolsheviks just across the water. In the central mountains of Iran the Bakhtiari and Qashqa'i tribes were all but independent of the central government. In the southwest, the oil-rich province of Khuzestan was dominated by a number of Lur and Arab chieftains. Finally, in the southeast, in the Iranian half of Baluchistan, warlords leading their starving troops, almost skeletons, into one futile battle after another, martyrized an already broken people. Throughout the country brigands roamed without fear. In 1921, Ruhollah's elder brother, Morteza, fell victim to a group of bandits when travelling to Qom from Isfahan where he had purchased a number of gifts for the young seeker. Morteza was allowed to keep his clothes because of his black turban which marked him out as a sayyed. All the other passengers in the coach were stripped of most of their clothes. The coach arrived in the holy city full of half-naked people, causing a near riot among the faithful.

Shaikh Abdul-Karim, although a theologian of eminent rank, made a point of living a modest life and avoiding the world of power and politics as much as possible. Unlike other leading mullahs of his generation, he had not been actively involved in the Constitutional Revolution. He had what amounted to a natural distaste for things political. As far as permissible within the narrow confines of Shi'ism, the shaikh seized every opportunity to probe the marvellous universe of Persian mysticism. The outside world, the world of reality, offered nothing but poverty and distress. It was a cruel world which took everything and gave nothing but death and desolation. A wise man's best course was complete withdrawal into the inner world, the realm of the *batin*, where only beauty and truth reign supreme. It was a fact known to more people than was prudent in those days of bigotry and prejudice that the saintly shaikh spent almost as much time reading the *diwan* of Hafiz, the great Persian poet of the fourteenth century, as studying the Qur'an. His love for Hafiz's mystical sonnets was such that at times he used to refer to the poet's *diwan* as 'the Persian Qur'an'.

Shaikh Abdul-Karim succeeded in communicating his love of poetry to his youthful disciple who at first had frowned on the idea of studying Hafiz as companion to the Holy Book. Ruhollah initially shared the Prophet's well-documented hatred of poets who were considered, in those days of 'emergence from the Darkness', as wizards of words determined to lead the people astray. Ruhollah had written some verses while at Maktab, but had been warned by his teacher that the pursuit of poetry could lead to damnation. Shaikh Abdul-Karim taught him that poetry was not incompatible with faith.

The advent of Islam in Iran nearly fourteen centuries ago led to what some Iranian thinkers describe as 'our national multiple schizophrenia'. Nowhere is this schizophrenia more evident than in the Persian language. An Indo-European language, Persian is, nevertheless, written in the borrowed Arabic alphabet. It is a language eminently suited to poetry; it has found its best expression in the writing of poetry. At the same time, it is Islam's second most important language and the Muhammedan faith has a traditional dislike of poets and poetry in general. This hatred is, understandably, strongest among the mullahs. For a mullah to love poetry is strange enough; actually to write poetry can amount to something of a scandal. To be sure, the mullahs, when addressing mourning assemblies, quote a number of approved poems, all praising the faith, the Prophet and the twelve Imams. But this limited use of poetry, like the use of music to enhance religious ceremonies, does not mean an overall admission that poetry and poets have a legitimate place in the Islamic society.

At any rate, young Ruhollah was soon completely enchanted with Hafiz. The *diwan* (book of verse) of the Shirazi poet became the novice's constant companion. For a while Ruhollah's supreme ambition was to write sonnets like those Hafiz had composed six hundred years earlier. It is difficult to be precise about the time of Ruhollah's first experiments in the Persian *ghazal* (sonnet), but it is almost certain that Shaikh Abdul-Karim saw and probably even liked some of his disciple's earliest compositions. It is equally possible that the matter remained a secret between master and pupil. A reputation as a poet would not have done Ruhollah's future as a mullah any service. To the mullahs, as we have already noted, writing poetry is a sign either of mental derangement or a propensity to blasphemy. The word *sh'ir* (poetry) is used as the contrary of *manteq* (logic). When an argument is described as belonging to the realm of the *sh'ir* it means that it can be discounted at least so far as the principles of theology are concerned. Writing poetry is also seen as a sign of weakness. And Ruhollah, even then trying to appear an iron-willed, level-headed man, would have done everything to keep his secret. At the same time, however, he was vain enough to want others to read and admire his poems. He read some to his fellow-seekers without revealing the identity of the poet. Every Persian poet ends his sonnets with a line that includes his *nom de plume*. Ruhollah chose the name Hendi (the Indian), and it was under that name that his *diwan*, consisting of thirty-five sonnets and twelve *qasidahs* (odes), was published in Tehran in 1979. The slim *diwan* contains Ruhollah's earliest exercises. It was quickly taken off the market on the Ayatollah's order. Once again the fear that the mass of the people might take the writing of poetry as a sign of weakness or even effeminacy had had an impact.[7]

Ruhollah's poems are solidly structured, following faithfully the classical rules of rhyme and metre. Although writing at a time when Persian poetry was entering an important period of revolutionary transformation thanks to the work of Nima Yushij, the poetical seeker of Qom preferred to stick to established forms. It is quite possible that he had not heard of any of the contemporary

Persian poets; the achievements of each generation had to wait at least a hundred years before penetrating the confines of most *madrasseh*. But even had Ruhollah known about the innovations of such people as Iraj Mirza Jalali and Mohammad-Taqi Bahar, he would certainly have rejected them as either irrelevant or, worse, positively harmful exercises.

In his poems Ruhollah offers a fairly narrow range; he limits his themes to nature, sorrow at the loss of dear ones, friendship and devotion to the faith. Love is conspicuously absent from Ruhollah's limited canvas. At best, there are only faint echoes of something vaguely resembling human love. The poems' form is that of Hafiz, the content undoubtedly that of Ruhollah himself. His is an austere bride, lacking in the endowments of provocative beauty but dressed in a robe borrowed from a queen. There are numerous references to 'the dear ones departed', but at no point does he directly refer to his father's tragic death. One poem describes a *mointat al-boka'a* (literally, a tears' assistant), a woman employed at mourning ceremonies to stage outbursts of profuse crying so as to encourage others present to weep. Ruhollah's own mother had on occasions, during the mourning months of Muharram and Safar in the Muhammedan lunar calendar, served as a *mointat al-boka'a* in exchange for alms and sundry gifts reserved for the widows of the sayyed. In Ruhollah's poem the tears' assistant cries for the martyr Hussein. But she is, in fact, also crying for her lost husband. We do not know how the woman's husband is lost but we learn that he has been 'a victim of the unjust rulers of this earth'. It is clear that Ruhollah, although he never spoke of his father's murder, neither forgot the tragedy nor forgave those who had perpetrated it. Many years later Ayatollah Khomeini's followers developed the theme of 'son avenging father' as part of the persona they created for him as the leader of the Islamic Revolution.

One advantage of being a seeker at a *madrasseh* was that one could practically live outside conventional time. A seeker did not have to plan his life in the same way that lesser mortals did. He did not know when he would complete his studies and did not have to think about a career. He had no use for worldly possessions but was, at the same time, certain that, in a country where more than half of the population starved at least half the time, he would never have to worry where his next loaf of bread was coming from. Each seeker received a stipend which, although modest, was sufficient for a hermitic life. The seeker lived in a small square room known as the *hojrah* (literally, stone cave), without any furniture other than a coarse tribal rug, a prayer mat, an old blanket often submerged under many patches, an earthen water jar and a bowl, and an oil lamp. The stipend Shaikh Abdul-Karim offered was among the most generous in Qom in those days, and yet it did not exceed the equivalent of £10 a month. Most of the seekers were too poor to have more than one meagre meal a day. Bread and cheese, sweetened with some grapes, constituted the usual fare. Meat was a great luxury, to be consumed a few times each year, on special occasions to mark the martyrdom of one of the Imams or to celebrate the birthday anniversary of the Prophet. A few dates, a handful of raisins, some pistachio nuts and sweet watermelons in summer provided occasional changes in an otherwise unvaried diet. Until the 1930s even tea was a luxury that the seeker could hope to enjoy only when visiting the houses of the rich on special occasions. The average seeker had only one change of clothes, which necessitated daily laundering. Cleanliness being a religious duty, the seeker had to wash at least once a day and complete the ritual of ablution five times a day. This may sound easy in these times of abundant piped water, but in those days in Qom, a city where lack of water was always a major problem, obtaining enough water for a daily wash was no easy task. Each seeker had an *aftabeh* or watercan which he filled three times a day from the nearest well. Not a drop of water could be wasted without incurring the wrath of Allah. Even today Ayatollah Khomeini does not allow half a glass of water to be thrown away. He may keep that water for several days before drinking it again. It was as a seeker in Qom that he learned the value of water. Wasting a single drop is like pulling a feather from the wing of an angel, according to a traditional saying among the mullahs. Thus, the seeker had to learn to make maximum use of a minimum amount of water. Of great help in fighting the inevitable odours of life in a hot and dusty place where most people rarely washed were the jars of rose-water donated to the seekers by pilgrims visiting the holy city. Ruhollah devoted an entire sonnet to praising rosewater, which, if we are to believe him, is a reminder to man of the 'perfumed eternity of paradise'.

A seeker's day began before sunrise when he would perform ablution and then face Mecca for the first of the five prayers that punctuate a Muslim's daily life. He would then drink a glass of lukewarm water sweetened with sugar or a few raisins. Some would supplement this with a bite of bread and goat cheese. The seeker would then go back to sleep for about an hour until the sun had fully risen. This short pre-sunrise sleep is known as the *ghaylulah* and reportedly was highly recommended by the Prophet.

The seeker then went to the *madrasseh* to attend discussions which would last until noon. The older seekers served as *modarres* (instructors) for the younger ones. The master, who formed the centre of the circle of seekers, did not attend the routine daily discussions. He provided what is known as the *dars-e-kharej* (literally, the outside lesson), which represented the highest degree of Shi'ite education. There was no set syllabus and each master chose both the form and the content of his lectures. He did not prepare any notes in advance of each lecture; a master was expected to know by heart whatever he needed for any given session. The seekers took notes during the lecture. These were later corrected and edited and presented to the master for final approval. The master could give his lectures at his own residence; the shrine of Ma'assoumah and the majestic mosque next to it were also used for specially important lectures. Both the master and his disciples sat cross-legged on the floor, which was covered with a straw mat or tribal rug. The seekers had the right to interrupt the lecture at any given time to pose questions or simply ask permission to leave. The master, however, did not answer each question immediately, preferring to respond to all questions in what amounted to a second lecture. It was not unusual for a master to announce that he did not know the answer to a particular question and to invite the disciples to help him with further research into the matter. To the typical seeker, the master was something more than a professor. He was a second father as well as a friend and confessor. Seekers were expected to confide in their master, keeping no secrets from him. They were also required, although never formally obliged, to provide a variety of services ranging from doing the shopping for the master to cleaning his house. Seekers who became favourites of the master were given the honour of becoming *kafsh-kan* (literally, one who takes off the shoes) whose task was to make sure that the master's shoes were always clean and ready for him. Since visitors to Muslim shrines and mosques must remove their shoes before entering the holy precincts, it is not unusual for shoes to be lost or mistakenly worn by someone else in the confusion of many people leaving at the same time. A master could not be expected to shove and jostle in search of his shoes. That was the duty of the *kafsh-kan*. The shoes in question were, of course, only modest slippers called *na'alayn* (literally, two horseshoes). It was early in 1921 that Shaikh Abdul-Karim chose Ruhollah as his *kafsh-kan*, a distinction that must have made some of the other seekers in the circle rather jealous of the dour-faced young man from Khomein.

Becoming a mullah is a vocation whose popularity varies with social and political circumstances. After the defeat of the fundamentalists during the Constitutional Revolution in 1906, the number of young men wishing to become mullahs showed a dramatic drop. That trend was further accelerated with the February 1921 coup d'état, which was to alter the course of Iranian history for over half a century. As a result, Ruhollah's generation was the last to consider becoming a mullah as one of the highest goals for a man. Becoming a mullah was one of the few ways of moving upwards in a society whose class structure, as developed in the sixteenth and seventeenth centuries, had been ossified into something resembling a caste system. For the son of a poor peasant family to rise in the world, so to speak, the choice was between becoming a mullah or joining one of the many private armies maintained by major landlords and tribal chiefs. The physically strong naturally tended to join the military elites, while the more intelligent sons of the people were attracted to religious studies. At times, as in the case of Ruhollah himself, a large number of relatives and friends would join forces to finance the studies of a local bright boy. The peasantry provided something like 80 per cent of the seekers. Many never reached the high status of ayatollah but returned to their villages to serve as *maktabdars*, judges or notaries public. Some, however, reached the very top of the religious hierarchy. Ruhollah was to be one of them. Another contemporary of Ruhollah in those early days at Qom was a shy peasant boy from Golpayegan who was many years later to become Grand Ayatollah Mohammad-Reza Mussavi-Golpayegani. Young men from the urban middle class, in those days forming a negligible percentage of the population, were attracted to a religious career either because of deep personal conviction or out of a natural yearning for speculative knowledge. Many did not stay long enough to become *mujtahids*, but they reaped immense benefits from their religious education in other fields, notably politics. Sons of aristocratic and wealthy families shunned the career of a mullah because it meant spending many years in hardship and self-abnegation. Some, however, welcomed the privations and went on to become notable exceptions to this rule.

Until the 1930s, when the mullahs were gradually marginalized by deliberate government policy, one could find mullahs in all walks of life. Many worked as part-time farmers, shopkeepers, teachers or members of the bureaucracy. For most, being a mullah was not a full-time occupation. They were expected to earn their living while attending to people's religious needs when required. The presence of a mullah was necessary for sanctifying a marriage, blessing a newborn child, reciting the proper prayers for a man who had just died, and delivering sermons at memorial services. But the function of the mullah extended far beyond these fairly routine tasks. Until the late 1920s, when an independent judiciary was created by Reza Shah and turned into a nationwide institution, the mullahs were the administrators of justice, based on Qur'anic law, throughout Iran. They registered virtually all contracts between private citizens and many of them served as trustees for sizable fortunes. They also had to administer the vast estates of various endowments. In 1962, when the reformist government of Ali Amini first launched the idea of land redistribution in Iran, a confidential report prepared for the Shah showed that more than 30 per cent of all cultivated land in the country either belonged to mullahs or was under their administration through more than 20,000 endowments. Bequeathing part of one's estate to one of the estimated 7000 saints of Shi'ism who are buried in Iran was considered the surest means of securing a place in the Islamic paradise. In 1978 the income from Imam Reza's endowments was estimated to be around £1000 million, making it one of the top three nongovernmental enterprises in the country. The Imam's endowments included a variety of businesses ranging from vast sugar plantations to super-luxury hotels.

Another traditional function of the mullahs was to provide what amounted to banking services in conjunction with the bazaar. Since usury is strictly forbidden in Islam, one way of getting round the inevitable problem of interest was to deposit money with a mullah so that he could lend it, supposedly without charging any interest. The borrower would return the money at the appointed time plus a 'voluntary' donation for 'charitable purposes'. Part of that 'donation' would then be transferred to the original depositor as a gift from the mullah. The operation was humorously referred to as 'finding a religious cap' (*kolah-e-shar'ee*). The finding of the proverbial cap was, arguably, one of the most important services rendered by the mullahs in a society which insisted on sticking to virtually inapplicable laws. A *mujtahid* could waive almost any and every rule, including some fully spelled out in the Qur'an itself. Like contemporary experts in legal wizardry, many mullahs developed admirable skills in getting the believers off the strongest of theological hooks. In 1811, for example, the chief mullah of Tabriz was asked by the royal court to find a way of allowing wine to be served at the wedding of the Crown Prince, Abbas Mirza. The proverbial cap was duly found by the mullah, who declared that the Qur'anic ban on wine would be suspended for the day in exchange for a cash gift to the poor by the bridegroom. The mullah cited a quotation attributed to the Prophet to the effect that no action which can lead to good being done can be bad.

The two imperialist powers of the day with direct interest in Iran were Britain and Czarist Russia. Both had recognized the important role of the mullahs in Iran at a very early stage in their quest for the domination and exploitation of the once glorious empire. The Russo-Iranian wars of 1813 and 1824 were both provoked by mullahs declaring jihad on the infidel Russians. Later, it was on the orders of the mullahs that a mob attacked and seized the Russian Embassy in Tehran in what now looks like an early version of the occupation of the US Embassy in 1979 by Muslim 'students'. The attack on the Russian Embassy ended with the murder of the Czarist Minister Plenipotentiary Alexander Griboïdev, a noted poet and writer, and his new bride. The incident shook the Russian aristocracy which counted Griboïdev among its heroes. It also persuaded the Czarist empirebuilders to seek friends and clients among the more powerful of the mullahs.

The British had recognized the importance of the mullahs earlier. They had on their payroll a substantial number of influential mullahs. Money was used with great care, through Indian Muslim agents of the Raj who would travel to Iran periodically to present the 'donations of the faithful' to the mullahs selected for their Anglophile attitudes. Mullahs who demonstrated hostility to British interests in Iran invariably found that they had suddenly ceased to have any followers among Indian Shi'ites. The British suffered a serious tactical setback in Iran when a leading ayatollah of Najaf declared the smoking of tobacco to be contrary to the laws of Islam. The *fitwa* had the effect of cancelling a highly profitable monopoly granted to a British company. The monopoly had been designed as the key element in a scheme to give British companies virtually unlimited rights in exploiting Iran's natural resources and trading potential. The Russians were alarmed by the success of their British rivals at the Qajar court and the tobacco boycott provided them with an opportunity to offset part of

Britain's recent gains. The boycott led to the cancellation of the contract by the Shah. But the mullahs, recognizing the importance of their own ties with the two imperial powers, did not go far enough in their sudden outburst of anti-colonial anger. At no point did they challenge the capitulatory rights granted to both Britain and Russia in Iran.

The division of the mullahs into Russophile and Anglophile factions continued until the Bolshevik Revolution of 1917 ended Russia's traditional colonial ambitions in Iran. From then on it was Britain that the mullahs considered as the dominant power in the region as a whole. The fact that the Bolsheviks openly advocated atheism and made a point of trying to uproot Islam in the Caucasus and Central Asia persuaded many mullahs that only British support could help counterbalance the emerging power of a heathen state dedicated to the destruction of Muhammedanism. This belief was soon to prove a mere illusion. The Bolsheviks succeeded in ruthlessly crushing a Shi'ite revolt, led by Imam Shamel, in the Caucasus while the British waited and watched. An attempt by Anglophile mullahs to secure British support for a jihad against Lenin's 'heathen hordes' failed miserably.

The Bolshevik Revolution and its subsequent efforts to de-Islamicize the Muslim-inhabited lands of the defunct Czarist empire reached Qom only in faint echoes. Ruhollah heard accounts of the Bolshevik Revolution and the massacres of Muslims in Azerbaijan and what was briefly to become an independent Armenian republic from Shi'ite refugees pouring into Qom after fleeing the Caucasus. Those who chose Qom as an abode of exile were especially devout Shi'ites. The presence of the Ma'assoumah shrine in the holy city made them feel secure and reassured them of the permanency of their faith. They described Lenin's movement as one aimed at legalizing polyandry and forcing the Muslims to shave their beards. Bolshevism meant *zan shariiki*, or the sharing of wives by two or more men. In a society where even an innocent glance at a married woman could lead to bloodshed, the idea of a political movement forcing Muslims under Russian occupation to share wives was, quite simply, the end of the world.[8] The émigrés also presented Bolshevism as a plot by Jews against both Islam and Christianity. Even Lenin and Stalin were 'militant Jews' taking their orders from a secret committee of rabbis working from an unspecified location in Central Europe. This belief was to remain with Ruhollah for the rest of his life.[9]

Preoccupation with the disastrous consequences of the Bolshevik Revolution for millions of fellow-Muslims was, however, to be soon pushed into the background as a result of equally alarming developments inside Iran herself. While Qom continued its seemingly eternal slumber, the whole of the country was, once again, stirring against the Qajars and their incompetent rule. The removal of the dynasty's Czarist protectors gave Britain the free hand she had seldom enjoyed in shaping the policies of the Qajar state. The pro-Russian faction within the ruling clique was suddenly rendered powerless and the Anglophiles could, for the first time in over a century, have it their own way. But the dynasty was by then too weak to hold the country together and make sure Britain's vital interests, notably the oil fields of Khuzestan, remained safe. The reigning king, Ahmad Shah, was too young, too inexperienced and too genuinely dedicated to the country's democratic constitution as well as the state of his own finances to be able to provide effective leadership in a basically medieval society attempting to imitate a Westminster-style parliamentary system. The Iranian intelligentsia, partly shaken and partly inspired by the success of the Russian Revolution, was crying out for reform and, taking its cue from what was going on in neighbouring Turkey, advocated the creation of a republic in Iran for the first time. Britain, which a generation earlier had sided with the constitutionalists against the Qajars, who had been backed by the Russians, was now forced to face the necessity of helping to destroy the selfsame system of constitutional monarchy it had formerly hailed as the panacea for all Iran's many ills.

# 4

# *The Turban and the Crown*

Perdition begins with but a small step, a tiny step that can be dismissed as insignificant. Man moves towards Hell step by step. All those who were lost did not become corrupt all of a sudden — with a giant leap as it were. They began with tiny insignificant steps and were soon beyond salvation. . . . There is a devil in every man, corrupting him little by little.

Ayatollah Khomeini

*T*he spring equinox, known as Nowruz (New Day) in Persian, marks the start of the Iranian calendar year. It is celebrated with great pomp and joy throughout the country, and also in Afghanistan, Soviet Tadzihkistan, Soviet Azerbaijan and northern Iraq. According to Persian mythology, it was on Nowruz that Jamshid, the first Shahanshah, was crowned. The tradition of Nowruz came into Iran at least a thousand years before Islam, and is therefore frowned upon by the mullahs as a relic from the 'pagan past' and a reminder that Iranians have not yet been fully converted to the Muhammedan faith. Numerous attempts at ending Nowruz as a national tradition have failed during the past thirteen centuries, the latest being Ayatollah Khomeini's own all-out attack on 'these paganistic rites' in 1979.

It was partly in order to soothe the mullahs that every Iranian king made a point of reaffirming his allegiance to Islam on the occasion of Nowruz. This often took the form of a pilgrimage to one of the holy shrines. Shah Abbas the Great, the most successful of the Safavid monarchs, showed his devotion to Mohammedanism by making the pilgrimage to the holy city of Mashhad on foot. That act of piety gave him licence to enjoy the excellent wines of Shiraz and the sophisticated music of Isfahan during prolonged ceremonies preceding the start of the pilgrimage. During the nineteenth century the tradition of visiting the holy shrine of Imam Reza at Mashhad was continued by the Qajar kings. But from 1916 onwards the tradition had to be modified. When Iran was occupied by the Allies during the First World War Mashhad fell into the Russian occupation zone. Later, after the Allies had withdrawn from Iran in 1918, Mashhad had still remained beyond the reach of the Qajar Shah as a result of Turkoman rebellions that virtually isolated the holy city. The only way to reach the shrine of Imam Reza was to take a boat to a Central Asian port on the Caspian and then travel through Russian-held territory southwards to Iran. Such a route was manifestly unsafe for the Persian Sovereign even at the best of times, and by 1921 the Bolsheviks were already firmly established in Central Asia and were beginning to foment revolution in Iran's own northern provinces as well. The only place Ahmad Shah, the popular but ineffectual Qajar monarch, could pick as the object of his Nowruz pilgrimage was the holy city of Qom.

News of the Shah's Nowruz pilgrimage to Qom was announced as early as January 1921 so as to give the pro-Qajar faction in the holy city time to prepare as impressive a show of loyalty to Ahmad Shah as they could organize in those days of dynastic decline. Special agents were dispatched to talk to the mullahs and seekers, playing on their fear of Bolshevism and the dangers that were beginning to engulf the only Shi'ite state in the world. The mullahs were told that the end of the Qajar dynasty could mark their end also, and that Iran's two super-institutions, the monarchy and the mosque, had to strengthen their unity in the face of exceptional domestic and external threats. The expulsion of mullahs from the newly created Soviet state and the murder of numerous Shi'ite preachers by Sunni Turkoman rebels in the Gorgan Plain, northeast of Tehran, were cited as examples of what could be in store for the turbaned guardians of the True Faith.

One leading mullah who needed no convincing was Shaikh Abdul-Karim, Ruhollah's master and benefactor. The Shaikh was determined to give a boost to the reportedly sagging morale of the Shah. He was to lead a welcoming party of thousands to the city's outer gate through which the Shah would enter, accompanied by his numerous suite. The demonstration was meant as a warning to both the Bolsheviks and the British that projects aimed at upsetting the traditional power structure in Iran could not be implemented without resistance. Ruhollah was put in charge of part of the arrangements, and he tackled his task with dedication and enthusiasm. That was his first and, for many years, his only experience of active politics.

The Shah was supposed to arrive in Qom in the second week of March and stay there until after the spring equinox. The city, usually covered with a thick coat of dirt and dust, was given a thorough spring-clean; many walls were given a new crust of bright mud and doors and windows were painted blue and white. The Ma'assoumah mausoleum was also given a good scrub, the first in decades. The vast army of beggars, forming something like a quarter of the city's estimated population of 20,000, were chased out and told to stay away until after the Shah had completed his pilgrimage. Some bazaar merchants offered cloth for new turbans or new *abas* (hand-knitted cloaks made from camel wool) to their favourite mullahs. A proclamation describing the Shah as Zel al-Allah fel-Ardh (the Shadow of Allah on Earth) was pasted on city walls, announcing the impending royal visit.

On 23 February, however, bad news arrived from Tehran. The so-called Brigade of Cossacks stationed near Qazvin, seventy miles northwest of Tehran, had staged a putsch and were marching on the capital. The earlier rumours spoke of the Shah as having been either killed or captured. Later, however, it was announced that the Shah had acceded to the putschists' demands by dismissing the government and appointing a new Prime Minister. The Shah's long-awaited visit to Qom would not now take place. In any case, even if the Shah were eventually to make the pilgrimage, he would have been little more than a shadow of his previous self. The putsch not only deprived Qom of the opportunity to honour a popular king, it also marked the beginning of a creeping revolution that was to lead to radical changes in Iranian society over the following six decades.

Two names were mentioned as the leaders of the putsch. One, the well-known Sayyed Ziaeddin Tabataba'i, was promptly appointed Prime Minister by Ahmad Shah. The other, Reza Khan, the brigade commander who actually carried out the putsch, received the post of War Minister as his share of the spoils. Both men represented social and political ideas which Ruhollah hated instinctively and he was later to describe them as 'agents of our ruination'.[1] They reminded Ruhollah and the world at large of the evanescence of power in fragile societies like Iran. Iranian folklore is full of stories about utter nonentities rising to power as a result of a lucky combination of events.

Ruhollah, as he was to recall decades later, could not decide which of the duo that had organized and carried out the putsch was the greater villain. But it is likely that, at least in the early days of the new regime, he directed much of his intense hatred towards Sayyed Ziaeddin.[2] Ziaeddin was something of a Judas in the eyes of the mullahs. He had trained to become a mullah, but had quickly discarded the turban and the long flowing robe of the Shi'ite clergy for an Ottoman-style cap and a European suit, complete with a deliberately provocative brightly coloured bow tie. Although a sayyed, and thus a direct descendant of the Prophet, Ziaeddin (who had come into contact with European ideas during his rather erratic studies in Palestine, then under British mandate) had the courage, or to the mullahs the gall, to speak of Iranian nationalism. In the eyes of the mullahs, Ziaeddin was the latest champion of Western-orientated intellectuals, whose secret wish was to secularize Iranian society and replace the idea of devotion to the Islamic faith with that of patriotism. Ziaeddin's connections with the British were all too apparent. It was obvious that the British had not been totally unaware of the putsch from its earliest planning stages. They saw in the move a means of helping Iran get out of the social and political impasse she had reached under the Qajars. Further, the British had not forgotten the generally Russophile attitude of the Qajars. Ziaeddin had quickly emerged as a leading voice for reform thanks to a daily newspaper he published in Tehran, probably with British moral and financial encouragement. He had created around himself a circle of intellectuals under the slogan *An-anat e Melli* (Nationalist Traditions). In masterminding the putsch his objective was to restore full constitutional government, retaining the Qajar monarch as a mere figurehead while an elected unicameral parliament would choose the Premier and Cabinet, and exercise full legislative power. Both the monarch and the mosque would become merely part of the political decor in such a system.

The mullahs, having identified Ziaeddin as their arch enemy, began fighting him almost from the first day of his premiership. They soon began to build up Reza Khan, the new War Minister, as the only man capable of getting rid of the treacherous sayyed.

They did not know that by doing so they were, in fact, jumping from the frying pan into the fire.

Reza took every care to curry favour with the mullahs. The man who was later to preside over a vast movement of secularization in Iran did not wish to reveal his hand at that early stage. During the month of Muharram when Shi'ites hold street processions to mark the martyrdom of Hussein, the third Imam, Reza would be seen weeping bitterly and beating his bare chest. His zeal allowed little doubt about his devotion to Islam, as interpreted by the mullahs. Not all mullahs were duped, however. Sayyed Hassan Modarress, a member of the Majlis, recognized the ambitious brigadier's true colours right from the start and opposed Reza Khan with remarkable dedication. Modarress was to pay for this with his life. His assassination, blamed on the khan's agents, silenced the one important voice among the Shi'ite clergy that might have posed a serious threat to the future Shah's schemes.

In the meantime, Reza Khan succeeded in sabotaging several hastily formed governments thanks to his friends in the Majlis and some of the big bazaar merchants who saw in him the only man capable of saving Iran from an eventual Bolshevik takeover. The Caspian province of Gilan was already more or less independent and the oil-rich Khuzestan, in the southwest, was fast becoming an Arab emirate paying only nominal tribute to Tehran.

Reza, combining the post of War Minister with that of Sardar-e-Sepah (Commander-in-Chief), appeared the providential man everyone had hoped for since the chaos following Iran's occupation during the First World War. In 1923 Reza managed to end the ephemeral Republic of Gilan set up by Mirza Kuchak Khan. Kuchak Khan's Republic of the Jungle (so called because of its stronghold in the dense forests of the Caspian littoral) was, in a sense, something of a dress rehearsal for Khomeini's Islamic Revolution more than half a century later. The charismatic ex-mullah used a mixture of religious passion and hatred for the rich as the basis for his discourse. He took from the rich and gave to the poor, and claimed that he was reviving the 'tradition of Medina' as the model for a truly Islamic state. The explosive potential of Kuchak Khan's synthesis of Islam and Communism was quickly recognized by Reza. He knew that the populist Islam of the Jungle could easily sweep the entire country. There is evidence that Ruhollah knew what was going on in Gilan and was strongly attracted to Kuchak Khan's teachings.[3]

Reza Khan made the destruction of the Republic of the Jungle a prime objective. But before he could use military force to crush the rebels he had to portray them as threats to Iran and to Islam. Through a careful propaganda campaign he persuaded public opinion, especially among the mullahs, that Mirza Kuchak Khan was a Communist and an atheist. The rebel leader was accused of being a Bolshevik agent although Lenin's still-fledgling Soviet state, which was, in fact, arming Kuchak Khan, considered the revolutionary ex-mullah as nothing but a petit-bourgeois opportunist. Mullahs financed by Reza Khan took to the pulpit throughout the country to demolish Kuchak Khan and Communism. The destruction of the Republic of the Jungle was seen as a joint enterprise of the newly organized army and the Shi'ite clergy, who both urged the peasants to join them.

The next step was the reassertion of central government authority in Khuzestan. There, Shaikh Khaz'al, an Arab tribal leader, had set up what amounted to a semi-autonomous emirate based on the port city of Muhammarah (which was later renamed Khorramshahr). The shaikh, enjoying a measure of British protection, had hoped that the Anglo-Persian Oil Company which exploited the region's oil resources would not allow him to fall into Reza Khan's hands. Khaz'al concluded a pact with the Bakhtiari tribes for common resistance against Reza's army. The Arab-speaking tribes of Bani-Ka'ab and Banu-Turuf could field a force of 10,000 rifles backed with a camel-riding 'cavalry' force of some 1000 seasoned fighters. The Bakhtiaris, under Amir Jahed, had some 15,000 armed men. Both Khaz'al and Amir Jahed soon realized that neither the British Government nor the oil company would be able or willing to help them win a war against Reza's much more disciplined and better equipped army. A few engagements proved sufficient for the destruction of the Arab emirate and its allied Bakhtiari tribal confederation. Unlike in Gilan, where the alleged Communism of the rebels had been the main theme of government propaganda, the struggle against Khaz'al in Khuzestan was presented as a confrontation between the Persians and the Arabs. Persian nationalism was to develop into one of the main ingredients of the ideology Reza Khan considered to be essential for the regeneration of the Iranian nation-state.

Qom had enthusiastically greeted Reza Khan's success in ending the Republic of the Jungle. But the defeat of the Bakhtiaris and the dethronement and capture of Shaikh Khaz'al in the name of Persian nationalism was a different matter. In the propaganda launched by Reza Khan, the mullahs of Qom detected national-istic themes that reminded them of Atatürk's already condemned exercise in nation-building in neighbouring Turkey. Ruhollah was one of the first mullahs to realize that the new strong man meant to follow in the footsteps of the Turkish leader who was already anathematized and declared a heretic by the traditional Muslim clergy. Islam could tolerate no rival ideology and Reza Khan's efforts to create a nationalist *prise de conscience* among the Iranians was seen as a direct attempt at creating an alternative source of legitimacy. Most Iranians had all but forgotten their pre-Islamic past and had little or no chronological notion of history. Persepolis, whose majestic ruins dominated the plain of Morghab near Shiraz, was not recognizable to the average Iranian as the once glorious capital of the Achaemenean empire. It was called Takht-e-Jamshid (Jamshid's Throne) and believed to be a relic of a mythological past. The tomb of Cyrus the Great at Pasargadae was believed to be the resting place of King Solomon's mother. Outside the small Zoroastrian community all ancient Persian names had been replaced by Arab Islamic ones. Even Shahnameh (Book of Kings), Iran's national epic, subsequently adopted as the holy book of Persian nationalism, was recited in public in praise of Ali, the first Imam. Darius the Great's famous edict, engraved on the face of a rock near the western city of Kermanshah, had been discovered and deciphered by the British archaeologist Sir Henry Rawlinson half a century earlier and later translated into both English and Persian. But most Iranians did not know of its existence and were therefore unaware of the King of Kings' great exploits. Over some four hundred years the mullahs had suc-ceeded in effacing the nation's collective memory of its pre-Islamic past. Iran's ancient history was considered a tragic tale of igno-rance and damnation that was best bequeathed to oblivion.

Reza Khan's wish to develop Persian nationalism as an alter-native ideology for Iranians was seen by many mullahs as yet another anti-Islamic plot hatched by the Christian powers. The West had failed to conquer Islam by the sword, and Christianity stood absolutely no chance of winning converts among the Mus-lims. It was, therefore, the mullahs claimed, necessary for the West to find other ways of weakening Islam. Nationalism was one such way.

Ruhollah put this view bluntly in an essay he wrote late in 1924. In it he indirectly attacked Reza Khan's advocacy of nationalism as a means of creating a powerful central government and ending the tribal and feudal structures of the society. 'Before Islam,' Ruhollah wrote, 'the lands now blessed by our True Faith suffered miserably because of ignorance and cruelty. There is nothing in that past that is worth glorification.'⁴ It is possible that the essay angered Shaikh Abdul-Karim who at the time strongly supported Reza Khan. Reza Khan's point of launching his campaigns against semi-autonomous provincial rulers in the name of 'our great Nation' rather than of Allah may have troubled Shaikh Abdul-Karim, but the fact that the Commander-in-Chief was restoring stability and security to the country was considered sufficiently important to offset his provocative playing up of the Persian past. On the eve of the campaign against Khaz'al, for example, Reza Khan had taken an oath either 'to end the last squeamish noises of feudalism' or 'to be buried under the ruins of Susa'. The mullahs may not have liked the reference to the pagan capital, but the fact that Khaz'al's dislodgement meant that the mullahs could once again freely operate in Khuzestan was greeted with gratitude in Qom and Mashhad.

Reza Khan's decisive manner in dealing with his opponents made nonsense of the attempts by traditional Qajar politicians to stop his ascendancy. The strong man who barely knew how to read and write proved to be a master strategist in the complicated politics of a society in turmoil. He engineered the sending of the Qajar king into exile to Europe and then began promoting the idea of turning Iran into a republic based on the model created by Atatürk. The changing of the national calendar, from Arabic and Islamic months, to an ancient Persian one, the creation of a national bank and the passing of the Military Service Act were all modelled on measures taken in neighbouring Turkey. By getting himself appointed Prime Minister by the Majlis, in the absence of the exiled Shah, Reza Khan had by 1924 become the unquestioned master of Iran. An earlier attempt by the Majlis to curb his powers had rebounded when the future king staged a dramatic departure from the capital after announcing that he planned to retire 'because of so many intrigues'. He was brought back from his temporary retreat in a village near Tehran by well-organized gangs of supporters roaming the streets of Tehran demanding his return. Similar demonstrations were organized in the provinces, notably in Qom, where a large crowd had gathered at the holy shrine to pray for Reza Khan's safe return to power. Post-revolutionary legend has it that Ruhollah 'resisted' the movement launched in favour of Reza Khan and even made a number of speeches in Qom in 1924. But there are no independent accounts of this.

In September 1925 Reza Khan used the same tactic of demonstrating his power over the crowd to intimidate his opponents, but this time for a final showdown. Calls for the end of the Qajar dynasty and invitations to Reza Khan to rule Iran as he wished came from every part of the country. In November a special session of the Majlis adopted a fifty-word resolution ending the Qajar dynasty and handing over the government to Reza Khan. By the time the resolution was tabled at the Majlis, Reza Khan had already chosen Pahlavi as his family name. The word Pahlavi, meaning 'heroic', comes from the version of the Persian language which had been in use until the Arab invasion of Iran in the seventh century AD.

It was as Reza Pahlavi, Prime Minister and Commander-in-Chief, that the now undisputed master of Iran organized a Constituent Assembly a few weeks later. In only five sessions the Assembly declared Reza Pahlavi Shahanshah of Iran and empowered him to found a new dynasty. Less than fifteen hours after the Assembly had ended its final session, Reza Pahlavi crowned himself King of Kings at the Golestan Palace. The mullahs who had fought against the idea of turning Iran into a republic were reassured. The sight of Reza Shah I sitting on the Peacock Throne and kissing the Holy Qur'an persuaded them that the change of dynasty would not mean a change in their power and fortunes. They were to be bitterly disappointed. Reza had failed in creating a republic but he had not abandoned his dreams of secularization. He was determined to destroy all traditional centres of power in the country so that the state could emerge as a super-institution dedicated to the task of nation-building. The tribal chiefs and provincial khans and emirs had been eliminated, as had the vast army of Qajar aristocrats. A brief edict cancelling all aristocratic titles and honours illustrated the republican style of the new king. Reza Shah, as he now was, knew that the last traditional centre of power belonged to the mullahs. He was to waste no time in storming that citadel as well.

The newly created army that provided the new dynasty's main power base naturally received privileged treatment. A military caste was quickly created bearing such titles as *sarkar* (used for officers below the rank of brigadier) and *timsar* (designating generals). These titles rivalled religious titles such as Hojat al-Islam and ayatollah in power and prestige. Reza Shah openly aimed at promoting loyalty to the burgeoning Iranian nation-state as the highest value in the Prussian-style society he wished to create. This made conflict with the clergy inevitable as the mullahs believed that Islam should have the highest value and that loyalty to the Muhammedan faith must remain total and unqualified.

The holy city of Qom, continuing its slumber in relative peace, was at first left alone by the new Shah in his increasingly disturbing attempts to revive the pre-Islamic empire of the Achaemeneans. Mullahs and *talabehs*, streaming into the city from Tehran, Mashhad, Shiraz and other cities where theological schools were closing down, brought with them many accounts of the new regime's irreverence and apparent determination to destroy the Shi'ite clergy. But these second-hand accounts of trouble and turmoil were not sufficient to persuade the mullahs of Qom that their turn might come soon. Things began to change from 1926 onwards.

To begin with, the new Shah, breaking the tradition of a New Year pilgrimage to the shrine of Ma'assoumah, went instead to the holy city of Mashhad to pray at the shrine of the eighth Imam. The shrine was cleared of all pilgrims, as well as the mullahs and other religious functionaries who worked or prayed there, so that the Shah could enjoy the privilege of meditative solitude. The move scandalized the mullahs since it meant that Shi'ism had no need of a clerical class and that the faithful could perform even the highest of rites without assistance from the turbaned specialists.

Returning from Mashhad in the spring of 1928, the Shah ordered the promulgation of two new edicts. The first made national service compulsory. The second ordered all Iranian men to wear a uniform version of the European suit complete with a specially designed kepi. The army was given the task of implementing both edicts. The theory behind both moves was that once all young men had spent two years together serving in the army, their tribal and ethnic differences would be blurred if not actually effaced. They would also learn Persian, the national language, and discover new values such as loyalty to a central state that stood above religious, ethnic and tribal feuds. The uniform dress would help not only to remove the appearance of diversity as far as tribal and provincial origins were concerned but also to destroy the most immediately noticeable aspect of a highly hierarchized society. Until then a man's ethnic and tribal origin and his station in life could be recognized from his clothes and hats. The uniform would end all that since all men would be wearing the same style of dress made from the same kind of material. The Shah hoped that this would remove not only the well-established ethnic and tribal differences but also class distinctions. The kepi, resembling that worn by French gendarmes, would replace the turban, which Reza Shah, wrongly, assumed to be an Arab headgear.

Once the edicts were promulgated, zealous army officers began implementing them with exceptional brutality. Tens of thousands of young men were torn away from their families and dispatched to provinces as far from home as possible so that they could train as soldiers, learn Persian and become worthy heirs to Cyrus the Great. In many city and village squares huge bonfires were built to burn thousands of turbans and tribal or 'guild' hats seized from bewildered men who suddenly discovered that the revival of the Persian Empire must be their chief goal in life. The more enthusiastic officers went even further and ordered that all beards should also be shaved. In some provinces local garrison commanders also banned the *na'alayn*, the slippers worn by the mullahs.

Ruhollah was in Arak, attending the funeral of a friend's father, when the new storm broke out. He was outraged by Pahlavi's frontal attack on traditional society. But his immediate concern was how to return to Qom without losing his turban and having his beard forcibly shaved off by 'modernizing' officers who seemed to take an almost sadistic pleasure in humilitating the mullahs. Ruhollah was proud of his beard, which was thick and full. In one of his poems he refers to it as 'the cherished friend of my face'. His turban was even more important. Its black colour denoted direct descent from the Prophet; thus to have it removed by a soldier would be an insult to the Messenger of Allah himself. Ruhollah had learned the art of rolling a turban with great dexterity and his turbans were often the smartest and the most elegantly rolled in sight. Rolling a turban may appear a fairly pedestrian enterprise, but in reality it requires a special touch, a certain sense of style. Ruhollah was gifted with such a touch right from the start and remains a turban-roller of style even in old age. In May 1979 he demonstrated his art in front of television cameras in Tehran by rolling a turban some six metres long. A turban can easily get out of control and become either too big and thus too pretentious, or tend to sag, denoting sloppiness on the part of the wearer.

Believing that the disturbances would not last beyond a week or two, Ruhollah decided to stay in Arak until the dust had settled. He lodged with a friend, Ali Emadi who, while sympathizing with

Ruhollah, considered Reza Shah's policies good for the bazaar. Emadi, a young merchant, argued that the security created by the new Shah's policy of tribal disarmament and the establishment of army garrisons in more than a hundred towns and villages would help create a national market economy. The two friends had heated arguments, with Ruhollah rejecting the benefits of this world that could cost the loss of the next. The unplanned stay in Arak lasted five weeks. It was a message from Shaikh Abdul-Karim which persuaded Ruhollah that it was time to return to Qom.

The easiest way to reach Qom from Arak was to travel to Tehran, and there board one of the coaches that left for the holy city on Mondays and Thursdays. But, for a mullah, if there were one place in the whole world to be avoided in those days it was Tehran. Passing through the capital would have almost certainly meant the loss of both beard and turban. Ruhollah decided to return to Qom via the mountainous region of Khamseh. That meant travelling on muleback for several days, with overnight stays at villages en route. The mountain tracks leading to the edge of the desert where Qom stood in its macabre glory were not patrolled by the Shah's army and therefore offered the prospect of unmolested passage. But even then Ruhollah was not sufficiently reassured. He took two more precautionary steps. The first was to perform the *estekhareh*, which literally means 'consultation'. One poses a question in one's mind and then opens a page of the Holy Book at random. The sura thus chosen is supposed to contain the answer to the question. All depends, of course, on interpretation. Ruhollah's *estekhareh* provided him with an affirmative answer to the question of whether he should attempt the return to Qom at that particular moment. The second step was to consult an eccentric luminary known only as Shebli who seems to have been a curious mixture of mullah, dervish and soothsayer. In exchange for a modest sum or a hot meal, Shebli, who also practised spiritualism and other occult arts, would tell his benefactor's fortune or ask the jinnis to drive his enemies away. It is difficult to decide how much importance Ruhollah attached to Shebli's predictions. But the vagrant saint-cum-conman was to become something of a friend to Ruhollah, visiting him whenever he was passing through Qom. At any rate, Shebli told Ruhollah that he could travel back to Qom in full confidence. 'You shall return to the shadow of holy Ma'assoumah's shrine safely and with both your beard and your turban intact,' Shebli told his client. 'I can also tell you that you shall die in Qom at a very ripe old age.'[5] When this latter part of the prediction was recalled by Ruhollah in later years he expressed confidence that he would return from exile to die in Qom.

The journey back to Qom, at last begun, proved especially arduous because of the heavy snow that blocked the mountain passes. And in many villages there was hardly anything to eat. It was the first time since his childhood that Ruhollah was confronted with the reality of life in the Iranian countryside where the passage of many centuries of tyranny and neglect had left a thick sediment of misery consisting of layer on layer of poverty and despair. In village after village he found broken men struggling to retain what seemed the very last grains of their humanity. In a sense, however, the most difficult part of the journey was its initial stage when Ruhollah had to pass through the streets of Arak on muleback, trying to avoid soldiers and local bureaucrats who were anxious not to allow a single turban to remain unrolled. To escape attention, Ruhollah arranged for his departure to take place shortly after sunset. He covered himself in a thick blanket and wrapped a big shawl around his face, carefully covering his threatened beard.[6]

Qom seemed like a haven of peace and plenty compared with the turmoil in Arak and the misery that gripped the villages on the way. For almost two weeks Ruhollah had survived on a diet of coarse black bread and sour yoghurt, washed down with huge bowls of pale tea sweetened with raisins. Only once or twice had he eaten a hot meal. This had consisted of ground millet mixed with onions and boiled in salt water to make a thick soup. Once a few extra coins had led to the magical appearance of half a dozen eggs, which provided the *plat de résistance* in an unexpected feast in which the local mullah and the headman had joined the young traveller. Besides better and more copious meals, Qom also offered the luxury of a hot bath in which Ruhollah could cast off what he jokingly described as his 'second skin' acquired during the journey and benefit from the services of the resident masseur. The public bath, not far from the holy shrine, was open from dawn to dusk every day. Men could use it every day except Saturdays which were reserved for women and children of both sexes aged under seven. One could spend the entire day at the bath, eating pistachios and melons and arguing about the finer points of theology. The bath was classless and those who could afford the price were treated as equals regardless of their social and economic status.

Only the higher-ranking ayatollahs and religious teachers such as Shaikh Abdul-Karim were allowed the privilege of a more or less private chamber. The centre of the bath consisted of a deep but narrow pool of lukewarm water in which the customers dipped their bodies and sometimes even tried to swim, often without much success, after a thorough scrubbing at the hands of the *dallak* (the brusher). The sight of so many mullahs and *talabehs* passing through the streets of Qom with their beards and turbans still intact was pleasant and comforting. To Ruhollah the image of a perfect Islamic city would not be complete without mullahs in their traditional gear.

The city's serene appearance, however, disguised a profound sense of malaise. The mullahs knew that their very existence as a privileged caste was threatened. They also knew that, sooner or later, Reza Shah's soldiers would also reach Qom. The Shi'ite clergy had never been so confused and leaderless. Many eminent ayatollahs had simply left Iran to take up residence in the holy cities of Najaf, Karbala and Kazemain in Mesopotamia. Going into exile was a long and deeply rooted tradition. Had not the Prophet himself left Mecca for Medina when the Meccites made life unbearable for him? Muhammed is quoted as having said that 'fleeing from bad rulers is a characteristic trait of the prophets'. The general feeling among the mullahs was that Reza Shah represented a passing storm. 'Let us bow our heads until the storm passes,' they said. This mood of resignation frustrated Ruhollah and those of his friends who preached immediate and strong action. They believed that Reza Shah and his army could be quickly isolated provided the Shi'ite leadership officially excluded them from the ranks of the believers.

Disagreements as to how to deal with the new regime's increasingly hostile policies was to affect Ruhollah's relations with his master Shaikh Abdul-Karim profoundly. While the young sayyed argued for energetic action, the septuagenarian shaikh recommended a wait-and-see approach. Ruhollah must have resented his master's apparent submission to what both agreed was tyranny of the harshest kind. But years later Ruhollah himself was to recommend to his own more zealous followers the virtues of patience.

Before long the new regime's reforms reached Qom itself. Some *talabehs* were virtually pressganged into the army while others sought sanctuary in the holy shrine. Reza Shah's troops respected the tradition that anyone seeking sanctuary at the shrine should be allowed to stay. Many mullahs found in Ma'assoumah's generous embrace the last bastion of Islam in the face of what they saw as a pagan power. By 1928 the new regime had ordered not only the removal of turbans and the shaving of beards as well as the wearing of uniform clothes but was also preparing a number of measures aimed at what Reza Shah described as the de-Arabization of Iran. The names of hundreds of villages and towns were changed as part of a sweeping programme of 'Persianization'. The names that were changed were often those of Shi'ite saints and were replaced with the names of pre-Islamic Iranian kings or mythological heroes. Later a special academy was created to purge the Persian language of as many 'borrowed' Arabic words as possible. The academy proved eminently successful and revived or coined thousands of Persian words, helping create a vocabulary which, to Ruhollah and other mullahs, appeared to be deliberately removed from the language of the Qur'an.

Ruhollah spent almost all of 1928 within no more than a mile of the holy shrine. Together with a few other young mullahs he rented a large house at the end of the sweetmakers' bazaar not far from the mausoleum. The idea was that they could immediately seek sanctuary at the shrine if and when Reza Shah's pressgangs appeared again. The house was only a few hundred yards from the large building where Shaikh Abdul-Karim lived and held most of his classes. Years later Ruhollah was to remember those 'days of terror' when every footstep heard in the narrow alleys of the neighbourhood in the moonless night was dreaded as belonging to the Shah's agents searching for more beards to shave and more turbans to burn in public.[7] That year of imposed seclusion, during which he did not leave his rented room for days except to wash, was punctuated only by a number of visits from his brother Morteza and a few of his friends from Arak.

The town of Arak had maintained its almost sinister fascination for Ruhollah. It was there that his father's murderers had been freed in a mockery of justice, and it had also been in Arak that he had spent some of the happiest days of his life. For a time Ruhollah thought of buying himself a small house, with a small garden, in Arak and getting married and raising a family. At least one of his friends from Arak tried to persuade Ruhollah to take a bride. The friend, Qanbar-Ali Ashtiani, had himself just married into a pious and wealthy local family of bazaaris and wished to have an eminent sayyed as his brother-in-law. By the Iranian standards of those days Ruhollah was already a confirmed bachelor and, at twenty-seven, was beginning to be considered almost middle-aged. Most men married between the ages of sixteen and twenty and by the time they had reached forty many were grandfathers. Ruhollah may have been tempted by Qanbar-Ali's offer of a marriage that promised both fortune and influence in Arak. After all, Ruhollah's only asset at the time was his title of a sayyed and the Araki family in question was reputed to be extremely rich. But Ruhollah had another option. During the 'year of terror' he had met a *talabeh* some eight years his junior. Sayyed Rahim Saqafi was the son of a wealthy Tehrani family which boasted as its head Ayatollah Mohammad-Hussein Saqafi, a pious and respected religious leader in south Tehran who complemented his income from donations by the faithful with occasional business transactions in the bazaar. The ayatollah had three marriageable daughters and, despite his being already 'too old' for marriage, Ruhollah could count on Rahim's support in seeking the hand of at least one of them. Another mullah, Mohammad Lavasani, was also related to the Saqafis and, as a friend of Ruhollah, was prepared to help make the match.

By the spring of 1930 Reza Shah's anti-mullah campaign had lost some of its ardour and turbaned heads were reappearing in the streets of Qom and Mashhad. Only Tehran itself remained dangerous to visit. Thus, when Lavasani suggested a holy pilgrimage to Mashhad there were many young mullahs to support him. Ruhollah welcomed the idea as a means of ending, more than a year of virtual imprisonment. By April nearly two dozen mullahs had put their names down for the pilgrimage. Shaikh Abdul-Karim strongly supported the plan but made it clear that he himself would not go. The risk of being arrested on the way and having one's beard shaved off still existed and an eminent religious leader could not take it. Eventually a group of twenty mullahs, led by Lavasani, left Qom for Mashhad early in May. The pilgrims were taking the long desert road that bypassed Tehran. This was to prove an eventful journey. The pilgrims travelled over seemingly endless tracts of desert dotted with tiny oases populated by 'wretches, vaguely resembling human beings'.[8] But everywhere, the poor of the desert, barely squeezing a life out of the salt-lands of the Kavir, did everything they could to make the mullahs feel welcome. The presence of so many mullahs convinced them that Islam was still alive and that the local clergy who had either been taken into the army or had fled to Mesopotamia would soon return. The pilgrims were also able to see how the Pahlavi state was making its presence felt throughout the country. Gendarmerie posts had been established in many villages and government offices already existed in the larger towns. In Semnan, once a sleepy desert town, the presence of an army garrison had created something of an economic boom and the mullahs were treated with less than respect by the local bazaaris who supported the new regime's policy of profitable progress. The Semnani merchants, at first, even refused to sell fodder for the horses drawing the four carriages that transported the pilgrims. The contrast between the treatment received at the hands of Semnan's merchants and the welcome extended by the poor peasants was to affect Ruhollah profoundly. Many years later, he developed his theory of 'the wretched of the earth' as the saviours of Islam.

It was also in Semnan that Ruhollah came face to face with the reality of the Baha'i faith in Iran. The Baha'is are considered a heretical sect by the mullahs, and could thus be automatically punished by death. For a mullah in those days, coming face to face with a Baha'i was far more dramatic than meeting Satan in person. The mullahs generally assumed that the followers of the detested faith kept their identity a secret. In Semnan, however, Ruhollah and his friends were told of Baha'i farmers, sheep breeders, artisans and shopkeepers who lived and worked openly and even preached their faith, protected by the Shah's gendarmes. Against his better judgement, Ruhollah tried to organize an anti-Baha'i gathering in the town's deserted and almost derelict mosque. But he was persuaded by his friends to leave that for later. It was this incident that earned Ruhollah the nickname of Sharur (Troublemaker) from Lavasani. The nickname was to stick for almost half a century and was dropped only after Ruhollah had become Iran's supreme ruler in 1979.

The caravan of pilgrims ran into further trouble in the Gorgan Plain where small bands of armed Turkomans were roaming the countryside, terrorizing peasants and robbing travellers. The main Tehran−Mashhad route, which passed through Turkoman territory, had been made safe by Reza Shah's army in 1923 after a massacre of tribal warriors. But the lesser roads, one of which was taken by Ruhollah and his companions, were still hazardous. Stopped by a group of Turkoman bandits near Quchan, the pilgrims escaped possible death thanks to the sudden arrival of a detachment of Amnieh (security guards). The Turkomans, being Sunni Muslims, would have been delighted to cut the throats of so many Shi'ite mullahs whom they considered to be the falsifiers of true Islam. The Amnieh guards graciously agreed to escort the pilgrims to the main route to Mashhad. But the timely service still did not convince Ruhollah that there was much good to be found in what the new regime was doing.

In Mashhad the pilgrims found lodging in a caravanserai not far from Imam Reza's mausoleum which, with its exquisite tilework and huge gold-plated dome, was a far cry from Ma'assoumah's neglected tomb. Compared to Mashhad, a great oriental metropolis even in those days of decline, Qom was nothing but a pretentious village. Mashhad's beauty was augmented by the many large gardens and tree-lined streets and alleys that had always distinguished it as the largest oasis between Samarkand in Central Asia and Rey, not far from present-day Tehran. Situated high on the Iranian plateau, Mashhad had a soothing climate and its perfumed air carried a mixture of exotic smells from hundreds of orchards and scores of gardens. The city's soft sweet spring water contrasted sharply with that of Qom. This was a city of radiant smiles and warm welcomes. Compared to Mashhad, then a city of no more than 180,000 inhabitants, Qom's sweltering heat, dusty air and noxious odours seemed but a bad dream. Mashhad also offered features of contemporary life that Qom had not even heard of, including electricity, provided for two hours every evening thanks to a second-hand generator bought from a German dealer a year earlier. That enabled the municipality to light some of the central streets long after sunset. The shrine itself was also illuminated with decorative multicoloured bulbs, presenting a spectacle of joy rather than the traditional one of tragedy and death. Some of the local hotels and a number of private homes also benefited from electricity. Most of the pilgrims were instantly seduced by the city which, for the most part, they were visiting after a lapse of many years. In Qom one could not have conceived of Islam as a religion of happiness and joy. In Mashhad the image of Islam as the faith of stern disciplinarians seemed totally out of place. Qom brushed its sins under the carpets and kept its skeletons well hidden in its cupboards. Mashhad recognized human frailty and tried to accommodate it openly. Life in Qom was designed to make one wish for and welcome death; in Mashhad, however, death remained a tragedy.

The group of pilgrims liked Mashhad so much that what was originally planned as a visit of days soon ran into weeks. Some members of the group even took temporary wives or *seeghahs*. It is not known whether Ruhollah was among those who took advantage of the *seeghah* rule but it is perfectly likely that he did. He had had a number of temporary wives in Qom, and in his subsequent writings he was to designate bachelors as 'prey to Satan', quoting the Prophet's celebrated dictum that 'marriage saves half of a man's faith'. The temporary marriage provided for under the *seeghah* rule is expected to be devoid both of love and lust. A man should satisfy his sexual needs which, if ignored for a long time, could lead to 'consternation, misery and even violence'.[9] But the prime objective of the contract was not the satisfaction of sexual needs. The *seeghah* or temporary wife was not even seen by her future 'husband' before the completion of the contract. In most cases, temporary wives were recruited amongst young widows, who used the opportunity for making ends meet. The temporary wife could be taken into contract for any length of time from a single hour to ninety-nine years. Every *seeghah* had to observe a period of a hundred days' abstinence after separating from a temporary husband before being allowed to enter another temporary marriage. In practice, therefore, no woman could become a *seeghah* more than three times in a single year. Temporary wives were in great demand in the summer when wealthy Muslims sent their full legal wives – sometimes four of them – to cooler mountain resorts and soon found themselves a 'prey to Satan'. In some cases the legal wife or wives chose the *seeghah* for the husband left behind in the dusty bazaar of a sweltering town. Often the same woman performed the task of *seeghah* for the same man every summer. Women were, of course, denied a similar arrangement as they were expected to remain scrupulously monogamous. The holy cities of Mashhad and Qom were important centres for women seeking temporary marriages. There were two reasons for this. First, both cities were full of male pilgrims who, having left their families behind, found it hard to spend several weeks or months without female company. The *seeghah* was needed not only for the carnal service she provided but also to offer the lonely pilgrim a steadying hand. She ran her temporary husband's temporary abode like any permanent wife looking after her own family residence. At the start of the contract the *seeghah* received the sum promised her under the contract. In addition, some *seeghahs* received cash or gifts in recognition of special services or the extra pleasure their company might have given to their masters. But any children born of the temporary arrangement were automatically denied any financial claim on their father or any estate he left behind. Thus, thousands of women had to work as temporary wives in order to support offspring produced as a result of earlier *seeghah* contracts. At the time Ruhollah and his friends were in Mashhad, taking *seeghahs* was far from being considered morally undesirable – as it was soon to be, thanks to government propaganda – but was seen as an act of piety towards poor and unprotected women. A man would be praised for saving a lonely woman from both solitude and poverty by making her his temporary wife; he could be equally sure of being envied for his ability to afford the costly enterprise. Although the cost of each contract naturally varied greatly in accordance with the age and status of the temporary wife and the length of time involved, such contracts could be afforded by only a very small percentage of the population. In that uncertain year of 1930 rumours that Reza Shah planned to make temporary marriages illegal – rumours that proved utterly wrong, as the *seeghah* system continued until the end of the Pahlavi dynasty and beyond – pushed the price of temporary wives through the roof. But the pilgrims from Qom were still able to foot the bill while cursing the Shah in the process.

Although various accounts of the pilgrimage to Mashhad show that the group had an enjoyable stay, it is clear that Ruhollah was far from happy. The relaxed version of Islam which permitted the full savouring of climate, food, music, sex and even the occasional smoking of opium was far from his idea of a militant faith which, rather than being content with a place as merely a part of life, considered all life as a tiny and insignificant part of itself. The group gathered on the mud-and-hay-covered terrace of the sprawling residence at night to enjoy the cool breezes of Central Asia, to marvel at the star-studded turquoise sky and to spend hours in chitchat. They would eat melons and watermelons, crushed pistachio nuts and dried pumpkin seeds, and stuff themselves with huge quantities of boiled rice and lamb grilled on an open fire. An elaborately decorated hooka, with rose petals dancing in its glass vase whenever the pipe was puffed, would be passed round at the end of the marathon meal, marking the point at which a teaboy would appear, almost miraculously, to fill the tiny tea-glasses known as *estekan* with thick, sweet liquid fire. Deep in the night the friends would pray together before retiring, each to his own room, often with a *seeghah* dutifully awaiting his return, for a few hours of intimacy and sleep before a new round of prayers at sunrise.

Ruhollah's evident displeasure at what he considered to be a glaring example of Islam's decadence – a decadence that had started with the cursed Omayyad caliphs and had led to the shrinking of the original Islamic empire over several centuries of *ghaflah* or slumber — was a factor in bringing about the group's division into two. Some of the mullahs decided to prolong their stay in Mashhad until the following winter. Ruhollah, Lavasani and a few other friends, however, chose to return to Qom. Probably under Lavasani's influence, they decided to make their way back to Qom via Tehran, even then cursed by the more ardent fundamentalists as a satanic city. The friends wanted to test the new regime's anti-religious measures yet again, this time at the centre of Pahlavi power. Ruhollah had never visited Tehran before and welcomed the opportunity of doing so. He may have also thought of using his visit to Tehran to test his chances of seeking the hand of one of Ayatollah Saqafi's debutante daughters. He bought an unusually large and varied collection of *soghati*, or gifts that each traveller, especially when returning from a holy pilgrimage, was expected to bring back for relatives and friends. He bought among other things a number of turquoise and lapis-lazuli stones as well as saffron, one of the province's greatest specialities, and a prayer mat adorned with an image of the black stone of Ka'aba at Mecca. Worry beads made of the earth of Mashhad, supposed to be specially beneficial because it held in its eternal embrace the remains of the eighth Imam, completed the young mullah's bag of *soghati*. At the start of the long journey to Tehran, a distance of nearly 1000 kilometres covered in three weeks under Amnieh escort, Ruhollah looked very much like a man plotting a marriage.

# 5

# *The City of Taghut*

It makes no difference which woman you marry. For all women feel the same, when you mount them in the dark.

Imam Ali Ibn Abitaleb

Do not marry the woman you adore; rather, adore the woman you have married.

Imam Jaafar as-Sadeq

*T*aghut, a Qur'anic term meaning 'rebel', is one of the many titles of Satan in the Muslim Holy Book. By extension, it is applied to all those who disobey the rule of Allah. Late in the summer of 1930, when Ruhollah eventually arrived in Tehran, Reza Shah had earned for himself the title of Taghut. In those days, of course, Ruhollah could not openly express his views on the despotic Shah whose hatred of the mullahs was only matched by his zeal to reduce their numbers in whatever way possible, including military conscription and plain murder. Many mullahs disappeared from their homes in the middle of the night, never to return. An unusually large number of turbaned heads 'fell' under military vehicles or were found on the roadside with bullet holes in them. Wisely, Ruhollah reconciled himself to the idea of replacing his black turban with a white *araq-chin*, a cotton cap still tolerated by the Pahlavi state, during his stay in Tehran. He also wore a *sardari*, an outfit representing a rather unhappy compromise between traditional Persian wear and the European-style jacketed suit. On one point, however, he was not ready to compromise: he did not shave off his beard and went only so far as to trim it. Ordinary passers-by would not have recognized him as a mullah; he looked like a pious bazaar merchant. More expert eyes, however, would instantly spot him as a *motohawwel*, meaning a mullah in the process of gradually changing both appearance and vocation. Many mullahs went all the way without hesitation, even sporting gaudy bow ties. Some did so out of opportunism, but most were simply making use of the psychological defence mechanism provided by Shi'ite tradition. They went along with the tide in the firm conviction that one day soon it would turn.

Ruhollah and his friends rented rooms at Shahr-e-Rey near Tehran, where a holy shrine had for decades housed a small theological centre. The centre was closed and its members scattered, but the shrine remained open, still attracting the poor and the downtrodden searching for solace in miracles that almost never materialized. Ruhollah refused suggestions for sightseeing in the satanic capital. Even the air seemed to him to be polluted with sin. Some of his companions wanted to visit the leading *motohawwels* who, having discarded their clerical robes, were fast rising as political stars in the new regime. Ruhollah, however, contented himself with making mental note of the names of those 'traitors to Allah' as he called them. The owners of some of those names were to be executed on Ruhollah's orders half a century later.

Within a few days of his arrival at Rey, Ruhollah asked Lavasani to open negotiations for the hand of one of Ayatollah Saqafi's daughters. Lavasani promptly agreed and recommended Ruhollah to the venerable ayatollah as a desirable future son-in-law. Saqafi agreed to receive the suitor a few days later. In the meantime rumours of an imminent marriage spread to the ayatollah's *andarun*, or inner harem, where it created great excitement. One of Saqafi's daughters, Batul, who was nicknamed Iran, was, at the age of ten, the most likely bride-to-be. When Ruhollah finally came to visit, it was Batul, suitably covered in a *chador*, an all-enveloping cloak which concealed every part of her body except her hands, who performed the task of serving tea to her father and his visitor. She could see her suitor, but all Ruhollah could see was a tiny creature covered in black. She did not speak, as a girl whose voice was heard by strangers would be doomed. Saqafi may have had some hesitations about the marriage, but these were soon allayed. Batul had a dream in which she was visited by Holy Fatima, the Prophet's daughter. Fatima told Batul in the dream,

'Oh sister, you are to marry a man who has been born on the same day as my birthday.' The dream was promptly reported to the sceptical ayatollah. A quick investigation showed that Ruhollah's birthday did, indeed, coincide with that of the Prophet's daughter. And since Batul could not have known this, it was decided that the dream was a sign from Allah giving his blessing to the forthcoming match.

Everything happened at a speed exceptional for Iran in those days. Ruhollah was received to present his gifts. A small ceremony was organized in which Saqafi himself performed the marriage rites. It was agreed that Batul should stay at her father's house for a few more months while her husband returned to Qom and found a new home for both of them. Before leaving for Qom Ruhollah was allowed a glimpse of his wife's face — the smiling face of a healthy child.

Ruhollah had made a suitable marriage. He was being taken into a wealthy, highly respected family. Batul was a sayyedah and the match, therefore, meant that the blood of the Prophet would not be mixed with that of outsiders. It was a late marriage by the standards of Islam, but it was to prove an enduring one. Ruhollah was to remain scrupulously monogamous all his life to the astonishment of friend and foe.[1] The newly wed mullah may have felt there was a lot of catching-up to do in those early autumn days in Tehran. Almost all his contemporaries had married years earlier and many had grown-up children. Had he looked at himself carefully in a mirror Ruhollah would, no doubt, have detected the first grey hairs in his much trimmed beard. At a time when most men died in their thirties, Ruhollah could not have been unaware of the seemingly short time left to him to raise a family, despite the soothsayer Shebli's prediction that the mullah from Khomein shall live to be eighty.

In Qom he had to return to his hermit's room at the Dar al-Shafa School for a few weeks while he looked for somewhere to live. The house he eventually rented had four big rooms, a small courtyard and an outside lavatory. It had two advantages: it was inexpensive and it faced Mecca. Batul, escorted by a sister and two brothers, arrived towards the end of December. The escorts remained for a month and then left a maid behind to help the new bride arrange her home. In January 1931 Batul began her eleventh year and was already expecting her first child. Her husband admired and adored her, although in deference to the rule that only Allah could be loved, he would not have said that what he felt for Batul was love.

Ruhollah was to prove a kind, considerate husband. Unlike many Muslim men in those days he did not treat his wife like a domestic servant who also shared his bed. Years later, the couple's daughters were to relate how their father never 'even asked our mother to bring him a glass of water' – something that, even in 1985, could well be thought part of a wife's duties.[2]

The dowry Batul brought with her enabled the couple to buy some furniture and improve their standard of living. Part of it was also used by Ruhollah for the purchase of a share in a farm not far from Khomein. That proved a fortunate investment as in the years that followed the farm prospered and enabled Ruhollah to purchase more land. In 1932 a second pregnancy, the first having ended in a miscarriage, produced the couple's first son. Ruhollah called him Mostafa, after his own father.

It was in the same year that a law under which all Iranians were expected to have identity cards and adopt family names was introduced. Until then there were almost no surnames. People were known as so-and-so, son of so-and-so. And women, of course, were never identified for any public purpose. A woman could only be known as so-and-so's sister, mother, daughter or wife. Her name would never be known to strangers or pronounced in their presence. The name of Ruhollah's wife, for example, remained a secret until 1979 when, urged by his Western-educated advisers, he agreed that it could be revealed to foreign reporters seeking more information on the life of Iran's future ruler. Before that, Batul was only known as Mostafa's Mother. Women who had no sons, and therefore could not be identified as someone's mother, were almost never referred to or, at best, known as 'Aqeemah (the Barren One). A woman who gave birth to boys immensely enhanced her status; one who produced only girls earned the title of Dokhtar-Za (Daughter-Maker) and was at best tolerated.

Ruhollah's brothers lost no time in securing their identity cards in Khomein. Morteza simply translated his father's Arabic name of Mostafa (the Chosen One) into Persian and thus created the new surname of Pasandideh for himself. The move must have angered Ruhollah since it clearly showed that Morteza had been influenced by Reza Shah's campaign of purging Persian of Arabic words. Ruhollah's younger brother Mohammad chose the surname of Hendi (the Indian), the name under which the family was known in Khomein. Ruhollah was loath to obey any of the Shah's rules and would have avoided doing so had there been the slightest opportunity. But without an identity card he risked becoming a non-person so far as the expanding and increasingly interfering administration was concerned. He also needed an identity card so that he could register the birth of his son Mostafa. Eventually, he registered himself as Ruhollah Mostafavi, a name he has continued to use in all official papers. Mostafavi simply means 'related to Mostafa'. In the case of Ruhollah this had a double meaning. It meant that Ruhollah was the son of Mostafa, but also that the family claimed ancestry from the Prophet, one of whose titles was Mostafa.

At the registrar's office, Ruhollah insisted that his title of sayyed be mentioned on the identity card but was rudely put down with the assertion that the Shah recognized no such distinctions among his subjects. Ruhollah had no intention of calling himself simply Mostafavi. By the end of 1932 he was already signing his letters in an entirely different name: Mussavi al-Khomeini. In this, he continued a long-established tradition under which men of mission had two or more names. Mussavi al-Khomeini was a *nom de plume* that was to become a *nom de guerre*. It described Ruhollah's identity the way he wanted it reflected. Mussavi showed that he descended from Imam Mussa Ibn Jaafar, the seventh Imam of duodecimal Shi'ism, and Khomeini meant that he knew where his roots were; it also distinguished him from the Mussavis of other regions in Iran. The Arabization of the Persian word with the use of *al-* as a prefix was a deliberate act of defiance against a regime which wanted to put seven oceans between Iran and the Arabs. It meant that Iran was at least partly Arabized with the advent of Islam, whether Reza Shah liked it or not.

In 1933, Shaikh Abdul-Karim, already ailing and disillusioned with Reza Shah, took the unusual step of allowing his protégé to serve as his stand-in even at the *dars-e-kharej* classes, the highest form of theological training. The move, which caused some controversy, was later to be seen as one reason for the future ayatollah's excessive 'narcissism'. To reach such a level of distinction at the early age of thirty-one would have gone to any man's head, and Ruhollah always had the feeling that he was destined for great deeds. When Shaikh Abdul-Karim died, in 1935, Ruhollah quickly moved to step into his master's shoes but was soundly defeated by the hierarchy at Qom. His attempt at delivering the memorial sermon was thwarted and within a few weeks he was even deprived of his seminary. Once again he became a tutor, working with a more senior doctor of theology, Ayatollah Hussein Sadr. During his brief moment of glory, Ruhollah, now referred to as Hojat al-Islam, had become the object of rumours and vindictiveness for his unorthodox sorties into the risk-ridden realm of mysticism which had been something of a taboo for generations. Mysticism was the realm of *shakk* (doubt) where Satan stood ready with a trap at every corner. Only teachers of great knowledge and unshakable faith were considered to be strong enough to venture into that universe of conflict between Allah and Taghut. The very fact that Ruhollah tried to do so was seen as a sure indication of his 'excessive conceit'.[3] Years later, it was claimed that Ruhollah's classes had been discontinued because of his indirect attacks on Reza Shah and at the instigation of the Pahlavi secret police. But although there is no doubt about Ruhollah's dislike of Reza Shah there is almost no evidence that he mixed theology and politics in those days. Few of his lectures from that time have survived. Those extant show a poetic rather than a political bend of mind. The Hojat al-Islam was still writing poetry and read the *diwan* of the poet Hafiz almost as much as he read the Holy Qur'an.

In 1935 what was to prove the last major religious uprising against the first of the Pahlavis broke out in Mashhad. A group of mullahs and *talabehs*, excited to fever pitch by the harangues of a magnetic and enigmatic holy man known only as Bohlul, sought sanctuary in the holy shrine, in effect occupying it. When peaceful negotiations failed to dislodge the group, who were dressed in white shrouds symbolizing their readiness to die at any moment, a detachment of gendarmes was sent to the scene. Most of the gendarmes threw their guns away and joined the group of candidates for martyrdom after listening to Bohlul, who described to them the thousand and one pleasures of the promised paradise compared to the utter misery of this world. Alarmed by this unexpected act of disobedience, Reza Shah ordered an army unit to quell the rebellion. The unit had to bring in heavy artillery and partly destroyed the outer wall of the shrine as well as the nearby Gohar-Shad mosque's courtyard before the zealots could be smoked out. Summary trials were conducted and the leaders of the revolt executed. The army detachment involved was led by a Captain Iraj Matbu'i. In 1979 he was executed on Ayatollah Khomeini's orders for his 'crimes' of 1935. Matbu'i was ninety-six years old when he faced the Ayatollah's firing squad.

Official rumours created in 1979 claimed that Ruhollah participated in the Mashhad revolt and was, in fact, its leader, having sown its seeds during his visit of 1929. But this is almost certainly not true and Khomeini himself has never made such claims.

Stories about Ruhollah's heroism in Mashhad can also be discarded, together with tales of his leading role in anti-Reza Shah marches and strikes in Tehran in 1924 and in Tabriz in 1927. Ruhollah never met the leaders of those tragic attempts at stopping the march of events. Ayatollah Nurollah Esfahani and Hojat al-Islam Mirza Sadeq were later to be honoured as the earliest 'martyrs' in Khomeini's cause, but in all probability they were not even aware of Ruhollah's existence.

The tragedy of Mashhad had a profound impact on Iran's religious classes. As usual, rumour multiplied the number of those killed in the incident to several thousands, although no more than ten or twelve people actually died. It was also rumoured that the army's fieldguns had completely destroyed the nation's holiest shrine and that Holy Fatima was appearing in dreams to mourn the destruction of her great-grandson's resting place. An earthquake in southern Khorassan, the province where Mashhad is situated, was promptly interpreted as a punishment and a warning ordained by Allah. The fact that hardly a year passed without some tremor in the region was, understandably, ignored. The bloody incident at the holy shrine marked the final rupture between the Shi'ite clergy and the Shah. From then on it was total war. The mullahs had very little room for manoeuvre. The mass of the people, still hopeful that modernization would improve their lives, were not prepared to follow them. The intelligentsia was becoming increasingly hostile, considering religion to be the root cause of Iran's backwardness and the abject poverty of its people. Reza Shah symbolized nationalist hopes. Had he not succeeded in abrogating unequal treaties that gave a number of European states capitulatory rights in Iran? Had he not renegotiated the oil treaty and forced the British company that tapped Iran's southwestern oilfields to more than quadruple the country's share of the income? Once again, a time-honoured rule for the understanding of the Iranian situation was proved right: the mullahs, lacking organization and economic independence, cannot, unlike the Catholic Church for example, exercise any significant influence on secular power without the support of the masses. The mullahs revived the old tactic of *takfir* (anathema) and *hijra* (withdrawal) as the only means of resistance then at their disposal. This meant that they anathematized the secular power and tried to remain aloof from it.

Barely had the dust settled at the Mashhad battlefield than Reza Shah dropped another bombshell. He ordered the abolition of the veil. Women appearing in public still wearing the *chador* or any kind of veil would be forcibly 'uncovered' by the police and if they made trouble in the process would be thrown into prison. The Shah's own wife, the official queen, and two daughters Shams and Ashraf, then in their teens, appeared in public without either *chador* or veil and wearing European dresses and matching hats bought in London or Paris. The forcible abolition of the veil, while greeted by Iran's progressives as an important step, nevertheless caused a great deal of distress among the people, particularly the women and even some of the Shah's most ardent supporters. It looked like a brutal, arbitrary measure that was being hastily introduced. Some officials preferred to resign from the government service when ordered to take their 'uncovered' wives and daughters to official functions. One army officer committed suicide, leaving a note saying he could not disobey the command of Allah that women must be covered and, at the same time, did not wish to ignore the Shah's wishes. Thousands of women fought the measure and were beaten up and imprisoned for a few days. Many more decided to stay at home until the dust settled. Batul did not step out of her house for nearly a year, and when she eventually did so she made a point of wearing both a veil and a *chador*. But by then the government had decided to adopt a less rigid policy on the issue. Hundreds of thousands of women, however, welcomed the measure and discarded their veils and *chadors* gladly until forced to wear them again in 1980 under Ayatollah Khomeini's rule. Years later, Ruhollah was bitterly to recall the abolition of the veil as one of the 'darkest moments in the history of Islam'. 'In those days,' he was to say, 'our women were given the choice of either becoming prostitutes or staying at home.'[4]

The 1930s, bad as they were for Shi'ite theology, proved fairly profitable for Ruhollah and others from an economic point of view. The stability created, combined with a sharp rise in oil revenue and the construction of a trans-Iranian railway linking the Caspian Sea to the Persian Gulf, enabled businesses to expand. Much of the new wealth went into the pockets of a few in the larger cities, especially Tehran itself. But many bazaar merchants also increased their donations to the mullahs in general and the sayyeds in particular. Hojat al-Islam Khomeini was by then sufficiently recognized to have acquired a following of his own. These were pious men who knew that if they paid part of their growing profits to a sayyed he would speak on their behalf in the next world. This was the price one had to pay for one's salvation. Ruhollah, with the help of his brother Mohammad, who proved to be a shrewd businessman, invested his extra income in a number of successful ventures, including the purchase of the first motor-driven coach linking Khomein to a number of nearby villages as well as Arak and Qom. By the end of the decade the now established Hojat al-Islam was sufficiently wealthy to take on a number of *talabehs* on his own, paying them a stipend comparable to that offered by the last remaining illustrious ayatollahs of the day. But Hojat al-Islam Khomeini still knew that he was neither rich enough nor senior enough to claim to be *primus inter pares* in the highest echelon of the Shi'ite clergy in Qom. With Mashhad seemingly irretrievably won by secularism, Qom was regarded as the last bastion of Shi'ite learning in the country. But it had no senior ayatollah who could be recognized as *a'alam* (most knowledgeable) so that his writ would run not only in Iran and Iraq, where Shi'ism predominated, but throughout the Muslim world. The Hojat al-Islam wrote a series of lengthy and passionate letters to the leading ayatollahs who had sought refuge in Mesopotamia, preferring to live under British protection rather than face Reza Shah's reforms. He invited them to come to Qom and create a new and universally admired forum for learning. It was not clear on whose behalf Khomeini, always signing himself as Mussavi al-Khomeini, was issuing the invitations. In any case, his letters either remained unanswered or were responded to with platitudes.

In 1937 Ruhollah performed the Haj pilgrimage, the highest of all Muslim pilgrimages. Since the pilgrimage is incumbent only on those who have become *mosta'tee* or well to do, presumably the Hojat al-Islam had by then accumulated something of a fortune. Having travelled to Mecca for the Haj in a semi-derelict steamer leaving Bushehr on the Persian Gulf, Khomeini decided to make the return journey less hazardous by taking the overland route. This offered the extra advantage of a visit to the holy shrines of Najaf and Karbala in Mesopotamia where he could pursue his campaign for the return to Iran of some of the Grand Ayatollahs of the day. In those days three Grand Ayatollahs were considered pre-eminent: Abol-Hassan Isfahani, Hussein Tabataba'i-Qomi and Mohammad Kazem Khorassani. All three were in their eighties and could not readily undertake the long journey to Qom. In addition, they hated Reza Shah and did not wish to risk falling into his hands.

Khomeini spent several months in Najaf. He disliked the city itself, which was an abode of smugglers, gun runners, undertakers and a variety of other suspicious characters. He could not then have imagined that one day he would return to Najaf an exile, staying there for some fourteen years. Najaf was, nevertheless, a much more exciting place than Qom. The newly formed Iraqi Government was certainly more liberal than that of Reza Shah, and Muslim activists from many countries were allowed to travel to Najaf and propagate their ideas without the fear of police intervention. In Najaf, Khomeini came into contact with two major political currents. One was that of the Ikhwan al-Moslemeen (the Muslim Brotherhood), a semi-clandestine organization created in Egypt in the early 1920s and by the 1930s active in most Arab countries. The Ikhwan were ready to kill and be killed in the service of Allah, and were already feared by many Arab politicians. The man who introduced Khomeini to the Ikhwan and their ideas was a young mullah by the name of Mohammad Nawab-Safavi who was both admired for his extreme good looks and feared for his power to mesmerize a crowd. The two men spent long hours together. Nawab-Safavi believed that the philosophy of the Ikhwan − based on the purification of Islamic society by ridding it of 'corrupting individuals' by carefully planned assassinations − had to be modified to take into account the specific features of Shi'ite society in Iran. Nawab-Safavi was an activist and did not care much about formal theological studies. His favourite phrase was 'Throw away your worry beads and find a gun. For worry beads keep you silent while guns silence the enemies of Islam.'

Khomeini may have been tempted to emulate Nawab-Safavi's example, but he was still strongly attracted to Persian mysticism and nurtured academic ambitions. He was already dreaming of becoming a'alam himself one day, ruling on all matters of the faith. While Nawab-Safavi spent every afternoon in target practice, for a while with the help of a cashiered Iraqi army officer, Khomeini preferred endless debates and polemics at the holy shrine of Ali. He accompanied Nawab-Safavi on a couple of occasions and was even persuaded to try his hand at shooting. But, whatever his feelings at the time, Khomeini did not join the ranks of the Muslim sharpshooters recruited and trained by Nawab-Safavi nearly a decade later in Tehran.

The second major political current with which Khomeini came into contact in Najaf was Nazism which, with its star rising in Europe, was proving very attractive to some sections of Muslim society in the Middle East. In Mesopotamia an anti-British movement led by Rashid Ali Guilani was openly pro-Nazi. In Egypt the movement called Young Egypt harboured similar sentiments. In Iran Reza Shah shared with many of the mullahs a deep admiration for Adolf Hitler. German agents active in the region fanned the flames of hatred for Britain as the colonial power of the day and for the Soviet Union as a heathen empire. They spread the wildest of rumours, including one that Hitler was a secret convert to Islam and that once he had exterminated the Jews and destroyed Britain and Russia he would come into the open and reveal his 'true Muslim identity'. The Shi'ites were told that Hitler's real name was Haider ('the brave one'), one of the titles of Imam Ali, the first Imam of the faith. Mullahs could be seen swearing with passion that Hitler was, indeed, a disciple of Ali and never went without a small silver-framed portrait of the saint which he kept close to his heart under his shirt.

While Khomeini, no doubt, shared in the general adulation of Hitler, he was far from convinced that the German leader could destroy both Britain and Russia at the same time. In a strange way Khomeini secretly admired the British. Years later, he was to speak of Hitler's mistakes including 'his failure to understand the character of his English [sic] enemies'.[5] One great novelty in those days was the wireless which enabled the mullahs of Najaf, and others, to listen to Persian and Arabic programmes broadcast by Berlin Radio. Germany's Persian service was, during the war, to enjoy the widest possible audience in Iran and Iraq. Khomeini listened to the programmes every evening. Later, he was able to compare Hitler's propaganda with that of the British Broadcasting Corporation which began its own Persian service as war in Europe became increasingly inevitable.

While in Najaf, Khomeini improved his knowledge of Arabic. He read with great interest, and often in secret, books written by Islamic reformers such as Shaikh Mohammad Abdoh as well as the pamphlets of Shaikh Hassan al-Bana, the founder and Supreme Guide of the Muslim Brotherhood. He tried to read as many books as possible since he knew that Reza Shah's police had instructions not to allow the import of any books in Arabic.

Khomeini may have made some half-hearted attempts to attach himself to one of the Grand Ayatollahs, but it must have been obvious after a few weeks that Najaf had no proper place for him. Further, he felt himself heir to Shaikh Abdul-Karim and still believed that Qom would, one day, become the major centre of Shi'ite learning, eclipsing Najaf. He knew that he could not, as yet, claim to be king himself, and was therefore determined to become king-maker. He knew that he had to find a new ayatollah to promote from among those teaching inside Iran itself.

By the time he was back in Qom in the winter of 1938 Khomeini had almost been forgotten in the holy city, which was beginning to attract a large number of *talabehs* and mullahs from all over the country. Khomeini had brought with him a radio receiver set made by the British company Pye which he had bought from an Indian Muslim pilgrim. The radio proved a good buy. Not only did it keep Khomeini informed throughout the Second World War of what was going on in Europe and North Africa but it also gave him a certain prestige. Many mullahs and *talabehs* would gather at his home, often on the terrace, in the evenings to listen to Radio Berlin and the BBC. In following the war communiqués on the two rival services, Khomeini developed a taste for military terminology. In a poem he wrote in the spring of 1941, for example, he used such words as 'bombardment', 'tanks' and 'maginot' to describe what an April hailstorm does to a flower garden.[6]

The war, which at first appeared to belong almost to another universe, soon reached Iran. In September 1941 British and Soviet troops invaded Iran from the south and the north. A few days later, Reza Shah was forced to abdicate after a sustained propaganda campaign against him by the Persian service of the BBC. Hojat al-Islam Khomeini was quick to try to seize the opportunity created by the apparent power vacuum in Tehran. He interpreted the British attitude towards the Pahlavis as hostile and organized a special trip by a number of mullahs to Tehran to campaign for an end to the dynasty. He did not at that time have any clear notion of how the country should be governed without a Shah but seemed determined to do all he could to prevent Reza Shah's son, Mohammad-Reza, then only twenty-one, ascending the throne. Khomeini and some of his companions may have managed to secure a meeting with a British political agent, although there is no proof of this. Years later, Khomeini himself referred to the episode without going into details. 'Once Reza Khan [*sic*] was gone,' he said, 'we told the British to allow monarchy to be ended so that our Muslim people could choose a government of their own liking.'[7]

Whether the British ever became aware of Khomeini's views or not, the fact is that they did try to end the Pahlavi dynasty then and there. They toyed with the idea of restoring the Qajar dynasty for a while but had to abandon this when they discovered that the Qajar pretender had become a British subject and spoke no Persian.

Then they half considered the idea of a republic, with Mohammad-Ali Forughi, the Prime Minister of the day, tipped as the first President. They had to give up such ideas, however, when Britain's Soviet allies, and Stalin in particular, insisted that there should be continuity in Iran for as long as the war lasted. The Crown Prince was, accordingly, allowed to drive through occupied Tehran to Parliament to take the oath as the new Shah.

Khomeini's opposition to the succession was certainly not based on deep convictions and may have been principally caused by opportunism and a vague notion of revenge. What is certain is that his activities remained largely unnoticed and he had to return to Qom without having made any impact on Tehran's confusing events. Back in Qom he took to the pulpit on a number of occasions to attack the exiled Reza Shah and to call on the faithful to pray so that 'the tyrant' would never return. Reza Shah was to return to Iran in 1944 in a coffin.

The economic boom brought about by the war had a very positive effect on Khomeini's personal fortune. The coach company he had set up with his brother had, by 1942, grown into a sizable concern and branched into haulage. Iran was called 'Bridge of Victory' by the Allies and used for supplying the USSR with food, arms and materiel. Khomeini's haulage concern received a tiny share of the booming transport business, but this was sufficient to alter the fortunes of the family. The extra money thus obtained was invested first in buying a larger house for Khomeini and his family at Qom's Gozar-Qazee district. By then the family had grown; another son, Ahmad, had been born in 1936, and two daughters, Farideh and Sadiqeh, followed within a year of each other. Once fully settled in his new home Khomeini began to hold court and create a religious and social following of his own. His circle could not rival that of the leading religious leaders of the day such as Ayatollah Sadr, but it was, nevertheless one of the city's busiest centres of religious and political activity. With more money at his disposal, the ambitious Hojat al-Islam took on more *talabehs*, paying them a modest stipend, and also secured a place at the Faizieh Theological School thanks to a shrewd combination of gifts and influence.

Towards the end of 1942 Khomeini published the first edition of a polemical pamphlet he had written under the title of *Kashf al-Asrar* (*Key to the Secrets*). He had begun writing the pamphlet in 1939 in an attempt to rebut criticisms of Islam by a growing number of secular intellectuals. The pamphlet was more specifically aimed against Ahmad Kasravi whose anti-clerical views were becoming increasingly popular among the intelligentsia. Kasravi saw the advent of Islam as a 'historical setback' for Iran and argued for a return to 'Aryan purity'. He supported Reza Shah's efforts to purge Persian of Arabic words and for a while even advocated the adoption of the Latin alphabet – a step that had already been taken by Atatürk in Turkey. Khomeini's pamphlet was vitriolic both in sentiment and tone and amounted to a virtual death sentence on Kasravi. Without naming the guilty intellectual, Khomeini denounced all those who criticized Islam as *mahdur ad-damm*, meaning that their blood must be shed by the faithful.[1] The pamphlet was almost totally ignored. In any case, it could not have attracted any public attention because those who were in the habit of reading books were on the side of Kasravi and those who were not did not know who 'the enemy of Allah', as described by Khomeini, was.

One man, however, read the pamphlet with great interest. He was Mohammad Nawab-Safavi, the militant mullah Khomeini had met in Najaf before the war. Nawab, as he was known to his disciples, had returned to Iran immediately after Reza Shah's departure and by 1943 had already established the first of the Islamic terror squads that were soon to shake Iran. Nawab believed that the enemies of Islam should be put to death instantly before they could do further harm. But a proper Islamic death sentence must come from a qualified *qazee*, or judge. Khomeini, because of his theological studies, could be considered to be a *qazee*. His pamphlet could, therefore, be interpreted as a death sentence that only remained to be carried out. Nawab visited Khomeini in Qom on a number of occasions during 1943 and 1944 and was the Hojat al-Islam's house guest. What the two men discussed is a matter for speculation; they often met in private and talked to each other deep into the night. But subsequent events showed that Nawab informed Khomeini of his plans to assassinate a number of leading intellectuals and politicians, including Kasravi.

Nawab called his terror squads the Fedayeen of Islam and recruited his future executioners of the enemies of Allah from Tehran's lumpenproletariat which at the time consisted of ruined peasants, unemployed artisans and bankrupt small shopkeepers. Each fedayee was assigned the task of murdering one 'enemy of Allah' but the sentence would not necessarily be carried out instantly. The fedayee had to keep a close watch on his future victim and be ready to strike him down the moment orders arrived from his *morshed*, or guide. The would-be assassins had at times to wait for years before receiving the longed-for orders. They would pray every night to Allah to hasten the moment of revenge, which would secure them a place in paradise. Although inspired by the Egyptian movement of the Muslim Brotherhood, the Iranian Fedayeen of Islam was, in fact, modelled on the group of assassins who, under Hassan Sabah, wreaked havoc in the Seljuk state as well as against the Frankish Crusaders in the eleventh century. The would-be assassin had to pass a number of moral and theological tests before being chosen for the task. Once chosen, he was given some training in the use of various weapons.

Curiously enough, the Allied occupying forces turned a blind eye to the gradual rise of the movement. The Soviets believed Islam to be a spent force and did not attach much importance to the activities of what seemed to them to be nothing but a group of deranged fanatics. The British may have tolerated the movement because they saw in it a potential means of checking the rapid advance of the Left in Iran. The Soviet-sponsored Tudeh (Masses) Party was beginning to attract a large number of intellectuals and workers. In 1944 the Tudeh, then openly advocating secularization and preaching atheism as one of its main slogans, even went so far as to organize a mass meeting at a factory on the outskirts of Qom. This storming-of-the-citadel tactic of the Iranian Communists was interpreted by the mullahs as a direct challenge to their authority. They dispatched a mob of their own, led by hand-picked *talabehs*, to break up the Communist gathering. But the emissaries of Islam were beaten back by the Tudeh's tough guards, who all sported Stalin-style moustaches.

Alarmed by the success of the Communists, who had already created a powerful nationwide trade union, the various traditional forces of society began looking for countermeasures. The new Shah, himself religious to the point of superstition at times, immediately recognized Islam as a bastion against Marxist ideology. Unknown to his sternly anti-mullah father, the new Shah had for years been a devoted follower of a mullah named Fakhreddin Jazayeri. The Shah, who believed that he had seen Imam Ali in a dream, was told by Jazayeri that one way of countering Communism was to create a strong centre of Shi'ite learning inside Iran. That meant building up ayatollahs whose authority would eventually rival that of the religious leaders in Najaf. Jazayeri especially recommended one man as a future Grand Ayatollah who could become supreme for Shi'ites everywhere: Mohammad-Hussein Borujerdi, a sixty-year-old mullah who had for years maintained a small seminary in the remote town of Borujerd.

It was at almost the same time that Khomeini reached exactly the same conclusion and sent a long letter to Borujerdi inviting him to come to Qom and 'revive this centre of science and save Islam'.[8] This was one of the few occasions on which the two bitter rivals of the future, Mohammad-Reza Shah and Khomeini, were, unknowingly, working for the same objective. The Shah dispatched special emissaries to Borujerd to invite the ayatollah to Tehran. The Shah's idea was to build up the small neglected seminary at Tehran's Sepahsalar mosque into a major centre of Shi'ite learning. But Borujerdi was allowed to make up his own mind as to where he would like to teach in the future. Naturally the holy city of Mashhad could not be considered as the venue for the holy enterprise as it was in the Russian zone of occupation. Borujerdi rejected the Shah's offer out of hand, pointing out that he was 'too ill' to travel. A physician was sent to examine the ayatollah and found him to be suffering from a bilateral hernia. The ayatollah was persuaded to go to Tehran and undergo surgery at the Firuzabadi Hospital. News of the ayatollah's visit was given unusual publicity thanks to a concerted campaign by the royal court and Khomeini's group. Khomeini led a delegation of over forty mullahs to Tehran to visit the ayatollah in his hospital room. Their message was simple: come to Qom and help us reorganize Islam's resistance against its enemies, especially the Communists. A few days later, the Shah himself came to the hospital to visit Borujerdi. Maximum publicity was given to the visit and Tehran's newspapers were filled with photos of the young monarch helping the elderly ayatollah stand up by his hospital bed. Borujerdi, a pious, good-humoured man, liked the young Shah instantly; the two men were to become friends in the following years.

Borujerdi had a faithful valet known as Shaikh Ahmad who was to become his right-hand man. In response to Khomeini's entreaties, Borujerdi dispatched Shaikh Ahmad to Qom to sound out the situation. Shaikh Ahmad spent nearly a month in Qom, watching and listening. During that time Khomeini launched a strong campaign aimed at building up Borujerdi. His defence of Borujerdi as the 'highest living authority in Shi'ism' at the time angered many supporters of the Grand Ayatollahs of Najaf. On at least one occasion Khomeini's campaigning zeal led him into a fist fight with opponents of Borujerdi. On his return to Tehran,

Shaikh Ahmad reported that Qom would welcome Borujerdi as a Grand Ayatollah. Khomeini, using the fleet of coaches he owned with his brother, ferried scores of mullahs to Tehran to serve as Borujerdi's entourage for the Grand Ayatollah's trip to Qom. The fanfare was designed to impress and quell any resistance that might be put up by supporters of the holy men in Najaf. Borujerdi arrived in Qom in great pomp and almost instantly captured the hearts of the people there thanks to his modesty and simple style of living. His success was, at least in part, due to Khomeini's resolution and hard work.

With Borujerdi in Qom, Khomeini could once again become the *éminence grise* of a powerful ayatollah. Borujerdi was, perhaps, not as learned as Shaikh Abdul-Karim, but he soon enjoyed a vast following throughout the country and became a real power in the land. The fact that the monarch himself paid visits to Borujerdi reflected a total change in the policy of the Pahlavis towards the mullahs and acknowledged the Grand Ayatollah's power. As one of Borujerdi's closest confidants, Khomeini was spotted by agents not only of the court but also of the various political groups which were competing for power. Towards the end of 1944 his name was mentioned as a possible candidate for Qom's seat in the Majlis. The mullahs, having been kept out of politics for nearly two decades under Reza Shah, were anxious to regain part of their lost power and Qom was considered as one of their natural constituencies. It was almost certainly Borujerdi's objection that prevented his protégé from contesting the following general election and obtaining a seat in the Majlis. Borujerdi's ostensible reason was that he still needed Khomeini at his side in Qom. Khomeini may have believed this explanation, which may have been a simple reflection of the truth. But the episode, none the less, marked the first instance of unease in the two men's relationship.

# 6

# *Encounter at the Marble Palace*

The fire that is rising out of the Temples of Fire in Persia and fed by the followers of Zarathustra and Mazdak must be extinguished, or else the fire-worshipping rabble shall lead you back to the heathen practices of the Magus.

Ayatollah Ruhollah Khomeini in *Kashf al-Asrar* (*Key to the Secrets*)

*H*aving established himself as Borujerdi's special adviser and troubleshooter, Hojat al-Islam Khomeini was by 1945 already thinking of building up an independent power base for himself. Borujerdi suffered from a variety of ailments and could be taken away by the hand of Allah at any moment. His death would leave Qom once again without a credible religious authority. Shaikh Ahmad, Borujerdi's influential valet and probably his natural son as well, disliked Khomeini intensely and did his best to prevent the latter's virtual takeover of the saintly household. But when it came to difficult missions, Borujerdi knew that Sayyed Ruhollah, as he liked to call Khomeini, was the man to turn to. During 1944 and 1945 Khomeini visited a number of provinces, promoting Borujerdi as the highest authority in Shi'ism and persuading scores of wealthy merchants to divert their voluntary religious donations from Najaf and Mashhad to Qom. The increased flow of money into Qom helped boost business there, adding to the once forgotten city's growing prestige. Khomeini, meanwhile, used his provincial journeys to create a network of personal loyalties for himself. On a number of visits to Tehran he made contact with Ayatollah Abol-Qassem Husseini Kashani, an openly political mullah who had been exiled by the British to Palestine in 1941 because of his pro-Nazi activities. Also in Tehran he deepened his relations with the Fedayeen of Islam's network of 'holy killers'. At Karaj he inspected the fedayeen training centre, a semi-derelict chicken farm where the zealots tried their hand at target practice.[1]

In 1945 the death sentence Khomeini had passed, in effect, on the intellectual Ahmad Kasravi in *Kashf al-Asrar* was finally carried out on the orders of Mohammad Nawab-Safavi. The assassin, a founder member of the Fedayeen of Islam, was one Hussein Emami, who was promptly arrested and sentenced to death. Kasravi's murder shocked the Iranian intelligentsia, uniting both Left and Right in a call for 'teaching the mullahs a lesson'.[2] The press, anti-clerical to a man, demanded revenge and many conservative mullahs, including Borujerdi himself, were alarmed by the fact that Islam was becoming associated with terrorism in the minds of the people.

Hussein Emami, himself a sayyed, appealed to other 'sons of the Prophet' to help save his life. He showed great courage by refusing to divulge the organization's secrets despite days of sustained physical and psychological torture. He branded his interrogators and judges as 'magi' and 'heathen Persians', and told the court that Iran was a Muslim land which had to be ruled by the descendants not of Zoroaster but of Muhammed. Khomeini must have loved his fellow-sayyed's eloquent defence of what to him was an act of piety. Kasravi was a *mufsed fel-ardh* (corrupter of the earth) and had to be eliminated. His murderer was a hero of Islam and not a common assassin to be committed to the gallows.

Ayatollah Kashani, who had just returned from exile, shared Khomeini's views. The young Shah was too weak to provide a focus of resistance to Kashani's hopes of securing the government of the country for the Shi'ite clergy. But without support from Borujerdi the mullahs had little chance of undoing Reza Shah's secularization programme. Hussein Emami's fate became a test case. The insistence that he should be judged by a religious court was an indirect demand for the dismantling of the system of civil justice created by the late Shah. Borujerdi was eventually persuaded to intervene in order to save Emami's life. He was not prepared to consider this as more than an isolated case and did not wish to have a direct confrontation with the government at a time when it had to cope with more serious problems. These included Stalin's refusal to take his troops out of the northwestern Iranian province of Azerbaijan in accordance with an international treaty. At the same time pro-Moscow Communists were showing their strength in the southern oilfields as well as in Tehran's few industrial centres. Borujerdi thought that the best way to solve the problem and prevent further complications was to ask the Shah to exercise his constitutional right of pardon and commute Emami's death sentence. Borujerdi charged Khomeini with the task of putting that demand to the Shah on his behalf. Khomeini was at first unwilling to undertake the mission and argued that seeking such a pardon was an open admission that the entire governmental system inherited from Reza Shah was now considered to be legitimate by the Shi'ite clergy. Eventually, however, Khomeini had no choice as a rupture with Borujerdi at that point could have wrecked all his plans for the future.

Setting out for Tehran, Khomeini took with him a delegation of five mullahs, including Morteza Motahari, a man who was to become one of his closest aides in the anti-Shah revolution of 1978–79. The Hojat al-Islam thought that by not going to see the Shah alone he would appear more important and thus more worthy of esteem. The delegation found rooms in a modest hotel in south Tehran's Amirieh Street not far from the Marble Palace where the Shah and his Egyptian-born Queen Fawziah lived at the time. Although Borujerdi's name opened many doors at the court, securing an audience with the Shah did not prove an easy task. Khomeini was asked whether he had a letter to deliver and when he said that his message from the Grand Ayatollah was a verbal one, he was told to return to his hotel and await further instructions. The mullahs had to wait ten more days before they were called to the palace by which time they felt deeply humiliated. At the palace they were told that only one of them could be received by His Imperial Majesty for an audience of fifteen minutes. Eventually, Khomeini was led into the Shah's private office and told to stand while awaiting His Imperial Majesty's arrival. A protocol officer also told the visiting mullah that he should not sit down unless invited to do so by the monarch. But once the protocol officer had left Khomeini simply sat down and waited for the Shah who arrived some half an hour later. The Shah, always extremely shy, was at a loss what to do for a few moments but eventually decided to sit down also. Khomeini's refusal to rise in front of the Shah was in full accordance with the tradition established from the sixteenth century onwards under which monarchs had to defer to the mullahs in exchange for the latters' tacit approval of their reign. The Shah was almost certainly not aware of that tradition and may have interpreted Khomeini's behaviour as a deliberate act of arrogance. The audience lasted barely ten minutes and the two men took an instant dislike to each other. 'This was hate at first sight,' recorded Ayatollah Shaikh Ali Tehrani who accompanied Khomeini during the Tehran visit.[3] Nevertheless, Khomeini delivered his message with both force and effectiveness and secured a promise of pardon from the Shah. Hussein Emami's life was spared and the mullahs won a major victory in which Khomeini could claim a part.[4]

Nearly a year later, Khomeini went on a second mission to Tehran and was, once again, received in audience by the Shah. This time he was asked by Borujerdi to seek the Shah's financial support for major repairs to the holy shrine of Ma'assoumah as well as a donation of land for the construction of a major new mosque in Qom. In this second audience Khomeini was a member of a six-mullah delegation and obeyed the rules of protocol to the letter. The Shah proved generous and offered much more than he had been asked. The gold-plating of the Ma'assoumah dome and the erection of a grand mosque could proceed immediately, becoming monuments to Borujerdi's tenure as the highest authority of Shi'ism in Iran.

Khomeini's growing links with Kashani and the Fedayeen of Islam began to irritate Borujerdi seriously from 1949 onwards. The Fedayeen had in the meantime carried out a number of other political assassinations. Among their victims were such prominent figures as Abdul-Hussein Hazhir, a former Premier and at the time of his murder Court Minister, and the Education and Culture Minister Ahmad Zangeneh. A year later, in 1950, they gunned down the Prime Minister Haj-Ali Razm-Ara. It is not clear whether the religious edicts sentencing these men to death were issued by either Khomeini or Kashani, but both men strongly approved the killings. Kashani, when elected Speaker of Parliament, arranged for a special Act to be passed quashing the death sentence on Khalil Tahamsebi, Razm-Ara's assassin, and declaring him to be a soldier of Islam. This incredible piece of legislation made nonsense of Reza Shah's secularization efforts and showed that a Parliament controlled by the mullahs and their allies among the large landowners was but a tool of reaction. Borujerdi disapproved of these measures but, at the same time, did not wish to split the clergy on what was, at least in part, a political issue. He showed his displeasure by refusing to invite Kashani to his house during a visit by the latter to the holy city. He also stopped sending Khomeini on any more missions and used a variety of excuses not to receive him. On a number of occasions Khomeini was told by the ever-present Shaikh Ahmad that the Grand Ayatollah was unwell and resting and thus unable to have visitors. Sensing that Shi'ism was heading straight into a political storm the consequences of which could not be guessed, Borujerdi decided to remain aloof. This was in accordance with a long-established and often tested strategy known as *tanfieh*, or the judicious doing of nothing. In a world where everyone insists on being a doer those who choose to be non-doers should maintain their positions and ignore the perpetual movement that surrounds them. The doers are bound to make mistakes, undoing themselves in the end. The agitated world will eventually spend its energies and return to *aramesh*, the point of tranquillity. All evil is done by those who do things for the sake of doing something. Sit back and do nothing, and you shall, in time, become the centre of gravity. Khomeini himself was to use precisely this strategy years later during his exile in Mesopotamia.

The oil nationalization fever that swept Iran from 1950 onwards brought to power Dr Mohammad Mossadeq, an aristocrat with strong nationalistic sentiments and a firm determination to make parliamentary democracy work in Iran. A secularist by both temperament and education, Mossadeq was aware of the danger the mullahs presented to Iran's democratic development. He advocated national sovereignty, urging that the nation should have supreme power over its own affairs. The mullahs argued that all power came from Allah and that the nation had only to obey the divine rules set out in the Qur'an. But Mossadeq and Kashani needed each other and became reluctant allies. Mossadeq needed the mullahs to counterbalance the power of the Left: the mullahs considered Mossadeq indispensable for reducing the powers of the court and thus making sure that no Reza Shah could emerge in the future.

In 1949 Borujerdi had convened an informal meeting of the leading mullahs in Qom, urging them to steer clear of 'political issues of the day'. Khomeini attended the meeting but remained silent, still hoping to stay close to Borujerdi while cultivating his relations with Kashani. Borujerdi's theses were later to be developed by some of his disciples, including the brilliant

Ayatollah Nasser Makarem-Shirazi. His central argument was that perfect government can only be offered by the Hidden Imam, in whose absence the mullahs could only act as watchdogs of society. 'We must be guardians of society's ethics,' Borujerdi argued. 'And in the politics of this world only a small place is reserved for ethics.'[5] Khomeini did not challenge Borujerdi's arguments and, at times, even gave him verbal support. In practice, however, he supported Kashani. This ambiguous stance, based on the traditional tactic of *ketman*, which advocates the pursuit of two different objectives at the same time, meant that Khomeini lost Borujerdi's confidence without gaining that of Kashani. By 1952 Kashani had broken with Mossadeq and was cooperating with the Shah in a united front against the threat of pro-Moscow Communism. Borujerdi, for his part, had never liked Mossadeq and suspected him of secret dictatorial ambitions.

In 1953 Mossadeq was overthrown and imprisoned and the Shah, who had briefly fled the country, was restored to his throne by a coup d'état led by General Fazlollah Zahedi. Kashani played a prominent role in the whole enterprise which enjoyed financial and logistical support from both the US Central Intelligence Agency (CIA) and the British Intelligence service. Sensational revelations by the recently formed Sazman Amniyat va Ettelaat Keshvar (SAVAK), the political police, spoke of deep Communist penetration in the armed forces and an elaborate Tudeh plot to seize power and invite the USSR to send in troops under an Irano–Soviet treaty signed in 1921. SAVAK published supposedly secret documents showing that the Communists would have preceded their attempt at seizing power with a series of assassinations in which some of the leading ayatollahs were among the main targets. Sufficiently scared by these revelations, the mullahs went out of their way to help the new military government root out what proved to be an extensive and well-organized network of secret Communist cells.

Borujerdi sent a cable to the Shah saying he would pray for the monarch's good health and success in 'serving the people of Islam'. The Shah, who, in 1948, had survived an attempt on his life by the Communists, appeared as the champion of all the traditional forces of society. He now represented the big landlords, the mullahs, the tribal chiefs and, above all, the military. With the exception of the military, all the Shah's new allies had been enemies of his father. He not only made a point of going on regular pilgrimage to Mashhad and Qom but was also prepared to call on

Borujerdi and even kiss the Grand Ayatollah's hand. The Shah also held secret meetings with Kashani in the latter's limousine which was parked just outside the palace at mutually agreed times. The ayatollah did not want to be seen going into the palace; that would have meant accepting the supremacy of the monarchy as an institution.

According to some accounts, Khomeini did not at first agree with Kashani's policy of full support for the Shah and warned that a son of Reza Shah could not but be a Zoroastrian 'fire-worshipper' at heart.[6] What is certain is that Kashani made it clear to the mullah from Qom that he was no longer welcome. Kashani described Khomeini as *sholugh*, meaning a busybody.[7] With Borujerdi also reluctant to readmit Khomeini into the closed circle of his confidants, the Hojat al-Islam must have felt like a man who has just tried to sit between two stools. Taking a cue from Borujerdi, Khomeini decided to forget about politics and instead began pursuing three objectives. The first was gradually to demolish Borujerdi, the second was to establish his own credentials as a teacher of theology and the third consisted of plans for reorganizing and expanding his estate. He began by referring to Borujerdi either as Rish-Ghermez (the Red-Bearded One) or Khaireddin after the Saracen buccaneer known in the West as Barbarossa. The reason for these unflattering nicknames was that the Grand Ayatollah, who had just married a new wife aged only fourteen, had taken to dyeing his beard with henna in order to look younger. Satirical rubáiyát about the Grand Ayatollah's beard and his procreational prowess were circulated among the mullahs and the *talabehs*. At least some may have been composed by Khomeini. The idea was to reduce the Grand Ayatollah to the level of a caricature so that when the time came he could easily be knocked off his pedestal.

By the mid-1950s Khomeini had his own circle of *talabehs* and was already recognized as a leading *modares* at the prestigious Faizieh School which had grown under the auspices of Borujerdi. He also completed his first and only work in Arabic, *Tahrir al-Wassilah (Liberation of the Means)*, which was circulated only in handwritten copies. The book's Arabic was so ungrammatical and peppered with Persian words no Arab would understand that it had to be almost entirely rewritten by a group of Lebanese Shi'ites before its eventual publication in Tehran in 1984. Khomeini also completed a 12,000-word commentary on the Hamd sura of the Holy Qur'an with the promise that he would offer similar commentaries on all other suras in the Holy Book. That promise was never fulfilled, however, but the lectures and books served to establish Khomeini's scholarly credentials. An increasing number of people now referred to him directly for answers to their religious queries. He would respond to each query in writing, taking care to have two copies made of each response and signing and sealing each copy. One copy would be handed over to the questioner and the other would be kept by Khomeini himself. A collection of these questions and answers was published years later under the title of *Towzih al-Masayel* (*Explication of Problems*). Publishing such an oeuvre is essential for those who claim the title of ayatollah (the sign of Allah).

Khomeini's third objective, that of expanding his financial resources, was achieved by a number of deals, including the sale of land to the government for the construction of a sugar refinery near Qom. The refinery was never built but the Khomeini family was none the worse for that. Morteza was by now fully established in Qom as a notary public and engaged in a number of business activities both on his own account and in partnership with his two brothers. Khomeini himself preferred investment in agricultural land and, as food prices rose, largely due to inflation in the late 1950s, he was proved right. By 1960 perhaps as many as 3000 families worked on the land belonging to Khomeini and his brothers. Khomeini was a generous, just landowner, popular with the sharecroppers who worked for him. He continued to live modestly and spent most of his extra income on stipends for more *talabehs*, especially from the villages. To him money remained nothing but a means. Although his parsimony was proverbial he did not wish to amass a fortune. All he was interested in was to have more and more pupils. And in the Shi'ite system of education it is the teacher who must pay the pupils and not the other way round. Thus the wealthier a mullah the better his chances of attracting a larger number of *talabehs*. And when it comes to recognizing a qualified mullah as an ayatollah, the number of students is a key factor. Having more money means that one can take on more students. And having more students means that one is more important as an ayatollah and therefore deserves greater financial support through the system of *khums* and voluntary donations. Even in the Shi'ite theological system, money brings in still more money.

By 1955 Khomeini had his own circle of disciples which, apart from Motahari, included such future prominent leaders of the

Islamic Revolution as Hussein-Ali Montazeri, Mohammad-Javad Bahonar, Shaikh Ali Tehrani and Shaikh Sadeq Khalkhali. Trying to build himself up as a religious leader with nationwide support, Khomeini also had 'representatives' in a number of cities. In Tabriz he had Ghazi Tabataba'i, while Shaikh Mahmoud Saduqi represented him in Yazd. In Tehran he had a special arrangement with the fiery preacher Shaikh Mohammad-Taqi Falsafi for mutual support. One man who was especially close to Khomeini in those days in Qom was Mohammad-Hussein Beheshti who was to emerge as 'strong man' after the Islamic Revolution until his murder by a terrorist group in 1981. Beheshti, although a mullah, was an employee of the Ministry of Education and had been sent to Qom as a teacher of English at a local secondary school. He spent almost all his free time either attending Khomeini's lectures or seeking to benefit from his knowledge at more restricted sessions. Handsome and wilful as he was, the charismatic Beheshti was both admired and feared by Khomeini. At one point Beheshti tried to teach Khomeini English. In those days there was much talk about the need for the mullahs to learn foreign languages so that they could gain first-hand knowledge of a world shaped by 'Cross-Worshippers'. The success of Ayatollah Shahabeddin Husseini-Mara'ashi-Najafi in learning French and thus being able to quote Descartes and Renan in routine conversations was the envy of more than one mullah. Shaikh Mohammad-Taqi Qomi, himself a notable mullah, had advanced the idea that learning at least one Western language should be mandatory for those seeking a place in the Shi'ite hierarchy. Beheshti offered Khomeini Longman's 'Essential English' series of textbooks but was apparently unsuccessful in organizing a regular course of study.[8]

Early in 1955 Khomeini had an important visitor from Tehran. This was Shaikh Mahmoud Halabi, an enigmatic mullah who had stayed on the sidelines during the stormy years of occupation and oil nationalization. Halabi had a single objective: to seek out and destroy members of the Baha'i faith. The Baha'is, representing less than 1 per cent of the population, had been able, largely thanks to education and hard work but also because of favouritism, to achieve economic power and social influence far beyond their numerical strength. They saw their faith as an independent, autonomous religion. To the mullahs, however, they were *mortad* (heretics) and thus had to be put to death. Halabi's scenario was simple: a national register of Baha'is would be compiled, enabling the mullahs to contact each follower of the faith and try to bring him back onto the right path; if they failed, the Baha'i in question would be put on a black list and boycotted by the Muslims. In some cases, the adamant Baha'is would be put to death. Halabi had discussed his project with Major General Teymour Bakhtiar, then head of SAVAK, as well as Lieutenant General Batmanqelich, the Amry Chief of Staff. Both endorsed his idea in exchange for a promise of support from the mullahs in the continuing campaign against the Left. The two generals charged Halabi with the task of convincing the mullahs of Qom that the Shah was not only far from his father's dreams of reviving aspects of Zoroastrianism but that he was prepared to allow the gradual liquidation of the country's largest religious minority after the Christians.

Halabi was politely received in Qom but was given no promises of support. Borujerdi contented himself with repeating the Qur'anic formula of 'May Allah lead all onto the Right Path'. Other ayatollahs such as Husseini-Mara'ashi-Najafi and Mohammad Ruhani even advised against the witchhunt, arguing that to accept the embrace of Islam was a blessing and should not be forced on anyone. All that was needed was 'better education' and a more forceful propagation of the tenets of the Mohammedan faith. Only Khomeini proved sympathetic to Halabi's enterprise and promised his full support. He could not forgive the Shah for the execution of Nawab and other members of the Fedayeen of Islam, including Emami who had received the royal pardon. But if the Shah now wanted to do something 'proper' by endorsing the destruction of the Baha'is, there was no reason why the clergy should not benefit from the opportunity. Falsafi, Khomeini's ally in Tehran, led the onslaught with an incendiary sermon at a mosque. The sermon, indirectly calling for the murder of thousands of citizens solely on the grounds of their faith, was broadcast by Tehran Radio. The following day a hired mob, armed with picks and shovels as well as more sophisticated demolition equipment, attacked and occupied the Hazirat al-Qods, the Baha'is' cathedral in Tehran. Having partly destroyed the Hazirat, smashing many ikons in the process, the mob then invited the faithful to come into the precinct to celebrate this latest conquest of Islam. A last-minute change of mind by the Shah, and Borujerdi's resolute opposition to the campaign, prevented widespread bloodshed. The two generals and their allies among the mullahs had to beat a retreat. It was during this episode that Khomeini and General Bakhtiar developed something of an affection for each other.

As the 1950s drew to a close Khomeini was already established as an ayatollah. During the turbulent days of 1978–79 the legend was put out by some of the Shah's supporters that Khomeini had been 'declared' an ayatollah by the leading mullahs of Qom only in 1964 and thus saved from the gallows. The truth, however, was that Khomeini was commonly included among the top twelve ayatollahs of the day as early as 1958. He belonged to a group that could be described as the second division of ayatollahs and thus was already in line for promotion to the first division which consisted of three Grand Ayatollahs with Borujerdi presiding over all. Endorsement by the royal court in general and the Shah in particular was an important means of reaching the first division. The fact that the Shah sent cables to Borujerdi on all major religious occasions was important for the Grand Ayatollah's position. By 1960 Borujerdi was already ailing and the succession seemed open. Khomeini knew that he needed the Shah's support in securing for himself the mantle of Grand Ayatollah. He also knew that the Shah did not like him and began to take steps to remedy that. He all but stopped his frequent attacks on the Shah's father and his policies. This did not mean that he genuinely changed his mind about Reza Shah and his record. All he was doing was making use of the dictum 'the end justifies the means', which in Shi'ite theology is more than a mere motto and can at times be taken as a principle of faith. Once convinced of the rightness of your objective, you are allowed to use practically any means, including murder, to obtain it. It was, perhaps, in this vein that Khomeini composed a series of lengthy and often flattering letters to the Shah in which the young monarch was given unsolicited advice on affairs of state, peppered with clever doses of sycophancy bolstering the addressee's ego without unduly compromising the writer. The ayatollah always dispatched his letters to the monarch through carefully chosen emissaries. One such emissary was Sayyed Mehdi Ruhani, then a young mullah. Ruhani was asked by Khomeini in the winter of 1960 to take a 'written message' to the Shah. He asked Shahabeddin Eshraqi, Khomeini's first son-in-law and by then one of his close confidants, what the letter was about.

'Nothing, my friend, nothing much,' Eshraqi replied. 'His holiness wants to attract the Shah's friendship.'

Khomeini was learning that his reputation as a radical could damage his chances of one day succeeding Borujerdi. In 1955 he had endorsed the anti-Baha'i campaign when Borujerdi had remained aloof. In 1957 Borujerdi had refused to call on the faithful to boycott the newly introduced Pepsi Cola on the grounds that its franchise holder was a Baha'i who sent part of his income to Israel. Khomeini, however, declared Pepsi Cola to be *haram*, warning those who insisted on quenching their thirst with the US-patented beverage that they would all roast in the fires of hell. The only practical result of Khomeini's move was to breach Pepsi Cola's monopoly of the beverages market in Iran. The breach was quickly occupied by Coca-Cola which, benefiting from the tacit approval of Qom, managed to capture part of the market. Pepsi supporters unjustly claimed that the whole issue of seeking religious approval for that type of beverage had been stirred up by the local agents of Coca-Cola who had not spotted the country's potential earlier.

Borujerdi's death in 1962 came at a time when Khomeini had not yet completed his plans for making a bid for the mantle of the Grand Ayatollah. He was still looked upon as something of a lone wolf. Theologically speaking he ranked below a number of others, including Grand Ayatollah Mohsen Hakim Tabataba'i, who lived in Najaf, Grand Ayatollah Ahmad Mussavi-Khonsari, who was resident in Tehran, and Grand Ayatollah Abol-Qassem Mussavi-Kho'i, who also lived in Najaf. As a Shi'ite scholar he belonged to a group that included such eminent teachers as Ayatollah Hadi Milani (in Mashhad) and Ayatollahs Shahabeddin Husseini-Mara'ashi- Najafi, Mohammad-Reza Mussavi-Golpayegani and Mohammad-Kazem Shariatmadari, who all lived and taught in Qom. Compared to them Khomeini had not handled the development of his theological career with adequate care. His flirtations with politics, his association with the Fedayeen of Islam and his love of poetry earned him the reputation of an eccentric. He also suffered from the fact that for years he had mixed mysticism and regular theology in his lectures, which were often delivered in a language deliberately designed to impress by its affected complexity. Was he a Sufi or was he a narrow-minded fundamentalist, people asked themselves without finding a satisfactory answer. Another problem was that Khomeini had earned the reputation of a miser in a society where leaders, whether religious or political, are expected to spend as much money as they can. Khomeini paid his pupils exactly the same stipend that Borujerdi offered. He also gave his sharecroppers a fair part of each year's harvest. But beyond that he loathed spending money as freely as other ayatollahs. He gave almost no receptions at a time when every ayatollah's house was full of all and sundry dropping in for a good meal or at least a cup of tea. He did not believe in offering gifts and marking special occasions with presents to friends and acquaintances. As campaign manager for Borujerdi only a decade earlier, he had made effective use of money to establish the supremacy of his candidate. But now that his own turn seemed to have come, he adopted a puritanical attitude. No one deserved to receive any money or other material rewards beyond that earned by his work. And that meant ignoring an important fact of life in poverty-stricken societies like Iran where one of the main functions of any leader is to distribute income and favours.

Once Borujerdi's death was announced, the Shah, in his constitutional capacity as Protector of the Shi'ite Faith, sent a number of cables expressing his feelings of bereavement. The longest cable was sent to Grand Ayatollah Moshen Hakim Tabataba'i and was, because of its length, instantly interpreted as the Shah's recognition of the recipient's theological supremacy. Within a few weeks, Hakim's agents in Iran and Iraq, aided by the Iranian court, had created a network of support for him as the undisputed heir of Borujerdi. A rumour was spread quoting Borujerdi as saying, 'Follow anyone you like, anyone except Khomeini. For following Khomeini shall lead you knee-deep in blood' [sic].[9]

Khomeini received no cable from the Shah and instantly interpreted this as a deliberate insult by the monarch. By then the Shah must have forgotten Khomeini's very existence and the fact that he was excluded from the list of those receiving standard condolences from the sovereign could have been due to a bureaucratic oversight. To Khomeini, however, this appeared a declaration of war. He told his confidants that it was a sign from Allah himself that the Shah had not sent him a cable. 'From now on it is we who have to defend the faith,' he boasted. While all other ayatollahs organized special mourning ceremonies to mark the third, the seventh and the fortieth day of Borujerdi's demise, Khomeini stayed at home and warmed himself under the korsi, a low table set over a brazier and covered with a thick eiderdown. He was practising the tactic of withdrawal; he wanted to be the only one who was absent from all those ceremonies and, therefore, the only one who retained his 'purity'. To a visitor who called on him and inquired why he was not organizing a memorial service for the Grand Ayatollah, Khomeini said, 'Things that can be done by others better be left to others.' When asked whether this meant that he was withdrawing from the race, he replied, 'Not at all. I am just waiting. Our turn will come when it will come.'[10]

# 7

# *The Road to Exile*

'With the Thirty Psalms in hand,
Thou hast entered a Quarantine.
I am the one torn into Thirty Parts;
Abandon thy quarantine. . . .'

Rumi, in the *diwan* of Shams Tabrizi

*T*hose calling at Ayatollah Khomeini's home in Qom's Gozar-Qazee district in the winter of 1962 were often told that His Holiness was in *cheleh*. The word *cheleh* means a cycle of forty, or quarantine. Going into *cheleh* thus signifies total withdrawal from the world for a period of forty days. This is an old-established tradition. According to Persian mystics, one should live in such a way as to be ready to die at any moment. That means leaving behind no regrets, no unsolved problems, no unpaid debts, no broken promises, no unfulfilled duties. The pace of life, however, is bound to carry one away, preventing the bringing of one's moral books up to date at any given moment. Knowing that the Creator can recall his creatures at any time without notice, it is incumbent on men to be always prepared to answer for their deeds. One needs to stop a while, stepping out of the infernal circle of daily deeds, and ponder one's life through the eyes of a detached observer – in other words, one should do *derang*, which means come to a halt. People going into *cheleh* to do *derang* often take with them an abridged edition of the Qur'an known as *Si-Jozve*, which includes only thirty of the passionate Meccite suras which portray the Muhammedan faith in an almost Manichean vision of the universe in which Good and Evil are locked in eternal combat.

Khomeini needed the break in order to reorganize his thoughts and also to plan future moves in what he was increasingly coming to believe was a divine mission. Looking back on the preceding decade, he might have thought that his life had been too complicated, almost too full, whereas the advice of the mystic was to retain in one's life adequate space, an 'area of emptiness' which could be filled by the painful presence of Allah. Men who do too many things cannot even hope to be considered as candidates for performing duties set by the Almighty. This is why Allah must deal with a chosen few so that his will is done on earth. Muhammed himself had given up his busy life as a successful merchant in order to do *derang*, to go into seclusion in the caves at Hara so that Allah could communicate His commands to him. He had had to empty his life, so that it could be filled by things not of this world.

A mullah is, by definition, a candidate for the performance of divine duties. Regardless of his rank and status, a mullah is not only meant to help implement divine laws already in existence; he should also be ready for new tasks. This is why mullahs, at least before they attained governmental power in 1979, made a point of keeping their lives as simple, as 'empty', as possible. They stuck to the routine of prayer and preaching, shunning all novelty and providing for themselves ample opportunities for *derang*.

During two or three consecutive *cheleh* Khomeini hardly ever left his room where he slept on a coarse tribal rug and observed a diet worthy of an Indian yogi. Only one man was allowed to meet him during those periods of withdrawal. He was Shaikh Hussein-Ali Montazeri, a thirty-six-year-old *talabeh* who had just established himself as Khomeini's favourite pupil. Montazeri was allowed to call on the Ayatollah after evening prayers and, twice a week, was invited to stay for a dinner of rice and sour yoghurt followed by cups of strong, oversweetened tea. He would give Khomeini a summary report of events at the seminary and in the rest of the world. The Ayatollah would simply nod or ask brief questions. Then he would dismiss his visitor with a curt 'Allah be with you'.

Khomeini emerged from his prolonged seclusion more convinced than ever that Allah meant him to perform major duties. Whether he believed that he had been in communication with the Archangel Gabriel, who in Islam serves as Allah's chief courier, remains a mystery. But the Ayatollah retained his *cheleh* sequences as a traditional feature of his life even after he became Iran's ruler and led an army of a million men in the war against Iraq. Members of his entourage have not hesitated to drop broad hints that Khomeini, when in seclusion, is in contact with the Hidden Imam and through him with the Almighty himself.[1]

It was after the *cheleh* periods of 1962 that the poet Nader Naderpour met Khomeini at the latter's house in Qom. Naderpour found the Ayatollah to be 'one of those black geniuses of history'.[2] In a conversation lasting several hours in the presence of other visitors, Naderpour was able to gain a first-hand impression of what was then a new Khomeini. He found the Ayatollah 'bitterly violent' and committed to the task of 'eliminating from the face of the earth every trace of corruption'.[3] He rejected any idea of social reform by arguing that 'pouring pure water in a cesspool would only be a waste of time'. Muslim society was gravely ill and he, Khomeini, was convinced that only surgery could save it from impending death. At about the same time the Ayatollah developed his celebrated formula according to which Islam was a tree that would continue to grow only if nourished by the blood of its youth. For too long Muslims had been afraid of death, to avoid which they had been prepared to pay a heavy price in the form of a wretched life under tyranny. He repeated the line from the great Persian poet Nasser Khosrow Qobadiani, who says, 'People's fear of death is a disease whose only cure is faith.'

With a single stroke the Ayatollah brushed aside all his previous dabblings with mysticism. It was almost certainly from then on that he also stopped composing poems. He must have worked out a careful plan in his head. First, he decided to simplify his language. He taught himself systematically to purge all words that might sound highbrow and thus be inaccessible to the largely illiterate masses. He knew that intellectuals would continue to laugh at him or dismiss him as an anachronism no matter what he did or how he wrote and spoke. It was therefore the downtrodden of the world who would provide him with his proper political province. The new vocabulary used by the Ayatollah consisted of about 2000 words which, by force of repetition, gain the effect of magic formulas. Second, he chose to present the world to his audience of the poor as an arena of conflict between Good and Evil. There were no zones of shade, no nuances; the world was not a spectrum; it offered a choice only between black and white. People were either friend or foe and no one could claim to be merely neutral. The Evil had to be put to death by the Good who, in themselves, were both the judge and the executioner. Third, Khomeini began propagating the idea that in any future movement against Evil, represented by the government of the day, the mullahs should exercise total leadership.

Khomeini had never been a particularly charismatic figure. A poor orator, speaking in a monotonous and often inaudible voice, he would have stood no chance against such magicians of the pulpit as Shaikh Mohammad-Taqi Falsafi or even his own pupil Shaikh Morteza Motahari. He appeared cold and distant if not utterly conceited and domineering. His deep black eyes looked like two wild ravens struggling to break out of iron cages. His bushy eyebrows added a further note of harshness to a face already harsh enough. And his beard, now uniting the conflicting extremes of black and white, denoted a passionately anarchistic owner. Gone were the days when Sayyed Ruhollah, simply continuing a well-established tradition among the mullahs, would spend a considerable measure of time ordering, arranging and occasionally even dyeing his proud beard. On the face of it there was no reason why Khomeini's new gospel should find an audience in Iran or anywhere else for that matter. And in the early 1960s the Ayatollah failed to build up a credible following for himself.

For some fourteen centuries the Iranians had mourned the death of Imam Hussein at Karbala as a great tragedy. To them Hussein's martyrdom symbolized a rejection of death and an affirmation of life. Now Khomeini was trying to tell them that it was, in fact, death that was to be coveted and life that had to be shunned. Death offered purification and the exalted status of the martyr, while life was pregnant with all manner of corruption and sin, the smallest of which would surely lead to hell. Hussein had been chosen by Allah and given the supreme honour of dying for Islam; he could, therefore, not be mourned as a mere victim of injustice. 'You should pray to Allah to grant you the honour of becoming martyrs,' Khomeini began telling the sparse crowds that heard his lectures. Later, he was to complete this line of reasoning by ordering that the deaths of young men in the service of Allah should become occasions for joyful celebration by the bereaved families and their neighbours.

Politically speaking, Khomeini believed that a state's supreme sanction remained its power to put its citizens to death. Remove that sanction, by making death a coveted prize, and the state is rendered incapable even of self-defence. It was in those days that Khomeini launched one of the famous slogans of his revolution some seventeen years later. The slogan, addressed to the forces of order, was: 'Oh please do kill us, for we, too, are going to kill you!' A man who was not only ready to die but passionately sought death would not be impressed by the fear of being sent to prison, beaten up or fined. The monster of the state would become a harmless circus lion.

Khomeini's new line was instantly recognized as a source of potential trouble. The Ayatollah had never been popular with his peers in the holy city but now he appeared as a tangible menace. The local leading ayatollahs were afraid that Khomeini's agitations might further reduce Qom's chances of regaining the pre-eminence it had lost because of Borujerdi's death. The Shah was bound to become annoyed with Qom and could well help build up the theological leadership in Tehran and Mashhad. The presence in Tehran of Grand Ayatollah Khonsari and in Mashhad of Grand Ayatollah Milani, both senior to those in Qom, gave the Shah ample opportunity to treat the troublesome town like a for-gotten oasis. Worse still was the fact that Khomeini's increasingly violent language was frightening the conservative merchants of the bazaar whose generous donations kept the Qom leadership going.

Most accounts of the Khomeini movement suggest that the Ayatollah did not think of exercising direct power until the middle of 1979, long after his revolution had triumphed. The truth, however, is that he had begun advocating direct rule by the clergy as early as 1961. During the 1978–79 revolution he simply kept that issue dormant in order not to alarm the Iranian middle class while also reassuring the United States. In *Towzih al-Masayel* first published in 1961, he says: 'What is the good of us [i.e. the mullahs] announcing rules set out by Allah when we have no power to make sure they are obeyed?'[4] The theme was taken up by several of Khomeini's disciples, including Motahari and Beheshti. In the winter of 1962 the two men organized a series of con-ferences in which direct government by the clergy was discussed and debated. Several secular supporters of Khomeini, including Mehdi Bazargan, also took part. The government did not consider these activities as threatening enough to interfere with them. The Shah was more concerned with fresh attempts by the pro-Mossadeq National Front to regroup and make a further attempt for power.

The Shah had another source of worry in the shape of the new Democratic Administration of President John F. Kennedy in

Washington. The USA had over the preceding seven years emerged as Iran's strongest ally. The Shah and President Dwight D. Eisenhower had even signed a mutual defence agreement that included a provision under which the USA would create a 'nuclear umbrella' in Iran's northern provinces, thus preventing a Russian advance in the event of Soviet invasion. The Soviets had turned the heat on the Shah and their propaganda openly called for his overthrow. Thus, the prospect of losing Washington's support at so critical a moment could not but disturb the Shah. Intelligence reports showed that Robert Kennedy, the new President's brother and closest aide, was in contact with the National Front opposition and openly advocated the overthrow of the monarchy. The State Department had even been asked to draw up a contingency plan for the replacement of the Shah's regime with a pro-National Front military government. The Kennedy Administration believed the Iranian monarchy to be moribund and incapable of resisting the advance of Communism. It further assumed that a government based on the legacy of Mossadeq would be in a better position to save Iran for the West. During a state visit to Washington the Shah was able to outmanoeuvre Bobby Kennedy and to reach an understanding with the new President. On his return home, the Shah appointed Ali Amini, a former Mossadeq Cabinet Minister and an ex-Ambassador to Washington, as Prime Minister, charging him with the task of carrying out a number of reforms. Amini, an attractive speaker and a clever manoeuvrer if not an imaginative leader, managed to create some excitement for his programme which included limited land reform. It was generally assumed that his government represented the emergence of the United States as the principal foreign influence in Iran. The Soviets, lacking a base inside Iran's establishment politics, remained outside players in an increasingly complicated game. That left the British, with their influence greatly diminished, as the only power capable of offsetting the American ascendancy to some degree. The Khomeini group tried to establish some form of dialogue with the British but failed. A little later, however, a lengthy essay by Miss Anne Lambton on the works of Motahari and Beheshti and Khomeini's ideas about direct rule by the clergy appeared in an English academic journal. This was interpreted by Khomeini's disciples as an endorsement of their views by Britain. Lambton was an old Persia hand and had for years served in Iran. She spoke Persian fluently and had studied traditional Iranian society both as an intelligence officer and as a scholar. Her essay has been described by opponents of the Ayatollah as the earliest version of the manifesto Khomeini was to publish years later under the title of *Hokumat-e-Eslami* (*Islamic Government*).

The Shah's difficulties did not end with the appointment of Amini. The much hated and overly ambitious General Teymour Bakhtiar, who had headed SAVAK for nearly seven years, was suspected of plotting to undermine the Shah's authority and was dismissed. Nursing his wounded pride, the general began contacting all active or potential opponents of the Shah, including Khomeini, but was forced into exile before he could put together anything resembling a serious coalition. The Shah also had to cope with a prolonged students' strike at Tehran University in which the National Front played a leading role. One Front leader, Shapour Bakhtiar, later to become the Shah's last Prime Minister, was already making his reputation as a magnetic speaker and a potentially dangerous opponent of the regime.

Throughout those hectic days, Khomeini stayed on the sidelines. His tactic was to allow all the secular opposition forces to try their respective strengths in challenging the Shah before the religious leaders stepped in and presented themselves as the only effective force of opposition left in the country. By the spring of 1963 that point had already been reached. Amini had been dismissed and replaced by Assadollah 'Alam, one of the Shah's closest servants. The National Front had once again been reduced to despair, and the striking students were hard at work trying to make up for the terms they had lost. Moscow was getting tired of the radio war against the Shah and probing chances of a fresh dialogue. General Bakhtiar was a vagabond in Lebanon, facing the threat of extradition. The Shah was in full command of the state and offering a programme of social and economic reform under the unhappy title of the 'White Revolution'. The six-point programme, to be the subject of a referendum, included the distribution of land among the peasants, the nationalization of forests and water resources, the sale of state-owned factories to private investors, a share for workers in the profits of the enterprises employing them, and the right of women to vote and to be elected to Parliament and local government bodies. The package seemed specially designed to provoke most of the vested interests, including the mullahs. Two key words in the programme had the same effect on the mullahs as waving a red cloth has on a wounded bull in a Spanish corrida. These words were 'land' and 'women'.

Iran had, over the two decades following the Second World War, undergone a slow but important process of urbanization and, thanks partly to the oil income, was on the threshold of industrialization. Nevertheless, the main form of wealth in the country remained land. Even the bazaar merchants and the newly rich factory owners of Tehran and Isfahan converted their extra profits into farmland. Some 3 per cent of the population owned more than 90 per cent of the country's arable land. The land reform programme would in effect dispossess hundreds of big landlords, including scores of top mullahs, offering them in return government bonds redeemable over twenty years at a nominal rate of interest.

The mullahs had always seen any programme of land redistribution as a direct attempt to destroy the economic base of their power. Even Borujerdi, a fairly liberal ayatollah by traditional standards, had successfully opposed the implementation of a much more limited land distribution scheme in 1959. Over several centuries the mullahs had grown into major landlords. Some owned hundreds of villages either directly or in trust for others. The new programme, immediately identified as only the prelude to much more radical land reform, was meant and over the subsequent decade proved to be an attempt at breaking the powerful coalition of the mullahs, the feudal barons and the tribal chiefs. The first attempts at resistance by the landlords themselves, however, were defeated as they all but lost their delaying powers when Parliament was dissolved. In subsequent general elections, the government, on the orders of the Shah, made sure that no big landlord won a seat at the Majlis. Some of the dispossessed landlords, joining forces with a number of bazaar merchants who had always distrusted the Shah, dispatched a large delegation to Qom to seek support from the ayatollahs there. Once again, only Khomeini promised action; the others just offered their prayers.

Khomeini was, indeed, angered by the land reform programme but his motives were far from selfish. To be sure, he stood to lose almost all his life's savings. But what worried him most was the prospect of the central government becoming too powerful to challenge as a result of the destruction of all other traditional centres of power in society. But what decided Khomeini to launch his campaign against the Shah there and then was the issue of emancipation for women. It seems almost certain from accounts by people close to the Ayatollah in those crucial days of 1963 that

Khomeini did not yet feel fully prepared to declare an open revolt against the government. His authority as an ayatollah was still too recent and too fragile to take such a major risk. The programme for giving women voting rights, however, appeared to Khomeini as the line at which battle should be joined. Two decades earlier he had described the abolition of the veil as 'a plan for turning Muslim women into whores'. How could he now tolerate a legislative programme that was bound to give women full equal rights with men? The Qur'an is explicit about the fact that Allah meant women to be dominated by men. The entire traditional society was based on a system of apartheid based on sex. Women could enjoy every right and respect and often did; but they could never be admitted as equals of men.

The Ayatollah fired his opening shots on 20 March 1963, the eve of the Iranian New Year. He had never been happy with the festival of Nowruz, which belonged to Iran's pre-Islamic days. Now he could use the occasion to reassert the authority of Islam as he saw it in a land he feared was 'drifting once again towards the Zoroastrian creed', as he had warned in *Kashf al-Asrar* two decades previously. In a *fitwa* he ordered all believers not to celebrate Nowruz since Islam was in danger. In the edict, breaking with the tradition that *fitwas* should be short and precise, he launched a bitter attack on the government's policy of reform. 'What is happening now is a dying man's conspiracy, but nevertheless a serious threat to Islam, the Muslim *ummah* and the independence of Iran. Apparently, it is the government which is responsible for such reforms; but, in fact it is the Shah himself who is facing us and now finds his position threatened. . . . He has been summoned to put this plot into effect at any cost.'

In yet another indictment of the regime he wrote: 'The ruling circles have violated the sacred rules of Islam and are heading for trampling underfoot the very tenets of the Holy Qur'an. . . . They consider Islam and the *ulama* hostile to their plans and interests. . . . In order to warn the Muslim *ummah* of the imminent dangers facing the Qur'an and this country of the Qur'an I declare the New Year to be a period not of festivities but of mourning. Oh Allah, I have performed my first duty and if you allow me to live longer and permit me, I shall shoulder other tasks [on your behalf] in the future.'[5]

The Ayatollah's appeal for mourning instead of feasting during the New Year was almost totally ignored outside the holy city of Qom. The Cabinet did not even hear about it until a day later when reviewing reports of disturbances in Qom itself. The government ordered counter-demonstrations in Qom and, failing to raise an adequate number of supporters in the holy city itself, dispatched over 2000 demonstrators from Tehran. These demonstrators, mostly recruited from among the employees of the Tehran Water Authority, received the equivalent of £2 each for their day in Qom. Some were dressed up as mullahs, complete with black or white turbans and beards. A theatrical accessories' firm helped with the scheme. The operation was led by Mansur Ruhani, the Water Authority's director and later a powerful Minister of Agriculture.[6] A unit of the special forces was also ordered to a village near Qom to be on hand to cope with any violence that might arise. The hired mob organized a demonstration in the vast courtyard of the holy shrine where, with cries of 'Long live the Shah', they tried to provoke the mullahs who, still uncertain of Khomeini's tactics, did not wish to get involved in a direct political confrontation with the government. Meeting with no resistance, the mob then attacked the Faizieh Theological School, the centre of resistance in future months. Khomeini himself had been warned in advance by his son Mostafa, who had been monitoring the situation in the city, and prudently stayed home. The mob ransacked a part of the *talabehs'* dormitories. Young mullahs were challenged and jeered at as sodomites and woman-haters. The demonstration coincided with the anniversary of the death of Imam Jaafar, the sixth Imam of the faith, and was bound to end in tempers boiling over. Emissaries from the moderate ayatollahs such as Shariatmadari and Golpayegani failed to calm the mob and end the demonstrations.

In the meantime, a rival mob had been organized by some of Khomeini's closest aides such as Shaikh Sadeq Khalkhali, later to earn the title of 'Judge Blood' as the Ayatollah's Islamic avenger. The two mobs clashed, using clubs, knives, sawchains and, as noon approached, shotguns which appeared as if out of nowhere. This gave the special forces unit the signal to enter the city ostensibly to restore calm between two feuding factions. By the time they reached the scene several thousand men were busy fighting each other. Shots were fired and two *talabehs*, Hassan Nejati and Karim Borhan, were fatally wounded; a number of others were injured. The pro-Khomeini mob fled in all directions, a large number seeking sanctuary in the shrine.

By sunset the city had calmed down and the mob from Tehran had returned home. Police and soldiers continued to guard key points and an armoured car was stationed not far from the shrine. The Ayatollah's house was bustling with activity as a continuous flow of mullahs poured in and out. Some were emissaries of other ayatollahs bringing messages of caution and prudence. Others had rushed to the holy city from surrounding villages on hearing rumours that the Shah's forces were burning the shrine. Many urged an immediate declaration of jihad on the government, but most showed they would be content with an amicable settlement in which the dignity of the clergy would be restored without the government being publicly humiliated. Sitting on a prayer mat and speaking not a word, Khomeini listened to the conflicting views. He eventually got up and, with a curt 'Allah be with you', left the room, retiring to his private quarters where he was fast asleep in a few minutes.

Rising before the sun as usual, he performed his prayers and took his breakfast of bread and goat cheese, washed down with hot sweet tea, before returning to the main reception room where heated discussions, interrupted only by prayers, had continued all night. As the Ayatollah entered the room, all murmurs died down. He motioned Montazeri and Motahari to sit on either side of him and ordered more tea. His face was as grim as usual but did not bear any trace of the struggle that was almost certainly going on in his mind. Keeping his eyes fixed on the patterns in the carpet, he pronounced, in his soft, monotonous voice, what amounted to a declaration of war against the regime. He did not mention the Shah by name, apparently even then not quite sure whether such a direct confrontation would prove wise. For the rest, however, he made no secret of his sentiments. Bahonar wrote down the Ayatollah's words, which were later edited into a declaration. 'By creating this catastrophe, the regime of tyranny has sealed its own doom; it is going to die and we shall be victorious. We have always prayed to Allah that this regime should reveal its true colours, bringing shame on itself. Our prayers have been granted.'[7]

The Ayatollah's brief remarks were printed the same day and distributed all over Qom. But their effect was so slight that the authorities did not even try to prevent the distribution. The government's leniency may have been due to the fact that the month of Muharram, when Shi'ites mourn the martyrdom of Imam Hussein, was approaching and there was every risk of violent clashes. The main reason, however, was that the reform programme offered by the Shah and approved by a huge majority in the referendum, in which women voted for the first time, was genuinely popular at the time, having aroused a number of hopes and expectations. Emissaries of Khomeini who had travelled to Tehran to sound out the popular mood reported back that the Ayatollah would have to take a stronger stance to have any hope of being followed outside Qom.

The government, however, was not prepared to take any further risks. It was announced that all religious processions during Muharram had to receive the written approval of the police authorities. The Faizieh School was to remain closed for the month and a number of popular preachers, such as Falsafi, were blacklisted and prevented from mounting the pulpit during mourning ceremonies. The officially approved preachers were strictly ordered to steer clear of political issues and focus their attention on ethics and personal morality. The state-owned radio also gave prominent coverage to an Islamic conference in London in which Iran was taking an active part both in the form of a generous donation and by sending a large delegation. Pro-government theology teachers broadcast special programmes designed to show that the emancipation of women and the distribution of land among the farmers who tilled it was not anti-Islamic.

The Ayatollah's hope of nationwide demonstrations against the reforms was quickly dashed when the overwhelming majority of the mullahs refused to be dragged into what appeared to be a dangerous adventure. Khomeini's emissaries also returned empty-handed from negotiations with the remnants of the Mossadeqist movement. The section of the intelligentsia that had always opposed the Shah proved equally unresponsive when invited by the Ayatollah's emissaries to oppose such eminently progressive measures as land reform and the emancipation of women. The only 'good news' came from the mountainous regions of the southern province of Far where a number of warlike clans in Boyer-Ahmad and Kohkiluyeh had staged an armed rebellion. The rebellion was to last nearly two years and engage more than 60,000 troops backed by aircraft. But even that could not have seemed encouraging to Khomeini since the rebellious tribes had never been known for their devotion to traditional Shi'ism and were fighting only to preserve the huge estates of their chiefs.

Khomeini's failure to secure any support from the middle class, confirmed his earlier conclusions that almost all of urban Iran was, he hoped only for the moment, lost to Islam. During the weeks that followed he spoke bitterly of the middle class, reserving his most caustic comments for the intellectuals who were either beginning to be coopted into the regime or who had already surrendered to despair. Islam, he concluded, had to find a new audience in a society that was being rapidly conquered by Western values and ideas. The intellectuals, even when they professed loyalty to Islam, were incapable of ordering their own lives in accordance with the strict rules of the Muhammedan faith. At best, Islam could become their ideology but never their life; at worst, they succumbed to the infectious charm of Western atheism which offered the illusion of boundless liberty. But where could he find his new defenders of Islam? Among the poor and illiterate peasants? Among industrial workers? Finding an answer to these questions was to take him another decade and a half. Of more immediate concern was the need to make a show of force. Having declared war on the regime, he could not simply sit back and watch as nothing happened. He had rejected the advice of those who would have been content with a government inquiry into the violent episode at Faizieh. He had become a general without many troops, engaged in a war in which the adversary did not even acknowledge his existence.

By now convinced that crying wolf over an alleged plot to destroy Islam would not mobilize many people, Khomeini added two new themes to his campaign. The first was xenophobia. In Iran, as in all the other countries of the Islamic East, the foreigner means the European or, more recently, the American and is both secretly admired and intensely hated. The notion that the poverty, backwardness and the generally dismal lot of the Muslim masses is mainly, if not entirely, due to the misdeeds of 'foreigners' (*farangi* in Persian and *agnabi* in Arabic) holds tremendous appeal for all sections of society. The rulers find this idea not only attractive but also profitable as it virtually absolves them of any responsibility for the existing state of affairs. They can claim to be doing their best in the service of the people, blaming their inevitable achievement of adverse results on scheming foreigners. The intellectuals also love the idea because it provides justification for their own laziness, their constant yielding to the temptations of money and power and, above all, their inability to offer a credible explanation for a complex situation. The cry of 'death to the foreigners' is certain to unite a much broader coalition of people in the Islamic East than virtually any other slogan. Even the non-Muslim minorities of the region are prepared to join in the cry because it provides almost the only sentiment they can fully share with their Muhammedan fellow-countrymen. While hatred of the foreigner offers a promising rallying call for any ambitious politician, it is fully effective only when the additional dimension of hating the Jews is also introduced. Most intellectuals and politicians in the Muslim East are not prepared openly to advocate hatred for the Jews, but this is mainly because they wish to describe themselves in terms borrowed from the West: Liberal, Democrat, Socialist, Social Democrat, Communist, etc. They also know that anti-Semitism is irrevocably associated with Nazism and distasteful to almost every major political movement in the contemporary world.

Khomeini, however, had no such inhibitions. He knew that preaching hate for the Jew and the foreigner would be popular and that was all that mattered to him in those critical days. He could not accept defeat, which would have meant slipping into oblivion. Accordingly, he chose an alleged plot 'by Jews and foreigners who wish to see Islam destroyed' as the main theme of his campaign, which was resumed in May. For stronger effect he also introduced the Baha'is, already considered heretics and thus automatically punishable by death according to him. This time, Khomeini avoided debating the actual reforms. He knew that calling on women to refuse the vote and expecting the peasants not to accept the land offered to them would only isolate him. He now concentrated his attacks on 'the enemies of the Qur'an'. In one speech he claimed that the Israeli Government had printed millions of copies of 'a falsified Qur'an' in a bid to 'destroy our glorious faith'. He also instructed his disciples to ignore the intellectuals and take the message directly to the illiterate masses. His advice was: 'An illiterate [man] can only pervert himself, while an intellectual who lacks moral [faith] can mislead a whole society.'[8] In a memo to emissaries sent to Tehran and other major cities he wrote: 'Remind the people of the danger posed by Israel and its agents. Recall and explain the catastrophes inflicted upon Islam by the Jews and the Baha'is. Declare your hatred for the traitor government. . . .'[9] He also asked that his emissaries should make maximum propaganda over the promotion by the government of a number of Jews, Baha'is, Zoroastrians and Christians to positions of responsibility within the civil service and the armed forces. General Assadollah Sani'i, a Baha'i who was to become a Cabinet Minister, was singled out as the first in a line of non-Muslims who would rule Iran in the future.

The new tactic proved far more successful and the Ayatollah's emissaries succeeded in organizing a number of meetings in Qom,

131

Isfahan, Najaf-Abad and Khomein. In Mashhad they won the support of Ayatollah Hassan Tabataba'i-Qomi who was also opposed to the Shah's reforms. Muharram's special ceremonies provided an ideal emotional setting for the preaching of hatred against Jews, Baha'is and foreigners who, nearly fourteen centuries after the martyrdom of Hussein, were now plotting to destroy Islam. In Isfahan a number of *mointat al-boka'as* (tears' assistants) were employed to encourage the audience to cry more profusely whenever a pro-Khomeini mullah mounted the pulpit. The ninth and tenth days of Muharram, when Shi'ite passion reaches its annual peak, were chosen by Khomeini as the climax of his campaign. He was determined to provoke an incident so that blood would be shed. 'Unless people see with their own eyes that the agents of Israel are shedding Muslim blood,' he told his disciples, 'we shall not be able to perform the duty set for us by Allah.'[10]

On Tassu'a and 'Ashura (9 and 10 Muharram) Qom plays host to tens of thousands of pilgrims from all over the country. According to Shi'ite tradition, praying at the shrine of Ma'assoumah on those days ensures a smooth passage into paradise. Some Shi'ite textbooks even claim that shedding 'sincere tears' at the shrine on 'Ashura is more meritorious than performing the pilgrimage to Mecca itself. The Tassu'a and 'Ashura of that year (3 and 4 June 1963) proved no exception. The size of the crowds may have been even larger because SAVAK also dispatched hundreds of agents to keep an eye on things and, if necessary, to break up anti-government demonstrations. The stage was set for a historic confrontation.

# 8

# *The Second 'Ashura*

The sky becomes black
Floods of tears are unleashed
Hussein arrives in Karbala
To sacrifice himself to Allah
This is the story of 'Ashura
Hear this tale of great sorrow
And shed tears for the King of the Martyrs
Who shall take you to paradise.

Popular mourning poem from the Ta'azieh Passion Plays

*T*he fifteenth day of the Persian month of Khordad 1342 (5 June 1963) is marked out in the history of Ayatollah Khomeini's movement as the Second 'Ashura. 'Ashura, the tenth day of the Arabic lunar month of Muharram, was the day on which the forces of the Omayyad Caliph Yazid put Imam Hussein to the sword in the Mesopotamian desert near the Euphrates nearly fourteen centuries ago. According to Khomeini, it was that rather bizarre episode in a remote setting which gave Islam a new lease of life by marking a clean break between Shi'ism and Sunniism. From the day when Reza Shah launched his original campaign against the mullahs Khomeini felt that a second 'Ashura was necessary. From 1962 onwards he became determined to secure a repetition of the tragedy in which he himself was prepared to play the part of Hussein. All that was now needed were a few mistakes from the Shah and his advisers so that the stage could be set for a re-enactment of the confrontation between Divine Good and Satanic Evil.

The Shah and his advisers did not hesitate to make the mistakes Khomeini was counting on. First, the Shah approved a series of measures designed to antagonize the mullahs, forcing them to bury their innumerable differences in the face of a common adversary. These included an order to force hundreds of *talabehs* into the army in accordance with compulsory national service laws. This was an unfair and illegal act since students were exempt from military service for the duration of their studies. The fact that the *talabehs* were not recognized as students was, rightly, interpreted as a prelude to closing down the theological schools. Next, the government, in what now appears as a dress rehearsal for their even more colossal mistake sixteen years later, cut off almost all the secret funds channelled to some key mullahs through the Owqaf or Endowments Office. Meanwhile, the government-owned radio in Tehran launched a campaign of abuse and ridicule against the mullahs. They were caricatured in radio plays and comedy programmes; they were portrayed as parasitical souls and as sodomites who were also capable of all other sexual deviations. Tehran theatre and cabaret, taking their cue from the resourceful Minister for Propaganda at the time, Jahangir Tafazoli, staged a series of farces aimed against the mullahs.

Having reached an understanding with the US Administration during his visit to Washington in which he had managed to win over President Kennedy, the Shah was now sure that there would be no American plot to overthrow him. He was, therefore, free to eliminate all his domestic opponents. Qom had represented a symbol of resistance to his father's reforms; now he was determined to break the holy city. Reviving the tradition under which the Shahs visited Qom for pilgrimage during the Nowruz festivities, the Shah organized a triumphal storming of the city for himself. In April 1963 he entered the city amid scenes of wild enthusiasm, directed by *metteurs-en-scène* dispatched from Tehran and played mostly by peasants paid to fill the streets. Out of the estimated 12,000 mullahs and *talabehs* who made up the city's clerical population, only a few agreed to welcome the monarch. He was not worried as a 700-strong detachment of his own bodyguard had been dressed as mullahs and provided all the local colour that was necessary for television and film cameras. The poor guardsmen had had to grow their beards for a full month before the visit.

Dressed in his uniform of Commander-in-Chief and adorned with full regalia, the Shah entered Qom not as a humble servant of the twelve Imams but as a reincarnation of Cyrus the Great. He was no longer the diffident Mohammad-Reza who kissed the hand of Ayatollah Borujerdi and held secret meetings with Ayatollah Kashani; he was the true son of Reza Shah, the dreaded dictator whose dream of de-Arabizing Iran had only been ended by the British who had sent him into exile. Addressing a large, and largely paid, crowd at the courtyard of the shrine, the Shah launched a bitter attack on the mullahs. He called them 'Black reactionaries' who did not wish to understand that the world had changed and that women could no longer be treated in the same way as children and idiots as far as the nation's laws were concerned. He said that his reforms would take Iran into 'the jet age' while the mullahs wanted to remain 'in the age of the donkey'. Later, receiving the few genuine mullahs who had risked their reputation by going to meet him, the Shah went even further and accused all mullahs of being 'sodomites and agents of the British'.

The Shah's aggressive remarks were promptly reported to the leading ayatollahs, giving them the impetus for a unity that had eluded them since Borujerdi's death. The four high-ranking ayatollahs of Qom – Shariatmadari, Mara'ashi, Golpayegani and Khomeini – issued statements condemning 'unjustified attacks on the dignity of the Shi'ite clergy'. The two main ayatollahs of Mashhad – Tabataba'i-Qomi and Milani – quickly followed suit. Milani, a deeply religious, almost saintly man, wept as he read a report of the Shah's sayings in Qom. 'The son was like the father,' he later recalled. 'Only he was more vulgar and lacked the moral courage of Reza Shah.'

The matter might have rested there had it not been for Khomeini's insistence that the clergy should counterattack before it was too late. The natural inclination of most of the ayatollahs was to seek refuge in silence and wait until the storm blew itself out. Some even began to think of moving to Najaf and Karbala in Iraq as a gesture of protest. Khomeini, however, was adamant that now was the time to make a stand. There is no doubt that he genuinely believed in the rightness of his strategy. At the same time, however, he knew that by pushing through with political confrontation he would secure ascendancy over all the other ayatollahs. From a purely theological point of view Khomeini still had neither the stature nor the following to enable him to claim supremacy among the mullahs. Grand Ayatollah Abol-Qassem

Mussavi-Kho'i, Grand Ayatollah Mohsen Hakim Tabataba'i and Grand Ayatollah Ahmad Mussavi-Khonsari were all by far his seniors. He would have to wait a very long time for all of them to die before claiming their mantle. And even then he would have very strong rivals in the ayatollahs Shariatmadari, Milani, Golpayegani, Mara'ashi, Tabataba'i-Qomi and Shirazi.

Khomeini was perfectly aware of the fact that none of those ayatollahs was politically inclined. Most were holy men content with teaching and praying. Some, like Mussavi-Kho'i, considered politics a pitfall to be avoided by men of goodwill. Others, like Mussavi-Khonsari, were so afraid of causing bloodshed that they were prepared to put up with almost any ignominy in order to prevent violence. Only two ayatollahs shared Khomeini's taste for politics. One was Shariatmadari, who had established himself as the leading authority on financial and economic matters according to Shi'ite Islam and enjoyed enormous popularity among the *talabehs*. The other was Tabataba'i-Qomi in Mashhad, who, although as passionate as Khomeini in his beliefs, was loath to promote himself as a political leader. Both men were to become Khomeini's mortal enemies from 1979 onwards. In those days, however, both of them joined forces with Khomeini in resisting what they saw as the Shah's plot to break the power of the mullahs. Shariatmadari, however, preferred secret negotiations with the government as a means of avoiding direct confrontation.

Sensing a mood of agitation among the mullahs the government ordered the arrest of sixty-three of the more militant of them. All the leading ayatollahs issued statements protesting against the arrests. But it was only Khomeini who called for 'strong action against the Administration of Tyranny'.[1] The Ayatollah had timed the start of his campaign to coincide with the start of the two mourning months of Muharram and Safar which began on 24 May. On 'Ashura, the tenth day of Muharram (2 June), sporadic demonstrations took place in Tehran and, for the first time, groups of militants attacked a number of public buildings with cries of 'Hail to Khomeini'.[2] Some militants managed to seize control of the Baharestan Square, where Parliament was situated, for a while and covered many walls with posters of the Ayatollah. Three men led the demonstrations: Tayyeb Haj-Reza'i, his brother Isma'il Haj-Reza'i and Sayyed Mehdi Araqi. All three were tough guys from the poor districts of south Tehran. All had helped the Shah regain his throne in 1953 by fighting Mossadeq and his Tudeh supporters. They had turned against the Shah for a variety of personal and political reasons. The two Haj-Reza'is had not even met Khomeini before and were now adopting him simply because they found him to be uncompromising and courageous.

Disturbed by the Tehran demonstrations, the authorities ordered security in Qom to be strengthened. Exaggerated reports of the events in Tehran had reached Qom, creating an atmosphere of defiance. Khomeini was sitting among a dense crowd of mourners in the courtyard of Ayatollah Shariatmadari's house when news of the events in Tehran reached him. It was 2 p.m. and Shariatmadari was delivering a traditional sermon. Khomeini was approached by Major General Nasser Moqaddam, a high-ranking SAVAK officer, who said he was bringing a message from 'His Imperial Majesty'. The message was: 'Keep quiet or we shall break your bones.' Khomeini, the expression in his face unchanged, replied, 'We, too, have our commandos; His Imperial Majesty should know that.'

The meeting at Shariatmadari's house broke up half an hour later and Khomeini returned to his home for a brief siesta. While he slept, an immense crowd gathered around his house and in the neighbouring streets. Many men had come dressed in white burial shrouds indicating their readiness to die at any moment. Men would embrace and sob uncontrollably as they said farewell to each other, convinced that they would be dead before the sun of 'Ashura had set. They were united in one thing: they all wanted Khomeini to speak.

An hour later, Khomeini emerged, flanked by his son Mostafa and also by Montazeri. Without raising his head he walked through the narrow path that opened up before him in the midst of the dense crowd of bearded men on the point of emotional explosion. Araqi, who had just arrived from Tehran, had brought with him a number of tough guys, known as *jahels*, to protect the Ayatollah. There were rumours that Khomeini would be killed by a SAVAK agent on that day. Khomeini himself, however, was totally oblivious of any threat to his life. Years later, he said that he had been told that he would die two years after the start of the fifteenth century of Islam, that is to say in 1981.[3] At that time, therefore, he was convinced he would not be killed. Finally, boarding an open car, the Ayatollah ordered the driver to take him to the Faizieh School. The choice was deliberate; he wanted to tell the Shah that Faizieh was now the heart of resistance against his regime.

At Faizieh, the Ayatollah did not mount the pulpit but, no doubt wishing to underline his modesty, sat on a platform facing the holy shrine and began to address the crowd. He used the technique of *rowzeh-khani*, a special brand of emotional oratory aimed at stirring up the deepest religious passions of the faithful. He was taking an unusual step, for ayatollahs usually shun *rowzeh-khani*, considering it to be a rather cheap and emotional means of extracting tears from the crowds. A *rowzeh-khan* is a low-ranking mullah whose function is to provoke tears. An ayatollah, however, aims at encouraging a more logical view of religious duties.

In his sermon he equated the Shah with the Omayyad caliphs who had usurped power that rightfully belonged to the descendants of Prophet Muhammed. The Omayyad had wanted to destroy the Bani-Hashem clan to which the Prophet belonged. Today, the Shah was trying to do the same by eliminating the sayyeds who also belonged to the Bani-Hashem clan.

The Ayatollah further claimed that the Shah's agents, in their raid on Faizieh, had torn up and burned copies of the Qur'an.[4] He then introduced one of his new themes: that it was Israel which was plotting against Islam.

'Israel does not want the Qur'an to be in this kingdom. Israel does not want the *ulama* of Islam to be in this kingdom. Israel does not want the rules of Islam to be in this country. Israel does not want [religious] scientists to be in this kingdom. Israel attacked the Faizieh School through its black agents.'

It was also Israel that wanted to dominate the Iranian economy and had taught the Shah to brand the mullahs as parasites.

The Ayatollah, by now visibly shaking with emotion, went on to say, 'Mr Shah, Excellency Shah, you poor, miserable man. I am giving you advice. Excellency Shah, I am warning you; stop these acts and change your manners. I do not wish to see the day that, when you are kicked out by your masters, people are giving thanks. I don't want you to become like your father. . . . Listen to me, do not listen to Israel. Israel is no good for you. Poor, miserable creature, you are only forty-five years old. Ponder a bit, have a bit of wisdom, think a little bit about the consequence of your acts.'

Revealing messages sent to him by SAVAK, the Ayatollah said that the security organization, which was rumoured to be directly trained by the Israeli MOSSAD and the American CIA, had asked the mullahs to avoid three subjects: the Shah, Israel and dangers to Islam.

'Why does SAVAK say that we should not speak of the Shah

and Israel?' he demanded, amid cries of 'Allah is the Greatest'. 'Does SAVAK mean that the Shah is an Israeli? Does SAVAK consider the Shah to be a Jew?'

He then introduced the threat of excommunication which, strictly speaking, does not exist in Islamic law. 'Shall I declare you, Mr Shah, to be a heathen so that you are chased out of this country?' the Ayatollah asked the absent monarch.

'You do not know that the day there is commotion and the page is turned, you shall have no friends. None of those now around you are your friends. They are friends of dollars. These people have no faith, no loyalty. They blame you for their [crimes].'[5]

The speech ran through the audience like an electric shock. It was the first time in nearly a decade that anyone had dared attack the Shah in so violent a manner and in public. Although the Ayatollah had tried to keep the door half open to the Shah by claiming that the monarch was being blamed for the misdeeds of others, the tone of his speech rendered any thought of a dialogue problematic. Shariatmadari was furious. He told Montazeri to tell Khomeini that the speech at Faizieh that afternoon had been 'too excessive'. Khomeini replied that his speech had been 'too moderate, compared to what they are preparing for us'.

Copies of Khomeini's speech were prepared throughout the night and sent to Tehran by special couriers. The following day thousands of copies of the speech were distributed at Tehran University but an attempt at forcing a closure of the university failed.

A copy of the speech was presented to the Shah by Police Chief General Nematollah Nasiri, who complained about what he termed 'the lax attitude of the government'. The Shah was furious. 'Why does no one reply to that miserable goat?' he demanded.[6] 'Alam, the Prime Minister, met an angry Shah later in the day when he called at the palace to present a report. He promised to 'pull their ears until they are blue', referring to the mullahs. The Court Minister Hussein 'Ala, however, was opposed to any use of force. 'These people,' he argued, referring to the mullahs, 'have kept their business going on the basis of martyrdom myths. They would love to have new martyrs. Our best course is to ignore them, let them bark themselves hoarse.'[7] 'Alam, however, saw 'Ala's stance as a shrewd manoeuvre to engineer the fall of the government. 'Ala had served as Prime Minister on two previous occasions and was suspected of having acquired a taste for the job. Also opposed to the use of force was Major General Hassan

Pakravan, the SAVAK director, whose policy of stick and carrot had failed to pacify the mullahs but who, nevertheless, thought that the bulk of the clergy wanted a compromise. It was because he suspected Pakravan of being 'too soft' that 'Alam eventually decided to use a detachment of Rangers to seal off Qom. All that the SAVAK agents had to do was to arrange for the Ayatollah's 'travel' to Tehran. At almost the same time over two hundred known opponents of the regime, including many mullahs, were rounded up in various cities.

It was shortly before 3 a.m. that the Rangers, moving in battle formation, encircled and sealed off the entire Gozar-Qazee district where Khomeini's house was situated. Taking position in a pomegranate grove behind the Ayatollah's residence, they poured into Khomeini's house from the rooftop, taking everyone by surprise. Amid the cries of women and the noise of doors being broken down by force, the Rangers searched every room and every nook and cranny in the house without finding the Ayatollah. They then rounded up the Ayatollah's domestic servants, who numbered seventeen at the time, and began beating them up so that they would reveal Khomeini's hiding place. Within less than an hour a fairly sizable crowd had gathered. The Ayatollah could hear the cries of his servants from his hiding place, an upstairs room in the house of his son Mostafa, just across the road. He had decided to stay there as a precaution against possible assassination attempts. There are different accounts as to why it took the Ayatollah nearly an hour before giving himself up to the soldiers sent to arrest him. According to Ahmad, Khomeini's younger son, the Ayatollah had locked himself in a room, hiding the key under a carpet. When awakened by the commotion he had quickly dressed and wanted to go out but forgot where he had hidden the key. But once the key was found he rushed into the street, accompanied by Mostafa. He asked Mostafa to go and inform the people of what was happening and then proceeded to his own residence. Arriving in the courtyard of his house, Khomeini was confronted with what resembled a battle scene. Going direct to the soldiers he shouted, 'Stop, I am Ruhollah Khomeini. You want me, so don't savage these poor people.'

The soldiers, at first probably fearing an imposture, hesitated but were finally convinced that the mullah facing them was Khomeini when they saw all present rush to him and kiss his hand and feet. The Ayatollah was led to a Volkswagen parked close by and pushed to the back where he was flanked by two huge

Rangers. At the end of the street the car had to stop as violent cries were heard. It was Mostafa who had run from one rooftop to another shouting, 'Oh, people of Islam, wake up!' Now he was shouting, 'I am going to jump from the roof unless you release my father.' He finally calmed down when the Ayatollah told him to go back home and look after the injured. The Volkswagen, escorted by two command cars, set out for Tehran just as the sun was rising.[8] The journey proved agony for the Ayatollah. One of the two officers sitting next to him in the back seat of the tiny car reeked of garlic and kept breathing in his direction. The other officer had a nasty habit of pinching the Ayatollah at the end of every cheap joke he related, giggling all the time. At one point one of the officers ordered the car to stop so that he could get out and attend to his natural needs in the desert. But by the time the convoy arrived in Tehran nearly three hours later the Ayatollah was fast asleep. One of the officers said jokingly, 'I wish your holiness was not angry with us.' Khomeini replied, 'You are just poor souls, my business is with your master.'

In Tehran the Ayatollah was driven to the Officers' Club, near the Foreign Ministry in the centre of the city. The officer in command, however, politely refused to put up the Ayatollah 'for a few days'. 'This is a club,' he said. 'We cannot admit non-members, unless orders come from His Imperial Majesty.' Rather than make an issue of it, the SAVAK officers decided to transfer Khomeini to the Qasr prison the same day. The Ayatollah was kept there for nineteen days and was then transferred to a room in Eshrat-Abad Garrison in east Tehran, thanks to Pakravan, who still hoped for a compromise.

Khomeini was not the only mullah arrested at the time. In addition to a large number of *talabehs* and lesser mullahs, SAVAK also seized Ayatollah Hassan Tabataba'i-Qomi, bringing him from Mashhad to Tehran. The preacher Mohammad-Taqi Falsafi had also been arrested in the capital after a sermon in which he had 'tried' the government for its 'crimes'.

By arresting Khomeini, the government was, in effect, recognizing him as the leader of the religious opposition. Qomi did not have Khomeini's theological rank then and was, in any case, not interested in a political career.

Meanwhile in Qom, Ayatollah Shariatmadari was already organizing a big demonstration for 'the release of our dear ones'. Shariatmadari, a calm, quiet man by temperament, must have seemed an unlikely leader for a religious revolt. But on that momentous day in Muharram he proved himself a master tactician. Exactly fifteen years later he was to assume precisely the same role when Khomeini was preparing to return from exile. At 5 a.m. Shariatmadari went to the holy shrine and led common prayers attended by some 3000 people. He then went to the Faizieh School, symbolizing by his presence the continuation of Khomeini's defiance.

Shariatmadari also published a statement calling for the release of the mullahs and *talabehs* who had been arrested and sent a number of cables to the ayatollahs of Najaf, inviting them to show solidarity with their brethren in Iran.

Shariatmadari had wanted the clergy to maintain a posture of helpless victims of tyranny. 'Our very force is in the fact that we have no force,' he told Mostafa.[9] But the young Khomeini and his friends had other ideas. They wanted to fight back. By noon they had organized groups of militants, armed with clubs, knives and even daggers, to attack the security forces. The tactic was to march with a group of women at the head of the crowd; once the police were sucked into the crowd they were isolated and beaten up. By early afternoon regular troops had been called into the city and, unnerved by the pressure of events, began firing on the crowd. A number of people were killed; many more were injured. Islamic historians have put the number of those killed on that day in Qom at 'many thousands' but the names of only four 'martyrs' have entered the revolutionary roll of honour. The government of the day put the number of the dead at only two.[10]

Qom was not the only place where trouble broke out. Shiraz also experienced demonstrations, provoked by a fiery speech from Ayatollah Fazlollah Mahalati. But by far the largest demonstrations took place in Tehran itself where crowds of women in black *chadors* and men in white burial shrouds started to move towards the city centre from the poor districts of the south. The crowd smashed everything on its route and grew bigger as it approached Arg Square where the radio station was situated at the time. The objective was, clearly, to capture the radio and transmit the tape of Khomeini's incendiary sermon. Tens of thousands of people took part in the biggest demonstrations against the regime that Tehran had witnessed for many years. The regime could no longer claim that it was being attacked simply because of its reform programme. It had now been identified as anti-Islamic and had thus isolated itself from the Tehrani proletariat which had supported it a generation earlier.

'Alam ordered security forces to shoot to kill 'if necessary' without first informing the Shah.[11] The Shah, briefed on the events in his capital, was totally unnerved and was already beginning to seek a way out without violence. But by the time 'Alam contacted His Majesty to discuss the events of the day, blood had already been shed and there was no choice but to declare martial law in the capital. At least a hundred people were killed, with hundreds more injured. Islamic legend, of course, has put the number of the dead on that fifteenth day of the Persian month of Khordad at 15,000, probably because the two figures of 15 offer greater dramatic impact.

Nasiri, the newly appointed Martial Law Administrator in the capital, had, at least in part, achieved his goal of provoking a direct and bloody confrontation between the government and the mullahs. According to some accounts, Nasiri had been influenced by Israeli Intelligence which at the time was doing everything in its power to worsen the already poor relations between Iran and the Arabs. Nasiri, probably taking his cue from MOSSAD, believed that Khomeini's sudden discovery of Israel as the main enemy of Islam had not been spontaneous and represented a success for Egypt's President Gamal Abdel Nasser's security forces. Nasser, in those days locked in a bitter personal struggle with the Shah, was known to have sent into Iran a number of agents recruited from among Iraqi Shi'ites. Some of them had contacted Dr Mossadeq, the fallen Prime Minister and long-term critic of the Shah, but had failed to persuade him to reactivate his support and launch a new attack on the monarch. Mossadeq, a passionate nationalist, had dismissed Nasser's agents politely but firmly. Nasser had then turned to the mullahs and contacted some of their representatives both in Iraq and Kuwait, offering them support and money through his own security agents. The Israelis, distrusting Pakravan, had given what information they had on Nasser's supposed links with the Iranian mullahs to Nasiri.[12] While Pakravan wanted to maintain the mullahs as a potential ally against the Communists, Nasiri considered them to be Nasser's fifth column and wanted to break up their organizational strength.

Nasiri and 'Alam were both in favour of an early trial of Khomeini, Qomi and thirteen other mullahs arrested in Qom, Mashhad, Shiraz and Tehran. 'Alam even spoke of trying the prisoners by a military tribunal and having them executed as soon as possible.[13] Pakravan stood firm and asked for time to negotiate with Khomeini and Qomi. In the meantime, Court Minister 'Ala brought together a group of seven elder statesmen to discuss 'these grave events'. The group sent an appeal to the Shah: Do not allow yourself to be dragged into a religious war. The Shah responded by dismissing 'Ala as Court Minister. He later told a confidante: 'Such elder statesman must be flushed down a lavatory.'

Meanwhile, Shariatmadari, hiding under a heap of rugs in the back of a truck so as to escape detection, managed to leave Qom and travel clandestinely to Tehran. He had also sent messages to other leading ayatollahs throughout Iran to make their way to Tehran as soon as possible. He believed that an assembly of the nation's religious leaders in the capital would prove strong enough to prevent the execution of Khomeini and Qomi. Pakravan endorsed the move and his agents turned a blind eye to the unusual number of mullahs arriving at the army-controlled capital. Shariatmadari took up residence at Rey, six miles southwest of Tehran, and was quickly surrounded by thousands of supporters. Since Rey was not under martial law, Nasiri's forces had no authority to interfere with Shariatmadari's activities. While in Rey, Shariatmadari received cables of support from the Grand Ayatollahs of Najaf with copies sent to the Shah. Scores of leading mullahs also joined him from all over the country. A solid front of Shi'ite clergy was in place and, before the month of Khordad had ended, it became obvious that the execution of Khomeini and Qomi would prove a very costly political blunder. Pakravan was given the green light to negotiate an amicable settlement. As a sign of goodwill he first allowed Grand Ayatollah Khonsari to visit Khomeini and Qomi in prison. He then went to Eshrat-Abad in person and spent several hours talking to both prisoners. He told them that politics was 'a dirty game, unworthy of men of God' and invited them to renounce interfering in politics.[14] Qomi said that the mullahs were not interested in politics as Pakravan described. Khomeini tried to appear to wish the Shah well and told Pakravan, 'All we are saying is that they are leading him [the Shah] towards disaster.'

Pakravan, a St-Cyr graduate and a deeply cultured man, was an unlikely SAVAK chief. He had stopped the torture of prisoners, believing that he could win over any opponent by being sincere and logical. He thought that Iran needed a generation of strong government combined with economic progress and social reform before being prepared for democracy. He tried to sell these ideas to Khomeini and failed. Later he recalled his negotiations with the ayatollahs like this: 'I felt like a helpless wave, smashing my head against solid rock.'[15] Nevertheless, having recourse to the traditional Iranian tactic of half-truth, Pakravan was able to report to the Shah that the two mullahs had agreed not to interfere in politics and that they should be set free. Pakravan's efforts to secure Khomeini's early release were to cost him dear. Soon after he was banished as Ambassador to Pakistan. After the Islamic revolution in 1979 he was executed without trial on Khomeini's orders and his body was badly mutilated. His corpse, or what remained of it, was left at the Tehran morgue for weeks as the Islamic authorities refused to issue burial permission because Pakravan had been a Christian 'at heart'.[16]

Meanwhile, Shariatmadari had returned to Qom to help prevent any fresh outburst of violence. In an important statement he tried to extend an olive branch towards the Shah. He claimed that the clergy were not opposed to 'genuine reforms' and all they were asking for was 'social justice and the implementation of the Constitution'. He criticized censorship and said that the mullahs were not 'reactionaries opposed to liberty and progress'.[17]

By August the Shah had been persuaded to order the release of almost all the arrested mullahs, Khomeini and Qomi among them. But neither was allowed to return to their respective cities and had to rent houses in Shemiran, a northern suburb of Tehran, where they were held under virtual house arrest for a further eight months. Khomeini and Qomi had become friends while in prison. They had been kept in facing cells and spent most of the day chatting through the iron bars. After the revolution in 1979, however, Qomi was one of the first leading ayatollahs to denounce Khomeini as 'an egoist, power-hungry politician, disguised in religious garb'.[18]

By the end of the summer Khomeini had been established as the unchallenged leader of the opposition to the Shah. 'Alam and Nasiri had accomplished for him what he could not have hoped to accomplish in a decade. All he had to do now was sit back and wait until his time came. It was 'Alam and his Cabinet colleagues who were on the way out as the results of a largely manipulated election gave a parliamentary majority to the Progressive Centre led by Hassan-Ali Mansur who soon formed a new government. Convinced that the mullahs would not be able to mobilize any mass support against a government that promised greater freedom and prosperity, Mansur allowed Khomeini and Qomi to return to Qom and Mashhad respectively. Khomeini arrived in Qom on 8 April 1964 and was greeted by a festive crowd never before seen in the grim city. Men and women, wearing colourful clothes and distributing sweets and fruits, were, however, not the type of crowd the Ayatollah liked. He told the organizers off by reminding them that 'we have had martyrs'. 'Our colour,' he said, 'shall remain black until we have avenged our martyrs.'[19] He also announced that he himself would be fasting every Thursday in memory of the martyrs. A few days later the Ayatollah addressed a crowd of several thousands at Qom's great mosque. Echoing a theme set by Shariatmadari, he said the mullahs were not opposed to progress and reform and, once again, bitterly attacked Israel.[20]

Anxious to consolidate his newly won position as a Grand Ayatollah, Khomeini made a number of manoeuvres. He called on the homes of the other Grand Ayatollahs, ostensibly to thank them for their support during his captivity. He then invited them all to his own house, where they were to meet together for the first time. Before the Grand Ayatollahs arrived at the Khomeini residence, Mostafa had spread the word about this 'historic event'. The fact that Khomeini, Shariatmadari, Mara'ashi and Golpayegani were coming together for the first time under Khomeini's roof was pointed to by his supporters as a sign of his recognition as the *a'alam*, or *primus inter pares*. At the meeting, the Ayatollah served a dinner of boiled rice, grilled lamb kebabs and yoghurt and suggested that the four should meet every Thursday at one of their houses. He also suggested a collective appeal to leading mullahs in other cities to organize similar committees, and that public meetings should be organized in the major mosques of every Iranian city to enable the mullahs to expand their audience and harmonize the thoughts of the faithful. The three Grand Ayatollahs agreed, no doubt with a certain degree of reluctance. None was too keen to see Sayyed Ruhollah build himself up as the rightful heir to Borujerdi.

By 1964 Khomeini had succeeded in persuading the hard core of Shi'ite fundamentalism that the Shah was drifting away from Islam and that no compromise with him was possible. This meant that from then on there were two rival and mutually exclusive visions of Iran's place in the world and its future. One was that of the Shah. He wanted to create a powerful, imperial state that would 'look after every Iranian from the womb to the tomb'.[21] Every reform proposed by the Shah was essentially aimed at increasing the power of the state at the expense of all other traditional institutions such as the clergy, the bazaar community, the semi-nomadic tribal confederations and Parliament. The Shah was convinced that Iran, a backward and still poverty-stricken nation plagued by illiteracy and ignorance, needed a benevolent dictatorship in order to bring her into the twentieth century. He wanted to Westernize Iran just as his father had tried to do. But his concept of Westernization was a physical one. When paying state visits to Western Europe, for example, he would admire the apartment blocks, the electricity pylons and factory chimneys. In later years he became obsessed with economic growth rates and figures concerning the GNP. On numerous occasions he could be seen dreaming aloud about the day Iran's GNP per capita would exceed $2000 a year. He believed that by the time Iran reached that lofty goal she would no longer be threatened by the dangers facing 'developing nations'. That figure was to be reached in the last year of the Shah's reign, thanks to several dramatic increases in the prices of crude oil, Iran's main source of wealth, as well as to assiduous manipulation of the figures by sychophantic bureaucrats. The Shah did not stop to think that a powerful state did not necessarily symbolize a happy nation and that Westernization, if confined to the creation of Western-style armies, secret police and bureaucracy, would not guarantee a transformation of the society. For him, the concept of Westernization did not include the rule of law, the recognition of basic human liberties and such principles as public accountability of government officials. In any case, under no circumstances would he allow Western-style political parties, trade unions and mass media to emerge and function. The material infrastructure for these was created but the prevailing political system prevented them from coming into being. The Shah's scenario for the transformation of Iran was eminently Prussian; the military, aided by a docile and sycophantic bureaucracy, had the mission of taking the empire of Cyrus the Great into the twentieth century.

The other vision of Iran, represented by Khomeini, was, in those early days of the movement, still quite blurred. But there is no doubt that it sought the ideal future for Iran not in a mythical Western model but in a still more mythical model supposedly developed in the early decades of Islam in Medina under the Prophet himself. Khomeini did not, as yet, advocate direct rule by the mullahs, but this was already implied. He saw almost all educated people as already tainted with corruption. He shared with the Shah one central belief: that the mass of Iranians were incapable of distinguishing right from wrong and, as a result, required a strong and uncompromising guide. The Shah had already decided to upstage his own father and become the second Cyrus the Great. Khomeini, for his part, was by then determined to succeed where even the Prophet himself had failed. The clash of two visions became a duel of two men as layer after layer of mutual hatred was deposited in minds extraordinarily bent towards bitterness. The two men and their conflicting visions were to represent two millstones between which any third idea of Iran's place in the world and the destiny of its tragic people would be crushed. From 1963 onwards anyone engaged in political activity in Iran was taking the side either of the Shah or of Khomeini, often without realizing it. People who opposed the Shah as Marxists or liberals were unaware that they were, in effect, strengthening the Khomeini camp. And democrats, atheists and socialists who advocated secularization while rejecting the Shah's dictatorship ended up endorsing him against the Ayatollah. Iran, the birthplace of Manicheanism, had, in closing the parenthesis created by the Constitutional Revolution of 1906, returned to its traditional 'either-or' style of ordering its political life.

The Ayatollah had tested some of his themes in practice, sounding out public opinion. He had discovered that xenophobia and anti-Semitism were powerful themes. The Shah could not use either since he was closely allied to the Americans on the one hand and was making increasing use of Israeli experts in agriculture and military training on the other. Furthermore, the Shah wished Iranians to copy the West as much as possible, provided, of course, that this did not extend to the realm of politics. Large sections of Iranian society, while tempted by the prospect of an improved material life, were scared of social and economic changes they had neither chosen nor helped to shape. It was among them that the Ayatollah would recruit his future volunteers for martyrdom. At the other end of the spectrum, there were many Iranians who, while genuinely attached to Islam, were frightened by visions of government by the mullahs in which life would be austere and dull if not downright cruel. In the 1960s the Shah could mobilize part of that opinion and this, combined with control of the armed forces and the bureaucratic apparatus, proved sufficient to isolate Khomeini and his supporters.

Throughout most of 1964 Ayatollah Khomeini played what amounted to a waiting game. He resumed his discourses at Faizieh and continued to receive a stream of militants from all over the country. Frequently, he spoke against the government and expressed concern about what he termed 'Israeli and Baha'i plots' to destroy Islam. But he was careful to modulate his attacks so as to avoid fever pitch. He dispatched trusted emissaries to various cities to recruit new supporters and raise additional funds. In Tabriz he had a powerful ally in the person of Ayatollah Ghazi Tabataba'i. In Yazd it was Ayatollah Mahmoud Saduqi, himself a former pupil of Khomeini's master, Shaikh Abdul-Karim, who represented the cause. More importantly, Khomeini ordered two of his closest aides, Morteza Motahari and Mohammad-Hussein Beheshti, to revive the secret cells of the Fedayeen of Islam. The two created the first cell in Tehran in August 1964 but dropped the name Fedayeen in favour of the more complicated *hayat-e-motalefeh-e-eslami* or the Coalescing Islamic Mission. The Mission, soon to be known in the clandestine movement only as the *hayat*, was to emerge as a vital link in the small but growing organization. The *hayat* brought together both propagandist and agitator. Khomeini would set the movement's general goals at any given time and a clandestine council, consisting of twelve trusted disciples, would translate these into concrete policies and communicate them to the *hayat*, which would then take charge of the implementation with the help of devoted militants.

Getting admitted into a *hayat* required passing a number of tests aimed at determining a candidate's loyalty, dedication and readiness to kill and die for the cause. The *hayats* had as members not only mullahs and *talabehs* but also bazaaris, shopkeepers, university students and teachers. Each *hayat* had a maximum of twelve members, the number twelve being considered sacred because of the twelve Imams, and acted autonomously. *Hayat* members did not meet at set intervals but would gather together at short notice. They were sure to meet on religious occasions, which are quite frequent in the Shi'ite calendar. The *hayat*, while an innovation, fitted well into traditional Iranian society. It acted like a traditional *dowreh* or circle, a structure loose enough to cut across class barriers and, at the same time, exclusive enough to foster intense loyalty. Members of the *hayats* were instructed to secure the leadership of as many religious organizations as possible. This proved a long and difficult process but, over the years, ensured the Ayatollah's domination of almost the entire religious apparatus in the country. That control enabled him to divide Iran into two parallel societies: the official one, headed by the Shah and supported by the army, the bureaucracy and parts of the middle and working classes; and the unofficial, the leadership of which passed to Khomeini from 1978 onwards.

During 1964 Ayatollah Khomeini made two attempts to repeat his success of 15 Khordad but failed. One was when he called on the faithful to prevent the execution of the two Haj-Reza'i brothers, who had been largely responsible for the disturbances in Tehran. His appeal, lacking the support of other ayatollahs, had almost no impact and the two men were hanged in Tehran. The Ayatollah's second unsuccessful attempt at provoking a new revolt came in June 1964 when he ordered nationwide demonstrations to mark the anniversary of the 15 Khordad riots. This time he was supported by Shariatmadari, Qomi and several other prominent ayatollahs but still failed to provoke a serious challenge. The only exception was the southern city of Shiraz, the cultural capital of Persia, where thousands of people went onto the rooftops to shout 'Allah Akbar' (Allah is the Greatest). This was also to become the battlecry of the movement during the revolution of 1978–79.

On the whole, however, the new government of Mansur succeeded in creating an economic boom and in distributing a greater share of the nation's wealth among broader strata of the urban and rural populations. Mansur was, at the same time, determined to strengthen further Iran's already close links with the United States. He negotiated a $200 million loan from the US which would enable Iran to re-equip her armed forces. While the loan was hailed by Mansur as a vote of confidence by the United States in the future stability of Iran, to Khomeini and his supporters this looked like a sellout. Securing foreign loans has always been and still remains one of the most unpopular policies in the Muslim East. Muslims remember that Egypt, in fact, lost her independence after being tied down with debts she could not pay. It was also foreign debt that virtually destroyed the Ottoman Empire. And in Iran herself the colonial powers of the day, Britain and Russia, used loans as a means of interfering in the country's domestic affairs throughout the nineteenth century. What was even worse in the case of the American loan was that it was accompanied by a bilateral agreement under which US military personnel who would be sent to Iran to help train the army in the use of new weapons were to enjoy extraterritorial capitulatory rights. A hastily drawn bill was pushed through Parliament depriving Iranian courts of the right to hear any complaints against American military personnel. The measure was resisted even in the docile Majlis, whose members had been handpicked by the authorities before the election. Some sixty out of the 271 members voted against the bill, which was, nevertheless, made law in record time. Some of the parliamentarians who had voted against the bill in October travelled to Qom and called on the ayatollahs to oppose it. They invoked a provision of the constitution under which no legislation could be valid without the endorsement of at least five Grand Ayatollahs. The provision had never been applied and the Shah was the last person prepared to revive it at that time. Once again, most ayatollahs were unwilling to take on the regime over this issue. But Khomeini promised to take action. The USA, anxious not to get involved in an Iranian political storm, dispatched one of its Iranian agents to Qom to 'explain things' to Khomeini.[22] This was the first time the Americans had contacted the Ayatollah. The agent's message was: Do not attack the United States. Attack the Shah, if you wish; that is not important. But if you attack the USA, there could be grave consequences.[23] The Ayatollah refused to see the agent personally but agreed that Mostafa should hear the verbal message. That proved the first of many blunders by the Americans in their dealings with the Ayatollah.

Through the *hayats*, Khomeini invited the faithful to travel to Qom from all over the country to hear what the Grand Ayatollahs had to say about 'some developments concerning Islam'. People began pouring into the holy city from Tehran, Isfahan, Shiraz and other major cities throughout the last week of October. On 2 November, the Ayatollah, accompanied by Shariatmadari and Mara'ashi, who, despite initial objections, were now ready to cooperate, appeared in the courtyard of his own residence which was teeming with an impatient crowd. The neighbouring streets were also filled with people who had arrived shortly after sunrise to hear the leaders. At about 8.30 Khomeini began to speak, as loudspeakers made his voice heard through much of the city centre. Once again he used the technique of *rowzeh-khani*. This time the main target for his attack was the United States and its 'agents'. Not once did he mention the Shah as he concentrated his fire on the Cabinet, the Majlis and the United States.

With his voice charged with emotion and often breaking down as he tried to contain his tears, the Ayatollah once again hammered his favourite themes. There was a plot to de-Islamicize Iran in the interests of the United States and Israel. All high-ranking officials and members of Parliament were agents of either the USA or of Israel. The only force capable of standing up to the USA and Israel was the Shi'ite leadership. This was why the authorities were trying to break up the organization of the mullahs and were still keeping so many mullahs in prison or in internal exile. The 'White Revolution' was nothing but a hoax.

In a passage that was to assume special significance in subsequent years, the Ayatollah had this to say: 'The source of all of our troubles is America. The source of all of our troubles is Israel. And Israel also belongs to America. Our MPs belong to America. Our Ministers belong to America. America has bought them all.'[24] He also said: 'The American President should know that he is the most hated man in the eyes of our people here in Iran. The United States Government should know that its [image] has been destroyed in Iran and its [position] ruined in Iran.'[25]

Expressing the deep resentment felt by many army officers, he said: 'They have dishonoured our army by setting an American sergeant above our four-star generals. The [military] have no prestige left in Iran. If I were [in their place] I would resign. If I were an army officer I would resign. If I were a member of the Majlis I would resign. I would never have accepted such a dishonour.'[26]

Probably foreseeing the government's response, he said: 'If the country is under American occupation, then tell us. In that case, seize us and throw us out of this country.'[27] This was precisely what was to happen a few days later.

Shariatmadari's speech, as usual, was far more moderate, while Mara'ashi, also using the technique of *rowzeh-khani*, delivered a passionate speech which outshone that of Khomeini, making the rather shy ayatollah the hero of the day. But Mara'ashi, uninterested in politics, was not prepared to join Khomeini in a popularity contest at that stage.

All three ayatollahs also issued statements condemning the Irano–American accord and declared it to be null and void under Islamic law. In this they were joined by Qomi, who organized a gathering of his own in Mashhad.

Contrary to Khomeini's expectations, the new agitation did not lead to nationwide demonstrations. The Ayatollah had miscalculated both the timing and the choice of his campaign theme. The United States was still regarded as a friendly power compared with Britain and the USSR which bore the heavy burden of their colonial past. The legal argument about who should try American military personnel if and when they broke the law in Iran was too complicated and abstract to be readily recognizable as 'a plot to destroy Islam'. In any case, there were very few American military technicians in Iran as yet. And, as the years went by, the capitulatory accord was allowed to die a quiet death and was hardly ever applied.

Nasiri, now chief of SAVAK, reported Khomeini's activities to Mansur and asked him to choose from among 'three courses open to us': to arrange an 'accident' for the Ayatollah; to send him into internal exile on a remote Persian Gulf island; or to exile him abroad.[28] Mansur immediately chose the last course and ordered his Foreign Minister Abbas Aram to contact the Indian and Pakistani governments on the subject. Both governments politely, but quickly, declined to offer Khomeini a place of exile. Aram then contacted the Turkish Government, an ally of Iran within the Central Treaty Organization (CENTO) and Ankara instantly agreed. Khomeini was arrested together with Mostafa and brought to Tehran where he was kept at a SAVAK 'safe house' for twenty-four hours before being flown to Ankara aboard a military aircraft on 4 November 1964. It was the start of an exile that was to last until 1 February 1979. Ayatollah Qomi was, at the same time, exiled to the Persian Gulf port of Bandar Abbas on the Strait of Hormuz.

Unlike the previous time, Khomeini's arrest had taken place smoothly and with full respect being paid to the Ayatollah. Khomeini had been offered facilities to take with him other members of his family but had refused. He had, at the same time, asked Mansur, through an intermediary, not to use violence against other mullahs 'because of me'. 'I am ready to pay for my own deeds,' Khomeini's message said. 'I do not wish anyone else to suffer on my behalf.'

Once in Turkey, the Ayatollah soon discovered that he was totally isolated. Turkey's secularism and the fact that Shi'ites formed a small minority there made Khomeini feel like a 'fish out of water', in the words of his younger son Ahmad.[29] More importantly, Turkish law banned the wearing of religious clothes and both the Ayatollah and Mostafa were politely told to wear European suits or else stay at home. Khomeini saw this as a deliberate insult and was deeply offended. He also did not like the cold. The Turks were, for their part, not sorry to see him go. So when he applied for permission to travel to Iraq and settle down in Najaf, there was little opposition. The Iraqi Ambassador in Tehran agreed instantly. 'There are so many mullahs in Najaf that one more or less would make no difference,' he commented. By January 1965 the family had been reunited in Najaf. The Ayatollah was specially glad to have his wife with him once again;

his attachment to Batul had not diminished with the passage of time. The family rented a mud-brick house not far from Imam Ali's golden-domed mausoleum while looking for a larger property to buy. Khomeini had expected prompt visits from the Grand Ayatollahs of Najaf – Kho'i, Hakim and Abdullah Shirazi. But a week passed and none appeared. So, swallowing his pride, he went to visit them.

# 9

# *Government as Allah Intended*

> Jews and their foreign backers are those who are opposed to the very foundations of Islam and want to establish an international Jewish Government; and, since they are a crafty and active lot, my fear is that, may Allah forbid it, they may one day succeed.
>
> Ayatollah Khomeini in *Kashf al-Asrar*

*B*y the time he had settled in Najaf, Grand Ayatollah Ruhollah Mussavi al-Khomeini was already written off as a political force by everyone – except a few devoted disciples like Montazeri and Motahari, who had remained in Iran to keep the torch burning. Khomeini was sixty-three years old, a grandfather, and already suffering from a weak heart, kidney trouble and chronic migraine. In addition, he was virtually without money as SAVAK had made sure that the flow of donations to His Holiness was cut off. A string of SAVAK agents, posing as servants, cooks or 'messengers' from Iran, kept a close watch on the Ayatollah and reported on those few partisans of his who made a point of calling on him during pilgrimages to Najaf and Karbala. Nasiri was able to report to the Shah that 'the old shark has had his fangs pulled out'. But the SAVAK chief was soon to be proved dramatically wrong.

Early in January 1965 the Ayatollah received a visit from Mohammad Mofattah who had been one of his pupils at Qom before moving to Tehran University where he obtained a PhD in

Divinity and thus was entitled to call himself Doctor, which he immensely liked. Dr Mofattah, on a regular pilgrimage to Najaf, had to dress up as a Bedouin Arab in order to reach the Ayatollah's residence undetected by both SAVAK and Iraqi secret police agents. He told the Ayatollah that a secret Islamic court, consisting of Motahari and Beheshti as judges, had sentenced Prime Minister Mansur to death on a charge of 'warring on Allah' as symbolized by the decision to send His Holiness into exile. Would the Ayatollah approve the sentence, Mofattah asked. In what was to become a regular ploy of his when facing difficult decisions, Khomeini rose and left the room with a curt 'Allah be with you' thrown at his visitor almost as an afterthought. Mofattah took the gesture to mean that the Ayatollah approved of the decision of the 'court', which had met at the granary of a semi-derelict house for only twelve minutes and 'tried' the Prime Minister *in absentia*.

Mansur had made himself unpopular not only because of Khomeini's forced exile but also for his almost monetarist approach to economics. He had ordered a steep rise in the price of petrol, which angered Tehran's 12,000 taxi drivers. To the nationalists he appeared as 'America's man' while the Left hated him for his reformism and populist slogans. Mansur was shot on 20 January as he walked out of Parliament in Baharestan Square. After a six-day struggle, he finally succumbed to his wounds and died. A youth, Mohammad Bokhara'i, was charged with the Premier's assassination, while two other men, Morteza Niknezhad and Reza Saffar-Harandi, were arrested and charged as accomplices.[1]

It is almost certain that all three men, who were later executed, suffered prolonged torture at the hands of their interrogators. But they did not speak and SAVAK was unable to link the murder directly to those who had ordered it. The secret Islamic court and the identity of its two judges were not revealed until after the Ayatollah's revolution had triumphed. Beheshti, one of the two 'judges' of the Islamic court which was to sentence other officials to death in the years that followed, continued his well-paid job as 'special religious adviser' to the Minister of Education and was soon posted to Hamburg as the dean of the Shi'ite mosque there with support from SAVAK. Motahari, the other 'judge' and a more substantial thinker, soon began writing a column in *Zan-e-Ruz (Today's Woman)*, the weekly magazine for women. Few people could have suspected the unassuming scholar who wrote tender, flowery prose was capable of ordering the cold-blooded execution of his guide's political opponents.

The enthusiasm rekindled by the murder of Mansur was, however, short-lived, and soon the Ayatollah was back with his many personal problems at Najaf. Chief among these was lack of money. Having no money meant that he could pay no stipends and thus could have no *talabehs*. And an ayatollah without a circle of students was no better than a general without an army. It must have been with a certain sense of bitterness that Khomeini heard reports of how the wealthier ayatollahs were surrounded by hundreds, if not thousands, of *talabehs* from all over the world. Grand Ayatollah Hakim, for example, paid stipends to more than 3000 *talabehs* and representatives in over a hundred cities in Iran, Iraq, Lebanon and India. Even Ayatollah Shirazi maintained a full seminary complete with an elaborate secretariat which handled his many international contacts with Shi'ites throughout the world. Khomeini, who doubtless did not consider himself inferior to any of the ayatollahs of Najaf in learning and piety, was, in those days of chagrin, left without even a *moharer* (secretary), the first of many status symbols associated with being a Grand Ayatollah. He had to be content with the services of his two sons Mostafa and Ahmad. Neither had managed to pursue an academic career and both were content to be considered as *talabehs*. Mostafa, by far the more passionate, was totally devoted to his father and had for many years been the Ayatollah's inseparable companion. He had inherited from Khomeini his deep rage at 'the wrongness of everything in this wrong world' and lost no opportunity to call for revenge against the heretical Pahlavis.[2] According to some accounts, Mostafa played a key role in keeping the flames of his father's volcanic anger alive. Mostafa was a charismatic, effective orator but a poor scribe. The many statements of his father that he took down were often full of grammatical and spelling errors. One word he never learned to spell correctly was *kahanevadeh*, which means family in Persian.

Ahmad, some five years younger than Mostafa, had grown up in the shadow of his elder brother. Ahmad took more after his mother and was calm, good-natured and more tolerant of human imperfections. He had for a while toyed with the idea of taking a university entrance examination in order to read chemistry but had been instantly discouraged by his father's stern rebuttal of the very idea. Once, in the early 1950s, Ahmad had incurred his father's wrath by going to a cinema while on a visit to Tehran. On his return to Qom he had confessed to the unthinkable 'sin' and asked for pardon. His father had remained silent; the Ayatollah did not forgive easily. Ahmad spent a minimum of time on learning Arabic, which he disliked intensely. Instead, he preferred to learn French and English. He tackled French with the aid of an 'Assimil' book in the late 1960s and continued with it during his subsequent stay in Lebanon. He also liked reading novels. It was Ahmad who persuaded the Ayatollah to read a number of novels, including Dostoevsky's *Brothers Karamazov* and *Ahu Khanom's Husband* by the Persian writer Mohammad-Ali Afghani. The Ayatollah did not stay with the Russian mystic writer right to the end of his epic of nihilism, but he liked *Ahu Khanom* immensely. The Persian novel, a chronicle of traditional Iranian provincial life, has as its main theme the oppression of women by men in the name of Islam.

In Najaf it was Batul who took charge of the household and, thanks to her natural talent for creating warmth, managed to hold things together. Her presence alleviated the Ayatollah's depression which, at times, created a tense atmosphere in the tiny house. The Ayatollah, now that he could no longer afford an army of domestics, took care to help his wife in as many of the household chores as possible. He would even go so far as to make his own bed and brew his own tea.[3] He also urged frugality. To his established habit of fasting on Thursdays in memory of the martyrs of his cause, he now added a second day of fasting once every other week. Almost nothing would be thrown away or wasted. The flesh of a watermelon, for example, would be eaten as fruit while its skin would be used for making jam or pickles; its seeds would be roasted and served as a delicacy to the family's rare visitors. The only luxury allowed in the household was a bottle of Paco Rabane aftershave which Ahmad had purchased from the local bazaar in an unguarded moment of extravagance. Since nobody in the family shaved, the eau de Cologne was used for lightly perfuming the household's three beards.[4]

The Ayatollah spent most of his day secluded in his tiny room where he read and prayed. He would rarely go out, not even to pray at the golden-domed shrine of the first Imam. He was already beginning to keep his distance from what he was many years later to describe as 'ceremonial Islam'. His evenings were reserved for listening to a number of radio programmes. These included Radio Iran's main news bulletin at 17.30 GMT as well as Baghdad Radio's international news and comment and the BBC's Persian service. He enjoyed playing with the radio and tuning in to different stations after hearing his favourite programmes. Often, Mostafa would be at his side and the two of them would discuss the events of the day and their implications for the future of Islam. Both tried to detect 'the inner meaning' of each news item, convinced that things were never quite as simple as they were reported on the radio. The Ayatollah was by now convinced that the central political theme of contemporary life was an elaborate and highly complex conspiracy by the Jews – 'who controlled everything' – to 'emasculate Islam' and dominate the world thanks to the natural wealth of the Muslim nations.[5] He would often ask Mostafa to find out whether a newly appointed high official in the government of any of the major powers was a Jew.

Contact with Iran was not limited to listening to radio programmes. The Ayatollah maintained a regular correspondence with a number of mullahs inside Iran through his son Mostafa who, at times, had to write as many as half a dozen letters a day. The letters would be posted to agreed addresses that would not arouse SAVAK's suspicion. Both Motahari and Montazeri were among those who regularly received letters from Mostafa on behalf of the Ayatollah. Ayatollah Mohammad-Ali Qazi-Tabataba'i of Tabriz also received many letters from Khomeini in those years.

Every now and then Khomeini would issue a statement on this or that event of note in Iran. These usually took the form of an open letter to Amir-Abbas Hoveyda, the jovial intellectual who had succeeded Mansur as Prime Minister. Hoveyda, who was related to Grand Ayatollah Kho'i through his mother, had at first thought of sending detailed replies to Khomeini's open letters but had been informed of the folly of such a course by Nasiri. Mostafa would send up to a hundred copies of each open letter to various ayatollahs as well as to newspaper editors in Iran. The fact that no photocopying machine existed in the whole of Najaf, outside the local secret police office where Mostafa was taken on a number of occasions, meant that the Ayatollah's two sons had to copy each letter at least a hundred times by hand. By 1970, however, Motahari had managed to purchase a second-hand Gestetner duplicating machine and the Ayatollah's statements could then be distributed in thousands of copies from a warehouse in south Tehran.

Khomeini continued to denounce every new stage of the land reform programme, which he described as 'a gimmick to cover up the regime's many crimes'. On the whole, however, he used relatively moderate language and did not mention the Shah by name. On one occasion, however, he gave free rein to all his accumulated hatred of 'the father and the son', meaning Reza Shah and Mohammad-Reza Shah. In a statement commenting on the Family Protection Bill, then being discussed in the Majlis in Tehran, Khomeini warned that legislation of this sort was aimed at 'turning our women into prostitutes and undermining the very existence of Islam'.[6] The Bill provided for a number of reforms including a virtual ban on polygamy which is allowed under the *shari'a* (Islamic law). To take a second wife, a man had to obtain the consent of his first wife and also convince a special court that he was willing and able to abide by a number of onerous obligations. The Bill also gave women the right to sue for divorce in a number of clearly defined cases. This was a truly revolutionary measure, making Iran the first Muslim country to recognize the right of women to sue for divorce in a secular court. The Bill fell far short of giving women full equal rights and protection under the law, but was, nevertheless, a courageous step. Premier Hoveyda, an astute diplomat, used the mullahs' own tactic of *ketman* (dissimulation) in order to minimize potential opposition to the Bill from the ayatollahs. He asked for a much more radical draft to be prepared and then sent the result to the Grand Ayatollahs of Mashhad, Qom and Najaf for comment. Khomeini was the only one not to receive a copy. Hoveyda's emissaries told the Grand Ayatollahs that unless they supported the government in pushing through a more moderate version of the Bill, the radical women's libbers, headed by the Shah's controversial twin sister Ashraf, would press for 'a complete break with Islamic rules'.[7] The tactic worked, and the government secured the tacit support of most Grand Ayatollahs while neutralizing the ambitious princess's drive for a 'fully Western' law of marriage and divorce. Later, Khomeini's opposition, however, succeeded in preventing the passage of a Bill legalizing adoption in Iran. Islam does not recognize adoption, and the new Bill, had it been enacted, would have revolutionized a good part of the Iranian legal system.

Khomeini must have suffered a great deal from isolation in Najaf. Of the Grand Ayatollahs of the city, only Shirazi had repaid his visit. Khomeini found out exactly when the other Grand Ayatollahs visited the shrine, thanks to Mostafa's vigilance and patient observation. That helped him avoid the shrine at certain times so that he would not run into them. Soon, this earned

Khomeini the reputation of being 'a cold and arrogant man'.[8] The fact, however, was that he felt hurt that Hakim, Kho'i and even Shirazi, who was of much lower rank, refused to recognize him as an ayatollah of equal stature. It was partly because of his solitude that he welcomed a visit in 1967 by an Iraqi mullah named Sayyed Mohammad-Baqer Sadr. Sadr, distantly related to Khomeini, was calling on all the religious leaders of the city to mobilize support for what he saw as a battle of destiny against Israel. The defeat of the Arabs in the Six-Day War had sent shock waves throughout the Islamic world. Khomeini had stayed awake almost every night during the war to hear the latest news bulletins on as many wavelengths as possible. On the first day of the war, a time when he, like most people in the Islamic world, expected an Egyptian victory, he had even invested in a new Telefunken radio set complete with a powerful antenna capable of expanding the Ayatollah's universe of news and views.

Sadr had called on Khomeini as just another mullah on a long list and had meant to stay only a few minutes. The meeting, however, went on for hours and Sadr was invited to stay for dinner after sunset prayers. After dinner, sitting on the floor in a circle, the Ayatollah, his two sons, Sadr and a young *talabeh* accompanying him engaged in a discussion about the fate of Islam. Sadr, probably the most 'modern' mullah of his generation and certainly the most erudite, argued that the Shi'ite clergy had to get acquainted with modern sciences, 'especially politics and economics', and prepare for direct rule. He said that Islam would 'be suffocated' if it remained confined to its present geographical limits and the sociopolitical ghetto into which heathen rulers had forced it. He discussed his plans for the creation of an organization to be called ad-Da'awah (the Call) whose task would be not only to propagate Islam throughout the world but also to prepare the ground for the establishment of a universal Islamic state. Sadr seems to have had the same effect on Khomeini that Nawab-Safavi had had almost a quarter of a century earlier. Sadr was charismatic but hid behind an unassuming appearance. He had completed his magnum opus *Eqtesadena* (*Our Economics*) which was, and remains to this day, the only serious attempt at presenting an Islamic economic alternative to both free enterprise and collectivism.

It was under Sadr's influence that the issue of the clergy's direct participation in politics and government became an important topic of discussion in the seminaries of Najaf. The death of Hakim in 1968 removed the only Grand Ayatollah still capable of claiming supremacy over all others. Hakim had been a resolute opponent of the mullahs' involvement in politics and his death proved a great help to Khomeini and Sadr. The Shah sent cables of condolences to all the Grand Ayatollahs in Mashhad, Qom and Najaf, once again excluding Khomeini, who quickly used this to his own advantage by announcing in a statement on Hakim's death that religious leaders 'are determined by the faithful, not by the sultans of the day'.[9] Kho'i, the most senior ayatollah after Hakim, tried to side-step the debate on the clergy's political role but was eventually dragged in by provocative questions from impatient *talabehs*. He started a series of lectures on the subject, opposing involvement in politics with the traditional argument that the mullahs had to remain above secular society so that they could serve as its watchdogs. Mostafa attended Kho'i's lectures, taking down detailed notes for his father. Khomeini read the notes and began writing a series of comments on them without ever mentioning Kho'i by name. He had decided to demolish Kho'i, the last of the Grand Ayatollahs still capable of barring his path to the summit. The comments later provided the basis for a lecture series delivered to the few *talabehs* who had gathered around Khomeini thanks to Ayatollah Sadr who wanted to promote his new friend and ideological ally. Those lectures were subsequently published in a slim volume, at first entitled *Valayat-e-Faqih* (*The Regency of the Theologian*, but more pedantically translated into English as *The Custodianship of the Jurisconsult*) and then reissued under the more accessible title of *Hokumat-e-Eslami* (*Islamic Government*).

Khomeini's central thesis is simple: all power has divine origin and such concepts as national sovereignty are, therefore, not only wrong but heretical. Allah transmits his power to the prophets, charging them with the task of ruling over men in accordance with Divine Law which has been set once and for all. Mohammed was the last of the prophets and exercised power on behalf of Allah. Muhammed was not a mere *rassoul* (messenger) simply informing people of their duties towards Allah; he was also a *nabi*, a vicar of Allah on earth, who served as head of state and a general in many wars. Allah has sent some 124,000 prophets, the first of whom was Adam. But of these only a few have belonged to the *olol-Azm* category, meaning that they could rule on behalf of the Almighty. Moses, Solomon and David were among them and had every right to be kings. Jesus was also *olol-Azm* but was not given an opportunity to form his government. 'Jesus would have used the sword like any other *nabi*,' the Ayatollah says. 'Those who say he was the type who would always offer his other cheek only degrade him.'[10] The Ayatollah also enlists the support of Plato, arguing that the Greek philosopher anticipated the rule of the clergy in his call for government by 'the pious and the wise, in *The Republic*'.[11] He quotes extensively from works of past ayatollahs, most notably, Mohammad-Hussein Kashef al-Ghita'a. The book is peppered with attacks on the Iranian Government of the day, on Israel and the Jews in general, and concludes with an oblique demand for the rule of the mullahs. Khomeini refrains from advancing his own candidature for the position of Supreme Guide of all Muslims but makes it clear that he is talking about a single universal Islamic state. The book, later assuming the status of the Islamic Revolution's *Little Red Book*, was at the time duplicated by Motahari and distributed among the Ayatollah's remaining devotees in Iran.

The book contains many of the themes Khomeini had already treated in his *Key to the Secrets* a quarter of a century earlier. 'What is the good of us [i.e. the mullahs] asking for the hand of a thief to be severed or an adulteress to be stoned to death when all we can do is recommend such punishments, having no power to implement them?'[12] Islam's rules are not meant only as recommendations for good personal conduct; Islam is a social religion which has strict rules concerning every aspect of life. Those who regard obedience to Islamic rules as merely optional are only paving the way for atheism and eternal damnation.

When writing the book Khomeini must have been aware of the two opposed views concerning the political role of the mullahs which had for centuries divided the seminaries. While Kashef al-Ghita'a interpreted the custodianship of the jurisconsult to mean direct rule by the mullahs, other leading authorities, such as Shaikh Ansari in the early nineteenth century, took it to mean only that orphans and widows with no next of kin should become wards of pious ayatollahs. The 'custodianship' in question should, in other words, be restricted only to vulnerable individuals and not to society as a whole. Khomeini's seizure of power in Iran has not ended the debate, which continues to divide the Shi'ite clergy.

In 1971 Khomeini met another holy man who was to leave a deep mark on his thinking. This new influence was Mussa Sadr, whose niece had become Khomeini's daughter-in-law by marrying Ahmad. Sadr, born in Qom and extremely ambitious, had forged a close and profitable link with the Shah and it was with the latter's help that he went to Lebanon to establish a Shi'ite charitable organization. Sadr had almost certainly been in contact with SAVAK but not as an agent, as was later claimed by Libya's Colonel Moammar al Gaddafi. Rather, he used SAVAK's support and resources in order to establish himself in Lebanon, where he quickly became the leader of the Shi'ites, who formed the largest community in that country, assuming the title of imam or 'guide'. The Shi'ite principle of *khod'ah*, or tricking one's adversaries in order to benefit from them, was used by Sadr against the Shah until the inevitable rupture that came in the mid-1970s.

In Lebanon, Sadr created the Shi'ite organization Amal (Hope), an umbrella organization covering all aspects of the community's life. Later, with financial help from Libya, he trained a militia for his organization and charged it with the task of defending Shi'ite rights against other armed bands in the country. But his most important contribution to Islamic revolutionary thought was his development of the concept of the division of any society into the *mustakbar* (the top dog) and the *mustadh'af* (the underdogs). Both words were directly borrowed from Jaafar Sadeq, the sixth Imam, who mentions them in passing and in a different context. The key concept is, of course, that of the *mustadh'af*, which, in Sadeq's work, designates the 'poor, half-witted wretches who cannot run their own lives without guidance'.[13] Mussa Sadr expanded the concept to include the entire Shi'ite community in Lebanon which suffered from social injustice and political inequality. On subsequent visits to Najaf he discussed the concept with Khomeini. The Ayatollah expanded it to include the overwhelming majority of Muslims in the world who suffered from impious or crypto-atheistic governments. The *mustadh'af* lack the intellectual equipment and the political maturity required to ponder their fate and organize their own affairs. They need to be treated as children, half-wits or other vulnerable individuals. The claim that the wretched *mustadh'af* can exercise democratic rights is, at best, a swindle and at worst a crime. The poor, illiterate masses are all too likely to sell their votes to the highest bidder, without the guidance of the clergy who are alone in having no worldly ambitions of their own. Later still, after the triumph of the revolution in Iran, the Ayatollah further expanded the concept to cover all the underdogs of the world regardless of their religious beliefs. His revolution was to address itself to the downtrodden and the poor everywhere. Allah would not allow his vulnerable children to remain objects of exploitation, humiliation and tyranny for ever; the Shi'ite clergy were there precisely to make sure that the *mustakbar* could no longer rule the world unchallenged. Returning to Iran's Manichean tradition, Khomeini turned the *mustakbar* into the earthly representatives of satanic evil while the *mustadh'af* represented only 'potential good'.

The triumvirate formed by Khomeini and the two Sadrs was supported by the increasingly powerful ad-Da'awah in Iraq and Amal in Lebanon. But the key country remained Iran, where the Ayatollah's persistent attempts at creating a nationwide organization met with little success despite tireless efforts by Motahari and Montazeri.

In the 1970s the newly established Iraqi Ba'athist regime felt itself so threatened by Iran, which fomented a Kurdish rebellion led by Mullah Mostafa Barzani, that it sought a counterbalancing force in the Soviet Union. The Soviet link led to a demand by the remnants of the Tudeh Party and the Soviet-sponsored Azerbaijan Democratic Sect for facilities on Iraqi territory for anti-Shah operations. Almost at the same time, General Teymour Bakhtiar, the former SAVAK chief who was now calling for the overthrow of the Shah, moved to Baghdad from Beirut where he felt himself threatened by assassins hired by Tehran. He was soon joined by almost the entire Tudeh leadership, headed by Secretary-General Reza Radmanesh, and the Azerbaijan Democratic Sect chief 'General' Danesh Panahian. Bakhtiar quickly created an alliance with Radmanesh and Panahian and the three men decided to invite Khomeini to join them. Bakhtiar had already established close ties with Mussa Sadr in Lebanon but now found it difficult to obtain an interview with Khomeini. Mostafa was dispatched to talk to the cashiered general, who was quick in promising 'everything needed'.[14] Bakhtiar suggested that he should visit the Ayatollah together with 'other leaders', presumably meaning members of the group he himself had put together. After seemingly endless negotiations Khomeini eventually agreed to receive the former SAVAK chief alone. When Bakhtiar arrived at the Ayatollah's house he was led into an upstairs room where he was kept waiting for over an hour while His Holiness ostensibly completed his prayers. The Ayatollah finally arrived, flanked by the inevitable Mostafa, and extended his hand towards the former SAVAK chief for him to kiss. A servant, who was later identified as a SAVAK agent, witnessed the scene and later served tea.[15]

Bakhtiar told Khomeini that the Shah was finished and that, having contacted the *khareji* (foreign powers), he was now confident that he could seize power with the help of the army 'very soon'. The former 'Butcher of Tehran' described himself as 'a devout man' and claimed that he aimed at the creation of a government based on the principles of Islam. Having listened to Bakhtiar for a full thirty minutes, the Ayatollah suddenly rose, saying, 'It is now time for prayers,' and began to leave the room. Before going out, he told the perplexed former general that his 'prayers were reserved for the people of Islam'. 'May Allah guide all of us onto the Right Path,' he added.[16] Despite subsequent propaganda by the Shah's regime, that was the only direct contact between Bakhtiar and Khomeini. And the Ayatollah also never met the pro-Soviet Communist leaders present in Iraq at the time.

By 1972 Khomeini had succeeded in putting his financial house in order and even bought a new and larger house. He now received regular donations from followers in Iran, Iraq and Lebanon and could offer stipends to over a hundred *talabehs* of his own. The larger house was necessary although Mostafa, who now had three children, had moved to a small residence of his own in the same street. Ahmad also had children but was not yet in a position to afford a separate house. In addition an increasing number of visitors came to stay for several days. Many travelled from Iran via Syria or even on flights from London and Paris. The Iraqi authorities had agreed not to stamp the visitors' Iranian passports so that they would not run into trouble with SAVAK. The Iraqis also allowed Khomeini air time on their radio for daily attacks on the Shah's regime. The Ayatollah himself never spoke on the radio directly, leaving the task to one of his close aides, Hojat al-Islam Mahmoud Doa'i. On at least two occasions the Iraqis also offered large sums of money to the Ayatollah but were turned down.

Both Mostafa and Ahmad became frequent visitors to Lebanon, where they received political and military training first at Amal camps in the south and later at an Al Fatah base near Beirut. Ahmad enrolled in Al Fatah as an honorary member and accompanied Yasser Arafat's fighters on a number of missions in Lebanon. The strained relations between Mussa Sadr and Arafat did not prevent the latter from winning the trust of the Ayatollah. On at least two occasions Arafat took time to call on Khomeini in Najaf during official visits to Iraq. The meetings led to an arrangement under which a number of Iranians would be trained under the auspices of the Palestine Liberation Organization. The first twelve, including three women, were dispatched in 1972 and 'graduated' in 1974, returning to Iran. Among them was Mohammad Montazeri, Ayatollah Montazeri's son, who subsequently won notoriety as 'Ayatollah Ringo' for his gun-toting antics. Candidates for guerrilla training were recruited through the *hayats* which continued under Motahari's leadership. By 1977, when the first rumblings of the Islamic Revolution began in Iran, more than 700 people had been trained by Amal, the PLO and, from 1974 onwards, Libya as members of the *hayats* devoted to Khomeini. They were by no means the only Iranians trained as anti-Shah guerrillas. The training of Iranian guerrillas became a major operation from 1970 onwards as the Shah, growing closer and closer to the United Sates under the influence of President Richard M. Nixon and Henry Kissinger (who later became Secretary of State), adopted an increasingly anti-Soviet posture. The Shah also began purchasing huge quantities of arms which disturbed Egypt, Syria and Iraq, all three Soviet allies at the time, forcing Moscow to adopt an increasingly hostile attitude towards Tehran.

In October 1970 the Shah organized a series of festivities at Persepolis, Shiraz and Pasargadae to mark the twenty-fifth centenary of the foundation of the Persian Empire by Cyrus the Great. Khomeini instantly denounced the enterprise as an Israeli 'plot against Islam'.[17] He recalled that Cyrus had liberated the Jews from their Babylonian captivity, thus 'preventing the natural disappearance of elements who would never be satisfied with anything less than world domination'.[18] It was implied that the Jews were now helping make the celebrations a success as a means of repaying their historical debt to Cyrus the Great. The colourful demonstration of Iran's rising power was attended by over seventy heads of state and government and scores of other international dignitaries. The Soviet President Nikolai Podgorny was there alongside almost every other East European head of state including Yugoslavia's Josip Broz Tito. The West was represented by half a dozen kings and queens as well as Britain's Prince Philip and Princess Anne. Nixon himself had wanted to come but had, at the last moment, explained to the Shah that such a trip would be hard to sell to the American public. Instead he sent Vice-President Spiro T. Agnew with the promise that he himself would pay a state visit soon afterwards. Queen Elizabeth had also wanted to attend but had been advised against the trip by her Ambassador to the Iranian court Sir Denis Wright.[19]

The long-term internal effects of the celebrations proved less positive and durable than the Shah had hoped for. But the 'party at Persepolis', as the event was referred to by enemies of the Shah, thoroughly frightened the Arabs, who saw a resurgent Iran claiming its imperial past as a springboard for future expansionist and irredentist policies. These fears were confirmed a few months later when the Shah's navy reasserted Iranian sovereignty over three tiny islands near the Strait of Hormuz. The islands, detached from Iran by Britain in the nineteenth century, were administered by the Arab shaikhdoms of Sharjah and Ras al Khaymah at the time of their seizure by Iran. The Iraqis, their relations with Tehran already at rock bottom, jumped at the opportunity provided by the invasion of the islands to sever diplomatic ties with Iran. From then on the two neighbours were in a state of virtual war. Egypt, still recovering from the shock of her 1967 defeat by Israel, maintained a low profile, but Libya, where Colonel Gaddafi was already claiming the mantle of Arab nationalism, reacted by offering money and training to any of the Shah's opponents who asked for help.

Throughout the early 1970s and until 1976 Iran was plagued by a very serious problem of terrorism and urban guerrillas. Hundreds of militants recruited from among the expanding population of Iranian students abroad, especially in the United States and Britain, received guerrilla training in Cuba, Libya, Lebanon, South Yemen, North Korea and, until 1971, the People's Republic of China. Some volunteered to fight against the Iranian forces which had been dispatched to the Sultanate of Oman to quell a rebellion in the province of Dhufar, neighbouring South Yemen. Others infiltrated the country itself and organized a series of bank robberies, assassinations, attacks on gendarmerie posts and other acts of sabotage. Most were Marxist–Leninists and were, at times, used for the specific purpose of exerting pressure on the Shah as part of the overall Soviet policy of countering American influence in Iran. At least a dozen Americans, including several army and air force officers seconded to Iranian units, were gunned down by the guerrillas, who also attempted to kidnap the US Ambassador, Douglas MacArthur III, but failed. The guerrillas trained on behalf of the pro-Khomeini *hayats* did not get involved in any of the spectacular attacks that hit the Tehran headlines on more than two dozen occasions. The *hayat* leadership, headed by Motahari, did not believe that power could be wrested from the Shah by a few dramatic acts of violence. The *hayats* concentrated their efforts on expanding their organizational network and improving the ideological as well as the military education of their members. The war between the Leftist guerrillas on the one hand and SAVAK's anti-sabotage agents, trained in Israel, South Korea and the United States, soon assumed the appearance of regular gang warfare. People in Tehran and several other major cities became witnesses to shooting battles and helicopter gunship attacks on 'safe houses' used by the urban guerrillas. According to one estimate, at least 150 guerrillas and more than thirty SAVAK agents were killed in action between 1970 and 1976. A further hundred guerrillas were sentenced to death and executed in the same period, nearly a third of all executions that had taken place in the preceding thirty-one years of the Shah's reign. The half a dozen or so guerrilla groups involved in the losing battle against SAVAK were eventually smashed, but they nevertheless succeeded in forcing the regime into violence that disturbed public opinion at home and further blackened Iran's image abroad. They also plunged the entire administration into a psychosis provoked by unknown and undefinable dangers. The duel gave SAVAK chiefs almost unlimited power and, from 1973 onwards, not even the Prime Minister was authorized to keep a check on their activities. The much dreaded political police used the war against the guerrillas as a smokescreen behind which it extended its influence in all walks of life. SAVAK propaganda was focused on retailing fear by means of exaggerated reports of its own power and efficiency. As a result, the number of people living in fear of the regime now far outstripped those whose support and good opinion might have been won by the continuing economic boom.

During 1973 and 1974 relations between Iran and Iraq worsened to the point where the two neighbours were involved in a prolonged border war. The Shah ordered his troops to occupy large sections of territory which the British had ostensibly handed over to their Iraqi protégés during the Second World War. The Iranian army also became directly involved in support of the Kurdish rebels in northern Iraq. SAVAK had earlier showed it could strike inside Baghdad itself by sending two of its agents, masquerading as hijackers of an Iran Air Boeing, to Iraq where they murdered Bakhtiar. Radmanesh and Panahian, who were also on SAVAK's death list, slipped out of Iraq before they could be hit. Nasiri had wanted Khomeini to be included on the hit list but changed his mind when he was advised by mullahs cooperating with SAVAK to 'forget about the troublemaker'. Khomeini was sometimes cited by the guerrillas standing trial as a leader who had opposed the Shah. But his supporters, grouped together in the semi-clandestine *hayats*, stayed mostly in the background.

The Iraqis retaliated against the Shah's aggressive policy not only by financing some of the guerrilla groups active in Iran but also by organizing a series of mass expulsions of Iranians living in the holy cities of Najaf and Karbala. The Ba'athist regime's move, directed against the Shi'ites in general and Iranians in particular, created a certain degree of sympathy for the Shah and was opposed by most Grand Ayatollahs. Grand Ayatollah Shirazi went so far as to accompany a group of expelled Iranians across the border on foot. A former opponent of the Shah, Shirazi, who was then eighty-five, became an instant hero in Iran and settled down in Mashhad. Some leading mullahs, notably Grand Ayatollah Milani, urged the government to arrange for the return of other Iranian religious leaders, including Khomeini, from Mesopotamia. Khomeini, arguing that he did not wish to be involved in the Ba'athist regime's 'war on the Iranian people', severed all contact with the Iraqi authorities and maintained almost total silence until Tehran and Baghdad ironed out their quarrels and signed an agreement in 1975. By then Khomeini had faded from view, at least so far as the Shah's regime was concerned. The Shah, when asked about Khomeini in the course of a long interview, had this to say: 'Khomeini? No one mentions him any more in Iran, except, perhaps, the terrorists. The so-called Islamic Marxists pronounce his name every now and then. That's all.'[20]

# 10

# *The Faith that Divided Islam*

The Imam [Ali] teaches that, as Allah is aware, we have not risen in order to secure positions of authority and become a government. We have no objective other than saving the oppressed from their oppressors. All that made me accept the rulership of the community is Almighty God's strict instruction that the clergy should not remain silent in the face of greed and oppressive profiteering and the soul-crushing hunger of the downtrodden.

Ayatollah Khomeini in *Valayat-e-Faqih* (*The Regency of the Theologian*)

*E*arly in December 1977 a number of Tehran newspaper editors received photocopies of a strange handwritten letter that was to become a key document in the history of the Ayatollah's revolution. The letter, on two pages and peppered with a number of amusing spelling errors, had been dictated by Khomeini and written by his son Ahmad. It was an unusual letter in more than one way.

Presented as a *fitwa*, which, according to traditional Shi'ite theology, has the force of Qur'anic law, the letter did not begin with the conventional formula 'In the name of Allah, the Merciful, the Compassionate'. Instead, it used another of Allah's 999 titles: 'The Punisher of the Tyrants' (Qassim al-Jabareen). Khomeini, referring for the first time to his 'responsibilities towards the Muslim nation throughout the world', effectively put himself above his peers, the five other Grand Ayatollahs of Najaf, Tehran and Qom. Although the *fitwa* was simply signed Ruhollah Mussavi al-Khomeini and sealed by the Ayatollah, it bore the strange title of 'A Fitwa from Imam Khomeini'. This was the first time in the history of Iranian duodecimal Shi'ism that the title of Imam was used to describe a theologian.

The title of Imam, used by Arab Shi'ites, notably in Lebanon, to describe religious leaders in general, is, so far as Iranian Shi'ites are concerned, reserved only for Ali, the fourth Caliph and the first Imam, and eleven of his male descendants. Thus the last person to have the title of Imam is Muhammed Ibn Hassan, the twelfth of the Alide line of authority who began his Great Occultation (Ghaybat-e-Kobra) nearly twelve centuries ago. During the absence of the Imam and until his eventual and inevitable, though unpredictable, return it is up to religious teachers (*ulama*) to instruct the faithful in the laws of Islam and to ensure their implementation. But none of these teachers is allowed the title of Imam.

It was not until the late nineteenth century that some of the *ulama* began to be described by the more enthusiastic of their *moreeds*, or followers, as *nayeb-e-Imam* or vicars of the Hidden Imam. The point is worth emphasis because Khomeini, often described in the West as a man of tradition, has, in fact, broken what is probably the most important traditional rule in Shi'ite theology. By allowing himself to be described as Imam he has initiated what could prove to be a major schism in Shi'ism after he is gone. We shall return to this point later. Suffice it to note for the moment that none of the Grand Ayatollahs, including those who have at times supported Khomeini's revolution, has ever agreed to endorse his title of Imam whether directly or by implication.

But let us return to the December *fitwa*. In it Khomeini said that, 'exercising my religious authority', he had 'deposed the Shah and abrogated the Constitution'. He ordered the faithful not to pay taxes and not to obey laws 'promulgated by the usurper'. He also called on 'true believers' not to attend schools or universities except to demonstrate their 'hatred of the dethroned Taghut' and his policies of 'Western corruption'. As far as we have been able to ascertain, this was the first time Khomeini had used the term *taghut* to describe the Shah. The term was later to gain popular currency and has now become an integral part of Persian political vocabulary. *Taghut*, literally meaning 'rebel', is one of the titles of Satan according to the Holy Qur'an. By using it to describe the Shah in his *fitwa*, Khomeini was, in effect, making use of 2500 years of Manicheanism in Iran. He now represented Allah, the Good; the Shah, on the other hand, was now the same as Satan, and thus represented Evil. There can be no compromise between Good and Evil. Allah can never make a deal with Satan, just as Ahura Mazda, the good god of Zoroastrianism in ancient Persia, would not have settled for anything less than total defeat of Angar Mainu, the Evil Spirit.

With hindsight, it is odd that the letter's urgent importance was not immediately recognized. Some of us at first dismissed it as a fabrication by SAVAK, designed to ridicule Khomeini while inciting other Grand Ayatollahs to anger over the use of the title Imam by one of their peers. It seems even more odd that SAVAK itself, despite the many mullahs it had in its pay and having learned of the letter almost immediately it had been posted to thousands of addresses in Iran (mostly to mullahs throughout the country), did not consider it of sufficient importance to be included in any of its daily reports to the Shah. At any rate, the Shah only learned of the letter more than a week after it had been sent. It was Foreign Minister Abbas-Ali Khalatbari, citing a report from the Iranian Ambassador to Baghdad, Sadeq Sadrieh, who reported to the monarch that an 'arrogant and ill-intentioned attempt at exploiting the religious sentiments of the people' had been made by Khomeini.

The report made the Shah furious. But this was nothing compared with his anger after reading the full text of the Ayatollah's *fitwa*. According to Amir-Abbas Hoveyda, then Minister of the Imperial Court, the monarch's first reaction was to blame his servants for 'allowing that vermin to continue to crawl'. The Shah recalled the earlier suggestions for a reconciliation with the Ayatollah so that arrangements could be made for his 'pardon and return to Qom'. He also saw Khomeini's *fitwa* as the first major impact on the Iranian political scene of Jimmy Carter's election as the thirty-ninth President of the United States.

In conversation, Hoveyda recalled the Shah's angry response and his suspicions concerning 'liberal circles in Washington'. But these may have been due to a momentary mood of pique. For, as the revolutionary process continued and developed, the Shah, in a number of other private audiences, blamed the British for his troubles.

Both Khalatbari and Hoveyda had tried to minimize the importance of the Khomeini *fitwa*, which amounted to an open declaration of war. Both reported themselves surprised at the Shah's almost violent reaction both to the letter and to their dismissal of it as the act of a senile man.

The Shah told Hoveyda that he was sure the country was facing 'a major, foreign-inspired conspiracy' in which the mullahs, representing what he termed 'Black Reaction', were to ally themselves to the Communists, seen by His Imperial Majesty as the party of 'Red Reaction'. The monarch also claimed that the major objective of the conspiracy was to 'destroy the Iranian armed forces' and prevent the emergence of Iran as 'a regional superpower'. He said that he sensed that an alliance of 'all our enemies' was taking shape, adding that Khomeini was to be their standard-bearer.[1]

The Shah received me in audience only a few days after he had learned of the Khomeini letter. He was still angry enough to mention it himself and to turn it into a major topic of conversation. He used the same Manichean approach as Khomeini. He represented progress, while Khomeini was a symbol of reaction. He would soon, he warned, call on all Iranians to choose sides. 'They must all decide,' he said in a tone of bitter determination. 'Do they want our great civilization or would they rather live under the great terror our foreign enemies are plotting with that crazy fanatic as their instrument?'

He dismissed a suggestion that there could be some genuine religious grievances – for example, over the replacement of the Islamic calendar by the imperial one. The Shah saw himself as the protector of the Shi'ite faith. A deeply religious or, as some would say, even superstitious man, the Shah was, nevertheless, ignorant of the deep-rooted doctrinal hostility of the *ulama* to the established political order. He knew that the mullahs, even those who benefited from state stipends and countless other advantages, could, somehow, never endorse his regime unreservedly. But he saw this as nothing but a tradition created by British money and intrigue so that the mullahs could, whenever needed, be used as a means of exerting pressure on the government of the day.

The mullahs, along with tribal chiefs and leaders of the bazaars in major cities, had often been drawn into anti-governmental activities because of British or Russian incitement, including bribery, during the nineteenth and early twentieth centuries. But the Shah was wrong in seeing them as nothing but instruments of colonial or neo-colonial intervention in Iranian politics. The mullahs themselves, even when favourably inclined towards the monarchy, knew that they could never totally endorse as legitimate a government that was not headed by the twelfth Imam. For centuries the mullahs, practising *taqieh* (dissimulation), a principle not only allowed but even recommended in Shi'ite tradition, had avoided direct confrontation over the issue of legitimacy. They had been content with the honours and advantages they enjoyed. They had secured a major share in the proceeds of mass exploitation of peasants and urban workers by the khans and the central monarchic state apparatus. All this, however, did not remove the fact that Shi'ism, even when declared a state religion, could not totally identify with the state.

Although duodecimal Shi'ism, as we know it today, is largely a product of the Safavid era (sixteenth and seventeenth centuries), its historic roots can be traced back to the earliest stages of the conquest of Iran by Muslim Arabs in the seventh century. It took the Arab invaders some fifteen years to secure control of the vast, though ramshackle, empire the Sassanids had left behind. The majority of the people in the newly conquered land, however, refused to become Muslims. It was not until much later, when the conquerors had succeeded in creating an organization capable of exacting *jeziyah*, the head tax for non-Muslims, that the poor peasants of the Iranian plateau, unable to pay, embraced Islam. Islam requires a verbal profession of faith as sufficient for new converts to be admitted into the community. According to the Hadith, a profession of faith, even if done without genuine conviction, should be taken by Muslims at its face value. In other words, a man who says he is a Muslim must be admitted and treated as one.

Some historians have developed the idea that many Iranians, including some who, like Sibouyeh, Ruzbeh or Mahyar, were to become masters of Arab grammar and literature, chose to wear an Islamic mask merely to destroy the new religion, imposed on the Persians by force, from within. The people who were accused of merely wearing an Islamic mask were designated *bateniyah* (introverts), meaning that they kept their true beliefs, presumably still based on the teachings of Zoroaster, to themselves. It was among these people that the so-called *shu-ubiyah* (ethnic) movement originally grew up. The movement represented the genuine grievances of the Ajam (Persians) against their Arab conquerors. The early history of Islamic Iran is full of accounts of popular rebellions against Arab rule. In every case, a revolt of distinctly economic or social origin was camouflaged as a movement of religious protest. This tradition has continued in Iran up to the present day. Only the Shah, unread in Iranian history as he was,

175

despite his sincere pride in Iran's ancient grandeur and resilience as a nation, remained unaware of this particular characteristic of Persian politics.

To the Sunnis (literally, the Traditionalists), who today form some 85 per cent of the world's estimated 900 million Muslims, Shi'ism, especially in its duodecimal form, is little more than an Islamic manifestation of Persian ethnocentricity, if not nationalism in the modern sense of the term. It is unclear when and where Shi'ism, which was at first little more than a sentiment, developed into a distinct faith claiming an independent existence of its own. But what is certain is that by the tenth century the Shi'ite version of Islam was already fully established and seen by the majority of Muslims as a continuation of Zoroastrianism.

Islam, as revealed in the Qur'an and the original traditions attributed to Muhammed, has only three principles. They are *towheed* (the belief that there is only one God), *nobuwwah* (the belief that God had dispatched prophets to guide mankind and that Muhammed was the last of them), and *ma'ad* (the belief that there will be a Day of Reckoning). Shi'ism adds to these principles two of its own: *adl* (the belief that the justice of Allah must be meted out in this world also) and *imamah* (the belief that Ali and his eleven male descendants represent the only legitimacy on earth before the Day of Reckoning). In the absence of the twelfth Imam, all government, even if exercised by Shi'ites, remains *ja'er* or illegitimate. Thus, right from the start, Shi'ism nurtured within itself a streak of anarchism which inspired and sustained more than one revolutionary movement. While Sunni theologians made it their business to justify the state right from the start and to bestow legitimacy on the ruler of the day, who won the title of Amir al-Mo'meneen (Prince of the Faithful), the Shi'ite doctors appeared as the guardians of a messianic dream that is to be fulfilled only for those who refuse the pollution of submission to earthly authority. This, to be sure, does not mean that Shi'ites are asked to live in a state of permanent revolt against temporal authority. All they are invited to do, even when forced to obey the rule of the illegitimate government of the day, is retain their true allegiance only for the Mahdi, the Hidden Imam who shall return.

The first great organizers of Shi'ism as a doctrine lived under the Dailamites in the tenth and eleventh centuries of the Christian era. The Dailamites, also known as the Buyids, were Persian Shi'ites from the Caspian region who traced their roots to the Sassanids. Unable to secure religious legitimacy for their own rule within Shi'ism, the Dailamites maintained in power the Sunni Abbasid caliphs of Baghdad as symbols of divine authority. The ambiguities thus created enabled such early Shi'ite theologians as Kolayni (d. AD 939), Shaikh Sadduq (d. AD 991) and Shaikh Tussi (d. AD 1067) to avoid direct confrontation with the problem of government. They remained content to await the end of the Great Occultation and saw in the deteriorating social and political situation in Iran a confirmation of their apocalyptic vision of a wholly corrupted and ungovernable world being rescued by the returning Mahdi at the eleventh hour, as it were.

Iran's invasion by the Mongols and then the Teimurid Tatars and the prolonged reign of various Turkic Ilkhanid regional dynasties further strengthened the alien character of all government in the eyes of Shi'ite Iranians. It is worth noting that the Pahlavis were, with the exception of the short-lived Zand dynasty which held ephemeral power in parts of the country in the eighteenth century, the only Persians to rule Iran since the eleventh century. Thus every dynasty and every government of the day could be rejected on both religious and ethnocultural grounds. One of Khomeini's greatest difficulties in his long fight against the Shah was to 'prove' that the Pahlavis were not only 'illegitimate' because they did not descend from the line of the Imams but also because they were 'foreigners' by adoption.

Right from 1962 the claim that the Shah had secretly been 'converted' to Judaism and taken up American citizenship became a favourite theme of Khomeini and his close associates.

In later speeches and countless leaflets over many years the campaign to identify the Shah with Israel and the Jews as well as portraying him as an 'agent of the USA' was relentlessly pursued. This was part of the long-established tradition of identifying Shi'ism with Persian nationalism. Let us also note that even the line of the Imams has been given some sort of Persian legitimacy through the myth that Hussein, the Prophet's grandson and the third of the Imams, married the youngest daughter of Yazdegerd, the last of the Sassanid kings. Thus, all Hussein's descendants, including the Hidden Imam, had some Persian blood in their veins while descending directly from the Prophet.

Between the eleventh and the fourteenth centuries Shi'ite theology was all but nonexistent. The rites and rituals were maintained and repeated, parrotlike, from generation to generation. Sympathetic chroniclers note that Shi'ism survived those long, dark centuries in the form of a low-burning fire waiting for the first breath of wind that would enable it to flare up once more. The teachings of Imam Jaafar Ibn Mohammad, nicknamed al-Sadeq (the Truthful One), continued to be taught to a diminishing number of theology students at the religious schools of Mesopotamia and Khorassan. But it was not until the early fourteenth century that Mohaqeq Hel'li and Najm-ed-Din Kobra revived Shi'ite scholarship by tackling subjects other than the traditional ritualistic questions concerning the 'clean' and the 'unclean'. But even they did not deem it necessary to probe the important issue of governmental legitimacy.

By the time the Safavids had established themselves as the ruling dynasty in the sixteenth century Shi'ism had all but died as an organized religion in Iran. Such important dates as the 'Ashura, the martyrdom of Imam Hussein, were still marked with ceremonies directly based on the tradition of mourning Siavosh, Iran's pre-Islamic mythical hero. But most of the theological schools had long been shut for lack of students and some parts of the country had even reverted to a pseudo-Mazdaen form of religious practice. The Safavids, themselves Sunnis from the province of Azerbaijan, were quick to discover the importance of Shi'ism as a means of mobilizing Iran's nationalistic energies against the Ottoman Turks who continued to dream of eastward expansion. Thus the revival of Shi'ism became an essential part of the Safavid programme for the restoration of the Persian Empire. As a first step in that direction, Shah Ismail, the founder of the dynasty, invented for himself an enviable genealogy that showed him to be a direct descendant both of the Prophet Muhammed and of the Sassanid kings of pre-Islamic Iran. The 'roots' linking him with the Prophet were clearly intended to obviate the traditional Shi'ite opposition to all temporal authority. The stratagem worked, but only for a while. Shah Ismail was obliged to import a number of mullahs from Lebanon to revive Shi'ite theology in Iran. Thus such eminent families of theologians as the 'Amelis and the Jabal-Amelis were brought to Iran and given title, land and money and assigned the task of training the mullahs needed for the reintroduction of Shi'ism into the vast empire.

The Safavid kings must have been aware of the ambivalent attitude of Shi'ite theology towards the state. This was why the phrase *as Sultan Dhil al-Allah fel-Ardh* (the King is the shadow of Allah on earth) was duly invented and attributed to the Prophet himself. Under the Safavids, who lasted until the early eighteenth century, the mullahs never secured enough strength or independence to think of challenging the authority of the Shah. They acted as agents of the Safavid state by keeping the peasantry quiet with strong doses of 'the opium of the masses'. The most successful of the Safavid kings, Shah Abbas the Great, described himself as 'the humble dog at the door of Imam Ali' but continued to indulge his inordinate weakness for strong wine despite the strictest of religious edicts forbidding alcohol. He held in high regard such theologians as Mullah Mohammad-Baqer Majlesi and Shaikh Baha'i, confident that their sterile exercises in forms long emptied of their content would not threaten the security of the state.

Majlesi has left behind thousands of pages on the minutest details of copulation, including with wild and domestic animals, but almost nothing that could even remotely be interpreted as a contribution to political thought. In his hands, Shi'ism, originally a political movement presented in a religious form, becomes a set of mechanically held beliefs in a universe of ignorance and superstition.

Shaikh Baha'i's poetical tone and his often amusing, if not provocative, ventures into the realm of Persian mysticism provide a better read. But even here we are faced with Shi'ism as a mere shadow of its tempestuous past.

With the advent of the Qajar dynasty in 1779 the long-established tradition of domination of the religious institution by the state was quickly questioned. The founder of the dynasty, Agha Mohammad Khan, a brilliant general and warlord, insisted on tracing his roots back to Genghiz Khan. His Turkoman tribe had only recently been converted to Shi'ism, while 90 per cent of the Turkomans living within the borders of the empire remained ferociously attached to Sunni Islam. Agha Mohammad himself had no time for the mullahs and succeeded in terrorizing them into silent submission for as long as he lived. Counting his money to the last penny, the agha, a dour-faced eunuch who lived by the sword and for the sword, expropriated many mullahs' incomes for his own benefit. The mullahs, long used to sweet parasitism under the Safavids and the brief Afshari dynasty which followed, were jolted out of their slumber when they began losing their unearned incomes. The best they could hope for under the first of the Qajars was to be allowed to keep their lives.

The experience forced some of the mullahs to seek alternatives to state patronage and revenue from land. The principle of *khums*, another specifically Shi'ite tradition, was revived. *Khums* is the form of taxation under which 20 per cent of all earned income must be 'presented' to the mullahs to be used in maintaining and furthering religious education as well as assisting the poor. In the strictest versions of duodecimal theology this is the only form of tax that can be legitimately paid. Not a penny should go to the state, which must provide its own finances either by forcing non-Islamic states to pay it tribute or, wherever possible, by exacting a headtax from non-Muslims. Yet another source of income for the state could be the proceeds of loot secured in wars against the infidel. But here, too, one fifth must go to the religious institutions. It was thanks to money raised from *khums*, as well as other voluntary donations received in exchange for promises of pardon for real or imagined sins, that the mullahs gradually regained an important measure of financial independence from the state under the Qajars.

Another factor that helped their independence was the loss of the two holiest centres of Shi'ism, Najaf and Karbala. The two cities are situated in Mesopotamia which, in the confusion that followed the withering away of the Safavid state, fell under Ottoman rule. Subsequent attempts by a number of Iranian kings failed to recover them. The Ottoman sultan, calling himself Caliph, did not pay much attention to the Shi'ites, who formed but a small minority among his subjects who were spread from Anatolia and Mesopotamia to North Africa and the frontiers of the Austro-Hungarian Empire. The Shi'ite doctors were able to revive the long-forgotten *madrassehs* of both cities, although it was Najaf that eventually emerged as the main seat of Shi'ite learning, a position it retained until the early twentieth century. From Najaf and Karbala the mullahs, whose principal source of support was Iran, were able to act as a power counterbalancing that of the Qajar court in Tehran. Away from direct state pressure and patronage, they revived the issue of legitimacy. Little theoretical work of consequence was undertaken during the period, but there are many records of revolts and rebellions in various Iranian provinces, all in the name of the Hidden Imam and invariably inspired, if not actually provoked, by the mullahs of Mesopotamia. Some of the tactics then used were later employed, to devastating effect, by Khomeini, who also operated from exile. The message was clear: the Shah has no right to be on his throne; government belongs to the Hidden Imam, who bears the title of Saheb-e-Zaman (Lord of the Time) and, in his absence, must be exercised by his vicars – the ayatollahs. It was during the reign of

Nassereddin Shah (1848–96) that the practice of having the reigning Shah 'endorsed' by the mullahs was firmly established. It was to this tradition that Khomeini referred in issuing his *fitwa* in 1977. After centuries of compromise and dissimulation, the mullahs came out to seek what they thought was their right by divine law: the government of Islam as a whole.

# 11

# *Fighting the Shadows*

The nation has nothing to worry about: as long as I am there and our glorious Armed Forces are there, neither Red nor Black Reaction can dream of imposing the reign of the Great Terror on this land.

Mohammad-Reza Shah Pahlavi

The Shah's armies are but shadows and shadows cannot fight.

Ayatollah Khomeini

*M*orteza Motahari, a mullah in his late fifties, was full of excitement as he waited in the upstairs room of his modest home in one of Tehran's poorest districts on a frozen December afternoon. His excitement was matched only by his anxiety as he pondered the task ahead of him. The moment for which he had waited for nearly fifteen years was, at last, approaching. He was going to unleash a movement which if successful would, so he hoped, lead to the revival of Islam after centuries of slow death. The white-turbaned Motahari, a respected Islamic scholar and a tireless preacher, had just received a message from his master, Grand Ayatollah Ruhollah Khomeini in Najaf, to prepare for jihad. In a message to Motahari the Ayatollah had announced the 'dethronement' of the Shah, the abolition of the two houses of Parliament, the suspension of all civil laws and the total boycott of 'the Government of Satan'. The message, written in Ahmad Khomeini's hand with a ballpoint pen on a page torn out of a school

182

notebook belonging to one of Ahmad's children, was meant to complement the Ayatollah's public *fitwa* posted to newspaper editors in Tehran earlier. The letter to Motahari contained in a postscript these words: 'This time either Islam triumphs or we disappear.'[1]

Despite his known sympathies for Khomeini, Motahari had managed to stay out of prison longer than most of his colleagues. He had also succeeded in allaying SAVAK's suspicions so that his home was no longer under surveillance. He had been taken off SAVAK's list of 'highly dangerous individuals' and was presumed to be mainly engaged in scholarly pursuits.[2] Now he was ordered to act as a general and organize a revolutionary uprising against the Shah. He must have wondered why Khomeini had decided that the moment was right for launching so hazardous an enterprise. Nevertheless, his faith in the exiled leader was so strong that it laid all his doubts to rest. For years he had included Khomeini's name in his prayers alongside that of Allah, the Prophet and the Imams, and he had drawn enormous strength from it.

By the time all of Motahari's guests had arrived it was already dark. The guests were Ayatollah Mohammad-Hussein Beheshti, special adviser to the Minister of Education, Ayatollah Mohieddin Anvari, Ayatollah Ali Golzadeh-Ghafouri and Ayatollah Ahmad Mowla'i. All four had been designated by Khomeini himself as members of a special secret committee charged with the task of 'supervising the defence of the faith' under Motahari himself.[3] To these, Motahari had added two others: Hojat al-Islam Ali-Akbar Hashemi-Rafsanjani and Hojat al-Islam Mohammad Javad Bahonar. So on that December evening in 1977 Motahari was presiding over a meeting of seven mullahs. The meeting, which lasted well into the night, did not discuss or debate the substance of the Ayatollah's orders. That would have been a total departure from tradition. The mullahs present had accepted Khomeini as leader and, conscious of the relationship between the Supreme Guide and his humble followers, would not have dreamed of questioning the Ayatollah's judgement. They knew that their mission consisted only of working out the best plan for organizing a nationwide uprising against the Shah. They were convinced, although none said so openly, that the Ayatollah had received a special signal from the Almighty that, as he put it in his message, the 'sufferings of Islam shall soon be at an end'.

Whether he had received any sign from Allah or not, Khomeini could cite a number of other reasons to support his optimism. Two months before he sent his letter containing instructions to Mota-hari, the Ayatollah had suffered a major personal loss. His eldest son Mostafa had died after a brief illness on 21 October. Khomeini had been temporarily broken by his bereavement and had, for three full days, stayed in his room, locked in prayers punctuated by uncontrollable tears.[4] Ahmad acted quickly to organize the burial ceremony and to inform contacts in Tehran and Beirut of his brother's death. News of Mostafa's death spread throughout Iran amid wild rumours that he had been murdered by SAVAK agents in cooperation with the Iraqi secret police. Claims that he had been poisoned by the Shah's agents reminded the faithful of the similar fate many of the Imams had suffered at the hands of cursed caliphs centuries ago. But neither Khomeini himself nor Ahmad ever even hinted at any SAVAK implication in Mostafa's sudden death, which was probably caused by a heart attack. At any rate, Mostafa seems to have had some premonition of his impending demise and had written and sealed his will, appointing his father as executor.

News of Mostafa's death provided the Ayatollah's supporters in Iran with an excuse to test and demonstrate their strength by orga-nizing memorial services. On 25 October an advertisement calling on the faithful to attend a memorial service for Mostafa at the Jam'e mosque in Tehran was published by the mass circulation daily *Kayhan*. The advertisement was signed by Ayatollah Mohammad-Hossein Saqafi-Tehrani, Khomeini's father-in-law, and referred to Mostafa as 'the offspring of the Exalted Leader of All Shi'ites of the World'. The fact that the advertise-ment was published in defiance of a formal ban by SAVAK was seen by many as a sign that the order forbidding any mention of Khomeini's name, outside slander and abuse, was being relaxed. Readers also noted with interest the fact that the paper itself had added its own condolences to the advertisement, referring to Kho-meini as 'Grand Ayatollah'. The publication of the advertisement encouraged scores of mullahs to come out and publish condolence notices of their own. One such notice was signed by no fewer than 300 leading mullahs, a roll call of the future leaders of the Islamic Republic.

The memorial service for Mostafa at the Jam'e mosque, Tehran's cathedral, was given the green light by the authorities only at the last minute. SAVAK had apparently decided to test Khomeini's appeal after so many years of exile. The service was attended by more than 3000 people and was addressed by Ayatollah Taheri Esfahani, who delivered a very moderate sermon.[5] Nevertheless, Esfahani made a point of inviting the congregation to pray for the good health and 'speedy return' to Iran of 'our one and only leader, the defender of the faith and the great combatant of Islam, Grand Ayatollah Khomeini'. The mention of Khomeini's name drew thunderous cries of 'Allah Akbar' (Allah is the Greatest). The Jam'e service was quickly followed with another at the Arg mosque near the Tehran bazaar and, within a few weeks, gatherings marking the demise of Mostafa Khomeini were organized in many cities, including Qom, Yazd, Tabriz, Kashan and Ahvaz. Worse still from the regime's point of view, the occasion was seized upon by a variety of opposition groups and personalities for publishing bitter attacks on the government in the guise of 'condolences' to Khomeini. One such letter, addressed to the Ayatollah in Najaf, was signed by over 150 prominent Mossadeqists, plus university teachers, lawyers, journalists, doctors and other professionals known for their opposition to the Shah. The snowball effect of the original memorial service continued for several weeks. The Grand Ayatollahs of Qom organized memorial services of their own, thus indirectly acknowledging Khomeini's position as supreme leader. Some half a dozen clandestine guerrilla organizations opposed to the regime issued statements describing Mostafa's death as a crime committed by SAVAK and praised Khomeini as both a religious and a political leader. By the time SAVAK realized what was happening, Khomeini's name was, after a lapse of more than fourteen years, on many lips as the Shah's leading opponent.

The Ayatollah, who had emerged from his seclusion still despondent, was greatly heartened by hearing the reports of what was going on in Iran. He consoled Batul with the words 'Mostafa was bequeathed to us by Allah, who has now taken him back.' But he also studied, with keen interest, a large number of photos sent to him by special courier from Tehran showing the crowds gathering to mourn Mostafa. He was specially pleased by a report of events in Qom, where two of his former *talabehs*, Sadeq Khalkhali and Abdul-Majid Maadikhah had addressed a crowd of mourners in passionately lyrical terms culminating in a blistering attack on the Shah. The two mullahs later led the crowd of chanting believers through the streets of Qom towards the Faizieh School, Khomeini's old citadel, which remained shut on the orders of SAVAK. The crowd had clashed with a detachment of police and forced them to retreat. Khalkhali had even managed to scale one of the walls of the school before the arrival of army troops, who scattered the crowd by firing at random, wounding a number of people. For the first time in years the holy city had witnessed a street battle between 'the soldiers of Allah' and 'Satan's mercenaries'.[6] Khalkhali, this time assisted by Ayatollah Rabani Amlashi and Ayatollah Ali-Akbar Meshkini, repeated his *tour de force* in Qom several weeks later on the occasion of the fortieth day of Mostafa's death.[7]

From the reports he received, complete with photos and recorded tapes of the sermons and crowd reactions, Khomeini apparently concluded that a broad consensus had taken shape around his name. Even those who had attacked his 'reactionary stand' during the 15 Khordad episode some fourteen years earlier now seemed ready to recognize him as leader. Khomeini saw this as an opportunity that should not be missed and set to work. Within a few days he sent more than four hundred letters and telegrams to supporters throughout Iran. Most of these were brief messages of thanks, consisting of a few sentences only. But they were sufficient to mark out the recipient as 'an approved representative' of the exiled Grand Ayatollah. The message to Motahari, ostensibly addressed to 'all the classes of our martyred nation', went beyond mere formalities and was to become a key document of the movement. In it Khomeini made a number of observations. First, he interpreted the gatherings organized to mark Mostafa's death as 'tremendous assemblies' which must be construed as 'a fit reply to the nonsense put out for so many years by that unfit element', meaning the Shah. Second, he noted that the gatherings were, in effect, a plebiscite for his opposition to the Shah. Third, he warned that the Shah's policy of 'liberalization', then in its early stages, was 'a big trick'. The Ayatollah then warned that any attempt at diverting 'the hatred of the people from the source of our miseries' to the government and individual officials ought to be resisted.

The message left no room for compromise. It also destroyed the prospect of any gradual progress towards a freer society, as wished by the Mossadeqists and other 'liberal' groups at the time. Launching a slogan which was to be on almost everyone's lips throughout Iran less than a year later, he wrote: 'The Shah must go', adding that the monarchy should also be abolished. In what can now be seen as direct political guidance to Motahari, then his plenipotentiary inside Iran, Khomeini also said that the leadership of the movement should be exclusively in the hands of the clergy so that 'the tragic experiences of the past' shall not be repeated. There was no longer any question of his playing the role of Kashani and serving as second fiddle to a secular politician. But the Ayatollah advised full use of the Shi'ite tactic of self-preservation in the struggle ahead. He emphasized the need to stay out of harm's way, noting that 'those key and committed personalities who have the [task] of leading should strongly avoid being recognized, learning from the experience of the past.'[8]

Motahari, known to his intimates for his firm belief that prudence was the best part of courage, must have noticed that the exiled leader in Najaf was attaching far more importance to the memorial services for Mostafa than they merited. Motahari was opposed to any frontal attack on the regime from what he thought was an eminently weak position. At the same time, however, he could not take issue with the Supreme Guide. So during the secret meeting in his house, Motahari emphasized Khomeini's own counsel of prudence. He argued that there was no point in exposing 'our best fighters' to unnecessary dangers.

The huge state apparatus over which the Shah presided was so vast, so powerful, that it appeared invincible. The imperial armed forces of which the Shah was Commander-in-Chief were nearly half a million strong and equipped with the most modern weapons available in any non-nuclear arsenal. There was also a 75,000-man national gendarmerie which kept the peace in the countryside. In urban areas a 65,000-man police force enforced the law and ensured security. At the same time the monarch had a variety of intelligence organizations at his disposal. There was the Imperial Inspectorate, at that time presided over by the enigmatic General Hussein Fardoust, a publicity-shy boyhood friend of the Shah, who reported only to the monarch himself. Then there was SAVAK, still headed by the sanguine General Nematollah Nasiri, who was then just getting used to the fourth star on his shoulder straps. The name of SAVAK had become synonymous with fear in all Iranian minds. Even the Shah's favourite ministers were frightened of SAVAK, which was rumoured to have as many as 500,000 full-time and part-time workers and informers. Several years of fighting the urban guerrillas had given SAVAK the image of a club of right-wing machos ready to shoot first and ask questions afterwards. SAVAK was also rumoured to have informers everywhere and people were advised not to trust anyone, including members of their own family. There were widespread reports of husbands and wives being denounced to

SAVAK by each other and SAVAK agents were reported to be active in all walks of life. Worse still, from the point of view of the conspirators who had assembled at Motahari's residence, was the certainty that SAVAK employed a large number of mullahs and *talabehs* as agents and informers.

The Shah's power was not limited to the coercive forces at his disposal. He was also a very rich ruler. Iran's income from exports of crude oil was hovering around the awesome figure of $20,000 million and the 'Imperial' state could, in the words of Amir-Abbas Hoveyda, for thirteen years the Shah's Prime Minister, simply 'purchase solutions' to many of its social and economic problems. The liberal injection of a good part of the oil income into the Iranian economy had created an atmosphere of prosperity and even mollified the bazaar which had been a traditional focus of opposition to the regime.

At the time the seven mullahs were assembling in south Tehran, there was virtually no organized opposition capable of representing a credible challenge to stability. Motahari and his friends had, without a doubt, the feeling that they were going to war against an invulnerable colossus. This, however, did not mean that they had no strength of their own. During Khomeini's exile, his supporters had not been content with periodical statements regretting his absence from Qom. They had created a nationwide organization which could mobilize mass support when and if the conditions proved right. The hard core of this organization, as we have already noted, was provided by the *hayats*. After years of infiltration and purges, SAVAK had succeeded in removing some of the more outspoken of Khomeini's supporters from the leadership of the *hayats* in Tehran. But the Shah's secret police could not destroy the *hayats*, which claimed to be purely religious organizations, completely. A strong faction within SAVAK considered the *hayats* to be potential allies in the fight against both the Communists and the so-called Islamic Marxist guerrilla groups. The mullahs made ample use of this delusion on the part of some leading SAVAK policy makers to escape the worst effects of the SAVAK-led repression of the 1970s. Even during the revolution the mullahs succeeded in deceiving successive governments in general and SAVAK in particular by claiming that they shared the regime's anti-Communist sentiments.[9]

The *hayats* were supposed to perform a number of important religious functions. They organized mourning processions in the months of Muharram and Safar. They also collected and distributed alms, looked after the needy and raised funds for the repair of mosques and other holy places. They operated either from the mosques or from the *mahdiehs* or *hosseiniehs* which existed all over the country. *Mahdiehs* and *hosseiniehs* are unassuming buildings which often consist of a vast courtyard and a few prayer chambers. They are used for religious assemblies and memorial services for leading citizens who have died. Control of the mosques, the *mahdiehs* and the *hosseiniehs* means the control of a ready network of community centres. By the end of 1977 most such religious buildings in Tehran and its environs were run by Ayatollah Khomeini's supporters.

Motahari had yet another organizational arm with which to challenge the regime. This consisted of a series of secret groups that had sprung out of the 15 Khordad movement and the Fedayeen of Islam before it. The fedayeen had reconstructed their organization under the leadership of the dynamic Shaikh Sadeq Khalkhali.[10] Other groups represented secret cells of the Islamic Nations Party which had been persecuted and apparently destroyed by SAVAK in the late 1960s. The party was, in fact, a loose organization of clandestine groups dedicated to the ideal of putting 'the enemies of Islam to death'.[11] Its original founder Sayyed Kazem Bojnurdi had escaped execution after being pardoned by the Shah. The party had continued to publish a newspaper named *Khalq* (*The People*) in Tehran, distributing it among the trusted supporters of the Ayatollah. All members of the party received military training and took an oath to assassinate anyone found guilty of 'warring on Allah'. During the early 1970s many members of the party had received training at various PLO camps in Lebanon as well as special centres set up by the Amal organization of Lebanese Shi'ites. Among the party's leaders and activists were several who subsequently organized the Islamic Revolutionary Guards. They included such militants as Javad Mansuri, Abbas Zamani, Abbas Douzdouzani and Hussein Sarhadizadeh.[12]

Another clandestine paramilitary group still active in a number of provincial centres was named Abazar after one of the early converts to Islam. The group, originally consisting of a dozen or so secondary-school pupils in the small provincial town of Nahavand, had been smashed by SAVAK a few years earlier. But its teachings as well as its name and insignia[13] had been adopted by other militant pro-Khomeini groups in Mashhad, Yazd and Kashan. The group had originally begun as an Iranian version of

Moral Rearmament and advocated a twenty-three-point manifesto which included a number of interesting stipulations such as 'combating narcotic drugs', 'fasting at least one day a week', 'showing kindness to animals', 'refusing to eat tasty meals and juicy fruit' and 'helping human beings under all conditions'. Another point on the group's list of resolutions demanded that every member should be 'submitted to torture one evening each week'. This was justified on the grounds that Abazar activists should prepare themselves for facing SAVAK and its torturers. The group's militants, who proved remarkably successful in escaping detection by SAVAK, carried out a number of 'Islamic operations' between 1970 and 1977, including setting fire to cinemas, restaurants, shops selling alcohol and some bank branches. They also organized an unsuccessful raid on the police headquarters in Kermanshah with the aim of stealing weapons. In addition, members of the group were responsible for a series of assassinations of a variety of people condemned as 'enemies of Islam'. Among the victims were notorious village usurers, gendarmes and schoolteachers found drinking vodka. SAVAK managed to identify and capture six members of the group. All were executed by firing squad in 1973. Among the group's founders and leaders were Bahman Monshat, Valiollah Sayf and Hojatollah Abdoli.

At least two other groups could be counted on by Motahari to provide the coming movement with coercive power when and if necessary. These were the Fajr-e-Enqelaab (Dawn of Revolution) organization and the Mahdavioun Society. The first group, known as Fajr (Dawn), had been founded by a number of students in Mashhad originally as a means of fighting the Baha'i faith, but it had quickly developed into an active paramilitary organization capable of carrying out assassinations and sabotage missions. Soon the group could boast a number of branches in Tabriz, Ahvaz and Qom. During the 1970s it was responsible for a bomb attack on a brewery near Mashhad as well as the burning of Qom's only cinema. This latter incident has entered the history of the Islamic movement as a major event. The opening of a cinema in Qom had been described by Khomeini as 'the greatest insult suffered by Islam in living memory'[14] and years of effort by Grand Ayatollahs had failed to secure its closure. What was more disturbing was that the cinema seemed to be doing excellent business, drawing a large number of believers away from the holy shrine and the mosques. In 1972 the screening of the American extravaganza *The Robe* was interpreted as the first step towards 'spreading the worship of the

*The Source of Imitation:* Grand Ayatollah Khomeini in exile in Neauphle-le-Chateau, near Paris, in 1979. Claiming the religious title of Marj'a Taqleed (Source of Imitation) he called on all Shi'ites to 'imitate' him in opposing the Shah.

*Two Young Seekers:* Khomeini and his friend Mohammad Lavasani (right) in Qom in 1928 when both were studying under Shaikh Abdol-Karim Ha'eri-Yazdi.

*The Light of his Eyes:* Khomeini with his eldest son Mostafa in exile in Najof in 1973. Khomeini referred to Mostafa as 'the light of my eyes'.

*The Revival of Islam:*
Khomeini, flanked by his son
Ahmad, responds to the
enthusiasm of his supporters in
Qom in 1979. He described the
revolutionary movement in
Iran as 'the revival of Islam'.

*'The Immortals':* High-ranking
officers of the Shah's 'Immortal
Guard' waiting for 'the King of
Kings' shortly before the start of
an official ceremony in Tehran in
1977. A few months later they
were fighting street-
demonstrations throughout the
country.

*An Uneasy Alliance:* Khomeini visits Grand Ayatollah Shariatmadari (centre) at the latter's residence in the holy city of Qom. Also present is Ahmad, Khomeini's son. The meeting in May 1979 united the top Shi'ite leadership in Iran, but only for a while.

*Allah, Qur'an, Khomeini:* Revolutionary women in a street demonstration in Tehran in 1978. They wear the authorised 'Islamic' dress in defiance of the Shah's efforts to westernise Iran.

*The Party of Allah:* Hojat al-Islam Hadi Ghaffari, leader of the Party of Allah, makes a point in Tehran in 1980.

*The Balancing Act:* Khomeini with his first Prime Minister Mehdi Bazargan (right) and Hojat-al-Islam Hashemi-Rafsanjani, leader of the main clerical faction in the Islamic Republic. Bazargan's resignation in November 1979 opened the way for a complete take-over by the religious faction.

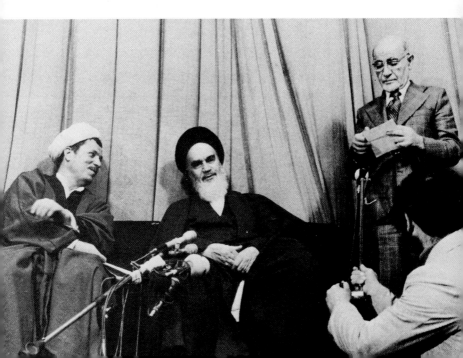

*Fighting 'Satan':* Members of the Imam's Committees round up women accused of defying Islamic laws in Tehran shortly after the triumph of the revolution in 1979.

*'Judge Blood':* Ayatollah Sadeq Khalkhali, nicknamed Judge Blood by the Western media, shows photos of the deposed Royal Family.

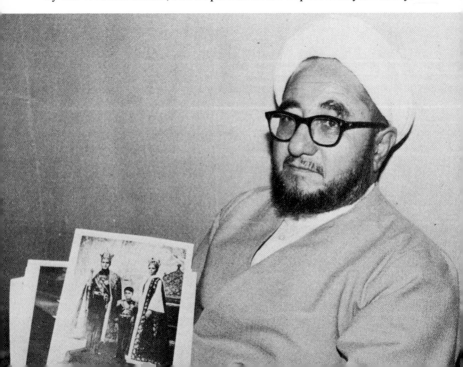

*Helping the Ayatollah:* Members of a Marxist-Leninist guerrilla group in action in Tehran in the last phases of the revolutionary struggle against the Shah in 1979.

*Moment of Revenge:* Revolutionary militants pose for a photo with the corpse of the Shah's Prime Minister Hoveyda in Tehran in 1979. Hoveyda was executed after being found guilty of 'corruption on Earth' by a secret revolutionary court.

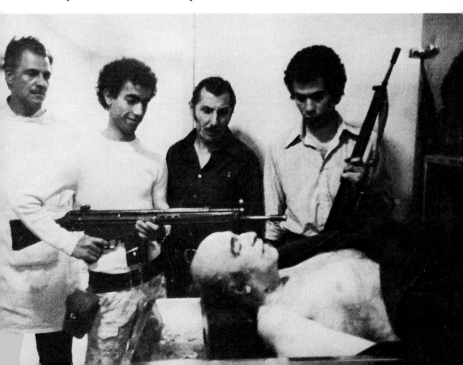

*'The Spiritual Son':* Abol-Hassan Bani-Sadr, described as Khomeini's spiritual son in the early days of the revolution, is escorted by armed supporters. He was dismissed by Khomeini in 1981.

*The Endless War:* A victorious mullah poses exultantly above a pile of Iraqi corpses.

Cross to the realm of Islam'.[15] The cinema had to burn, and burn it did, thanks to a commando led by Mohammad-Reza Fatemi who was later to be killed in a gun battle with SAVAK agents. The Fajr group claimed credit for the operation which was hailed in the holy city as 'a sign of divine favour to Islam'.[16] The cinema's frustrated owner, having suffered losses thanks to previous smaller attacks, agreed to sell his land at a giveaway price to Grand Ayatollah Mara'ashi-Najafi, who instantly ordered the construction of a theological school on the site, bearing his own name.

The Mahdavioun Society started as a circle of friends devoted to the study of the Qur'an, but it soon developed into a paramilitary organization offering its members training in the use of light arms, homemade bombs and plastic explosive devices. Led by Ali-Akbar Nabavi-Nuri and an enigmatic character known only as Mahdi (Guide), the group, which began in Tehran, was by 1977 boasting branches in more than a dozen provincial centres. Members of the group were involved in a number of gun battles with SAVAK agents but had nevertheless managed to keep most of their strength intact.

All these and many other smaller groups were directly loyal to Khomeini and could be counted on to fight for him when given the necessary signal. Some, like the Hadafi group in Qohdarijan, near Isfahan, were village terror gangs, while others, like Ghad Islam (Islamic Rendezvous), led by Mir-Hussein Mussavi, who was to become Prime Minister in the Islamic republic, were little more than semi-secret debating societies.

During the fourteen years following Khomeini's exile hundreds of mullahs had been imprisoned for speaking in his support; dozens had died in prison in suspicious circumstances, some under torture, and thousands had been pressganged into the army. Hundreds more were in exile, while scores were forbidden to mount the pulpit and address religious gatherings. Many mullahs were periodically subjected to attacks on their homes and to brief periods of detention during which they had their beards shaved off. Thus, Khomeini, by appearing first and foremost as a defender of the rights of the clergy, could expect much sympathy among the mullahs.

At least one more important religious organization could be counted upon to support the movement in its purported aim of making Shi'ism the basis of Iranian life once again. That organization was the Hojatieh Society. The Hojatieh had been founded in 1954 by the Tehrani mullah, Shaikh Mahmoud Halabi, who had known Khomeini in the 1920s in Qom. Halabi considered the Baha'is to be the most immediately important enemies of Islam in Iran and dedicated himself to the elimination of what he considered to be 'a lethal heresy'. Promising SAVAK full cooperation in fighting 'other heathen forces, including the Communists', Halabi enjoyed what amounted to *carte blanche* from the authorities to recruit militants for his organization and to raise funds in the bazaar. By 1977 Halabi boasted an organization of more than 12,000 members throughout the country. Most members were part-time volunteers and their task consisted of keeping an up-to-date list of Baha'is in their neighbourhood and trying to reconvert as many of them as possible. Halabi did not like Khomeini personally but could be counted on for support in any fight against a government which allowed the Baha'is ample scope for social advancement and economic profit.[17]

SAVAK could not have had any serious appreciation of the strength of the religious opposition. But an assertion that Motahari was even then able to field as many as six hundred highly trained guerrillas and determined would-be assassins would have surprised the secret police. These militants were to provide the hard core of the Tehran crowds which became the hallmark of the Islamic Revolution. They would protect the crowd against police attack and Left-wing infiltration, while using the crowd as a shield behind which to keep their own identities hidden as long as possible.

Motahari, however, decided to begin at the beginning, keeping his trained military cadres in reserve. He began by alerting the open religious network of support that he could command on behalf of the exiled leader. In 1977 Iran was estimated to have around 85,000 mullahs and *talabehs*.[18] Many of them received stipends and indirect financial support from various government agencies. Some 20,000 of them were teachers, employed by the Ministry of Education. Motahari himself was one such ministry employee along with Beheshti and Bahonar, who wrote religious textbooks for the government. Some 1200 mullahs were considered to be of higher rank and used the title either of ayatollah or of Hojat al-Islam. An ayatollah is a Hojat al-Islam distinguished enough to run an independent seminary of his own. Almost all *talabehs* were attached to one or more of the ayatollahs and received stipends from them. Motahari knew that the vast majority of the mullahs consisted of poor, semiliterate rural preachers who were too hungry, too frightened and too ignorant of the world to play an active political role. All that was needed was to secure the support of a few hundred leading mullahs in Tehran and the provinces to be able to mobilize every turbaned head in the country. The meeting at Motahari's home chose as its first task the preparation of a list of mullahs who would support Khomeini's claim to exercise power in the name of Allah without any reservation. The list as it finally emerged contained no more than seventy-five names. Many of them did not command much public support at the time. A few, however, were already established as major sources of power and influence in their own towns. Among them was Ayatollah Mohammad-Ali Qazi-Tabataba'i, who had secured a following for himself in Tabriz, especially among university students disillusioned with the many different brands of Marxism. Another key figure included in the list was Ayatollah Mahmoud Saduqi, who dominated the religious scene in Yazd. A third major name on the list belonged to Ayatollah Mahmoud Salehi of Kerman. Some of the senior leaders of the movement were in prison at the time, notably Ayatollah Hussein-Ali Montazeri, who was to emerge as Khomeini's heir presumptive after the revolution.

Motahari and his colleagues knew that almost all of traditional Iran had been abandoned by the Shah's regime over the preceding decade of modernization. The bazaars, important commercial and social institutions in every city of any size, had their own organizations in the form of guilds, fraternities, trade associations and informal *dowrehs* or 'circles of friends'. They were connected with a string of associations representing people of the same provincial origin in the capital and other major cities. The Association of Azerbaijanis in Tehran, for example, boasted a membership of over 5000 and could mobilize more than 100,000 on special religious occasions.

There were numerous other traditional organizations which, believing they were either ignored or duplicated by regime-sponsored bodies, felt threatened, and were as a result hostile to the government. These included the Zur-Khaneh (House of Force) where hundreds of men, aged between sixteen and sixty, followed special body-building courses and trained as traditional wrestlers. There were also the so-called 'interest-free' loan funds which provided many banking services and, benefiting from the country's economic boom, mobilized popular savings on a large scale. One such fund, essentially used as a cover for channelling funds to Khomeini's supporters throughout the country, was headed by a young mullah, Mohammad Mussavi-Khoiniha, who was to gain international notoriety as the leader of the 'students' who occupied the US Embassy in Tehran in 1979, seizing its diplomats as hostages.[19] In 1977 Khoiniha was handling something like £15 million through his *sanduq* (fund) which operated from the back of a carpet shop in Qom. Finally, the *dasteh* (group) brought together believers who assumed the task of leading mourning processions during Muharram and Safar.

Taken together, these traditional organizations covered almost all Iranian society. Only a tiny part of Iran's 'modernized' society was left out and increasingly pushed into isolation. In most cities and in most districts of Tehran it was virtually impossible for an individual to stay outside the traditional organizational networks. In neighbourhoods where everyone knew everyone and most people were related to one another by blood or through marriage, there was no room for lone wolves. Islam's tradition of emphasizing the communal at the expense of individual interest allowed .little scope for stepping out of the crowd. This traditional society did not see itself reflected in the Shah's slogans and policies.

The Shah's ministries, factories, new urban development centres, supermarkets, cinemas, casinos, opera house, country clubs, American-style hotels, dance halls, universities, cabarets and parliament appeared as if imported from a different planet. 'Real' Iran remained in the narrow alleys, the mosques, the roofed bazaars and the Islamic schools where turbaned teachers emphasized the importance of the Qur'an. Women dressed in miniskirts and driving fast cars, boys with long hair and wearing jeans, stately matrons resembling painted peacocks strolling in their expensive fur coats, gentlemen in Cardin and Dior ensembles ordering this or that French wine in posh restaurants, bespectacled intellectuals quarrelling about whether Camus was right or Sartre, modern revolutionaries offering new interpretations of Trotsky and Gramsci, fat, cigar-smoking cynics playing baccarat and technocratic ministers boasting about facts and figures in a strange jargon, were all just so many manifestations of an alien world to the Iranian in his *kucheh* (alley). The 'alien' Iran often did not even speak Persian; official memos and even *billets-doux* were exchanged in English or in French. It was not unusual for young Iranians to court each other in English. There were two English- and one French-language dailies in Tehran. The television offered a whole channel in English and there were two English-language radio stations. By 1976 Iran had become the largest importer of

French *haute couture* between West Europe and Japan. This 'alien' Iran educated most of its children abroad and had already bought tens of thousands of houses and flats in France, Britain, the United States and Canada. It spent almost all its holidays abroad and was increasingly treating Iran as nothing more than a place of work and a cultural desert. By 1977 the number of Iranians spending their holidays abroad had risen to nearly one million. Iran's oil-lubricated economic boom of 1971–76 had, without a doubt, benefited almost everyone. The gross national product (GNP) had risen from around $700 per head per annum in 1970 to over $2000 in 1978. Tens of thousands of new housing units had been built and mostly sold to low- or middle-income groups. Almost every child of school age was receiving education for the first time in the nation's history. Infant mortality had fallen by threequarters. But the gap between the rich and the poor had become much wider than before, while official propaganda continued to create new needs and new desires. The Shah might have expected a measure of support from the middle and upper classes of his emerging dreamland.

But even this assessment was to prove wrong. The new rich hated the Shah even more intensely than did the traditional poor. Most of the rumours against 'His Imperial Majesty' and members of his family were fabricated in the rich salons of north Tehran and reached the poor districts of the capital many days later. The Iranian middle and upper classes disliked the Shah for what they saw as his Bonapartist policies. They believed that the Shah relied on the poor as a reserve force to tame the rich when and if the latter threatened to get out of hand. Such schemes as profit-sharing and the sale of industrial shares to factory workers were seen as royal bribes to the 'lower classes'. A good section of the urban middle class disliked the Shah for political reasons. Middle-class Iranians who travelled to the West did not take long to start comparing their political situation in Iran with that of their peers in Europe or North America. They enjoyed almost the same measure of material wealth and well-being as the middle classes in the West but had virtually no political rights. The Shah wanted his regime to stand above social class, while the middle class wanted their real economic power to be translated into political power.

Thus, by the time Motahari was positioning his forces for an assault on the imperial regime, Iran was feeling two different revolutionary undercurrents. One was that of the middle class who, having gained tremendous economic power, now wished to turn

Iran into a Western-style constitutional monarchy in which the Shah would cut ribbons and kiss babies, leaving the real domain of politics to parties, Parliament and the press. The Iranian middle class were badly divided politically; some were liberals, others socialists. But they were all unanimous in wanting the powers of the Shah reduced and a multiparty system installed. For years this middle class had tried a variety of stratagems for imposing the reforms they desired but had failed. To them only the army seemed capable of counterbalancing the monarchy's historical weight in Iranian society.

In some Islamic countries, notably Egypt and Iraq, middle-class intellectuals had succeeded in whetting the appetite of the military for political power by promoting nationalist or socialist ideologies. In both countries the army had toppled the monarchy by staging a coup d'état. In Iran, however, such a scenario would have had little chance of succeeding, as the monarchy itself, in the form it had taken since Reza Shah, symbolized rule by the military. The Shah's opponents had to look for another force with which to topple him, a force large and strong enough to counterbalance that of the army. Some of the middle-class opposition had hoped to provide precisely such a force by organizing a variety of urban and rural guerrilla groups. Between 1970 and 1976 these groups had fought a number of losing battles with the security forces. By the time Khomeini was launching the new phase of his struggle against the Shah it was obvious that the guerrillas, despite their courage and ruthlessness, had slipped into a historical footnote. The question of finding a counterbalancing force against the Shah's army remained unanswered. Right from the start, however, Khomeini thought he had the answer. He was convinced that only huge street crowds could neutralize the Shah's security forces. And the masses, who had to produce the crowds, could not be mobilized in sufficiently large numbers around socialist or nationalist slogans. The average Iranian would not be prepared to die for the ideals of Lenin or Mao; but he would, given the right circumstances, sacrifice his life in defence of 'the honour of Imam Hussein' and the Muhammedan faith. The language of class struggle, used by almost all the guerrilla groups, frightened the urban bourgeoisie without mobilizing the peasants and the working class. The appeal of the European-style Left did not extend beyond the universities, the secondary schools and certain strata of the lower middle class. None of the major social and economic groupings found their aspirations and interests reflected in the hotchpotch of proto-Marxian and pseudo-religious ideologies espoused by the guerrilla groups.

Khomeini's instructions to Motahari made this abundantly clear – the movement was to act exclusively in the name of Islam. It also included the basic elements of a coherent strategy. The first step was to destroy the regime's legitimacy. This was to be achieved by a persistent and savage campaign of character assassination, rumours and the exposure of the regime's links with the Zionists, the 'Cross-Worshippers', the Baha'is and other 'enemies of Islam'. There was to be no discussion of the Shah's policies as such and it was to be argued that the Shah, regardless of what he did or said, had been 'excluded' from the Islamic community and should be put to death. Hahsemi-Rafsanjani, in one of his earliest 'guidelines' to militants, put it this way: 'Today, saying "Allah is the Greatest" without immediately adding "Death to the Shah" can only mean that we only half believe in Islam.'[20] He added, 'The Shah must die so that Islam can resume life, after centuries of slow death.'[21] The powerful traditional rumour mills of the mosque and the bazaar were set to work to attribute to the Shah every sin in the book. The monarch was accused of plundering the nation's wealth, being a heroin addict and, at the same time, an indefatigable womanizer. It was rumoured that the Shah had secretly converted to Judaism, Zoroastrianism or Mithraism. The conversion of Princess Shams, the Shah's elder sister, to Catholicism, which was true, was seized upon as an example of the Pahlavi family's disregard for Islam. 'Your Shah is a Jew,' screamed one of the early leaflets, probably written by Ayatollah Beheshti. 'He is a Jew just like his sister has been a Cross-Worshipper for years.' In addition, the Shah was in turn accused of homosexuality, feeble-mindedness, impotence and sadomasochistic habits.

The Shah's close collaborators were not spared either and within a few months were turned into hated caricatures who deserved to be put to death. The regime, content with its hold over the Western-style media, radio, television and the press, totally ignored the tremendous power of traditional media such as the pulpit, the bazaar teahouses and, above all, the nationwide network of rumours. The Islamic East's love of rumour cannot be overemphasized; it is virtually impossible for the community as a whole to accept a straight account of events as such. In almost every case fiction is preferred to fact. Money and sex were the two key elements in almost all the rumours. The message was that the Shah, his family and a tiny group of officials – who were all

Baha'is, Jews or atheists – were spending their time amassing huge fortunes and fornicating, while the mass of deserving believers had to struggle with the problems of everyday life. Within a few months the appellations *Shah-e-Emrika'i* (the American Shah) and *Shah-e-Esraili* (the Israeli Shah) were on many lips throughout the country. The leaders of the movement justified the use of such dirty tactics against their hated enemy by reference to the celebrated maxim that 'the end justifies the means' which, in its Shi'ite version, reads 'All means are justified in the service of Allah.'[22]

Motahari believed that destroying the regime's image and persuading a sufficiently large number of people that the Shah was an illegitimate ruler would require 'at least a year or two of hard work'.[23] In the event, however, the objective was achieved much more quickly as the Shah failed to counterattack while also preventing his supporters from reorganizing themselves in his defence. For months on end people were to hear abuse and invective aimed at the Shah, who remained silent or only spoke in apologetic terms that reinforced the claims of his adversaries.

Next to establishing the regime's lack of legitimacy on religious as well as moral and political grounds, Khomeini aimed at creating alternative sources of authority. Reviving his theory of 'opting out', he called on the faithful to reduce their contact with the established order to a minimum. The faithful were to withdraw their money from the 'satanic' banks, refuse to pay taxes or electricity and water bills, refuse conscription and not defer to the courts of justice. Government employees were ordered to create 'Islamic' committees that duplicated the formal managerial structure of each Ministry. The tactic was slow to start but once it had gained momentum it proved lethal to the regime. Ministers, under-secretaries, directors-general and other high-ranking officials were quickly turned into mere actors each playing a part. They lacked all authority, unless, as was increasingly the case from the middle of 1978 onwards, they contacted the 'Islamic' committee and swore loyalty to the Ayatollah.

The third point put forward by Khomeini in his strategy was to neutralize or, if possible, to win over the regime's coercive forces. As we have already noted, the Ayatollah could field several hundred fighting men and women trained in Lebanon, Libya, South Yemen and, from the middle of 1978, Iran itself. These militants, when using large crowds as shields, became far more effective than their actual numerical strength would allow. But the

Ayatollah knew that his army of street fighters would be no match for the Shah's well-trained and highly disciplined armed forces. Thus a vast campaign of hearts and minds directed against regular army troops, members of the police force and even SAVAK personnel was launched. The campaign had only limited success so far as the actual number of recruits to the Ayatollah's camp was concerned. But it nevertheless hurt the regime by casting doubt on the loyalty of the forces at its disposal. And once the revolutionary movement began to gain momentum the remnants of the Leftist guerrilla groups joined forces with it and gave it additional strength in facing the Shah's forces. The most important of these groups was, without a doubt, the Mujahedeen-e-Khalq-e-Iran (the People's Combatants of Iran), which was based on an ideological marriage between Shi'ism and socialism. The group, followers of the writer Ali Shariati, at first advocated Shi'ism without the mullahs. But by the summer of 1978 the Khomeinist movement was so strong that they had to join forces with it, acknowledging the Ayatollah's supreme leadership. The fact that almost all the principal leaders of the Mujahedeen were in prison at the time made it difficult for the badly battered organization to force Khomeini into any concessions as the price of this additional support. The Marxist–Leninist Fedayeen of the People organization also went the same way, being sucked into the ever growing movement of the mullahs. The pro-Moscow Tudeh Party, having just revived its organization inside Iran, was the last to join the Ayatollah's movement. But Tudeh, when it finally acknowledged Khomeini's position as 'supreme leader', was able to provide invaluable service thanks to its expertise in psychological warfare, sabotage and the organization of industrial strikes.

The fourth and final point in the Ayatollah's strategy was based on the assumption that the Shah's regime would not be overthrown unless a credible and more or less acceptable alternative to it emerged. Such an alternative, Khomeini realized, had to reassure the middle class, who were sure to be frightened by the prospect of living in a strictly Islamic society, as well as the outside world, which was worried about its vital interests in Iran and the Persian Gulf region as a whole. The Ayatollah was to leave this last point aside until the final stages of his revolution. All he did was order one of his pupils, Jalaleddin Farsi, of Afghan origin, to prepare a new edition of *Islamic Government* for publication in Iran. Azra Bani-Sadr, the wife of Abol-Hassan Bani-Sadr, a student of economics in Paris and a long-time supporter of Khomeini, prepared a French translation of the Ayatollah's little book. Thus, without going into details that risked antagonizing sections of the broad coalition he was creating against the Shah, Khomeini, at the same time, took care to make his blueprint for the future government of Iran available to anyone sufficiently interested in the subject. Strangely enough, almost nobody bothered to read the book which is crystal clear on at least one point: Islamic communities must be ruled by the Muslim clergy in accordance with the laws of the Qur'an.[24] The fact that few of the middle-class and Leftist leaders who sided with Khomeini took time to read his books and find out what he was really talking about was to cost them dearly. Many paid for that omission with their lives while others still languish in the Ayatollah's prisons or are fighting him from exile. But all that came much later.

The seven mullahs who met at Motahari's home were to form the nucleus of an expanded Shuray-e-Enqelab-e-Eslami (Council of the Islamic Revolution) several months later which managed to escape detection by SAVAK right to the end. The group took Khomeini's advice and gave top priority to self-preservation. For months other mullahs were promoted as leaders of the movement together with a wide range of ambitious politicians who suddenly found themselves veritable heroes of large and 'spontaneous' crowds. Motahari and Rafsanjani would dispatch hundreds or thousands of screaming, fist-shaking volunteers for martyrdom to the homes of long-forgotten Mossadeqist politicians or even members of the Shah's parliament who had shown a penchant for dissent. The crowds would, by their mere presence, force essentially conservative, and in some cases frankly cowardly, politicians to adopt a militant stance against the Shah. Karim Sanjabi, a rather shy septuagenarian who had briefly served as a Minister in Mossadeq's Cabinet in 1952, was, in 1977, living a quiet life as adviser to the Ministry of Science when he suddenly discovered a vast following he had never suspected. His luxurious villa in north Tehran became a point of pilgrimage for hundreds of demonstrators each day. The result was that when SAVAK was finally ordered to make a move months later, it was Sanjabi who was arrested as the leader of a movement he did not even understand. The mullahs' tactic worked admirably. The real leaders remained safe and secure, shielded by their anonymity, or even tricking SAVAK into thinking that all the trouble was coming from 'the Communists and terrorists'. A SAVAK report in February 1978 cited several of the key figures in the Khomeinist movement as 'our potential allies' in the fight against 'Communist and terrorist groups'.[25] Between January 1978 and 1 February 1979, when the Ayatollah returned to Tehran, more than 10,000 people were arrested and held for varying lengths of time in connection with riots, demonstrations and acts of sabotage. Only two were mullahs and neither was in any way connected with the tightly knit group of conspirators who led the revolution.[26] It was only in the last six or seven weeks of the regime that SAVAK, the Cabinet and the imperial court reached a consensus that a fully fledged and independent nationwide organization of Khomeini's own supporters existed and was in operation. Before that Khomeini was considered to be a mere figurehead who was being used by a variety of Leftist, Mossadeqist and pro-Soviet Communist groups as a symbol. Apart from the Shah himself, who nurtured a profound personal hatred for the Ayatollah, there was almost no one in the higher echelons of the regime who recognized the movement's profoundly religious personality. The leaders of the regime fell so wide of the mark as to think of making a deal with Khomeini himself against the unknown forces that were setting the country ablaze day after day, burning banks, cinemas, libraries, women's clubs, restaurants and other 'Western' oases in the Islamic desert of Iran. Jaafar Sharif-Emami, who was to serve as an ephemeral Prime Minister towards the end of the regime, was so confident that Khomeini would respond to his invitation and return to Iran to help combat Communism that he even ordered a special jet to be kept ready at the airport.[27] His government also ordered the arrest of a number of people who had dared to insult the Ayatollah in public. The illusion that the Mossadeqists and other middle-class politicians, such as Mehdi Bazargan, were leading the movement or were, at least, key figures in it had the additional advantage of reassuring the well-to-do in the towns while persuading the international media, often bitterly hostile to the Shah, that Iran was experiencing a democratic, middle-class revolution against a medieval and tyrannical regime. Motahari described the tactic adopted as one of 'leading from behind'; so long as middle-class politicians spoke the slogans and espoused the themes set for them by the religious organization there was no harm in allowing them to stand in the limelight. The general assumption among the middle-class and liberal opponents of the Shah was that Khomeini, already in his late seventies and reportedly in poor health, could not have any political ambitions of his own. Nevertheless, the middle-class politicians who were promoted by the clandestine religious leadership were kept on a very tight leash. Dariush Foruhar, a leader of the National Front, was rudely reminded of the real extent of his party's popular appeal when addressing a crowd in north Tehran in January 1978. Foruhar's mention of the name of Dr Mossadeq, the idol of liberal middle-class politicians, provoked prolonged noises of disapproval followed by the by now customary cries of 'There is no leader but Ruhollah.' In other words, Foruhar could enjoy all the glory and power of riding the tiger so long as he did not try to dismount and go his own way.[28]

The Shah, however, identified Khomeini as his number-one enemy right from the start and felt a profound hatred for the Ayatollah. In 1976 a suggestion by Hussein Shahidzadeh, Iran's Ambassador to Iraq, that a dialogue be established with Khomeini with a view to arranging for his peaceful return to Qom made the monarch so angry that it virtually ended the career of the enterprising diplomat.[29] The Shah was scandalized by the sharpness of the language Khomeini used against the Pahlavi dynasty. The terms Khomeini used to describe Reza Shah and his son included such unflattering ones as 'bastard', 'dog', 'lackey', 'traitor', 'rascal', 'blood-sucking' and 'jackass'. Many middle-class politicians opposed to the Shah blushed when reading or hearing the Ayatollah's torrents of abuse. But Khomeini knew that he had to demystify the monarch and show the illiterate masses that even the King of Kings could be dragged into the mud with impunity. During the course of the revolution the Ayatollah coined a number of slogans directly aimed at dispelling any fear of the Shah by subjecting him to the most violent kinds of personal attack. One slogan was: 'Farah, where are your gloves? And where is your pimp of a husband?' And another was: 'When we have killed the Shah, Farah will rush into the arms of Carter.'[30]

It was in more or less the same terms that the trusted mullahs of Motahari began attacking the Shah from the pulpit and at meetings of students or bazaar merchants from the autumn of 1977. Since the Shah had been declared *mahdur ad-damm* by the Ayatollah, there was no reason why he should be spared any verbal injury. Towards the end of December 1977 the Shah ordered the creation of an ad hoc committee to prepare plans for countering the Ayatollah's growing militancy. The committee was to report to him directly through the Court Minister and act independently of SAVAK.[31] The committee recommended what the Shah himself had already decided – to present Khomeini as the real challenge to the regime. Khomeini would be portrayed as a mad mullah seeking personal power to return Iran to the 'dark ages'. While the Shah boasted about his dynasty being the first 'purely Iranian and Persian-speaking' family to rule Iran in nearly three centuries, Khomeini was to be presented as an 'Indian' charlatan who had been trained by the British to Arabize Iran. Thus started a slanging match in which the head of state and one of the nation's highest-ranking.religious leaders described each other in terms more suited to fist-fighting incidents in south Tehran bazaars. The committee prepared the drafts of two 'letters' which were supposedly written by two individuals to the editors of *Kayhan* and *Ettelaat*, Tehran's two main dailies. Both letters described the Ayatollah as a mad Indian poet with homosexual tendencies and a long record of serving British colonialists. Although Khomeini was directly named in both letters, the vile language used was extended to cover almost all mullahs, who were described in one of the letters as 'a race of parasites, engaged in sodomy, usury and drunk most of the time'.[32] The Shah personally read, edited and approved the letters, which were dispatched through the Information Minister Dariush Homayun.[33] One of them, signed by a fictitious Ahmad Rashidi-Motlaq but in fact written by a freelance journalist who had once been a member of Iran's tiny Fascist Party, was published by *Ettelaat* on 7 January 1978.[34] The following day the letter was discussed at an emergency meeting of the seven-man committee under Motahari in Tehran. Everyone agreed with Motahari that the letter marked the start of a crackdown and it was decided that attacks on the Shah should be toned down pending the full revelation of the regime's intentions. Even a suggestion that *Ettelaat* be boycotted for having published the letter was brushed aside as too risky. But the committee had underestimated the appetite of the mullahs at large for militant action against the hated regime. During the following thirteen months, until the revolution triumphed, there were to be many more occasions when the central leadership proved far too cautious for the rank and file. Copies of *Ettelaat* containing the incendiary letter were rushed to Qom by groups of militants within two hours and proved a bombshell. A group of some fifty *talabehs*, led by Khalkhali, began roaming the streets of the holy city and burning *Ettelaat*'s newsstands. The following day Qom experienced more demonstrations. By this time almost every mullah and *talabeh* in the holy city had read the paper and felt personally insulted. Even Grand Ayatollah Shariatmadari, by temperament a man of peace and understanding, was so angered by the letter as to say that 'no punishment would be too harsh for the writers of that letter'.[35] On 9 January the holy city's bazaar was shut down and thousands of people began gathering around the shrine with cries of 'Hail to Khomeini' and 'Death to the Shah'. Khalkhali and Maadikhah, who led the main procession, made brief speeches before directing the growing crowd to the Faizieh School. The outnumbered and frightened police quietly withdrew from the main streets and a crowd of some five thousand frantic mullahs, *talabehs* and bazaaris virtually seized control of the city. The crowd made maximum use of the opportunity offered it and went on the rampage against all symbols of the Shah's rule. Banks, government offices, girls' schools, bookshops selling non-religious publications, the homes of officials and the city's only two restaurants where men and women could dine under the same roof were sacked and set on fire. By early afternoon the crowd, which had now grown to some 20,000 and was led by overexcited *talabehs*, felt confident enough to head for the central police station with cries of 'Muslims, take 'up arms, Islam is in danger'. Seeing the angry crowd approach, the nervous police began firing from the rooftop of the central police station. At least seven demonstrators and two policemen were killed in the shooting and the subsequent clashes in front of the police station.[36] It was the arrival of army troops on the scene shortly before sunset that finally restored peace. Over a hundred people were arrested and held for a few hours before being released as a gesture of goodwill to Shariatmadari, who telephoned the police chief asking him not to inflame passions further. The movement had its new martyrs as well as heroes. The martyrs were mostly schoolchildren. The heroes were, in addition to Khalkhali and Maadikhah, a group of militant *talabehs* describing themselves as Hezb-Allah (the Party of Allah). Their leader was a young, white-turbaned mullah named Shaikh Hadi Ghaffari. Ghaffari's father, also a mullah, had been imprisoned by SAVAK for five years and had died under torture in 1975.

There is no doubt that the Shah did not see the violent events of Qom as a warning, for on the evening of the following day he addressed a women's rally in Tehran and strongly attacked the mullahs. Without naming Khomeini, he referred to the Ayatollah as 'the dog that barks at the moon'. The Shah told the women that he was determined to pursue his reforms regardless of 'the coalition of Black and Red Reaction' forming against his regime. 'My father ended the tyranny of feudal tribal chiefs,' he said, 'and I continued his task by smashing the landed barons — giving land to the peasants. But I know that the supreme test of my reign will be the establishment of full equality for women.'[37] The Shah's tough, fighting speech was, in fact, a reply to a relatively mild statement put out by the three Grand Ayatollahs of Qom — Shariatmadari, Golpayegani and Mara'ashi-Najafi. This was the first time in nearly forty years that three ayatollahs of such high rank had put their signatures to a single statement. The fact that the statement also referred to Khomeini as a *marja-e-taqleed*, the highest title used for a mullah, showed that an unprecedented degree of unity had been achieved at the highest echelon of Shi'ite religious leadership. Only two other Grand Ayatollahs remained uncommitted: Khonsari in Tehran and Kho'i in Najaf. But Khonsari was known to everyone as a holy man totally uninterested in the affairs of this world and almost Augustinian in distinguishing between the 'kingdom of this world' and that of the hereafter. And Kho'i, while not endorsing the movement, had on a number of occasions refused to condemn it either.

# 12

# *The Chain of Martyrdom*

The Iranian nation has risen against tyranny and corruption. The revolution of the Iranian nation cannot but be endorsed by me both as the Monarch and an individual Iranian. . . . I hereby guarantee [to achieve] what you have offered your martyrs for. . . . In this revolution of the Iranian nation against colonialism, tyranny and corruption, I am at your side. . . .

Mohammad-Reza Shah Pahlavi

The Shah is saying that he is granting liberty to the people. Hear me, you pompous toad! Who are you to grant freedom? It is Allah who grants freedom; it is law which grants freedom; it is Islam which grants freedom; it is the Constitution which grants freedom. What do you mean by saying: we have granted you freedom? What has it got to do with you anyway to grant [us] anything? Who are you anyway?

Ayatollah Ruhollah Khomeini

Grand Ayatollah Kazem Shariatmadari would have been the last person to be considered as a revolutionary leader. Already in his late seventies and suffering from a heart condition, he was certainly in no state to take up arms against the Shah's huge, American-equipped armed forces. And yet before the end of January 1978 this quiet, saintly man was threatening the Shahanshah with an armed uprising. Shariatmadari's modest house, made of mud brick, in the centre of Qom had become the focal point of the Islamic movement. The reason was that on 11 January a group of *talabehs*, being chased by troops, had sought sanctuary in the ayatollah's house, having recourse to a long-established and respected tradition under which the residence of a top religious leader was treated as a holy place and considered inviolate. The commander of the troop on that day, however, knew nothing of the tradition and was determined to capture the troublemakers come what may. Thus he ordered his men into the Grand Ayatollah's house where they fired shots killing a young *talabeh*.[1] They then withdrew, taking with them half a dozen other turbaned militants, who were released the same evening. The dead man's corpse was quickly removed from the ayatollah's reception room but his blood-stained white turban remained, becoming a symbol of martydom in the service of Islam. That austere reception room, containing the bloodied turban, became a place of pilgrimage in the subsequent twelve months. Shariatmadari was aware of the dangers involved in the revolutionary movement both for the country as a whole and for the Shi'ite clergy in particular. He neither liked nor trusted Khomeini but, as one of the most senior ayatollahs inside Iran, he could not appear indifferent when the regime began firing on the mullahs. Shariatmadari now began a complicated game which, he hoped, would save the situation both for the Shah and for his opponents, and save the country from what he feared would be a bloodbath. Shariatmadari's moderation reflected the mood of the majority of the mullahs even at that late stage. The Grand Ayatollah wanted a number of quick and effective concessions from the Shah aimed at taking the steam out of Khomeini's radicalism. But the Shah was as determined as Khomeini to force things to their inevitable violent conclusion.

The Shah did not recognize the fact that he was entering that deadly arena from a position of weakness. The oil-propelled economic boom of the seventies had already peaked and inflation had risen to double figures. The ruling elite was running out of fresh ideas and was showing the inevitable signs of lassitude after over a decade in power. The Shah had distanced himself from the people over the years and was no longer seen rubbing shoulders with workers, peasants and other ordinary folk. People saw him on television or in newspaper photos only in the company of foreign dignitaries. He gave numerous interviews, but always to foreign journalists and never to the Iranian press.[2] The people had to find out about their monarch's future intentions and policies through translated accounts of interviews published by often obscure foreign journals. The Shah was already operating as a world leader; Iran had grown too small an arena for his wisdom and energies. His Majesty's rather inflated view of himself as a towering giant of the twentieth century, a Persian version of Charles de Gaulle, was to a large extent a reflection of his own natural penchant for megalomania. A shy, sulky and eminently fragile person, the monarch used affected grandeur as a shield behind which to hide from the dangers of the outside world. But there is little doubt that a number of foreign leaders and politicians were, perhaps unwittingly, responsible for steering the Shah's already wayward vessel into the unknown seas of excessive pride. Richard M. Nixon, US President between 1969 and 1976, must bear part of the burden of responsibility. Next to him stands Henry Kissinger, Nixon's security adviser and later Secretary of State, who gave the Shah the illusion of being a great intellectual. Throughout the 1970s the Shah sat on his Peacock Throne and received an endless string of foreign dignitaries who queued to pay their respects and, if lucky, go home with multi-billion-dollar contracts. None dared draw his attention to reports indicating that all was not well in Iran. 'Aren't we lucky in Iran?' His Majesty would often demand. 'Today, the whole world admires us.'[3] In private conversations the Shah would brush aside any suggestion that Iran might have any major domestic problems and would quickly turn to his and Iran's 'international role'. Encouraged by Kissinger, the Shah developed the idea of an Indian Ocean 'common market' in which Iran would be the central partner. Another pet idea, also at least in part inspired by Nixon and Kissinger, was that of the triangle bringing together Australia, Iran and South Africa as guardians of peace in the Indian Ocean. The Shah believed that the so-called Nixon Doctrine had been inspired by him and amounted to the recognition of Iran by the United States as a regional superpower. The only foreign states-man to lecture the Shah on human rights and the need for demo-cratic development was the Federal German Chancellor Willy Brandt. The Shah was angered by Brandt but later dismissed the Chancellor's lecture on ethics as 'utter rubbish' after hearing reports that his critical visitor had broken into song after imbibing an appreciable quantity of alcohol at the Omar Khayyam Bar of the Shah Abbas Hotel in Isfahan the day after concluding nego-tiations with His Majesty in Tehran. The Shah often cited Brandt as typical of Western politicians, 'living one way and talking another'.[4]

During some thirty-six years of rule the Shah had made the acquaintance of scores of foreign leaders and was genuinely convinced that he himself was better than most of them. With a few he had forged relations bordering on friendship, but only just. These included Egypt's Muhammed Anwar El Sadat, Jordan's King Hussein, Rumania's Nicolai Ceausescu, Yugoslavia's Josip Broz Tito and, of course, Nixon. Those he admired, for different reasons, included Fidel Castro, whom he had never met in person, the Federal German Finance Minister Helmut Schmidt,[5] General Francisco Franco of Spain, the British Conservative Prime Minister Edward Heath and Singapore's Premier Lee Kwan Yu.

From 1976 onwards, convinced that he was destined to reshape the history of the world, His Imperial Majesty spent a great deal of time worrying about the problems of other countries. For him, without his realizing it, Iran had become just one country among many about which he had to worry. There is no doubt that he loved Iran above all; but his love and attention were no longer exclusive. In 1977 he asked one of his ministers to organize an international 'think-tank' to meet periodically and find solutions to the world's problems. The final list, approved by His Imperial Majesty, included, in addition to Premier Lee and Edward Heath and the inevitable Kissinger, the following names: the French philosopher Raymond Aron, the former International Labour Organization director David Morse, the American banker David Rockefeller, the American politician George Shultz and the Bavarian political leader Franz Jozef Strauss.[6]

On 18 February 1978, however, His Imperial Majesty was rudely reminded of the fact that his own problems in Iran were far more acute than those of the other countries he loved to discuss with his hand-picked 'international brains'. Marking the *arba'een* of those killed in Qom during the anti-Shah riot, thousands of people poured into the streets of Tabriz, Yazd, Isfahan, Jahrom, Shiraz and Ahvaz to chant anti-regime slogans and attack banks, cinemas, alcohol shops, government offices and the headquarters of the Iranian Women's Organization. Holding *arba'een* (fortieth day) ceremonies was to become the regular pattern for the movement as in every memorial march a number of new martyrs was created, giving fresh occasions for future rounds of demonstrations. The uprising in Tabriz, organized by Ayatollah Mohammad-Ali Qazi-Tabataba'i, that old war-horse who had spent years in the Shah's prisons or in exile, was by far the most violent. At least fourteen people were killed and some two hundred injured when troops fired on mobs attacking police stations and government buildings. After a day of street fights Tabriz looked like a war-torn city. The Shah, still confident that he could 'flush out and crush' the 'Red and Black Reactionaries', ordered films of the incident to be shown on national television with full commentary detailing the activities of 'a mob, led by foreign elements who had crossed the borders of Iran illegally'.[7] The incidents in the other cities did not lead to deaths, except in Jahrom, where one man was shot dead, but were massive and violent enough to indicate the existence of a nationwide malaise. In every case, the presence of militant mullahs was the root cause of the disturbance, indicating the growing power of the clergy. In Yazd, Ayatollah Mahmoud Saduqi urged an all-out revolt against the regime, despite advice from Motahari to adopt a more gradual approach. In Shiraz, Ayatollah Bahaeddin Mahalati, a veteran of many anti-Shah campaigns, revived the tactic of asking the faithful to gather on the terraces of their homes at sunset and, on hearing the muezzin from the mosque, shout 'Allah Akbar' in unison. This ritual was to be adopted by millions of people throughout the country later on as the movement continued to grow. There is no doubt that some of the militants trained by the PLO in Lebanon had returned to Iran and played a part in organizing the revolts in Tabriz and Isfahan. But it is almost certain that there were no Palestinians among them as the authorities claimed at the time. A degree of confusion may have been created by the fact that an increasing number of militant supporters of the Ayatollah wore the Palestinian headgear, the *kufiah*, often as a *cache-col*, to symbolize their hatred of Israel as 'the number-one enemy of Islam'.

The Shah's response to these disturbing events was almost nonchalant. To be sure, the Governor of Azerbaijan, of which Tabriz was the capital, was dismissed and replaced by General Mohsen Shafeqat, who had served as Commander of the Imperial Guard. An inquiry into the incidents was ordered, but the Shah, once again commenting on events through interviews with foreign journalists, said that his policy of 'an open political atmosphere' would not be altered. That reassured Motahari, who consistently feared a nationwide crackdown by SAVAK, and convinced many militants that the regime, strangely confident of its political strength, would not field its awesome machinery of repression in the near future.

The so-called 'open-atmosphere' policy had been designed by the Shah back in 1976 following the failure of his attempt to make his newly created one-party system work. The party he had created, known as Rastakhiz (Resurgence), had at first generated a mood of optimism and might have succeeded in growing into at least as effective a political machine as any other single-party structure in the Middle East or the Soviet Bloc. But the Shah was not prepared to allow even his own party to assume a meaningful political role and Rastakhiz was soon dismissed by both friend and foe as just another part of the imperial decor. In 1976 the Shah was also disturbed by Jimmy Carter's emphasis on human rights and his criticism of Iran's record during the presidential primaries. The Shah's government did all it could, probably including generous financial donations, to ensure Gerald Ford's victory, but by August 1976 it was sure that Carter would win. For years the Shah had depended heavily on US support and was now, despite his appetite for playing a world role, unable to recognize his and Iran's own strength. He was convinced that the loss of American support would leave his regime exposed to intrigues by both Russia and Great Britain, the two colonial powers of the past which, according to the Shah, would never recognize Iran as master of its own destiny. So, in order to avoid a repeat of the initial troubles he had had with President Kennedy, the Shah embarked on a policy of 'liberalization' even before Carter had won his party's nomination. Several of the Shah's closest aides had for long believed that Iran had to reform its political structure to take into account the economic changes of the preceding decade. Some like Hushang Ansary, the Finance Minister and later chairman of the National Iranian Oil Company (NIOC), argued that Iran could not run a liberal economic system together with an autocratic political set-up for ever. It was partly due to Ansary's influence that the Shah agreed to allow the emergence of two 'wings' to his single Rastakhiz Party. One wing, known as 'constructive liberal', was led by Ansary, while the other, the 'progressive', had Interior Minister Jamshid Amuzegar as leader. Ansary's group urged dialogue and compromise and tried to put its theories to the test by organizing a number of meetings, rallies and 'dialogue sessions' in Tehran and several other cities, but failed to alter the basic course of His Majesty's policies.

Carter's election, which had set the Shah worrying about the future course of his relations with the USA, at the same time encouraged the regime's opponents. They, like the Shah, overestimated Washington's knowledge of the Iranian situation and its role in shaping the Shah's policies. They conceived of the United

States as a traditional imperial power for which long-term planning of policy by experts would be the norm. Both the Shah and his opponents underestimated the profound changes Iran had experienced since 1963 and were, at least until the autumn of 1978, unaware of the power of the masses in reshaping the country's destiny. Ibrahim Yazdi, a naturalized American of Iranian origin and one of Khomeini's closest aides during the revolution, details the impact of Carter's election on the Shah's opponents in a book entitled *Last Efforts in Last Days*.[8] Yazdi writes that he was convinced that the US 'liberals' would want to help get rid of the Shah once they were back in power. As early as November 1976, immediately after Carter's election, Yazdi advised the Ayatollah in Najaf that 'the Shah's friends in Washington are out. . . . It is time to act.'[9] Mehdi Bazargan in his book *Iran's Revolution in Two Moves* also reports that he and other opponents of the Shah resumed their activities as soon as Carter won the Democratic Party's nomination.[10] Two other middle-class opponents of the Shah, Dariush Foruhar and Rahmatollah Moqadam-Maragheh, said in separate conversations in 1976 that Carter's election would 'alter the general outlook'.[11] Foruhar believed that 'the American liberals' would no longer insist on backing the Shah 'against the express wishes of the whole Iranian nation'.[12]

Soon after Carter's election a number of incidents were interpreted, probably quite unreasonably, as signals that Washington meant to end its support of the Shah. Carter's reply to a cable of congratulations from the Shah was, inexplicably, delayed for more than two weeks, giving rise to rumours that the new US president was already dissociating himself from the policy of his predecessors. And the reply, when it eventually arrived, sounded merely polite and bore no resemblance to Nixon's messages and speeches during banquets with the Shah in which the monarch was praised beyond recognition. The next episode was the serialization by *Ettelaat* of Carter's little book entitled *Why Not the Best?* The book was later published in a pocket edition and became a popular gift among opponents of the Shah. Early in the life of the new Administration a speech by Cyrus B. Vance, Carter's Secretary of State, which was indirectly critical of the Shah's human rights record, was translated into Persian and distributed by the US Information Office in Tehran in the usual limited number of copies. But the speech was reprinted by mysterious entrepreneurs and distributed in thousands of copies throughout the country with the heading 'Even US Recognizes the Shah's Savagery'.[13] The resignation of Richard Helms, a former CIA director, as Ambassador to Tehran further strengthened the impression that the period of special relations was drawing to a close. Helms had, in fact, been sent into a respectable exile by Nixon after refusing to cooperate in the Watergate cover-up. But the Shah's opponents had seen Helms's appointment as a sign that Iran was now considered America's main ally in the region. Another incident which emphasized the impression of malaise in relations was Carter's refusal to invite the Shah to Washington until the end of his first year in office.

The Shah's visit to Washington, in the company of Empress Farah, when it eventually materialized in November 1977, was to prove less than a success. The Shah himself raised the question of human rights in Iran and informed the President of fresh measures taken to improve the situation. These included regular inspections of Iranian prisons by the International Red Cross and a royal decree that all torture should cease. In addition, the Shah pointed to his policy of 'open atmosphere' as proof of his goodwill and determination to liberalize the system. Carter, and more especially his wife Rosalynne, were charmed by the Iranian royal couple; Ardeshir Zahedi, the Shah's Ambassador to Washington, was later able to report that relations will be 'as warm as with Nixon, if not warmer'.[14] The Shah, however, could not bring himself either to like or to trust the new President. 'Those frozen blue eyes,' he remarked after meeting Carter. 'Somehow there are no feelings in them at all.'[15] The Shah also believed that Carter had deliberately allowed Iranian opposition groups to demonstrate close to the White House during the royal visit. Supporters and opponents of the Shah clashed violently during the welcoming ceremony on the White House lawn and police were forced to use teargas, as a result of which everyone present, including the Shah, his wife and Carter had to reach for their handkerchiefs. The whole episode was telecast live to Iran and millions of Iranians saw the humiliation to which the King of Kings was being subjected in the capital of his closest friend. The average Iranian, not understanding the niceties of American law on public demonstrations and the First Amendment, interpreted the incident as a deliberate plot by Carter to show that the Shah faced strong and determined opposition from his own people. It is almost certain that the Shah, his sister Ashraf and some of the monarch's closest advisers were of the same opinion and believed Carter to be guilty of hypocrisy. In retrospect, however, it is difficult to imagine that the Carter Administration had worked out any consistent attitude towards the Shah at that early stage. Carter gave the Shah all he had asked for. The Administration would continue to help the Shah acquire all the non-nuclear weapons he wished to buy in the United States. And the President reaffirmed his support for the bilateral defence agreement signed by the late President Dwight D. Eisenhower and the Shah in 1959. The agreement, as the Shah interpreted it, committed the United States to help defend Iran in case of a direct threat from the USSR.

The 'Washington tears', as the incident at the White House was to be called, was taken by the Shah's opponents as a clear signal that the Carter Administration was standing off from the Shah. Ibrahim Yazdi, who was working on a pharmaceutical research project in Houston, Texas, at the time had, in his capacity as president of the Muslim Students' Association of North America – the main pro-Khomeini organization outside Iran – participated in the Washington demonstrations and was able to report to the Ayatollah back in Najaf that the Iranian regime was being abandoned by its principal ally.[16] He also advised the Ayatollah to increase his contact with the people and make more frequent statements.

Carter and Rosalynne repaid the royal couple's visit to Washington by arriving in Tehran for a twenty-hour state visit on 31 December 1977. As a result Carter had to send his televised New Year message to the American people from one of the Shah's palaces in Tehran. The coincidence was seized upon by courtiers in Tehran as a sure sign that the imperial capital was now the nerve centre of the 'Free World' and that Carter, whatever his initial reservations about the Shah, was now as converted as his predecessors. The opposition did not share this view and more than a dozen 'open letters' addressed to Carter were circulated in Tehran. They all praised the new President for his stand on human rights and called on him to extend his campaign promises to Iran also. Khomeini issued an uncharacteristically moderate statement from Najaf, an indication of Yazdi's success in urging a conciliatory attitude towards the new Administration.

In Najaf, the Ayatollah, accepting Yazdi's advice, worked out a programme of regular appearances at the holy shrine of Imam Ali. He would arrive at the shrine around 10 p.m. when it was virtually empty of the mass of pilgrims, preachers, soothsayers, undertakers, healers, dervishes, luminaries, exorcists, water-bearers, dispellers of charms, casters of leeches, vendors, Iraqi and Iranian secret police agents easily recognized by their light-coloured Dacron suits and dark sunglasses, *talabehs*, temporary concubines, opium and hasheesh-pushers, reciters of the Holy Book, barbers, removers of unwanted hair from female faces, interpreters of the astrolabe and part-time butchers ready to cut the throat of a sacrificial lamb for a modest fee. The Ayatollah could, in fact, have the whole shrine to himself and his supporters. In that impressive setting the Ayatollah would sit on a prayer mat and welcome his supporters to 'this resting place of my martyred ancestor, Ali, Commander of the Faithful'. He would first lead his followers in common prayer, fulfilling one of the most cherished dreams of every Shi'ite. According to tradition, those who pray at Ali's shrine will be given larger rooms in paradise. The Iranians who visited Najaf in those days belonged to a small privileged minority.

Iranians had been prevented from visiting Najaf and the other holy cities of Mesopotamia since 1968 when deteriorating relations between Tehran and Baghdad led to the interruption of travel links between the two neighbours. A limited number of Iranians, about 1200 a month, were allowed to visit Iraq from the middle of 1976 onwards after relations between Tehran and Baghdad had warmed up once again. At first, few of these visitors dared establish contact with Khomeini. But by the beginning of 1978 the Ayatollah's nocturnal assemblies at the shrine attracted hundreds of Iranian pilgrims. The Ayatollah would bless all those present and then embark on his usual tirade against the Shah and his father. He would tell them that the Pahlavi dynasty had been established by the British and was now sustained by the Americans for the sole purpose of destroying Islam in Iran. The Zionists who ruled America had allied themselves with the Cross-Worshippers in order to accomplish what the Crusaders failed to do. 'If the Shah is not destroyed,' the Ayatollah would tell his incredulous and yet no less attentive audience, 'you shall all become slaves of pagans. Foreigners shall take your womenfolk; they shall plunder all your natural wealth and put the Muslim community to eternal shame.'[17]

Members of the audience would tape the Ayatollah's sermon and take it back to Iran as a curious souvenir from the holy land. At the end of his sermon the Ayatollah would suddenly rise and leave the shrine, allowing only a few lucky believers to kiss his hand or the hem of his *'aba* (a kind of thin overcoat made of camel hair) before boarding a ramshackle Magirus Deutz minibus driven by Ayatollah Doa'i. Ahmad would stay behind for another hour to answer questions, exchange addresses and reassure yawning Iraqi security agents who had been ordered to prepare regular reports on the Ayatollah's nocturnal sorties. During the summer of 1978 Khomeini was drawing between 3000 and 4000 people to meetings at the shrine and was also having an impact on the local Shi'ite population. At times he would be joined by his friend Mohammad-Baqer Sadr, who was already emerging as the Iraqi regime's *bête noire*.

It is impossible to estimate the exact number of Khomeini tapes distributed in Iran during 1978. But Parviz Sabeti, head of SAVAK's 'anti-subversion unit', believed that the number exceeded 100,000. That meant that millions of Iranians were able to hear Khomeini's uncompromising condemnation of the Shah directly and were encouraged by his total lack of regard for conventional rules of politesse when speaking of 'the hated Shah, the Jewish agent, the American snake whose head must be smashed with a stone'.[18] On a number of occasions, SAVAK suggested a crackdown on distributors of Khomeini tapes as well as a temporary ban on visits to Najaf by Iranians. But the Shah would have none of that. He had promised Carter, and apparently himself, that he would liberalize the regime and was not ready to change his mind. The sale of the Ayatollah's tapes was quickly taken up by regular networks of the trade and the octogenarian exile joined the hit-parade charts of the capital. Khomeini tapes were simply marked '*Sokhanrani Mazhabi*' (Religious Sermon) and sold alongside the latest offerings of popular singers like Gugush and Dariush.

The tapes helped inflame passions in a country already well on the way to compensate for nearly twelve years of silence and docility. It seems that every society needs a normal dose of strikes, demonstrations, protest movements and other acts symbolizing dissent at any given time. Iran had, at least since 1966, been denied its normal dose thanks to the Shah's pathological fear of any manifestation of dissent. The Shah believed politics to be the curse of human society and politicians to be cynical rogues who would think nothing of causing death and misery in the pursuit of their abject ambitions. He had been determined to make Iran a society free of politics and one totally devoted to economic progress and social advancement on the basis of tight control and 'iron discipline'. At a meeting of leading industrialists in 1970 the Shah had advised all managers to anticipate the wishes of their workers so that these could be granted 'even before any worker has formulated them'. When Mahmoud Khayyami, a car manufacturer, suggested that workers should be allowed to strike so that they could feel they had won something through their own efforts, the Shah all but lost his temper. 'We are here to give our people everything,' he observed. 'We shall look after every Iranian from the womb to the tomb.'[19] The Shah also disliked crowds and believed that human beings can be creative and accomplish 'positive deeds' only as individuals or by working in small groups. Large crowds could lead only to frenzy, unleashing man's 'inner urge to destroy'.[20] In 1978 the Shah was to have more than his share of strikes and face ever growing crowds of opponents. He looked like a man whose luck has run out and every time draws a blank.

Jamshid Amuzegar, the American-trained engineer who had replaced Hoveyda as Prime Minister, lacked the political experience and the nervous stamina required for coping with a burgeoning revolutionary situation. Unlike Hoveyda, who had been a political animal, Amuzegar was the archetypal technocrat and believed that every social, economic or political problem would, eventually, have a technical solution. He identified inflation and the slowdown in economic growth as the main problems his government had to solve. To achieve this he adopted Carter's favourite 'zero-based budgeting', and organized a 'monetarist' onslaught on government expenditure across the board. Among the items he cut, no doubt without paying the matter much attention, was some £20 million which the Prime Minister's office spent on humouring thousands of mullahs every year. Many mullahs were dependent on the secret donations they received from the Premier's office; many more used the money as welcome additional income. The sudden cut meant that a large number of mullahs no longer had any reason to support the regime. Some of the mullahs went straight to the opposition while others slipped into the background. By September 1978 Sayyed Hassan Emami, the Friday Prayer Leader of Tehran and the only high-ranking mullah still close to the Shah, was bitterly noting that the regime was, for the first time, left without any friends in Qom or Mashhad.[21] Motahari, always quick to exploit every opportunity, put the more vocal of the jilted mullahs on the payroll of his growing organization.

In Tehran the massive demonstration marking the feast of Fitr, at the end of the fasting month of Ramadan, put forward the movement's basic slogans. These could be divided into three categories.

The first, and by far the largest, consisted of slogans emphasizing Khomeini's leadership. The most celebrated among these were: 'Allah is the Greatest, Khomeini is the leader' and 'Allah, Qur'an, Khomeini'. The second category consisted of slogans against the Shah and his dynasty. These included 'Death to the Shah' and 'This American Shah must be put to death'. The third category included slogans exalting martyrdom and promising the ideal Islamic society, more notably 'The only way to Salvation is Faith, Holy War and Martyrdom'.[22]

The pattern of the movement's activities was by now clear. It brought people together for religious occasions, of which there are over a hundred in each Iranian calendar year, or for mourning ceremonies marking the fall of the martyrs. The crowds attending the ceremony at a mosque, *hosseinieh*, *mahdieh* or *takiyah* would then pour into the streets and launch attacks on 'places of sin' such as cinemas, banks, girls' schools and cafés. Whenever there was a chance of confrontation with the security forces, the crowd would organize itself into a peaceful procession, at the head of which were schoolchildren followed by women and old people. The idea, suggested by Khomeini himself, was that the security forces should be faced with a choice between firing on children and women or doing nothing. 'The death of a child is especially important,' the Ayatollah said in one of his taped instructions. 'When a child dies the true nature of this Zionist regime becomes clear.' The mullahs were instructed to avoid confrontation with the security forces and to encourage other people to do the fighting on their behalf.

The typical Khomeini crowd in Tehran numbered around 2000 to 3000, representing a surprisingly wide cross-section of the population. The only social groups conspicuously absent from these crowds until the very last weeks of the struggle consisted of factory workers and peasants. Shopkeepers, lumpen elements, middle-class merchants, intellectuals, teachers, students, high-society ladies in expensive fur coats and, of course, mullahs and *talabehs* formed the crowds. Bazargan who was present in most demonstrations notes that very few mullahs took an active part in the early marches, presumably on instructions from Motahari to 'lead the crowd from behind'.[23]

The government's attempts at staging pro-Shah demonstrations in Qom, Isfahan and Tehran proved a failure, and Amuzegar, visiting Tabriz after the uprising there, did not convey any mood of determination to the 300,000 people who had been brought to the central square to listen to him. Almost daily statements by Khomeini, Shariatmadari, Mara'ashi and other leading mullahs continued to inflame passions and fan the fires of revolt. A standard tactic was to force the bazaars to close so as to keep tension high. Shopkeepers who refused to comply with instructions from the local organizers of the movement would find their shops locked by strangers in the night or simply burned down. People reputed to be supporters of the regime were given a chance to prove they had changed their ways or they would see the windows of their homes broken and dead cats thrown into their gardens. In some cases, such culprits would have their cars set on fire. In some localities the 'Shah-lovers' would suffer a social boycott with everyone refusing to trade with them or even talk to them. An attempt by Abdul-Majid Majidi, leader of the progressive wing of the Shah's Rastakhiz party, to organize community defence groups met with some success in the western Iranian city of Reza'iyeh but had to be abandoned, leaving Motahari's militants a completely free hand.

By the summer of 1978 Khomeini had consolidated his leadership of the movement and was able to announce in a statement sent from Najaf that the large number of political parties and groups then active against the Shah were joining 'the nation, only in the pursuit of their own interests'. He wrote: 'This holy movement which began on 15 Khordad was founded by the powerful hand of the clergy with support from the great Iranian nation. It is being led by the clergy without the interference of any party, front or personality. Our movement, which is now fifteen years old, is purely Islamic and shall continue under the leadership of the clergy without the slightest participation of anyone else in leading it.'[24] He also warned those who were trying to 'appear as leaders' that the clergy would 'in time make their fate clear'.[25] That could mean assassination.

Khomeini's messages, now being regularly broadcast by the Persian service of the BBC from London, established him as the undisputed leader of the movement. He continued to radicalize the crowds, to urge them to attack the Shah more violently and to encourage clashes with security forces. 'Our movement,' he said in a message, 'is but a fragile plant as yet. It needs the blood of martyrs to help it grow into a towering tree.'[26]

Despite the Ayatollah's claim that no one else played a part in leading the movement, a variety of political organizations were intimately involved. The pro-Soviet Tudeh Party, using its small but effective clandestine organization, played a key role in waging psychological warfare against the regime. The Mujahedeen and Fedayeen guerrilla organizations were also making their presence felt by organizing attacks on police stations and murdering specially selected SAVAK agents and other officials. Tudeh and the Fedayeen also began campaigning for industrial strikes at factory level. But the Left's main contribution came in the form of a series of attacks on American military personnel in Isfahan. These attacks developed into a serious security risk for the US military authorities when the presence of scores of guerrillas trained by the PLO or the Libyan government was signalled in the Isfahan region. These guerrillas were led by Mohammad-Ali Montazeri, nicknamed 'Ayatollah Ringo' for his agility with a Magnum which he constantly carried under his *'aba*. 'Ringo' was a close friend of Libya's Colonel Moammar al Gaddafi. He had spent three years in Libya as an honoured guest receiving 'military training' and had been Gaddafi's partner in countless games of backgammon. Having tasted torture at the hands of SAVAK in the 1960s, 'Ringo' had vowed to devote his life to bringing down the Shah. Returning to Iran on a false passport a few months earlier, 'Ringo' had set up headquarters in his native Isfahan, where he founded the Sazaman Towhidi e Saff (the Unitary Organization of the Line), known as Saff for short. In only eleven days in August, Saff was able to burn eighty-five bank branches and destroy one cinema in an explosion. It also organized a Molotov-cocktail attack on two hotels, the Shah Abbas, Iran's most luxurious, and the Pol, which was a popular meeting place for the high bourgeoisie of the city. Probably helped by the Mujahedeen and other Leftist groups, Saff also attacked several municipal offices and set fire to thousands of rates records. Hundreds of anonymous letters were posted to Americans living in Isfahan inviting them to return home before they 'lose your good health'. Finally, the Iranian wife of an American teacher was attacked in the bazaar by two youths who threw acid on her face. 'Ringo' and his group also organized a crowd of some 30,000 people to welcome Ayatollah Sayyed Jalal Taheri Esfahani who was returning home from exile. Esfahani had been allowed to end his internal exile at the same time as Ayatollah Hassan Tabataba'i-Qomi, who had been under house arrest in Karaj, near Tehran, for over twelve years. Esfahani's first move was to call on the faithful to 'get rid of American Zionists'. This led to an attack on his house by SAVAK agents who were apparently looking for 'Ringo' and his Libyan-trained companions.

The ayatollah's wife had two front teeth broken by a SAVAK man who did not appreciate her screams. The ayatollah himself was once again transferred to Tehran. Esfahani left a message calling on the faithful to 'cleanse the city'. He said: 'Isfahan is now hosting the drug-addict American rejects of Saigon. These broken bits of America's Zionist army have come here to impose on this city of Islam their civilization of prostitution, sodomy, addiction and acoholism.'[27] The ayatollah's house became the scene of endless meetings in which the frequency of anti-American slogans and speeches indicated a strong Leftist presence.

It was partly to reassure American military personnel, who were beginning to talk of leaving Iran because of the troubles, that the government decided to impose martial law on the city. As Isfahan began experiencing a sinister calm under General Reza Naji, instantly dubbed 'Boris Karloff' because of his physical resemblance to the British actor, the militants who had provoked martial law left for other cities. Travelling in minibuses, they went from one town to another, burning banks, cinemas, cafés and government offices. Very soon the Tudeh Party provided invaluable help by resuming broadcasts from Baku, in Soviet Azerbaijan, in Persian. The Soviets had at first dismissed the Khomeini revolt as a bubble that would burst, noting that no 'large popular classes' were involved. But Tudeh was finally successful in persuading Moscow to hedge its bets by allowing the resumption of the Baku broadcasts after nearly a decade. These Persian programmes were entirely devoted to teaching techniques of demonstration, the production of Molotov-cocktails and plastic bombs and what tactics to adopt when fighting security forces.

The merchant class, including the bazaaris and the high-street shopkeepers, were already angry with the regime. For over a year they had suffered a crackdown from the government in its anti-inflation campaign. No fewer than 250,000 merchants and shopkeepers, including some of the wealthiest in the country, had been fined, imprisoned or exiled, or had had their places of trade shut for weeks as punishment for alleged overcharging and violation of fixed prices. Still recovering from heavy losses and hurt feelings caused by the anti-inflation campaign, the bazaaris and shopkeepers were hit by another new governmental measure in 1978. The Ministry of Social Security and Health announced that insurance schemes covering industrial and office workers would now be extended to employees in the distributive trades as well. That meant a hefty bill for over 2 million bazaaris and shopkeepers at a time when they had to cope with problems caused by an overall reduction in demand.

Until the summer of 1978 the Shah was convinced that the industrial workers and the bulk of the peasantry who had benefited from his land reform projects would support his regime. With their help, he felt confident that he could eventually crush any revolt by the bazaaris and the mullahs who had been his traditional enemies, while the new-rich middle class played a double game. Very soon, however, his regime was under attack both in factories and in villages. A group of militant power workers began pulling the plugs out for several hours each day as a sign of 'protest against state violence'. Before long it became impossible not to strike, at least for a few hours each day, as crowds of women and children, led by mullahs, surrounded the factories, weeping and wailing and shouting: 'They are killing our husbands and fathers, how can you work, O Muslims?' Daily street marches, strikes and attacks on 'symbols of Western corruption' became routine in more than two dozen cities, although Tehran itself remained relatively calm. Islamic committees headed by mullahs were now in existence in almost every district of the major cities. The committees had at their disposal full-time volunteer 'marchers' and motorcyclists, organized in bands of between three and thirty, who were used for hit-and-run attacks against banks, government buildings and other designated targets. These motorcyclists, wearing green armbands, were mostly aged between twelve and twenty and called themselves Motorihay-e-Allah (Allah's Motorized Ones). In Tehran alone their number was estimated at around 70,000. An attempt by the government to stop this army of motorcylists by imposing a blanket ban on all imports of spare parts failed when it was revealed that enough spare parts were already in stock for at least two years. A further decision by the government that motorcylists should obtain special permits was never taken seriously and never applied.

Motahari's Islamic committees were already beginning to manoeuvre themselves into position as alternative sources of authority. They would, for example, take over traffic control in key squares, forcing the regular police off the scene. Another favourite tactic was to occupy a major street and close it for several hours in a show of force and in defiance of the police. While under 'occupation', the street in question would be covered with pictures of Khomeini and slogans against the Shah. Every shop in the street would be forced to display a portrait of the Ayatollah while residents of every house or block of flats would be contacted and told to join the movement or risk 'being left exposed to the anger of our youths who have had so many of their friends martyred for Allah'.

This almost routine pattern of events was shattered on 18 August when what was without doubt the single most horrible event in Iran's recent history took place. The Rex Cinema, one of the best theatres in the oil city of Abadan, was offering a special late-night programme consisting of a short documentary on the Shah's achievements followed by a feature film by leading film-maker Massoud Kimaa'i, when a fire broke out. Within a few minutes the entire cinema was engulfed in rapidly spreading flames. The audience, more than a thousand strong, soon found to its horror that all the exit doors had been closed and blocked from the outside. Fire engines arrived on the scene within fifteen minutes but could not begin operations, ostensibly for lack of water in the pipes in the street, for a further half an hour, by which time the smell of burnt human flesh had spread to much of the city. At least six hundred people were burned to death while a further three hundred were rushed to hospital. The tragedy created such widespread shock that for two full days neither the regime nor its opponents knew how to react. The indecision was broken by Khomeini, who sent a message, broadcast by the BBC, accusing the government of having planned and executed 'this horrendous crime'. The Tudeh Party's clandestinely produced daily news bulletin *Navid* (*Good News*) took up the theme and claimed that the Shah had personally dispatched a Brigadier General Razmi to Abadan to 'arrange this tragedy'.[28] Neither the Ayatollah nor *Navid*, however, condemned attacks on cinemas as such and the planting of bombs in cinemas continued as a key revolutionary tactic right to the end.

The Shah was left with the choice of either donning his iron gloves once again or pressing on with his 'liberalization' policy. He chose the latter and dismissed Amuzegar, appointing in his place Jaafar Sharif-Emami, the President of the Senate. Sharif-Emami was supposed to have a number of assets in dealing with the mullahs, who were by then recognized as the principal force of opposition. He was related to Grand Ayatollah Golpayegani and was himself the son of a mullah. But Sharif-Emami, who had spent the previous fourteen years mostly looking after his own numerous business ventures as well as running the Pahlavi Foundation for the Shah, was totally out of touch with the country's political and social issues. He saw 'these troubles' as the result of intrigues by SAVAK, which did not like 'liberalization', and also blamed the British for 'wanting to show their displeasure at the appointment of Amuzegar', who was supposed to be pro-American.[29]

Sharif-Emami immediately announced a number of measures aimed at meeting some genuine religious grievances. These included reversion to the Islamic calendar which had been replaced by an imperial Persian one two years earlier on the orders of the Shah. The government also pledged to organize a return to 'real Islamic time' instead of official time, which meant that the faithful had to say their prayers one hour late. Sharif-Emami also ordered the closure of Iran's four casinos and the banning of films 'containing suggestive scenes'. Some restrictions were also imposed on night clubs and restaurants serving liquor and wine. The new government's 'evil genius', Manuchehr Azmun, also announced that a special delegation would be sent to Najaf to invite 'His Holiness Khomeini' to return home and resume 'his services to Islam in the holy city of Qom'.

The arrival of Sharif-Emami and his conciliatory gestures were instantly interpreted as signs of weakness on the part of the Shah. Azmun was seen on television indirectly criticizing the Shah himself and adopting pseudo-revolutionary language. The opportunity provided by Sharif-Emami's obvious hesitation and lack of orientation was seized by thousands of anti-Shah militants who had spent years in Europe, the United States and the Middle East to return to Iran en masse and strengthen the ranks of the leadership at middle and lower levels.

Among those returning were guerrillas trained by Al Fatah in Lebanon, including Mohammad Gharazi, the future Islamic Oil Minister, Jalaleddin Farsi, Khomeini's special representative to the PLO, and Ayatollah Ali Janati, who had taken part in several Al Fatah operations against Israel. Scores of Lebanese Shi'ite fighters, organized in the paramilitary group Amal under Mostafa Chamran, also arrived in Iran and played an active role in the revolution.

The net result of Sharif-Emami's policy of 'national reconciliation' was a further blow to the morale of the armed forces and an open invitation to the opponents of the regime to intensify their campaign. But the new government went even further and began releasing the three thousand or so political prisoners still held. All those released joined the anti-regime movement without a moment's delay, further fanning the fires of revolt. Among those released was Ayatollah Hussein-Ali Montazeri, later to become Khomeini's designated heir as Jurisconsult, who had spent seven years in prison. Montazeri was released on the express understanding that he would not leave Tehran, but was on his way to Najaf, where he met Khomeini, the following day.

Sharif-Emami and Azmun, whose official title was Minister of State, also worked out a Machiavellian scheme under which Imam Mussa Sadr, the leader of the Lebanese Shi'ites, would be invited to support the Shah. Sadr had been close to the monarch for years but had broken with him after a quarrel with the Iranian Ambassador to Beirut, Mansur Qadar. But the Shah still believed that their old friendship could be revived. The trouble, however, was that Sadr had mysteriously disappeared during a visit to Libya and could not be traced. The Shah sent a special emissary, Hushang Moqtaderi, on a tour of Arab capitals and specially enlisted the help of Jordan's King Hussein to find the missing Sadr and presumably build him up against Khomeini. Sadr, although related to Khomeini, had never sided with the Ayatollah openly and was closer to the more moderate Grand Ayatollahs. It was, perhaps, partly to pre-empt any attempt at building up Sadr that Khomeini's supporters began calling the Ayatollah 'Imam' as a regular title, despite Motahari's initial objections. Sadr was never found and there is almost no doubt that he would not have cooperated with the Shah in any case. But the episode further illustrated the regime's disorientation and helplessness in the face of events.

Early in September the demonstrations, which had partly ceased as a result of the Rex Cinema fire and the formation of a new Cabinet, resumed throughout the country. Tehran, however, was still relatively calm. It seemed as if the clergy wanted to conquer the whole country first before launching their final attack on the capital. But many activists were too impatient and did not see the logic of Motahari's gradualist strategy. They were convinced that they could simply attack and occupy the main official buildings and invite Khomeini to return to Tehran. The militants also multiplied the number of small clashes with the security forces. And on 5 September at least a dozen police stations in Tehran were attacked and, in two of them, the officers on duty were disarmed. These attacks were almost certainly the work of the Mujahedeen, the Fedayeen and other maverick groups anxious to wrest control of the movement away from the mullahs by upstaging them. The government, under strong pressure from the new Interior Minister, General Abbas-Karim Gharabaghi, decided to impose martial law on Tehran and twenty-three other cities. An announcement on 6 September said that nearly 10 million Iranians were to be put under martial law from midnight. All public gatherings of more than three people were banned and army units were moved into the city centres. Sharif-Emami believed this show of force would pacify the military while giving him enough time in which to negotiate a deal with Qom and Mashhad, isolating Khomeini in Najaf. As a sign of goodwill the proclamation of martial law was not accompanied by any arrests. The following day, a Friday, the capital was unusually quiet, but around Jaleh Square, near the Parliament building, small groups of demonstrators began assembling for a meeting announced a week earlier. It was obvious that they had not heard of the imposition of martial law and thought that they were attending another routine meeting at the invitation of the local mullah, Shaikh Mohammad Nasiri, alias Yahya Nuri. Troops guarding the Parliament building about a mile away reported the gathering on their closed-circuit radio and were instantly ordered to disperse the crowd. A detachment of infantrymen was also dispatched as reinforcement. When the soldiers and the crowd came face to face, it was all smiles at first. The crowd began to scatter when some of the Motorcyclists of Allah suddenly turned back and drove into the troops' formation shouting 'Allah is the greatest.' Nervous soldiers began to fire and several riders were killed instantly. The crowd returned and began charging the troops. Someone shouted over a loudhailer that the troops facing the people were Israeli soldiers. The soldiers were, in fact, Kurdish and because the Tehrani crowd did not understand their dialect they could be mistaken for Israelis. 'Massacre the Jews!' thundered the loudhailers from among the crowd and some snipers began firing from a water department building on the square. By the time the crowd had been dispersed at least two hundred people had died, the largest number of casualties after the Rex Cinema fire. The religious leaders in Tehran immediately announced that 'thousands have been massacred by Zionist troops'.[30] The government put the number of dead at fifty-nine. Later, the number of Jaleh Square martyrs was inflated to 15,000.[31]

The killing, so obviously wanton, ended all chances of Sharif-Emami's attempt to achieve a measure of calm and appeared a deliberate act of violence on the part of the regime which had tolerated scores of much larger demonstrations before. Later government claims that demonstrators aimed to occupy Parliament convinced no one. The incident at Jaleh Square marked the end of the regime.

# 13

# *The Face in the Moon*

The Day the Imam Returns

The day the Imam returns
no one will tell lies any more
no one will lock the door of his house;
people will become brothers
sharing the bread of their joys together
in justice and in sincerity.
There will no longer be any queues:
queues of bread and meat,
queues of kerosene and petrol,
queues of cinemas and buses
queues of tax-payments,
queues of snake poison
shall all disappear.
And the dawn of awakening
and the spring of freedom
shall smile upon us.

The Imam must return . . .
so that Right can sit on its throne
so that evil, treachery and hatred
are eliminated from the face of time.
When the Iman returns,
Iran — this broken, wounded mother —
will for ever be liberated
from the shackles of tyranny and ignorance
and the chains of plunder, torture and prison.

Taha Hejazi's poem calling for Ayatollah Khomeini's return to
Tehran[1]

*O*ne typically hot evening in September 1978, when Tehran was still recovering from the latest round of street battles between the supporters of Ayatollah Khomeini and the Shah's troops, an Iraqi Airline Boeing arrived at Mehrabad Airport on an unscheduled flight. Aboard was only one passenger: Barzan Takriti, half-brother of Iraq's strong man Saddam Hussein and that country's secret police chief. Barzan was taken directly to the Shah's Niavaran Palace, which, suffering like the rest of the capital from power-cuts ordered by the Ayatollah. looked like the haunted abode of ghosts rather than the residence of the King of Kings.

Barzan's message on behalf of his brother was simple: His Majesty must stand firm and Iraq would be prepared to help in every way. The security chief more than hinted that the physical liquidation of the troublesome mullah could be arranged.

The Shah, expressing his gratitude for President Hussein's concern and offer of help, ruled out any suggestion of organizing an unfortunate accident for Khomeini. Instead, however, he asked the Iraqis to force the Ayatollah to leave their country. Barzan instantly agreed. This was the second time he had been helpful. Earlier he had helped SAVAK 'capture' the man who was to be presented as the ringleader of the group responsible for the fire at Abadan's Rex Cinema. The man, Abdul-Reza Ashur, twenty-two, was an Iraqi security agent serving in the Iranian port of Khorramshahr. He was ordered to organize a fake escape by boat through the Shatt al-Arab waterway so that he could be 'captured' by Iranian guards. Ashur was further ordered to confess instantly to having acted on direct orders from Khomeini himself. The show was designed to cool tempers in Iran and to exonerate SAVAK, which was wrongly but plausibly accused of having organized the Abadan tragedy.[2]

The reason why the Shah refused to have Khomeini murdered was plain enough: such a move would have inflamed passions in Iran beyond all possible control. Khomeini was no longer just a spiritual leader but commanded a strong nationwide political network complete with hundreds of heavily armed, highly trained urban guerrillas. It had been his tactic to retain the posture of the weak, wronged party and to speak on behalf of 'the helpless victims of armed tyranny'. This had kept the armed crowds seeking vengeance under control. The Ayatollah's death would change all that. Khomeini wanted to win a spiritual victory, to show the superiority of the faith over the sword, as he put it. The younger revolutionaries, on the other hand, were bent on guerrilla warfare and on using the many machine guns they had smuggled into the country with so much difficulty. Further, they did not believe that only a few messages from Khomeini could end the Shah's regime; a revolution without some dramatic fighting would lack much of the glory it deserved.

The Shah's reasons for asking the Iraqis to expel Khomeini were different, and eventually they were proved wrong. The Shah believed that Khomeini's presence in Najaf, one of the holiest cities of Shi'ism, gave the Ayatollah a degree of religious authority which he would lack anywhere else. The Shah also thought, and said so on a number of occasions, that the Western world, which by now he believed to be mortally opposed to his rule, should see 'the alternative'.[3] The Shah was warned that the West would instantly approve 'anything exotic' and was reminded of how a new film version of *King Kong* in 1977 had resulted in a great show of sympathy for the captured beast. 'The West would find Khomeini colourful and would adopt him instantly,' the Shah was advised.[4] Nevertheless, the monarch's will prevailed and Khomeini was ordered to leave Iraq within forty-eight hours.

The Ayatollah had prepared himself both for death and for expulsion, and Barzan's order occasioned no surprise. Khomeini immediately wrote and sealed his will, as was his habit at the start of every major journey. He also informed his supporters abroad. One of them, Ibrahim Yazdi, flew into Iraq and reached Najaf in time to accompany the Ayatollah to the Kuwaiti border. Kuwait seemed a natural choice: it was not far from Iran and contained a strong Palestinian presence; Yasser Arafat could ensure the Ayatollah's safety, while Shi'ites of Iranian origin, forming some 10 per cent of the population, would enable the exile of Najaf to be surrounded by sympathetic crowds. The Kuwaitis, however, refused Khomeini and his party entry into their territory. Yazdi's request for a forty-eight-hour stay in Kuwait were also rejected and the small band of exiles was caught in no-man's-land between the two Arab states. The Iraqis eventually allowed the Ayatollah and his companions to travel to Baghdad under guard and there to seek visas from other countries. In Baghdad the Ayatollah was soon informed that France had agreed to issue visas, thanks to the efforts of Sadeq Ghotbzadeh, the future Foreign Minister, who lived in Paris. The Ayatollah was reluctant to travel to Paris, which he referred to as 'the capital of the Franks' recalling the role 'that tribe' had played against Islam in the Crusades. Sayyed

Ahmad, having unsuccessfully tried to contact the Syrian Embassy for temporary visas, urged his father to accept the French offer and the prospect of spending months, if not years, in a land of Cross-Worshippers.

Khomeini's transfer to a Parisian suburb early in October, however, was to have the opposite effect to that which the Shah had expected. It took the Ayatollah a few days to resign himself to the idea of living in a non-Muslim land. He was careful not to touch unclean objects and not to have his eyes polluted by looking at impurities. Throughout the journey from Orly-Sud Airport near Paris to the suburb of Cachan, the Ayatollah kept his head down so as not to see the surrounding scenery. He spent a few days in Bani-Sadr's small flat while a house in another suburb was being made ready for him. The house, in Neauphle-le-Château, had to be fitted with a 'Turkish' lavatory as the Ayatollah would not use the European-style one that already existed. Part of the house also had to be separated from the reception area so that Batul and Sayyed Ahmad's wife, still in Najaf but soon to join their husbands, could enjoy the proper measure of seclusion from the world of men. The local municipality at first warned that issuing licences for such alterations could take months but subsequently gave its consent within a day after being approached by the Quai d'Orsay.

Once joined by Batul and fully settled at Neauphle-le-Château, which he referred to as 'Noffal', the Ayatollah set to work with an energy that surprised friend and foe. Sayyed Ahmad headed an informal action committee consisting of Bani-Sadr, Ghotbzadeh, Yazdi and Hassan Ibrahim-Habibi. They held long meetings with Khomeini and advised him on the themes that should be developed in order to win support from the West. Khomeini was to stop, or at least to limit, attacks on the United States and 'the corrupt West', and to concentrate his fire against the Shah. The Ayatollah was also to avoid being drawn on the subject of equality for women and his plans for the literal implementation of *shari'a* law. A network of direct contact with Tehran was quickly established with the help of the local post office, which provided two telex and six telephone lines within a few hours. For the first time in nearly sixteen years Khomeini could be in almost hourly contact with Motahari, his field commander in Tehran. Breaking a life-long tradition, the Ayatollah began using the telephone personally and held long conversations with both Motahari and Montazeri, who was once again back in Tehran. A local tape-recording studio was approached and agreed to leave all other business aside and produce thousands of tapes of Ayatollah's daily messages and interviews for dispatch to Tehran. Khomeini's messages now reached Tehran hour by hour, and journalists from all over the world flocked to photograph, film and interview the holy man. A stream of religious and political leaders also visited 'Noffal'; they included Bazargan, Karim Sanjabi of the pro-Mossadeq National Front, Motahari, Ayatollah Mohammad-Hussein Beheshti (who was emerging as a key figure in the movement even then) and scores of leading bazaar merchants who brought with them donations of more than £20 million in cash.

Yazdi, worried that SAVAK might make an attempt on Khomeini's life, organized a special bodyguard for the Ayatollah. This consisted of some fifty men brought from Tehran and allowed to bear light arms while on duty at 'Noffal'. A few months later, they were to form the nucleus of the Islamic Revolutionary Guards which Yazdi created together with Chamran. Yazdi also suspected the CIA of having bugged the Ayatollah's residence and using an ice-cream van for the purpose of listening to the telephone conversations of the revolutionary leaders. The suggestion to invite the French to inspect the house was, however, rejected for fear that the inspectors themselves might install electronic devices of their own.[5]

In that Parisian suburb the Ayatollah gave a total of 132 radio, television and press interviews during his four-month stay. He issued some fifty declarations which were quickly published and distributed in Tehran. He also addressed a total of 100,000 Iranians who came at an average rate of over a thousand each day to pray with him, hear him speak or simply kiss his hand and depart. Many brought with them cash gifts but most were students pouring into France from Britain, West Germany, Italy and even the United States. The Ayatollah sat under an apple tree on a tribal rug and poured out his sulphuric hatred of the Shah at meeting after meeting, describing him as 'a wounded snake' and calling on his followers to 'finish him off, lest he finds new life to bite back'. He rejected Bazargan's suggestion of more gradual progress towards a change of regime, and expressed the fear that the people faced the danger of 'cooling down with the passage of time'.

Keeping quiet about his radical views on social and legal issues, he put himself forward as a moderate man who asked only for an end to tyranny and corruption, and went out of his way to reassure the Iranian middle class that the fall of the Shah would not change the country's social and economic system and that every 'rightful privilege' would be retained. He also allayed the West's fears that an 'Islamic' government might threaten the flow of oil and trade in the Persian Gulf.

The French were the first to be persuaded that a government under Khomeini would offer them a golden opportunity in Iran. Valéry Giscard d'Estaing, the French President, also began advising his Western allies not to try to prolong the Shah's regime.

Khomeini had warned his field commanders in Iran to stay out of the limelight as much as possible, but to control the movement more firmly than ever. He did not want the mullahs to give the impression that they were seeking to exercise power directly. The mullahs, he said again and again, would not serve in executive positions, and would be content with the moral and spiritual guidance of society. He whetted the appetite for power of numerous politicians and encouraged them to believe that they would be the future rulers of Iran. At the same time, however, the Ayatollah made absolutely no concessions to anyone and made it clear that he alone was in charge of the revolution. For example, he told Bazargan to organize his friends for 'responsibilities you will assume in future'. The frustrated Bazargan, who was worried that the country was heading for a bloodbath, gained the impression that the revolution was already victorious as far as Khomeini was concerned.[6] Hassan Nazih, a lawyer turned politician, also visited Khomeini at Neauphle-le-Château and found him to be 'a cold and determined man'. 'He was convinced that he is in direct communication with Allah,' Nazih later recalled. 'Khomeini's arrogance shocked me even then.'

Others, however, did not detect arrogance in the old man's attitude and admired him both for his energy and his modest way of life. A man who was content to sleep on the floor and eat bread, cheese and pistachios could not be accused of arrogance. Further, in speech after speech addressed to 'my suffering but brave people' the Ayatollah took care to refer to himself as 'your servant', 'a nobody', 'a mere *talabeh*' or 'an old man in his last days'. Many people, including some foreign leaders, saw Khomeini as a holy man expressing an entire nation's outrage against a corrupt and tyrannical regime. Andrew Young, the US Permanent Representative at the United Nations and a close friend and adviser of President Carter, described Khomeini as 'a twentieth-century Saint'.

During his stay at Neauphle-le-Château Khomeini used all the traditional techniques of Shi'ite leadership. These included *khod'eh*, which means tricking one's enemy into a misjudgement of one's true position. Khomeini did not tell direct lies but used many half-truths based on well-established *khod'eh* tactics. Later, in 1984, he admitted having used *khod'eh* in order to trick 'the enemies of Islam'. One example was his repeated assurances that women would enjoy every freedom and be treated as the equals of men. Another example was his pledge of full press freedom. He did not lie, in the strictest sense, because he qualified every pledge with phrases such as 'in accordance with Islam' or 'on the basis of the Qur'an'. Few people wanted to notice these important qualifications and the various political factions began to consider Khomeini as one of their own. To the liberals he was a man fighting a dictatorship and calling for the people's right to choose the government. The Left loved him for his demands for 'justice and equity' and 'an end to exploitation'. The conservatives saw in him a champion of tradition against the hasty and harmful innovations of the Pahlavis. Since everyone assumed that Khomeini and other mullahs would return to their mosques once the Shah was overthrown, Iran's future was depicted by almost every faction as one of democratic development and pluralistic politics. Khomeini actively encouraged such illusions in accordance with another Shi'ite tactic – that of *tanfih*, which means taking the sting out of one's potential rivals or enemies. The tactic of *taqieh* – which means misleading everyone about one's true beliefs in a hostile environment – was also used by Khomeini and his adjutants inside Iran. Motahari and Beheshti, now the key partners in the Khomeini set-up inside Iran, had used *taqieh* for years. Motahari had even agreed to become a member of the so-called Imperial Board of Philosophers under Empress Farah's chairmanship. And Beheshti had drawn close enough to SAVAK to accept the post of prayer leader of the Iranian-financed mosque in Hamburg, West Germany, in the early 1970s. In Tabriz, Ayatollah Qazi-Tabataba'i continued secret meetings with the Shah's Minister of Endowments and Religious Affairs, Alinaqi Kani. He kept reassuring Kani that the mullahs were taking a radical line only in order to steal the show from the Left.

It was under Khomeini's orders that such outsiders as Ayatollah Mahmoud Taleqani and Grand Ayatollah Shariatmadari were promoted as leaders of the movement inside Iran without, however, having any real say in key decisions. *Khod'eh*, *taqieh* and *tanfih* were also used, together with *ketman* (dissimulation) in opening negotiations with the Americans. Yazdi established contacts of his own and in Tehran itself Ayatollah Abdul-Karim Mussavi-Ardabili met the American Ambassador William B. Sullivan to tell him that the future 'Islamic' government would continue to maintain close ties with the USA. It was also on the basis of *khod'eh* that the Ayatollah never even pronounced the word 'republic' until after he had won power. His slogan was 'Islamic Government', a phrase that gave the impression that there would be no drastic constitutional changes and that even monarchy could continue without the Pahlavis. The Ayatollah's choice of Bazargan as head of the provisional government was yet another example of *khod'eh* in practice. Bazargan was liberal enough to win the confidence of the middle class and weak enough to keep alive the ambitions of the Left. At the same time, however, Bazargan was not allowed to exercise real power. In November Khomeini asked Bazargan to organize a leadership group. 'Suggest some names to me,' the Ayatollah said, 'for I do not know anyone in Iran.'[7] Bazargan did not know that the secret committee under Motahari was already running the movement and promptly created an eighteen-man council which included only six mullahs. The body continued to be considered the leading organ of the movement until after Khomeini was back in Iran and sure of his grip on power.

While the Ayatollah worked between twelve and fourteen hours every day, stopping only for prayers and an hour of seclusion, presumably to communicate with the Almighty, the Shah in Tehran was sinking deeper and deeper into despair. Under chemotherapy for an old and eventually fatal cancer, the monarch, a full twenty years Khomeini's junior, was by the end of October unable to do more than two or three hours' work a day. And this consisted mostly of useless meetings with old politicians who had no real power, and with the ambassadors of the United States and Great Britain, who soon began to advise him to leave the country. The Shah was convinced that the revolution was organized and fomented by his two Western allies. The British wanted to 'punish' him for bringing the Americans into Iran, and Carter, representing the American 'liberals', wanted him removed because of Iran's role in raising oil prices.[8] Sitting in a large, half-lit office whose pink velvet wall covering was already fading and dusty, the Shah took a variety of pills and drank endless glasses of Contrex mineral water from France. To his visitors he complained of the 'ingratitude' of the Iranians and their readiness to be manipulated by 'our foreign enemies'. The Sharif-Emami government, torn by internecine feuds and discredited by its incompetence and crude opportunism, was falling apart, and clashes between demonstrators and troops continued to increase the number of casualties. The consortium of British, American, French and Dutch companies purchasing more than 90 per cent of Iran's oil was beginning to press for price reductions and other advantages from what they saw as a regime under siege and thus vulnerable to pressure. Talks between a consortium team and the National Iranian Oil Company in Tehran finally broke down after Iran refused to offer a 22 cent per barrel 'bonus'. The oilmen's hasty departure from Tehran was seen by the Shah as another indication that London and Washington wanted to destroy his regime.

The Russians, who had up to the end of October refrained from any action that might appear hostile to the Shah, now joined the other major powers in establishing secret contacts with the opposition. A sure sign that they considered the Shah doomed came when an invitation to the NIOC chief Hushang Ansary to visit Moscow was withdrawn at the last moment.

The Shah received conflicting advice. His ambassador in Washington, Ardeshir Zahedi, now staying in Tehran all the time, led the hardliners who urged a military crackdown and a Pinochet-style regime. He gathered around him a large number of high-ranking officers including Major General Manuchehr Khos-rowdad, the special forces' commander. Zahedi wanted the job of Prime Minister and believed that the movement in the streets did not represent the will of the people. To put this theory to the test Zahedi paid two sudden visits to the holy cities of Rey and Mashhad and drew crowds of supporters for the Shah. But the fact that some of his closest friends refused to accompany him on these visits showed the fear that Khomeini had inspired among the ruling elite.

Countering Zahedi's hard line was another influential faction led by Sharif-Emami himself, who still hoped that his many concessions, including guarantees of full press freedom, the release of thousands of prisoners, the raising of minimum wages and the arrest of dozens of high officials (including three ministers) would in time cool tempers down.

The Shah vacillated between the two. Egypt's President Sadat counselled a firm line, as did Jordan's King Hussein. Carter, when listening to his national security adviser Zbigniew Brzezinski, advocated a tough line but urged 'moderation and concessions' when reflecting the views of Secretary of State Vance.

Empress Farah counselled a direct appeal to the people and volunteered to stay behind and fight even after the Shah had left for his much discussed 'brief trip abroad'. The Shah, however, dismissed the suggestion angrily. 'You cannot be our Joan of Arc,' he told the enthusiastic Empress. Empress Farah had already established contact with Shariatmadari through one of his cousins, Ahmad Ansari. Shariatmadari, now convinced that Khomeini's seizure of power would lead to a bloodbath, went out of his way to help Sharif-Emami's faltering government but failed, largely because of the Shah's inability to offer firm leadership. When contacting Shariatmadari by telephone or special messenger, the Empress used the codename Madar-e-'Ali (Ali's mother).

All sorts of strange ideas were aired as remedies for the persistent revolt. General Gholam-Ali Oveissi, the military governor of Tehran, wanted some 20,000 activists arrested and imprisoned on the island of Kish in the Persian Gulf. Others suggested that Iran should invade Afghanistan in the name of defending Islam and as a means of diverting attention from the domestic revolt.[9] General Mir-Shapour Mir-Hadi, Military Governor of Qazvin, wanted authority from the Shah to order the shooting of anyone who dared appear on the streets after sunset and before sunrise. Sayyed Hassan Emami, the Imam Jum'a of Tehran, believed that spending an adequate sum of money among the mullahs would do the trick. 'The mullahs cannot resist two things: money and women,' he told a meeting.[10] The Shah was asked to make some funds available from his own fortune and refused. 'We don't have that kind of money,' he said when Emami mentioned a figure of one billion rials (about £9 million in those days). Kani, the energetic Endowments Minister who was officially in charge of relations with the mullahs, also believed that the huge amounts of money distributed by the Khomeini network among the poorer mullahs and *talabehs* should be more than matched by government handouts. Sharif-Emami, adamant that the government should not spend a penny without the approval of Parliament, refused to dig into the sum of more than £150 million available to him as 'secret funds'. Possibly with the Shah's knowledge, Kani began seeking money from 'Arab friends'. Shaikh Zayed Ibn Sultan al-Nahiyan, the Emir of Abu Dhabi, obliged by providing £14 million. The money was, however, instantly transferred to the government's 'general fund' on Sharif-Emami's orders and could not be used for financing friendly mullahs.[11]

Meanwhile, Tehran's international airport witnessed an endless stream of dignitaries, princes and princesses, former premiers and ministers, governors-general, high court judges, wealthy tycoons, leading film stars and middle-class families leaving the country for what only a few of them could have believed would become a more or less permanent exile. Between 1 October 1978 and 31 January 1979, the day Khomeini flew back to Tehran, some 100,000 people left the country. The Shah felt bitter about this mass flight of his supporters and observed that the one thing he and the late General de Gaulle had in common was that at times of danger supporters of both of them marched down the Champs-Elysées. The exodus was accompanied by an unprecedented flight of capital. Iran had abolished all exchange controls years earlier and feared no loss of native capital as interest rates remained high and the regime maintained its stability. But in the last three months of 1978 the trend was completely reversed and middle- and upper-class Iranians sent some £1500 million of their savings abroad.[12] This represented less than 9 per cent of the nation's currency reserves but was, nevertheless, seen as a vote of no confidence in the Shah's regime by its most natural supporters.

As the Shah dithered and sulked the Ayatollah's movement launched its second phase. This consisted of full-scale strikes and sporadic stoppages throughout industry. The small Leftist parties, notably Tudeh, played a crucial role in extending the struggle into the industrial sector. Very soon the vital oil industry itself was crippled by strikes and the flow of Iranian oil was halted for the first time since 1954. The Shah had to be content with a small oil heater as he sat in his huge reception room, where so many kings and queens and other great world leaders had been entertained, cursing everything and everyone and constantly saying that his time was over. He only took time off from the pressure of events to play gin rummy with the few trusted companions who had not yet fled the country.

A coalition of hardliners, including Zahedi and Oveissi, finally decided to allow the revolt to assume its 'natural proportions'.[13] On 4 November Oveissi ordered his 100,000 troops in the capital to stand aside and allow the mobs to burn and destroy to their hearts' content. Back in September Oveissi and Zahedi had successfully negotiated another 'cease-fire' under which the army had withdrawn to the northern portion of the capital and allowed the pro-Khomeini crowds to demonstrate in the central and southern districts. Anti-regime crowds, estimated at between 250,000 and 3 million according to who counted them, had the habit of breaking into smaller groups after every demonstration and going on the rampage against banks, cafés, girls' schools and other 'places of corruption'. The army's presence usually reduced the damage they could do without, however, stopping them altogether. On 4 November there was to be no army intervention and there was none. It is even possible that gangs hired by SAVAK started the wrecking spree in Tehran on that most bizarre day of the revolution.

The conspirators, helped by the excessive zeal of their revolutionary opponents, succeeded beyond their wildest expectations. Thousands of shops, banks, restaurants and other public buildings were attacked, set on fire and partly destroyed. The middle class, still hoping its bread would be buttered on both sides, was suitably alarmed. Sharif-Emami, now bitterly attacking Oveissi for his disobedience, was forced to resign. The Shah was left with no choice but to ask the generals to form a government. The army expected Oveissi to be named Prime Minister and the general had already contacted a number of people to serve in his government of 'national salvation'.[14] But the Shah, showing one last sparkle of his old self, stepped in and wrecked the whole game. He named as his new Prime Minister the army's Chief of Staff, the four-star general Gholam-Reza Azhari. At the same time, however, the Shah, who had not been seen or heard by the public for weeks, went on television to read what became his last message to the nation as reigning monarch. In it he admitted that much of his rule had been marred by 'corruption and cruelty' and demanded the nation's forgiveness. He became the first person to describe what was happening in Iran as a revolution rather than a movement, as Khomeini liked to call it, or a case of sedition as Oveissi believed. An astonished nation heard the Shah say: 'As the Shah of Iran as well as an Iranian citizen, I cannot but approve your revolution.'[15] He recalled his many efforts to form a coalition government with the help of various Mossadeqist politicians and added that having failed to bring civilian leaders together he was left with no choice but to ask the military to intervene.[16]

The policy of the new military government reflected the Shah's inability to stick to any course of action. Azhari, more of a poet than a soldier and totally without political ambition, decided to pursue Sharif-Emami's pseudo-legalistic course and appeared in front of Parliament for a vote of confidence. At the same time he ordered the arrest not of the revolutionary leaders but of 132 high-ranking officials, including Hoveyda and Nasiri. Within two days

Azhari, at first nicknamed 'Iran's Pinochet' by the Leftists, was seen as a paper tiger. In Parliament he read poems, burst into tears and finally clinched a vote of confidence. But the spectacle, seen by millions on television, killed his government by portraying him as a rather inoffensive old gentleman in a luxurious uniform. Azhari, like the Shah himself, was not prepared to order the massacre of thousands and the imprisonment of many more in the name of a totally discredited regime. In any case, the army was already crippled for lack of petrol needed for the tanks and armoured cars. And General Mir-Hadi's experiment of shooting everyone on sight had proved a disaster in Mashhad and there was no reason to believe it could succeed elsewhere.[17] Oveissi, angry at the turn of events, resigned and was replaced by General Mehdi Rahimi. Oveissi quietly left the country soon afterwards. In 1984 he was 'executed' by unknown gunmen in a Paris street.

As the oil strike, the powercuts and the almost total paralysis of the economy continued, the Ayatollah prepared to implement the final stage of his strategy. He had succeeded in the first two stages: the regime was already discredited and considered as illegitimate by the majority of politically active Iranians, and the armed forces could no longer be counted on to side with the Shah automatically. The third stage of the strategy was to establish the Khomeini network as the real source of authority in the country. The Ayatollah did this by issuing decrees appointing special missions to 'regulate' the oil strike and the paralysis of the customs entrepôts. Ali-Akbar Hashemi-Rafsanjani was named Representative of the Imam and sent to the oilfields together with Bazargan to ask workers to produce enough oil to cover domestic needs. Within a few days the country had two governments: one consisting of the traditional bureaucracy and the other formed by 'Imam committees' springing up everywhere. The contacts already established with various foreign embassies now assumed the character of negotiations at an official level. Gerhard Ritzel, the West German Ambassador, was the first leading Western diplomat to realize that Iran's future ruling apparatus was already in place. He was quickly joined by others including the Israelis, who were wise enough to withdraw their personnel from Iran then and there.[18] The Ayatollah's secret committee in Tehran also established contact with a number of SAVAK and military leaders. General Nasser Moqaddam, the new head of SAVAK, was among them, together with General Hussein Fardoust, then serving as chief of the Imperial Inspectorate. More importantly, perhaps, the revolutionary leaders opened channels to General Abbas-Karim Gharabaghi, the new Chief of Staff. Gharabaghi had served as Interior Minister in Sharif-Emami's Cabinet and was deeply suspected by the hardliners as a capitulationist. Gharabaghi was already developing his theme of the army's neutrality in what was so manifestly a political struggle. He argued that the army should not play a political role, especially when this meant firing on its own people.

The Shah's army, rated the sixth most powerful in the world, had neither the training nor the equipment to fight street battles. It had been shaped by the Shah as an instrument of regional power and not as a police force. The Shah's much taunted 'police state' was more imaginary than real. The police's central archives, for example, boasted the fingerprints of only 5000 people, for a population of 38 million. The country lacked a riot police unit and limited quantities of teargas had to be flown in at the last moment. During the revolution Britain sold the Shah some plastic bullets, but the consignment arrived after the Ayatollah had taken over. The National Police's special commando units, trained in South Korea and Taiwan, had for long been reorganized as a club for Asian martial arts and were not prepared to fight mullahs on the streets of Qom. The army's conscript soldiers could not understand why they should suppress a revolution which the Shah himself had so lavishly praised and approved. Very soon the army was faced with a growing problem of desertion. And in some barracks, notably one occupied by the Imperial Guard, known as the Immortals, men and junior officers revolted against their commanders. The urban guerrilla groups were impatient to engage the army and thirsted for blood. Khomeini's firm opposition to any attack on the army, prompted by his hope of winning over the high command, restrained many guerrilla groups. Nevertheless some groups were determined to fight their own revolutionary war with or without Khomeini's approval. These groups at times dressed their fighters as women, wearing the *chador*, which had become a symbol of opposition to the Shah, and attacked police stations and isolated army posts.

Hoveyda's arrest sent shockwaves throughout the bureaucracy. For thirteen years he had presided over an expanding state apparatus which had trebled in size in a decade. The majority of high- and middle-ranking members of the state's functionaries were Hoveyda appointees and many of them considered him as their godfather. His arrest was seen as an act of betrayal by the Shah and accelerated the pace of departures from the country. By the end of November, when Azhari was carried out of his office on a stretcher after suffering a stroke, the Shah had lost all effective control of the civil service and was on the point of losing his tenuous grip on the armed forces as well. The Shah decided to leave the country as quickly as possible. His problem was to find someone to serve as Prime Minister. He had agreed to the appointment of a Regency Council and seemed to care little who served on it. The country was left without a nominal government for several days as the Shah looked for a Premier. Dr Hussein Saddiqi, a highly respected former colleague of Mossadeq, was approached and agreed to serve provided the Shah did not leave the country. The Shah could not accept the condition. The Mossadeqist Karim Sanjabi, now in his seventies, refused to serve. There were only two candidates for the post no one else wanted and the Shah talked to both. Mohsen Pezeshkpour, leader of the tiny ultra-nationalist Pan-Iranist Party, who had forged some links with Grand Ayatollah Shariatmadari, was the more enthusiastic of the two. But the second was Shapour Bakhtiar, another Mossadeqist. Unlike Saddiqi, Bakhtiar insisted that the Shah leave the country and this was precisely what the ailing monarch wanted to hear. But as soon as news of Bakhtiar's efforts to form a government was published, Khomeini denounced the whole enterprise and thus doomed its chances of success which would have been slim in the best of circumstances.

Khomeini had already unleashed the last stage of his strategy which consisted of emerging as the only credible alternative to the Shah. A poem promising that Khomeini's return would end all hardship and usher in a period of peace and plenty was genuinely believed by millions of exhausted Iranians who privately longed for an end to their ordeal. This longing for Khomeini was dramatically illustrated by what was, no doubt, one of the most unusual episodes in the revolution. A rumour spread like a fire through the bush that a pious old lady in the holy city of Qom had found a hair from the Prophet's beard in the pages of her Qur'an. The same evening an apparition had informed the saintly lady that the faithful would be able to see the face of Imam Khomeini in the full moon on 27 November. No one bothered to ask how the old lady knew that the hair belonged to the Prophet or whether any such old lady existed in the first place. Within a single day almost everyone had heard the rumour and millions of people gathered on the rooftops on the promised day and waited for the full moon, shouting '*Allah Akbar*'. It was also rumoured that only miscreants and bastards would fail to see Khomeini's face in the moon. Tehran and other major cities experienced a festive moment that sharply contrasted with the rest of that bleak, bitterly cold and bloody autumn. Tears of joy were shed and huge quantities of sweets and fruits were consumed as millions of people jumped for joy, shouting 'I've seen the Imam in the moon.' The event was celebrated in thousands of mosques with mullahs reminding the faithful that a sure sign of the coming of the Mahdi was that the sun would rise in the West. Khomeini, representing the sun, was now in France and his face was shining in the moon like a sun. People were ready to swear on the Qur'an that they had seen Khomeini's face in the moon. Even the Tudeh Party shared in the collective hallucination. Its paper *Navid* wrote: 'Our toiling masses, fighting against world-devouring Imperialism headed by the blood-sucking United States, have seen the face of their beloved Imam and leader, Khomeini the Breaker of Idols, in the moon. A few pipsqueaks cannot deny what a whole nation has seen with its own eyes.'[19]

The episode, a masterly coup probably plotted by Beheshti, who had a remarkable understanding of popular psychology in Iran, soured Khomeini's already troubled relations with the other Grand Ayatollahs even further. Khomeini's peers saw the 'moon trick', as Grand Ayatollah Khonsari called it, as a cheap attempt at exploiting the people's religious sentiments. Grand Ayatollah Qomi, Khomeini's former fellow-captive in the 1960s, was 'shocked and alarmed' by the carnival organized in the holy city of Mashhad to mark the appearance of Khomeini in the moon. He rang Khomeini in Neauphle-le-Château and asked the Ayatollah to issue a denial. Khomeini refused, arguing that he would not act against 'the spontaneous initiatives of the people'.[20] Qomi decided to avenge himself and a few days later told his aides to spread the rumour that he had seen Imam Reza, the eighth Imam, who is buried in Mashhad, in a dream and had held a fairly long conversation with His Holiness. Imam Reza had ostensibly confided his concern for the sad events of Iran to Qomi and added that true Shi'ites should not oppose a Shah who was named after both the Prophet and the eighth Imam.[21] The Imam finally asked the Grand Ayatollah to make sure that a statue of the Shah that had been pulled down by a mob in one of Mashhad's squares several days earlier should be restored to its place. The rumour proved instantly effective in Mashhad and the Shah's bust was put back on its pedestal. The few diehard supporters of the Shah who were still around jumped at the opportunity and tried to turn the Mashhad episode into a nationwide turning of the tide. Khomeini, informed of Qomi's counterattack, acted promptly and ordered Motahari over the telephone to spread the rumour that the ayatollah of Mashhad suffered periodic moments of hallucination prompted by an upset stomach. Motahari was also to make sure that the restored bust of the Shah was not only taken off the pedestal once again but also smashed to pieces. Qomi was forced to beat a hasty retreat, acknowledging the fact that at that time no one could challenge Khomeini.

By mid-December even those who did not desire the advent of Khomeini to power considered this as inevitable and were resigning themselves to such an eventuality.

Motahari, once again using the tactic of *khod'eh*, agreed to help organize the Regency Council so that the Shah could leave the country quickly. In giving the impression that he was prepared to cooperate with the regime at least to some extent, Motahari aimed at securing a majority in the council so that he could announce its dissolution the moment the Shah flew out of Iranian air space. Tipped off by Javad Sa'id, the Speaker of Parliament, that Motahari was less than sincere in his offer of cooperation, the Shah refused all the names suggested by Khomeini's field commander. The Regency Council was eventually created with a retired astronomer at its head. The 82-year-old astronomer, Jalal Tehrani, promptly flew to Paris and offered his resignation to Khomeini. The Shah was no longer concerned with what was happening and thought only of flying out of Iran as quickly as possible. For months he had been a virtual prisoner in his gloomy palace which was surrounded by tanks pointing their guns ominously towards the King of King's private apartment. He was beginning to hate the people he had loved all his life. He told one visitor, 'For me everything is at an end. Even if I return to Iran one day as Shah, nothing will be the same again. It is like a beautiful crystal vase that is broken for good; repair it and it will still show its cracks.'[22] He was so depressed as to forget even Hoveyda, despite earlier promises that the former premier would not be abandoned to his fate.

The Shah and the Empress eventually left on 16 January, only an hour after Bakhtiar had been approved by Parliament as Prime Minister. News of the Shah's departure was followed by scenes of wild jubilation in the streets of Tehran and within hours almost every sign of the Pahlavi dynasty had been removed. Militants changed the names of streets and other public places, burned photos of the Shah, smashed his statues and cried themselves hoarse with endless shouts of 'Death to the Shah'. In France, Khomeini announced that he would now return to Iran and establish a new government to replace that of Bakhtiar, which he described as 'illegal'. Bakhtiar responded by announcing that he would not allow mullahs to intervene in the affairs of the state. After rumours circulated that Khomeini was planning to arrive at one of the provincial centres and declare jihad on the government in Tehran, the new Prime Minister closed all of Iran's airports.

Meanwhile, the army chiefs saw themselves as the only alternative left to a Khomeini takeover of the country. At least two of them, General Abdul-Ali Badreh'i, the new commander of the ground forces, and Khosrowdad, still commanding the special units, were thinking of staging a coup d'état without knowing quite where and when to start. The USA, determined to help the Bakhtiar government stick, believed an attempted coup to be the worst possible course for the army. Carter accordingly dispatched the deputy-commander of NATO, General Robert C. Huyser, to Tehran to discourage any thought of a putsch by the generals. Huyser succeeded in sowing enough dissension among the generals and creating a sufficient degree of confusion to render any serious attempt at a military move virtually impossible. Secret contacts between senior officers and revolutionary mullahs rose dramatically once Huyser had left Tehran.

The Shah spent some time in Egypt, being received there by his friend Anwar Sadat as a head of state, but soon moved to Morocco and was thus removed even farther from the Iranian political scene. Several of the generals who still considered him to be Commander-in-Chief tried to contact him but were told that His Imperial Majesty the King of Kings was on 'a private visit' and that all matters should be referred to the Regency Council in his absence. General Gholam-Reza Rabi'i, the air force commander, was determined to shoot down any aircraft bringing Khomeini to Iran, but wanted his decision approved by the Shah. Having failed to talk to the monarch in person, he abandoned the plan altogether.

By the end of January it was obvious that no one could prevent Khomeini from landing at Tehran's Mehrabad Airport without provoking a bloodbath. From 30 January the airport fell under the control of armed members of the Imam's committees. The Ayatollah arrived at Mehrabad aboard a chartered Air France Jumbo jet two days later, amid scenes of jubilation never before witnessed

in Iran. On hand to greet him were all but one of Iran's Grand Ayatollahs, and they paid him respect never paid to anyone else before
or since. Far more important from Khomeini's point of view, however, was the presence of between 1 and 4 million people who had
come to see 'the Imam'. To make sure that no one else could claim
any part in his triumph, the Ayatollah refused to start his first day
in Iran by visiting Tehran University, where an imposing array of
intellectuals and liberal politicians would have gathered to emphasize their own share in the end of the Pahlavis. Instead, Khomeini
decided to visit Tehran's new graveyard, Behesht-e-Zahra.

At the graveyard he made a long and bitter attack on the Pahlavis
as a whole and on the departed Shah in particular. He accused him
of having 'destroyed our universities and expanded our ceme-
teries'. He also made a number of promises to the poor –
including free housing, electricity and water – under the Islamic
regime. The Ayatollah said he would not accept Bakhtiar's
government and, shaking his fist in the air, shouted, 'I shall kick
their teeth in.'[23]

This was the first time the people of Tehran were seeing Khomeini in person in nearly sixteen years. To them the man who had
chased the Shah out of Iran, as he had promised many years
earlier, appeared as an elemental force of destruction. The violence of his language, the bitterness of his tone and the mixture of
passion and cynicism he so ably demonstrated contrasted sharply
with what other Iranian politicians had offered for generations.
Khomeini deliberately cultivated his image as a tough leader. One
of his first orders to Motahari soon after his arrival in Tehran was
to make sure that only approved pictures of him be printed and
displayed. He especially objected to two of his own pictures then
widely on display. One showed him wearing spectacles, which
might create an impression of frailty, if not of outright disability.
The other showed the Ayatollah smiling benevolently. Islamic
tradition maintained categorically that the Prophet never smiled,
and dismissed those who did as superficial and morally loose.
Within a few days all the objectionable portraits of the Imam were
replaced with new ones, showing him knotting his bushy eyebrows in a posture of angry determination. Khomeini knew that
the average Iranian respected strong leaders and had turned away
from the Shah partly because of the monarch's manifest weakness
and vacillation. Reza Shah had succeeded because everyone feared
him, his motto being: I don't care whether they love me or not, all I
want is that they should obey me absolutely.[24] Khomeini had

learned that much from the long-buried enemy of the mullahs. He told his close confidants the same evening that the Shah's 'regional superpower' was 'as hard as candyfloss' and could no longer resist.[25]

Khomeini settled in a school not far from the Parliament building and ordered his followers to defy martial law as before, until the defiant Bakhtiar capitulated. He presided over a meeting of his Islamic Revolutionary Council, but this lasted for less than an hour as the Ayatollah retired to sleep on the floor of a converted classroom. Bakhtiar, however, stayed awake all night still hoping against hope.

# 14

# *The Taste of Triumph*

Islam was dead or dying for nearly fourteen centuries; we have
revived it with the blood of our youth. . . . We shall soon liberate
Jerusalem and pray there.

Ayatollah Khomeini in Qom, 1979

*T*he Refah School for Girls is situated in a mud-brick building
in a narrow alley behind the Sepahsalar mosque, not far from
the former Qajar Palace that had housed the Majlis for more than
seven decades. Early in November 1978 the school had been
closed down, together with the rest of the nation's educational
network. The quickening pace of the revolution wooed both
teacher and pupil into the streets where history could be made
rather than studied. So when Ayatollah Khomeini arrived at
Refah, none of its three hundred girls were present to greet him.
Refah was to serve as the Imam's headquarters as well as his residence. Motahari had already taken a number of precautions as
rumours persisted that Khomeini might be the object of an assassination attempt. The piercing of several communicating walls
allowed secret doors to be installed connecting the Refah building
with several neighbouring houses. Khomeini was to spend each
night in one of the buildings. The Ayatollah insisted that all
members of his immediate family, including fourteen grand-
children, should also be housed in the same alley so as not to face
any direct danger. All the streets and alleys leading to Refah were
also sealed off as some eight hundred heavily armed guerrillas,
many of them Lebanese and Iraqi Shi'ites, guarded the area.

The impressive security measures taken were not gratuitous. Documents seized after the revolutionaries finally took control of the state machinery showed that General Amin Afshar, an officer fiercely loyal to the Shah, had prepared an elaborate plan to arrest Khomeini, try him and have him executed soon after the Ayatollah's return. It is not known how or why the plan failed or was shelved, but one reason may have been US pressure, exerted through General Huyser, aimed at discouraging any move by the military that might upset Bakhtiar's heroic but tenuous hold on power.[1]

The Ayatollah was also concerned about the possibility of being poisoned by his enemies. He had not forgotten that all but two of the twelve Imams of Shi'ism had died as a result of poisoning. Accordingly, a special taster was appointed at Refah. He was a former schoolteacher by the name of Mohammad-Ali Raja'i who was to become Prime Minister and President of the republic before dying in an explosion organized by counter-revolutionaries.

Refah quickly became the Mecca of the revolution as mullahs, politicians, journalists and wave after wave of the faithful, wishing to see the Imam in person, crowded there every day. Among the mullahs calling at Refah was Hojat al-Islam Abdul-Karim Hejazi, who had once been a pupil of Khomeini but had subsequently abandoned him. Hejazi had been a favourite of Khomeini's because of his deep, emotional voice which, when reciting the sonnets of Hafiz in the special style of the mullahs, left few people unmoved. On one evening the Imam, now in his private quarters and with only a dozen or so confidants present, invited Hejazi to recite Hafiz. Hejazi did and, for a brief moment, the Imam had some difficulty restraining his tears.[2] This was, perhaps, the only time in years that the 'iron-willed Avenger of Allah', as some of Khomeini's supporters called him, succumbed to emotion. Hejazi was never invited again.[3]

The Imam was in almost continuous session both with his secret Cabinet and the scores of politicians who hoped to have a place in the future government. On 5 February the Imam announced that he had asked Mehdi Bazargan to form a provisional government and supervise a referendum and subsequent general election. The choice put Bazargan in a difficult position. He had been a close friend of Bakhtiar for some thirty years and had, until Khomeini's arrival from Paris, tried to arrange a compromise with the Prime Minister. Bazargan made one last feeble attempt to persuade the

Imam to accept a step-by-step progression towards full power but was firmly told off and ordered to select his ministers.

Bakhtiar dismissed Bazargan's appointment as Prime Minister as a joke and warned that any act of disobedience would be dealt with by force. The Imam's inner Cabinet retaliated by ordering civil servants to prevent Bakhtiar's ministers from entering their offices.

Why did Khomeini choose Bazargan? Two reasons seem likely. First, the Imam was still unsure of his real strength in the country and needed an outer shield of politicians to protect his intimates against violent action by the military. Right to the end the majority of the high command believed that Khomeini and the mullahs were simply helping politicians like Bazargan and Sanjabi. Secondly, Bazargan would serve as a front man in an exceptionally difficult period when hundreds of people had to be executed and thousands thrown into prison. Khomeini did not want the mullahs to be immediately spotted as the real force behind the inevitable repression. Bazargan's regime would therefore serve as a smoke-screen behind which the inevitable final battle of transition from the old order to the new one could be fought. Bazargan, a well-intentioned man but a poor politician, agreed to play the part in the hope of outmanoeuvring the mullahs within a few months.

History continued to hesitate; in that fateful February almost anything could have happened in Iran. No one, least of all Khomeini himself, had any clear idea as to how the transition would take place. Few people expected the army to melt away so quickly, leaving the crumbling imperial state to its fate. The Leftist guerrillas had converged on Tehran from all over the country; hundreds had also returned from abroad. They wanted to force the pace of the revolution, and from 6 February onwards they seized the initiative. Khomeini, after a moment's hesitation, decided to side with the most radical elements, rightly sensing that the popular mood was against any unnecessary prolongation of the political struggle. He called on the people to defy martial law and invited the soldiers either to desert and return to their villages or to join the revolutionaries. For a whole week the Imam was the hero of the Left which, jumping at the opportunity provided by the general confusion, acted decisively to strengthen its position. Scores of banks were attacked by guerrillas who 'confiscated' substantial sums of money in the name of the people. Army and police arsenals were raided and looted and the guerrillas even succeeded in stealing tanks, anti-aircraft guns and rocket launchers. Large numbers of conscripts, NCOs and junior officers joined the various guerrilla groups and turned them into an even more formidable force.

On 11 February, the Chief of Staff, General Gharabaghi, tried to convene one final meeting of the high command and, when this failed to materialize, announced the army's 'neutrality'. The announcement served as a signal for an armed insurrection in Tehran. The Immortals, the only unit still loyal to the Shah's regime, was dispatched by its commander, General Ali Neshat, who had failed to make a deal with the mullahs, to 'punish' air force cadets who had dared salute Khomeini instead of the Shah. While the Immortals were fighting the air force cadets, helped by the technical personnel and some NCOs, the Marxist–Leninist Fedayeen guerrillas arrived on the scene, and what was to be the only real battle of the revolution was fought. The Immortals won the battle but lost the empire. Before the sun had set the Shah's last Prime Minister was in hiding and most of his generals were either shot on the spot by guerrillas or arrested. A nationwide search for Bakhtiar proved fruitless as the former Premier remained hidden in a safe house provided for him by his old friend and new rival, Bazargan. Bakhtiar was later able to leave Tehran disguised as a French businessman aboard an Air France jet.[4]

On the morning of 12 February the Imam had only his instinct to guide him; no one knew exactly what was happening in the country, or in the capital for that matter. He had the keys of the empire and did not know what to do with them. Every minute a new van arrived loaded with former officials of the regime who were handed over to the Imam's self-styled bodyguards at the door of the Refah School for Girls. Sometimes those bringing in the captives demanded receipts. But in most cases they were content with simply announcing: Here we bring you a four-star general, five three-star generals, a Prime Minister, seven ministers, etc. The captives were glad to be in the hands of Khomeini's men. Those who had been captured by the guerrillas of the Left had been murdered on the spot. Among them was General Ali Badreh'i, commander of the ground forces. In those early days no one expected the mullahs to order summary executions and few people were aware of the existence of Ayatollah Sadeq Khalkhali, who was to win the title of 'Judge Blood' within a few weeks.

For at least the first week of the new regime Tehran was at the mercy of the Leftist guerrillas who, unaware of their real organizational strength and badly divided, were unable to make a direct attempt at seizing power. Khomeini hugely radicalized his vocabulary and, for the first time, made use of such typically Leninist terms as 'imperialism'. In almost every speech he bitterly attacked the United States, giving the Left the impression that he was on their side in global terms. The Imam was anxious that no one should appear a more radical or more ardent revolutionary than himself. The prevailing mood favoured the most extremist slogans. The Imam also put the emphasis on 'social justice', 'looking after the dispossessed' and 'making fat cats pay'. Without being conversant with the intricacies of class-war politics, the Imam robbed the Left of its vocabulary and slogans. The middle classes were now frightened and did not pose a threat. In any case, Bazargan's presence was sufficient to allay middle-class suspicions and encourage their almost inbuilt talent for self-deception. What mattered now was the support of the small shopkeepers, students, schoolchildren, workers and the lumpenproletariat which could be seduced by the Left.

The Left's demand for instant social justice, symbolized by wholesale nationalization and an almost immediate distribution of land among the peasants, could be accepted verbally and postponed. But the Left also wanted blood, and clamoured for the execution of former officials. While still at Neauphle-le-Château Khomeini had made it clear that he would put a number of former officials on trial. Motahari had been given to understand that the Imam had had only the SAVAK 'torture masters' and at most thirty high-ranking politicians in mind. The trials, Motahari naively thought, would be principally aimed at fully establishing the legitimacy of the revolution. There was no reason to believe that Khomeini himself had thought of any exact figure for the envisaged executions. Bazargan, in any case, wanted none and was even toying with the idea of announcing the abolition of the death sentence.[5]

By the third week of February Imam committees, known as *komiteh*, had sprung up everywhere in the capital and proceeded with the arrest of former officials and local rich people. Khomeini was deeply disturbed by the class character that his revolution was beginning to assume. For him the revolution had mainly cultural aims. He wanted to eliminate the Shah and his close supporters because they were 'evil' and 'satanic'. He also wanted to end foreign, non-Muslim influence in Iran so as to foil what he considered to be 'a Jewish plot to destroy Islam'. He further wanted to eliminate the Baha'i 'heretics'. He believed that the clergy should have the final say in the affairs of the state and that the rules of Islam, which basically concern personal behaviour rather than social and economic matters, should be strictly applied. His opposition to the Shah's land reforms had not been motivated either by personal loss of wealth or because of class solidarity with landlords. He saw the Shah's moves as a means of increasing his own 'satanic' powers at the expense of the mullahs and the landlords. He hated the Pahlavis not for Leninist reasons but because they had tried to loosen the hold of Islam on Iran.

Islam does not believe in a classless society in the Marxist sense and Khomeini had little or no regard for the economic status of his aides. The composition of the Revolutionary Council itself illustrated the point. Five of the eighteen members of the council were multi-millionaires, while at least five others were genuinely poor. The rest of the membership consisted of people who could be described as comfortably off. The revolution had advanced no economic promises and Khomeini's talk of free housing, electricity and water during his speech at Behesht-e-Zahra had been an exception. The speech was, in fact, later relegated to oblivion and its taped or printed copies seized and destroyed on the orders of Khomeini himself.

The overwhelming majority of the revolutionaries were children and young people who cried out for action. In a country where some 60 per cent of the population consisted of those aged below twenty, Bazargan's brand of conservatism would have quickly isolated the Imam's party and opened the door for a victory of the Leninist Left. Khomeini was determined not to allow this to happen and accordingly ordered a number of high-ranking military officers to be executed. Among those chosen as the first victims of the soon to be notorious Islamic courts were General Nasiri, for years head of SAVAK, and General Rahimi, the last martial law administrator of the capital. The executions were aimed at both pushing the Left out of the limelight and discouraging any crazy notion of a putsch among the remains of the shattered imperial army. The five generals chosen for execution on St Valentine's Day had already been badly beaten before they were finally delivered to Refah School. Not knowing what to do with them, the *komiteh* revolutionaries had brought them to the Imam's own residence. Sayyed Ahmad signed the receipt for them. The next problem was to find a judge to preside over at least a token trial. Several mullahs were approached but politely declined this historic role. In the end the Imam ordered Khalkhali to do the job. 'These people are guilty in any case,' he told Khalkhali. 'So hear what they have to say and then send them to hell.'[6] Khalkhali acted quickly and using a converted classroom as his courthouse sentenced the five generals to death after a brief recital of the Holy Qur'an and a few minutes of abuse and counter-abuse. The Imam had ordered a quick execution but the condemned had to wait another eighteen hours before a firing squad, the first of many, was put together. The squad was led by Mostafa Chamran, who was later to be named Defence Minister. The generals were taken to the roof of the school building and blind-folded. Their earlier stormy meeting with Sayyed Ahmad in the school's canteen had not helped their case. Sayyed Ahmad had taken one of the generals, Nader Jahanabani, who was blond and blue-eyed, to be a 'foreigner' and had suggested that he be released. The suggestion had infuriated the captive. 'You are the foreigner, not I,' Jahanabani had retorted. 'You are the one who openly boasts about being of Arab ancestry.' General Rahimi had gone even further and slapped the Imam's son in the face. He had been punished by having his right arm smashed with the butt of an Israeli-made Uzi machine gun. Nasiri started to cry, with blood dripping down his long tawny face. Khosrowdad, the most dashing of the Shah's generals, had remained haughty and aloof, while Naji continued to demand a quick end to the ordeal.

The execution of the generals broke the atmosphere of fear that still persisted among most of the revolutionaries, who could not believe that the Shah's regime was dead and that its powerful ally, the United States, would not lift a finger to help save its friends. The Imam himself climbed the narrow, winding steps to the terraced roof of the school building to inspect the corpses and embolden his followers. He spent less than a minute contemplating the naked, still bleeding corpses. 'Allah gave them their just deserts,' he observed, motioning to Ahmad to accompany him downstairs. Bazargan learned of the executions through Ghotbzadeh, now heading the radio and television organization. Ghotbzadeh had been asked to send a film crew to make the footage necessary to convince viewers that Islamic justice was being set in motion. The Left loved what it saw on television and demanded more. It urged an immediate dissolution of the armed forces and their replacement by a people's militia. The fear that the army would be reconstituted and used either for a coup d'état or as means of defending a conservative Islamic government was the chief concern of the Left in those days. The least the various

Leftist groups would accept was the execution of more generals. The Imam was to meet them halfway and order some more military commanders to be shot. At the same time the new Defence Minister, Admiral Ahmad Madani, unveiled a plan for reducing national service to six months and endorsed the desertion of more than 80 per cent of the conscripts.

The Left's wooing of the poor was countered by a new move from the Imam. He ordered some hundred mullahs to fill suitcases with banknotes and travel to the provinces distributing money among the *mustadh'afin*. Hojat al-Islam Ali Khameneh'i, for example, received some £1 million for distribution in Baluchistan where he had been in exile under the Shah. Central and local authorities were also advised, behind Bazargan's back, not to insist on collecting taxes or cashing bills. Tens of thousands of lumpen elements were allowed to share the loot from the homes of the rich who had either fled abroad or were in hiding. South Tehran's slumdwellers were allowed to occupy vacant or even half-built flats in the well-to-do districts of the north. Thousands of cars, including very expensive luxury limousines, were confiscated by the *komitehs*, enabling many young and poor men to drive in luxury for the first time in their lives.

The Imam sought to emphasize the revolutionary nature of the new regime further by inviting Yasser Arafat, the leader of the Palestine Liberation Organization, to Tehran and embracing him in front of Ghotbzadeh's television cameras. Arafat had tried to visit Tehran for more than a decade but had met with the Shah's categorical refusal.[7] He brought with him his 'ambassador', Hani al-Hassan, who declared that the PLO, having trained more than 10,000 anti-Shah guerrillas, considered itself to be a full partner in the victory of the revolution.[8]

Meanwhile, the debate concerning the future form of government dominated the political scene in Tehran. But the Imam quickly ended it by calling on the people to vote for an Islamic republic – 'not a word more, not a word less' – in a referendum in March. Khomeini received the approval of the usual 98 or so per cent of the electorate which is the outcome of almost every referendum in developing countries. The Left and the monarchists boycotted the polls but failed to have any impact on the masses, who voted for the Imam. Most political parties and some of the mullahs frankly admitted that the very term 'Islamic republic' was still an unknown quantity to them. Islam had never advocated or experienced a republican form of government. And there was little that could be described as republican in the brief caliphate of Imam Ali, which was at times referred to as 'the ideal Islamic political model'. Bazargan made no secret of his opinion on the matter and, provoking Khomeini's displeasure, announced that there was no theoretical basis for an Islamic republic. To most people the Persian term *jomhuri* (republic) simply meant that there would be no monarch. Iran had no republican movement at the time and the profound differences between republican and monarchical systems of government had never been studied even by the parties of the Left.

The nearest thing to a model for Khomeini's Islamic republic was the Imamate of Yemen which had been overthrown in 1963 in an Egyptian-backed coup d'état. The Yemenis, Zaydi Shi'ites, had lived within the system of Valayat-e-Faqih (the Regency of the Theologian) for centuries, with imams serving as both the temporal and spiritual head of the community. In Oman a similar experience by the 'Abadhiah community had ended in the nineteenth century with the sultans of Muscat capturing the last strongholds of the community.

It was not only uncertainty about a model for the future government of the country that troubled the Imam in those crucial days. Khomeini could sense that the vast coalition built around his name was already beginning to disintegrate. The Left had more than 300,000 weapons, and ignored appeals by Khomeini to hand these over to the authorities. The many thousands of exiles who had returned home during the revolution felt frustrated as Bazargan refused to give them jobs, preferring to retain the bulk of civil servants who had served under the Shah. The new Chief of Staff, Brigadier General Mohammad-Vali Qara-nay, was reconstituting the army high command much faster than the revolutionaries wanted. Rumours that both Qara-nay and Madani, the Defence Minister, were thinking of a coup were rife in Tehran. Women were beginning to demonstrate against incidents of acid-throwing by zealots against all those who did not wear the veil. The press, now dramatically expanded and reaching an ever greater readership, was already propagating such 'dangerous ideas' as democracy, multiparty parliamentarianism, human rights and the separation of mosque and state. The mullahs could see history repeating itself. In 1906 they had mobilized the illiterate masses against the despotic Shah and had ended up with only a chair in the aisles of a basically Western-style constitutional system. Now, once again, the 'Westernized' middle classes, which would not have been able to overthrow the Shah without the muscle mobilized by the mullahs, were trying to steal the victory.

Far more dangerous than any of these developments, from the Imam's point of view, were the cracks that were beginning to appear in the alliance formed by the mullahs themselves. In Tehran, Sayyed Mahmoud Taleqani, who had been quickly promoted to the rank of ayatollah by his followers, was emerging as a symbol of the Islamic Left and, although a member of the Revolutionary Council, openly criticized much of what was done or said by the hard core of Khomeini supporters. In Qom, Shariatmadari, although opposed to the direct involvement of the clergy in politics, was already established as a source of power. His supporters in Tehran and Azerbaijan, his native land, were organizing themselves into a People's Islamic Republican Party. In Khuzestan, Ayatollah Shubayr Khaqani was successfully mixing tribal and ethnic loyalties with his own brand of Shi'ism. Inside the Imam's own serail the *fokoli*, meaning those who wore European dress, were fighting with the mullahs as well as among themselves.

It had always been Khomeini's tactic to fight his opponents one by one, starting with the most vulnerable. He knew that he had to retain his hold on the religious network or he would soon be isolated. He was the hero of the mullahs and had no intention of losing that position. He had even refused to approve the execution of more than a hundred mullahs who had for years cooperated with SAVAK and who were now fully exposed. Only one particularly troublesome mullah, Gholam-Hussein Daneshi, had been shot with the Imam's consent. Khomeini insisted that defrocking would be punishment enough for mullahs who had served the Shah. 'A mullah does not kill a mullah,' he reportedly told Khalkhali, who wanted some turbaned heads to roll. The divisions within the Islamic coalition could prove fatal if each group were to be led by one of the leading ayatollahs. He had to return to Qom, the throbbing heart of the revolution, and there assert his supremacy over the 'sources of imitation'. But before he did that he appointed Mohammad-Reza Mahdavi-Kani, an ambitious, wealthy mullah, to assume control of the *komiteh* and turn them into an effective instrument of coercion. He also settled the dispute among his *fokoli* supporters concerning the creation of a Revolutionary Guard, asking Yazdi, Chamran, Farsi and Mohammad Montazeri to work together in shaping the force which was, at first, to number only 10,000. He also dismissed

Qara-nay but, fearing his possible influence in the army, called him in for a private interview in which the ambitious general was led to believe that his dismissal was merely a prelude to his impending appointment as Prime Minister. Using the technique of *Khod'eh* (trickery), the Imam told the general that the country needed a strong, dedicated government and that everyone should be ready at any moment to assume any task that the nation might deem necessary. 'You, too, must be ready for service and sacrifice at the highest level,' the Imam told the general, who was suitably overjoyed.[9] A few days later Qara-nay was shot dead by a shady terrorist group describing itself as the Forqan (Distinction between Good and Evil).[10] Madani was eased out of his job in a slightly different way. He was called to a private meeting with the Imam and told that the best way he could serve the country now was to become Governor of the oil-rich province of Khuzestan which was 'threatened by the Arabs and Communists'. Madani, an admiral, would also hold the post of commander of the navy. 'I want you to go a long way,' the Imam told the delighted admiral. 'Prove yourself in Khuzestan and Allah knows what other tasks you may be invited to perform.'[11]

The Imam's stay in Qom was, by all accounts, an exceptionally happy one. In his sixteen years of exile he had always spoken of returning to the holy city, and now he was back in the modest brick and mud house where he felt so much at home. He could also witness the revival of the Faizieh Theological School, the symbol of opposition to the Shah's rule. In Qom he could walk from his home to the holy shrine or the school without being surrounded by hundreds of armed men. He could also prevent any possibility of Shariatmadari, Golpayegani and Najafi forming a triumvirate against him. He called on the three Grand Ayatollahs one by one, appearing to pay them full respect while encouraging their mutual jealousies. None of the three had political ambitions but any of them could cause a great deal of trouble by allowing political parties to be formed in their name. He managed to persuade Golpayegani and Najafi that all the Grand Ayatollahs should have just one common representative in each city. That, in practice, meant that Khomeini himself monopolized the religious network. Shariatmadari refused the offer without, however, forcing a rupture. The break between them was to come much later.

In Qom the Imam acted as if he had once again become a teacher of theology and his involvement in the affairs of the state were of a purely ethical order. In reality, however, no major decision or appointment could be made without his consent. Bazargan reported to him at least twice a week and other top officials followed this pattern. If he did not like a particular government policy, all he had to do was to have Sayyed Ahmad ring Ghotb-zadeh to broadcast the Imam's displeasure. Bazargan was at first shocked when he heard over the radio that his Cabinet's decisions had been made null and void with a simple declaration from the Imam. 'I am like a knife without a blade,' the Prime Minister told the nation in a television appearance. Nevertheless, he did not resign.

The assassination of Motahari, also by the Forqan group, proved a serious blow to Khomeini. The Imam had been genuinely attached to his former pupil and mourned his demise with deep grief. The murder, soon to be followed by a series of other assassinations, exposed the vulnerability of the leadership. Khomeini ordered the strengthening of the Revolutionary Guards and the creation of a semi-secret organization which grouped together the Hezb-Allah, Saff and half a dozen other Islamic groups with long records of violence. Hadi Ghaffari, a young mullah whose father had died under torture in a SAVAK prison in 1974, headed the new organization, which retained the name of Hezb-Allah. Hezb-Allah consisted of several thousand lumpen elements who received a monthly allowance in exchange for parti-cipation in street battles whenever necessary. They were used for attacking the headquarters of opposition parties and the homes of anti-Khomeini politicians. Hezb-Allah also made a habit of setting fire to the printing houses of newspapers critical of the regime and wrecked opposition rallies, beating up everyone with clubs and 'teaching a lesson' to the activists with a meticulous use of jack-knives, sawchains and meatchoppers. Women's lib activists were disfigured with razor blows or acid. The war cry of *'Hezb faqat Hezb-Allah, Rahbar faqat Ruhollah'* (Only one party: the party of Allah; only one leader: Ruhollah) was to become the fighting slogan of the Islamic Republic.

Despite rising violence and the gradual emergence of the true colour of the revolution's real leaders, the spring and summer of 1979 was a period of unprecedented freedom in Iran. It was justly described as *'Bahar Azadi'* (the Spring of Freedom). With fear of SAVAK gone and fear of Hezb-Allah not yet sunk in, the people basked in the sun of liberty. Everyone talked to everyone, and politics, a taboo subject for years, was the most popular topic. Lenin's works, banned under the Shah, were a dime a dozen, and young bearded Marxists heatedly debated such original topics as 'socialism in one country' and 'the role of the vanguard party'. Che Guevara T-shirts were worn by many revolutionaries and khaki and camouflage-style clothes, often crowned with the Palestinian *kufiah*, made Tehran resemble war-torn west Beirut. The smart ladies and gentlemen of the Shah's era had all but disappeared, with their *haute-couture* clothes and impeccable hair-dos. The new male Iranian wore the mandatory beard, or at least a moustache in the case of Leftist revolutionaries, and would not be seen dead wearing a necktie. The new female wore the *charqad*, a headdress of white, black, navy blue or brown cotton that covered the hair but left the face fully exposed, much like the headgear of Christian nuns. Many young men carried as an accessory a machine gun or, at least, a revolver. The revolution had succeeded too quickly for many would-be guerrillas who had prepared themselves for 'a second Vietnam' in Iran.[12] In the absence of an opportunity to fight an exciting revolutionary war, no one could now begrudge them the chance to look like guerrillas who had just emerged from the forest. Some young Marxist–Maoists even called their group Sazman Jangal (the Forest Organization) and ended up attacking a gendarmerie post in the Caspian littoral woodlands. Almost all were shot on the spot or executed after summary trial.

The revolution, which in fact represented four different and parallel revolutionary traditions – religious, nationalistic, ethnic and Marxist – had generated much more energy than was needed for the overthrow of the Shah. This energy continued to seethe under the surface and erupted whenever it found an opportunity. Bazargan wanted a return to normality without any further transition, pointing out that all the aims of the revolution had already been realized. The Shah was gone, Khomeini was the supreme leader and a republic had been declared. The largest of the guerrilla organizations, the Mujahedeen Khalq, quickly had been neutralized thanks to its own internal divisions. One faction, headed by Moussa Khiabani, had all along called for preparations for an armed uprising in the 'second phase' of the revolution. But those advocating the legal electoral path had carried the day and the Mujahedeen began reconstituting themselves into a political party in order to fight presidential and parliamentary elections. The second largest guerrilla organization, the Fedayeen Khalq, was split into two factions – the Bolsheviks and the Mensheviks. The Bolsheviks formed an alliance with the Tudeh Party and threw their support unconditionally behind Khomeini. The Mensheviks organized armed uprisings among ethnic minorities, notably the Turkomans on the Soviet border and the Arab-speaking tribes of southwestern Khuzestan. They were brutally crushed by the army and the Revolutionary Guards.

A far more serious attempt at guerrilla warfare was made by the revived Kurdistan Democratic Party of Iran (PDKI), whose leader, Abdul-Rahman Qassemlu, had returned from exile in Czechoslovakia to rekindle the flames of Kurdish autonomy. Within months he had some 1200 fighters at his side. A smaller group of Marxist–Maoist guerrillas, the Komalah, also became active in Kurdistan. The capture of an army garrison and the expulsion of central government officials from several Kurdish towns gave Khomeini the impression that the PDKI was heading straight for secession. The Imam declared the Kurds to be 'children of Satan' and ordered the army and the Revolutionary Guards to crush the rebels.

The void left by Motahari's assassination was quickly filled by Beheshti, who was soon to prove himself an able administrator as well as a clever manoeuvrer. Beheshti had never been as close to the Imam as Motahari and had no qualms about seeking a separate power base for himself. He founded the Islamic Republic Party and before the summer of 1979 was over he had emerged as the strong man of the new regime. It was Beheshti who organized the election of an Assembly of Experts which approved the text of a constitution written by one of his protégés, Hassan Ibrahim-Habibi. The constitution provided for the election of a President and a unicameral Parliament and a theoretical separation of powers. But it was Khomeini, as Faqih (Theologian or Juris-consult), who received the essential part of power. The ratification of the constitution under less than correct circumstances ended whatever illusions may have remained concerning the clergy's determination to rule the country. Bazargan had tried to contain the mullahs by giving them subordinate posts at various ministries. But the mere presence of a mullah in a ministry was sufficient to make him the real centre of power. Bazargan's ministers came to resemble actors playing the part of decision-makers. One of them, Sanjabi, the the Foreign Minister, was quietly advised to resign and gladly obliged. The others stayed on until they were forced out by events in November.

Neither the internal rivalries nor the need to contain the Left prevented the Imam from attending to the other requirements of his revolution. He ordered the executions to continue and

Khalkhali had to issue many death sentences each day, including a record fifty-three sentences in October during a thirty-minute stopover at Sanandaj Airport where he judged Kurdish rebels. All the sentences were carried out before the ayatollah's jet had taken off. Over two hundred former officials, including twenty-three ex-ministers, were shot. The mullahs made a point of executing anyone who had at any time in his life committed 'a grave offence' against the clergy in general and the Imam in particular. Mohammad 'Alameh-Vahidi, aged 102, was shot because of 'insulting remarks' he had made about the Imam in 1963 during a speech in the Senate. His fellow-senator, Jamshid 'A'alam, shared the same fate for the same reason. The trials usually lasted less than an hour and were held in rooms packed with former political prisoners or relatives of those who had died under SAVAK torture or during anti-Shah demonstrations. Bazargan's attempt to prevent the summary execution of Hoveyda in April had failed after Khomeini had given Khalkhali the green light. Khalkhali accordingly half strangled the former Prime Minister after having taken him to a car parked in the courtyard of the prison. It was a dying Hoveyda who fifteen minutes later received bullets fired from Hojat al-Islam Hadi Ghaffari's gun.[13]

The purge of the army was also continued energetically. Chamran, who was soon appointed Defence Minister, took charge of this, and by the end of 1979 between 8000 and 12,000 officers, including all those ranking above brigadier, had been retired or cashiered. Of the eighty or so generals who had formed the top brass of the Shah's army, at least seventy were executed together with more than two hundred other officers and NCOs. The executions shocked the helpless middle class but helped the Imam outmanoeuvre the Left which still clamoured about the 'insufficient' number of executions.

The Imam, commenting on the execution of Hoveyda which had led to protests both at home and abroad, defended Khalkhali by saying that those who protested had 'only animal under-standing'. 'They cannot understand that killing Hoveyda should cause no grief whatsoever.'[14] The Imam declared that those executed were *mufsed fel-ardh* (corrupters of the earth) and had to be eliminated like pests. Khalkhali, expanding on the theme, said, 'It is a human right to destroy a snake in one's home. . . . Human rights mean that unsuitable individuals should be liquidated so that others can live free. This is made clear in the Qur'an.'[15]

Bazargan and his ministers protested every time an execution was announced, but did little to stem the tide. Ahmad Sadr Haj-Sayyed Javadi, Bazargan's Minister of Justice, expressed regret at Khalkhali's exploits in Kurdistan. He said, 'I was moved when I saw the photo of a twelve-year-old boy who had been executed. I was moved when I saw that even wounded men had been executed by firing squad.'[16] The Minister also related how Khalkhali had refused to commute the death sentence he had passed on a sixteen-year-old boy who continued to plead his innocence. 'Well, my boy,' the Islamic judge told the condemned adolescent, 'if you are truly innocent, as you claim, you shall go to paradise. And if, as I am sure, you are guilty, you will be receiving your just punishment.'[17] Photos of a man who had been executed while receiving treatment in a hospital and with his legs still in plaster, created further revulsion. But the executions consolidated the crucial support given to the Imam by former political prisoners, mullahs seeking to avenge themselves for over half a century of humiliation under the Pahlavis and militants who believed that anyone who had worked under the Shah was, by definition, an enemy and deserved to be put to death. Khomeini had succeeded beyond his most exaggerated expectations in portraying the regime of the Shah as 'satanic' in the eyes of the 'small people' who, having become masters of the land, thirsted for bloody revenge. Domestic servants came out to denounce their former masters and mistresses. Tenants wanted their landlords put to death as SAVAK agents. The Islamic rule under which the testimony of two men, or four women, is sufficient proof of guilt was often used to accuse innocent people of crimes they had never committed. Personal jealousies and rivalries as well as a desire for gain prompted many denunciations. Shopkeepers would drive their competitors out of business by branding them as SAVAK agents, Baha'is, Zionist spies or simply as counter-revolutionaries. Almost any excuse seemed to be good for sending people to the firing squad. Mrs Farrokhru Parsa, a 63-year-old veteran of the women's emancipation movement in Iran and a former Minister of Education, was accused of 'immoral acts' and shot. In Sanandaj a surgeon was shot after he was found 'guilty' of treating wounded anti-Khomeini demonstrators. The former Foreign Minister, Abbas-Ali Khalatbari, a saintly and highly respected man, was executed after being accused of 'having contributed to strengthening the Pahlavi regime'.

In most cases the terms 'corrupter of the earth' and 'warring on

Allah' were deemed sufficient for a death sentence. These terms were not reserved for former officials or ethnic rebels alone. They were also used as justification for the execution of homosexuals, lesbians and people charged with other 'sexual crimes'. Khalkhali organized the execution of half a dozen prostitutes in a south Tehran street where they had practised their profession. A woman accused of adultery was stoned to death in Kerman. Homosexuals were hanged from the trees in Semnan and Najaf-Abad. And in Behshahr an eighteen-year-old pregnant woman was executed by firing squad on a charge of fornication.

The revolution, lacking any serious programme of economic and social reform, tried to maintain its momentum through executions, purges, growing violence against women not wearing the veil, pressure for a total ban on music and dance, and continued attacks on the Shah and his late father. The militants felt they were accomplishing their divine role by raiding people's homes at night in search of musical records and instruments and other 'objects of corruption' such as playing cards, chess sets and backgammon tables. The Imam had no comments on land-ownership, beyond allowing the mullahs to appropriate some 30,000 hectares of land in five provinces. Nor did he have any ideas concerning the control of industry, banks and mineral resources. To him exploitation of man by man was not a result of systems in which small minorities controlled the bulk of the means of production, distribution and exchange. Exploitation was a result of 'satanic' tendencies in certain individuals, who all had to be eliminated. Khomeini's disregard for economic issues contrasted sharply with his strong opinions concerning what he described as 'the essential ethical questions of mankind' in his *Kashf al-Asrar*. He was to propagate his favourite themes in speech after speech made in Qom.

Receiving the directors of Radio Iran in Qom, the Imam urged them to combat music 'with all your might'. 'Music corrupts the minds of our youth,' he declared. 'There is no difference between music and opium. Both create lethargy in different ways. If you want your country to be independent, then ban music. Music is treason to our nation and to our youth.'[18] In a separate meeting with university students the Imam claimed that the introduction of music into Iran had been 'a plot by foreigners' to 'lead our youth astray'.[19] He poured scorn on the Arabian Nights' vision of an Islamic society. His Islam was stern, tough and uncompromising. 'Allah did not create man so that he could have fun,' he told another meeting in Qom. 'The aim of creation was for mankind to be put to the test through hardship and prayer. An Islamic regime must be serious in every field. There are no jokes in Islam. There is no humour in Islam. There is no fun in Islam. There can be no fun and joy in whatever is serious. Islam does not allow swimming in the sea and is opposed to radio and television serials. Islam, however, allows marksmanship, horseback riding and competition in [such sports].'[20]

Having succeeded in preventing the emergence of a triumvirate of Grand Ayatollahs in Qom, the Imam ordered the dismantling of the Islamic People's Republican Party that had been set up by Shariatmadari's supporters and was fast becoming a powerful political instrument. The fact that Shariatmadari, always anxious to prevent violence, swallowed the humiliation without protest dealt a serious blow to his authority. From then on he had nowhere to go but down. Afterwards Khomeini turned his attention to Taleqani who, although of junior rank in strictly theological terms, had established himself as the spiritual leader of the Islamic Left. A series of provocative acts, including the abduction of Taleqani's two sons, proved that the ayatollah had no real power. And Khomeini, receiving him in Qom, referred to him only as 'mister', indicating that Taleqani was not recognized as an ayatollah. Taleqani was broken and died soon afterwards. Like Shariatmadari, he had not wanted to provoke a violent confrontation between his supporters and those of the Imam, and had simply backed out of a duel. Other ayatollahs, such as Golpayegani, Najafi and Mahalati in Shiraz, issued periodic protests against the summary trials, executions and confiscation of property but stopped far short of challenging Khomeini's authority. Khomeini counted only on those who were ready to die and, perhaps more important, to kill for his revolution. It is entirely possible that he was fully aware of the injustice caused by the executions, confiscations and widespread purges but saw it as the inevitable result of revolution. 'Our people are like a volcano that has been kept down for years,' Mahdavi-Kani said, in a speech that interpreted the Imam's thoughts. 'When a volcano erupts no one can restrain it.'[21]

The Imam's endorsement of acts that appeared to other ayatollahs as manifestly unjust, and therefore un-Islamic, was not, however, entirely motivated by tactical considerations. Khomeini had always believed that Islam should be enforced both through individual example and collective coercion. Earthly life, he argued, consisted of evanescent facts that had to accord with the eternal truth revealed in the Qur'an. What was important was that everyone should behave according to Islamic principles whether or not he or she believed in Islam in private. Rather than create an Islamic society from a community of already practising Muslims, the process was to be reversed. An Islamic society had to be imposed from above, and by this means render individuals good Muslims. The individual begins by having *iman* (faith) when he learns the truth of Islam. The next step is to acquire *taqwa* (piety) and organize one's own life in accordance with the rules of Islam. But no 'good Muslim' could stop there, as most ayatollahs seemed to recommend. A 'good Muslim' would seek the next stage of his development, which is *tasdeeq*. Now, the term *tasdeeq* is a difficult one to translate in a single word. It means the realization in this world of the eternal truth revealed to Muhammed by Allah in the Qur'an.[22] Islam's kingdom is of this world and must be constructed, by force and through violence and bloodshed if necessary. People who are forced to obey the rules of Islam, even grudgingly, will end up living by those rules as if they formed their second nature. Most people would go astray and be lost if left to their own intellectual resources and moral strength, and it would be cruel to subject such weak souls to constant temptation and expect them not to succumb eventually. Only a small minority of the exceptionally strong can remain pure in a world of sin and corruption. Islam is the rope that prevents the climber from falling into the abyss, the buoy that saves the shipwrecked souls of the universe, who form the majority of mankind, from drowning. It is not a set of rules which one adopts voluntarily; even its optional rules, known as *khiarat*, cannot be violated.

Making full use of radio and television as well as the pulpit, Khomeini and the younger generation of mullahs supporting his view that Islam must be imposed, not merely recommended, succeeded in impressing their ideological domination on Iran at the expense of all rival ideologies. For the first time in centuries every aspect of the nation's life had to be discussed in terms of Islamic ideology. The Imam's vocabulary extended its influence throughout the political discourse. Even Marxists were obliged to adopt his language and bow to his ideological ascendancy. Only a few years earlier no Persian article dealing with this or that political issue would have been complete without quotations from Western philosophers and intellectuals. Even Jalal al-Ahmad's anti-foreign pamphlet *Gharb-zadehgui* (*Westoxication*) started with a quotation from Ernst Jünger and included numerous citations from other

Western gurus such as Jean-Paul Sartre, Raymond Aron and Albert Camus. Now all this was changed, and every political essay, including many by intellectuals with a dialectical or 'liberal' past, was peppered with Arabic quotations from hitherto unknown Muslim saints and thinkers.

Montazeri used his position as the Friday Prayer Leader of Tehran to turn the Tehran University lawn into an open Islamic seminary. Using a simple language directly addressed to the illiterate masses and adopting the traditional style of storytelling, he reminded the Iranians of their Islamic heritage in a way never considered before.

Works by Shi'ite scholars, previously available only in manuscript, were printed and published in tens of thousands of copies, attracting a vast readership for a while. Radio, television and most newspapers were turned into mere extensions of the mosque's traditional propaganda network.

Khomeini, for his part, continued to dismiss all Western philosophy as 'a cobweb of intrigues concocted by Jews', and began developing the theme that only Islam could solve the modern world's 'seemingly incurable diseases'. He announced a television series in which he would offer a weekly two-hour commentary on the various suras of the Qur'an. In the end only one programme was produced and broadcast, in which Khomeini offered a commentary on the Hamd Sura. For the first time a typical Faizieh School lecture was brought to millions of Iranians. Khomeini's refined and sophisticated vocabulary and his rhetorical prowess revealed an aspect of his personality that had remained unknown to the public. This was no longer the vengeful mullah speaking the language of the poor and the illiterate and reducing all phenomena to good and evil, black and white. The opposition intellectuals were jolted out of their comfortable assumption that Khomeini was 'a semi-literate village mullah', and extended to him a grudging respect. He had shown that Shi'ite tradition could still offer fine examples at least of exciting sophistry if not of genuine philosophical speculation. The illiterate masses, however, were confused. Having listened to their Imam for nearly two hours they had understood nothing. Some began murmuring that even Khomeini may be 'one of them', meaning those who, thanks to their education and position, had looked down on the *mustadh'afeen* until the revolution. They also detected in him a soft streak which sharply contrasted with the macho image he had cultivated for himself. The series was not to be, and the Imam recorded no further programmes. Instead he resumed his usual attacks on 'satanic forces', promising to 'kick their teeth in'.[23] The mass of his followers were reassured; the Imam was not 'one of them'.

# 15

# *Taking on the Great Satan*

America cannot do a damn thing.

Ayatollah Khomeini

*F*or years the Shah had warned successive American admin-
istrations that his removal from power would mean an end
to US interests, not only in Iran but also in the Persian Gulf region
as a whole. But by the autumn of 1978 the Carter administration
had already thought about the unthinkable, and a year later
relations between the United States and the Islamic Republic
appeared promising. During his stay in France Khomeini had
promised to continue normal relations with the United States.
And the provisional government had kept that pledge. The huge
contracts signed by the Shah for the purchase of arms from the
United States had been cancelled by Bakhtiar during his brief
tenure as Prime Minister but the revolution had taken no specifically anti-American action. The mullahs had allowed an orderly
departure of thousands of American technicians from Iran in the
last days of the Shah's regime, and had acted in time to prevent
pro-Soviet guerrillas from stealing sensitive equipment from
listening posts stationed in northern Iran to monitor the SALT
agreements. Bazargan's government had a solid majority of
members who favoured close ties with the United States.
Bazargan's first Foreign Minister, Karim Sanjabi, had dispatched
his children to the USA for further education. One of his sons had

become a naturalized American in the 1960s. Sanjabi's successor as Foreign Minister, Ibrahim Yazdi, was himself a naturalized American. It was he who announced the cancellation of the 1959 military agreement between Iran and the United States, but he did not take the necessary legal steps for a full abrogation, and the agreement, technically speaking, remains in force even today. Yazdi had also balanced his move by simultaneously announcing the abrogation of the 1921 treaty with the Soviet Union. Bazargan's energetic deputy and government spokesman, Abbas Amir-Entezam, was an open advocate of strong ties with the USA as a means of offsetting the pressure exerted by the fact that the USSR shared a 2535-kilometre frontier with Iran. Many people in the Imam's entourage privately believed that Carter had helped speed up the triumph of the revolution by abandoning the Shah to his fate. Thus they did not include the United States among the long list of the new regime's enemies. The USA was seldom attacked as an imperialist power and, when mentioned on rare occasions, was criticized only for having supported the Shah for so long and for her continued assistance to Israel. Efforts by the Left, especially Tudeh and the Fedayeen guerrillas, to give the revolution an anti-American edge did not succeed. Khomeini's revolution was not a class-based movement at home and could not develop into one so far as international relations were concerned. Attacks on American embassy and consulate buildings by Fedayeen and Mujahedeen elements had been firmly dealt with by the authorities. And an attempt by the Soviets to secure a list of purported CIA agents in Iran via the Mujahedeen failed when the Revolutionary Guards arrested Mohammad-Reza Sa'adati shortly before meeting his Russian contact. Night after night, hundreds of mullahs used the pulpits in mosques throughout the country to denounce communism and attack the Soviet Union for its role in Afghanistan and 'the captivity of our Muslim brethren' in Soviet Azerbaijan and the Central Asian republics. A constant theme was that the Shah would have been unable to prevent the takeover of Iran by Communists in the long run, and that the Islamic Revolution could now make sure that this did not happen. Thus when the Shah was given permission to travel to New York for medical treatment in October few people either in Tehran or in Washington expected the move to cause a major upset in the tenuous relations between the two countries. They were to be proved wrong. Bruce Laingen, the American chargé d'affaires in Tehran, had already warned the State Department that the Shah's admission into the United States could lead to trouble. But everyone assumed that any crisis caused by this would be manageable and temporary. Laingen had established strong ties with several of Bazargan's ministers, notably Yazdi, and Washington considered him capable of handling an Islamic loss of temper.

News of the Shah's arrival in New York did not draw much comment from Tehran and Qom at first. Only Tudeh and the guerrilla groups began speaking of a plot. They claimed that Washington was plotting a repetition of the 1953 CIA-backed coup that had restored the Shah to his throne. Satellite footage showing the Shah holding court at his New York hospital and receiving, among others, Henry Kissinger, David Rockefeller and several former Iranian ministers, gave the impression that the dying monarch was planning something. This coincided with a sudden surge in pro-Shah activities by a group of rebel soldiers under General Palizban in the Western province of Kermanshah, where Jaaf tribal warriors also raised the banner of revolt in the name of the Pahlavis. General Gholam-Ali Oveissi was reported to be in Iraq at the head of a counter-revolutionary force consisting of deserters and tribal mercenaries. Tudeh magnified all these reports and was soon able to create a new anti-American atmosphere. November 4, the anniversary of Khomeini's exile to Turkey, was to be marked by nationwide demonstrations, and each group and party tried to think of something dramatic. A group of students under the influence of a militant pro-Palestinian dentist, Habibollah Payman, decided to demonstrate in front of the US embassy compound on Takht Jamshid (Taleqani) Avenue. The demonstrators quickly found that they could enter the compound without encountering resistance and therefore did so. They had not planned what to do once they had entered, and must have surprised even themselves when they announced that they would stay in the building together with everyone else in it, until the Shah was extradited to Iran together with his wealth. Since then millions of words have been written about the takeover, often claiming it to be the result of a Machiavellian plot. But there is no evidence to suggest that anything more than an attempt by some enthusiastic students to perform a dramatic act was involved. The episode was, to be sure, later exploited as part of the power struggle that was already going on between the mullahs and their political rivals. The fact that the students stole the show from everyone else and became the focus of universal attention, thanks to television and satellite transmission, made any quick settlement impossible. The 'heroes of Islam', as they were instantly labelled by Tudeh propaganda, could not simply bow out after sunset. A group of students who had previously been just part of the grey mass of frustrated revolutionaries craving dramatic action now felt they could dictate the future of the country – indeed, of the whole world.

Khomeini could have ended the episode on the first day, but he would have had to accept some loss of revolutionary prestige in order to do so. He had no accurate information on the crisis, and was further handicapped in making a decision by the fact that three of his closest advisers were unavailable. Rafsanjani and Khameneh'i were in Mecca, performing the Haj, and Beheshti was in the Isfahani countryside and could not be reached. Sayyed Ahmad was dispatched to Tehran and visited the embassy the same afternoon. When he returned he advised what seemed the easiest course: wait and see. Ahmad had always been far less radical than either his father or his late brother Mostafa, but he had over the years learned that the Imam would always choose the most extreme course of action. The students asked the Imam to send them a spiritual leader and Khomeini at first wanted Hojat al-Islam Mohammad Yazdi to take charge. Yazdi could not be found in time, and the Imam gave the mission to Khoiniha. The many versions of the fable that Khoiniha was a KGB agent and had been trained in Moscow and was the leader of the students right from the start must be discounted although they have been adopted as part of American mythology. But Khoiniha's choice was to prove crucial. The young mullah, aged thirty-nine at the time, had distinguished himself as an able organizer and belonged to the hard-line faction in Khomeini's entourage. He hated the USA for its support of Israel and had deep sympathies with the Palestinians who had trained him in the art of guerrilla warfare in Lebanon in the 1960s.

Within forty-eight hours, what was to be named 'the second revolution' was in full swing, attracting millions of people, especially children and teenagers throughout the country. Life was, once again, exciting as Islam took on the 'Great Satan'. The speed with which the Bazargan Cabinet disintegrated left the regime's moderate elements with little chance to rally and prevent a full takeover by Beheshti, who was then in alliance with his future rival and enemy Bani-Sadr. It was Bani-Sadr who was asked to form a government that would have no Prime Minister. Ghotb-zadeh was moved to the Foreign Ministry and almost immediately saw himself as the great diplomat who would quickly settle the crisis and win universal acclaim. The Revolutionary Council gave its formal approval to the occupation of the embassy and the holding of the hostages a few days later, thus directly implicating the regime.

The seizure of the embassy gave the 'Muslim Students Following the Imam's Line', as the group called itself, direct access to a mine of highly classified, sensitive information on virtually all aspects of Irano–American relations over some thirty years. The documents had been moved to Washington during the revolution but had been returned after Bazargan formed his Cabinet and resumed dialogue with the embassy. For the next five years the publication of a selection of these documents was to serve as a means by which the radical factions eliminated their rivals from the political scene. By June 1985 sixty-one volumes of selected documents had been published, often in bilingual editions. They provide invaluable insights into the methods of intelligence and diplomatic operation used by one of the two superpowers in a country as sensitive as Iran.

An analysis of these documents falls outside the scope of our study. But a few observations might be in order. The USA had roughly five thousand 'sources of information' in Iran, ranging from paid CIA agents to voluntary informants. These 'sources' were recruited from all walks of life and included almost all the Shah's known non-clerical opponents over some twenty-five years. The embassy in Tehran and the CIA station which worked alongside it did an excellent job of reporting. US policy-makers could have known almost everything about Iran had they chosen to study their own files. But, in what remains an astonishing oversight, they omitted to do so; and, as a result, understood almost nothing about their key ally in the Persian Gulf. During the Nixon–Ford years, the documents demonstrate, Washington did not even want to hear any bad news about the Shah. Washington insisted on being deceived and was suitably obliged. The documents also show that many Iranians agreed to become informants, informers or outright spies partly in order to advance their own various careers in business or the civil service. As a result they fed the Americans information that suited their own personal schemes. In the 1970s this meant that an unusually high percentage of the information gathered was biased or totally unreliable.

The documents show with what naiveté the Shah's traditional

opponents had over the years tried to persuade Washington to abandon him and help them, instead, to create a nationalist government that could fight the Soviet Union with a 'potent ideology'. Some American agents understood the intricacies of the Persian character and showed a certain degree of sophistication in recruiting new informers. Others, however, seemed to believe that Iranians were inferior beings who could be bought with a bottle of Bourbon. One agent wanted to employ Bani-Sadr, then a key member of the Revolutionary Council, for a monthly salary of £700 in 1979.

The publication of these documents, carefully selective to be sure, discredited most of the middle-class politicians who still insisted on a share of power. Many of them had to escape the country to avoid arrest and possible execution as CIA agents. Some, like Amir-Entezam and Dariush Foruhar, who had been Bazargan's Labour Minister, were imprisoned, the former for life. The documents provided the excuse for a fresh purge of the civil service, the media and the armed forces.[1]

The continuing drama at the embassy, with its endless twists and turns, helped Beheshti speed up his drive for full power. Beheshti used the embassy episode as a means of signalling to Washington to recognize the mullahs as the real force of the revolution and the future rulers of Iran for decades to come. The Carter administration had written off the Shah as early as November 1978 but had persistently refused to recognize the mullahs as his inevitable heirs. At first it had tried to prop up Bakhtiar's government, which was instantly dismissed as a non-starter by most of the 'sources' in Tehran. Later, it backed Bazargan who, as a conservative in a revolutionary time, was bound to fail in his efforts to send the jin back into the bottle. The seizure of the embassy did not change Carter's policy of looking for 'moderates' in a radical situation until much later. And his administration was to draw two more blanks by trying to back Bani-Sadr and Ghotbzadeh. By the time Carter had established contact with Beheshti, through Hamilton Jordan helped by a French and an Argentinian lawyer, the issue of the hostages had become far too complicated to admit of a quick resolution. Carter's own decision to freeze Iranian assets in US banks and his ill-fated military rescue attempt had added new dimensions to the crisis. But the contact with Beheshti, and through him with Khomeini himself, eventually paid off and the hostages were released on the same day Ronald Reagan took over from Carter as President.[2]

In the meantime, Beheshti suffered one major setback when he failed to persuade the Imam to allow him to run for President. Anticipating Beheshti's ambitions, Khomeini announced that none of the mullahs wished to be a candidate in the presidential election which was held in February 1980. Forced out of the race, the ambitious Beheshti set to work to ensure the election of one of his protégés, Jalaleddin Farsi. But when Farsi filled in the forms needed for his candidature it was revealed that this former pupil of Khomeini in Najaf was, in fact, an Afghan citizen. The Islamic Republic, although claiming to be the universal state of all Muslims, could not allow an Afghan to become its first President. Beheshti quickly fielded another candidate, Hassan Ibrahim-Habibi, who had represented him in secret negotiations with Hamilton Jordan.[3] But Habibi, a lacklustre sociologist from the Sorbonne, failed to get his candidacy off the ground. In the poll he collected only 5 per cent of the votes. The two main contenders were Bani-Sadr, who secured some 11 million votes (75 per cent of the total) and Admiral Madani, who collected over 2 million votes. Bani-Sadr's candidacy was helped by the fact that he was generally recognized as the Imam's 'spiritual son'. Khomeini himself had not recommended any candidate and probably voted for Ghotbzadeh but Sayyed Ahmad declared for Bani-Sadr together with Eshraqi, the Imam's son-in-law.[4] The bombastic Ghotbzadeh, who had tried to improve his chances by falsely announcing that the Shah had been arrested in Panama as part of a secret deal with that country's dictator General Omar Torrijos, suffered a serious blow by receiving less than half a million votes.

In January the Imam had moved to Tehran to receive treatment for a heart condition at a hospital built by the Dowager Empress shortly before the revolution. Khomeini was sure he was going to die in the course of that year, and was anxious to set up the new institutions as quickly as possible. On 4 February he took Bani-Sadr's oath as the first President of the Islamic Republic. A visibly moved Bani-Sadr kissed the Imam's hand in front of television cameras. Khomeini, tearing a sheet from a writing pad still bearing the insignia of the Dowager Empress, wrote a sixteen-word edict appointing Bani-Sadr Commander-in-Chief of the armed forces. He warned the new President against 'egoism, excess of ambition and seduction by the world'.[5] A man who only a year earlier had been a student in Paris was now at the head of the region's richest and most powerful country.

The parliamentary elections which followed in the spring provided Beheshti with an opportunity to remedy his defeat in the presidential race. His party, mobilizing the mullahs and through them millions of the Imam's devotees, won the majority of the 271 seats in the unicameral Majlis Shuray Islami (the Islamic Consultative Assembly). Rafsanjani was quickly elected Speaker and began to purge opposition deputies even before the first month of the Majlis was out. Several deputies, including Madani, had to flee the country after documents showing them to have been in contact with US officials were suitably leaked by the 'students'. Others, like Khosrow Qashqa'i, a tribal chief from Fars, had their credentials thrown out. Qashqa'i was later executed as a CIA agent. The Majlis finally began work with only some thirty deputies opposed to the Beheshti faction still present. Half of these supported Bani-Sadr, the rest were grouped around Bazargan, who sat as a member for Tehran.

After weeks of wrangling the Majlis forced Bani-Sadr to accept Raja'i as Prime Minister. Bani-Sadr hated Raja'i and considered him to be 'a paragon of stupidity'. Khomeini, hearing of Bani-Sadr's remark, came to the defence of his former taster at Refah School and said, 'Mr Raja'i may not be the most intelligent of men but he is devoted to Islam.'[6] The remark launched the debate on ability versus loyalty. The Imam was to side with those who believed loyalty to be by far the more important quality.

The continued confrontation with the United States strengthened the position of the Left which hoped the Imam's movement would lead to a pan-Islamic revolt against 'American imperialism'. The subject of 'exporting the revolution', first raised by Bani-Sadr in his election campaign, was seized upon by the Left and the Islamic radicals as a proper avenue for the energies of Islamic Iran. The Imam had until then promised to work for the liberation of Jerusalem and the destruction of the Jewish state. But now that he had proved that 'America cannot do a damn thing', he was beginning to talk about the overthrow of 'puppet regimes imposed on Muslim peoples everywhere'.

Tudeh encouraged what it described as the revolution's 'international duties'. The party's secretary-general Nureddin Kianuri, himself the grandson of Shaikh Nuri who had died for the cause Khomeini now represented, told Bazargan that the Imam was 'applying exactly our policy' and that the Communists would 'separate our path' only if the anti-imperialist strategy of the revolution was abandoned.[7] Tudeh's aid, reflecting support from the Soviet Union, proved crucial in the summer of 1980 when Kianuri informed the Imam that the Iraqis were preparing a surprise attack on Iranian airfields aimed at destroying the air force on the ground. Bani-Sadr was later able to secure similar information, possibly with Syrian help, and arranged for Iranian fighter-bombers to be transferred to airfields beyond the range of the Iraqi air force. The transfer dramatically reduced Iraq's chances of a quick victory when its forces launched a massive invasion of Iran on 22 September after weeks of sporadic border clashes. The Iranian air force was able to knock out Iraq's oil-exporting facilities and provided effective cover for the nation's disorganized forces.

The Iraqi invasion took Iran by surprise. Almost no one in the leadership had taken the trouble to interpret the numerous signals from Baghdad to mean that an attack on Iran was imminent. The Beheshti faction tried to dismiss the Iraqi move as a limited show of force. The Imam was at first inclined to share that view, and accordingly told the nation in a message that the Iraqis had acted like 'a thief who throws a stone in the garden and flees'. The Islamic leadership was not psychologically prepared for war and both Bani-Sadr and Raja'i were, at first, inclined to look for a quick cease-fire. Raja'i even began preparing the political ground for such a cease-fire by announcing that Islam attached no importance to 'land and water'. The Iraqis interpreted this as a signal that the Islamic Republic would be prepared to offer concessions on the Shatt al-Arab waterway as well as parts of Khuzestan which Baghdad claimed to belong to 'the Arab nation'.

Bani-Sadr was the first to lose his illusion of a quick end to the war, but he succumbed to another. He thought that the war would end the internecine feuds and that, as Commander-in-Chief, he would emerge victorious in his duel with the detested Beheshti. But the Commander-in-Chief, who had not even performed his national service, did not know even where to begin. The army had only two divisions in more or less fighting shape and only one of them was in the war-struck region. Under the Shah, Iran had constantly treated Iraq as enemy number one and had based her strategy on taking the war into Iraqi territory as quickly as possible once conflict appeared inevitable. Iraq, a country lacking in depth and geographically dominated by the Iranian plateau, was never expected to launch a fullscale invasion on so broad a front. The Iraqis, for their part, had for years trained themselves to fight a defensive war against Iran. Thus, when the Iraqi President Saddam Hussein took the decision to invade Iran his army had to copy a plan used by the British in 1941 to send troops into Khuzestan. The Iraqis had no doubt been indirectly encouraged by the USA which apparently hoped that the war would force Tehran to speed up the process of releasing the fifty-two American diplomats held hostage. President Hussein had also been fed highly optimistic reports from anti-Khomeini exiles showing that the regime of the Imam would be unable to fight a fullscale war. Hussein had calculated the war would be over by 5 October and had prepared himself for a dramatic announcement of 'the second Qaddessiah'. Qaddessiah is the name of the decisive battle in which the forces of Islam broke the Sassanid army some fourteen centuries earlier. The Iraqi advance was quick and largely unopposed; within a week some 7000 square kilometres of Iranian territory were captured. People began to escape from the border provinces, creating a mood of fear and despair throughout the country.

The second Qaddessiah, however, was not to be. Khomeini, once again using the technique of *rowzeh* which is used for mourning the martyrdom of Hussein, the third Imam, told the nation that this was a dramatic repetition of the tragedy of Karbala, with the difference that this time the forces of Good were to triumph over the forces of Evil. He fixed as the objectives of the war the destruction of the Iraqi regime, the establishment of an Islamic republic in Baghdad and the continuation of the struggle until Jerusalem was liberated. The Imam's fighting words had the tonic effect expected. In many towns and villages mullahs called on volunteers to gather at mosques, and within a few days a stream of young men thirsting to kill and be killed started in the direction of the wartorn provinces. Young boys who had reluctantly returned to their classrooms after nearly two years of exciting revolutionary activity were now once again able to seek adventure and martyrdom in the name of Allah.

Saddam Hussein had declared the Iranian port of Khorramshahr, which he called Muhammarah, to be the main prize of the war. The port city was to be annexed by Iraq 'until the end of time'. The local army and Revolutionary Guard commanders wanted to abandon the city almost immediately, preferring to draw the Iraqi forces farther inland before engaging them. But a group of local boys decided to stand and fight. Soon they were reinforced by the arrival of some 1200 boys from Ahvaz who, led by one Gholum-Deraz (the Lanky Gholum), otherwise known as 'the John Wayne of the poor', came to the port city to die the death of martyrs. Every one of them died during nearly three weeks of fighting which included several days of house-to-house and hand-to-hand combat. The Iraqis conquered the burned shell of the city which was almost totally abandoned by its 120,000 inhabitants. Khorramshahr's heroic resistance transformed Iran's fortunes and enabled Khomeini to dismiss any further suggestion of a negotiated end to the war. For a brief but glorious moment, Khomeini, a man dedicated to the destruction of Persian nationalism, became its living hero and symbol. The frontier between loyalty to Islam and love of one's homeland was effaced, and patriotic songs, banned since the Islamic Revolution, were once again broadcast by Radio Iran.[8] By mid-October the Iraqi offensive had run out of steam and a war of attrition began. It was to end nearly a year later when the Iranians took back Hamid and Sussangerd and finally liberated Khorramshahr. A new deadlock was reached when Iranian forces penetrated into Iraq in the summer of 1982 at the start of a long and endless confrontation which by 1985 had claimed at least 300,000 dead on both sides.

The war halted all propaganda aimed at the abolition of the armed forces. The army, at first hesitant, soon rallied and spearheaded the reconquest of national territory. As Commander-in-Chief, Bani-Sadr spent much time at the front and played a valuable role in restoring the morale of officers and NCOs. It was thanks to his intervention that a number of army and air force officers were released from prison and allowed to take part in the fighting. Bani-Sadr hoped to use the army as a force capable of counterbalancing the organization of the mullahs. The Chief of Staff, Brigadier Valliollah Fallahi, had gained nationwide popularity and headed a group of officers who seemed to prefer almost anyone to the mullahs. But Fallahi and most of the key members of his group were to be killed before the first year of the war was over in an air crash, the circumstances of which remain shrouded in mystery. The fact that the commission of inquiry charged with the task of investigating the crash has failed to offer any report or, indeed, to complete its work at all has fostered rumours that the Beheshti faction may have had a hand in 'organizing' the disaster.

Reports of millions of children and adolescents pouring into mosques to beg to be sent to the front persuaded the Imam that, contrary to the advice of those who preached a return to normal, the revolution had not yet run its course. The war had come at a time when the leadership was locked in petty intrigues and the people were beginning to withdraw into indifference. The vast political coalition that had swept the Shah out of Iran had disintegrated and Khomeini himself was prey to more and more frequent fits of despondency. The minor heart attack he had suffered in the spring of 1980 had left him in a morbid mood. He was not, as Bani-Sadr was to suggest two years later, afraid of death; he had always believed Shebli's prophecy and did not expect to live much longer. What he was concerned about was that his revolution seemed to be dying a slow, inglorious death. The seizure of the US Embassy in Tehran had given the revolution a second wind but had failed to reverse the overall trend of decline. It was the Iraqi invasion of Khuzestan that rekindled the dying flame. The Imam described the war as 'a blessing from Allah', and decided that, more than ever before, he should listen to no one except those teeming masses of children and teenagers craving martyrdom. Without the war, these children and young people, radicalized to a degree unknown anywhere else in the world, might have been attracted to the various Leftist groups which advocated the continuation of the revolution and accused the ruling factions of conservatism. The Mujahedeen, for example, had been able to recruit thousands of additional members, mostly from among teenagers in the poor districts of major cities. They gave the recruits arms, military training, frequent periods of 'simulation clandestinity' in safe houses and a full chance for a wide range of revolutionary activities that the all too sudden victory of the Ayatollah had prevented millions of young Iranians from experiencing. The Mujahedeen offered a simple and attractive ideology. They were as Islamic as Khomeini, if not more. At the same time, however, they campaigned for the abolition of the army and the 'protection' of society by a militia consisting precisely of the teenage and young armed volunteers. The war gave these young volunteers for martyrdom a chance to become heroes in the service of the Imam. The Baseej Mustadh'afeen (Mobilization of the Dispossessed) organization, established in 1980, was to provide the nucleus of an army of 20 million youthful fighters.

Bani-Sadr's fortunes were not helped by the war as he had naively expected. The Commander-in-Chief continued to write the editorial of his daily newspaper, *Enqelab Islami* (*The Islamic Revolution*), often from the war front, offering details of future military moves by Iran. This was a daily intellectual striptease of a very original type, and it soon persuaded Khomeini that his 'spiritual son' was suffering from an acute case of *folie de grandeur*.

Bani-Sadr began describing himself as the original architect of the revolution and even claimed that it was he who had given Khomeini the idea of an 'Islamic government'. The President's enemies used his daily column as a means of discrediting him. And one pro-Beheshti firebrand, Hassan Ayat, even accused Bani-Sadr of high treason for publishing Iran's war plans in advance. Khomeini was getting tired of Bani-Sadr's endless complaints against almost everyone else. The Imam had supported Bani-Sadr's demand for a unified military command and had prevented a move by the Beheshti faction to divest the President of his responsibilities as Commander-in-Chief in December 1980. But now Bani-Sadr seemed to be trying to create a new coalition around himself. He was already in touch with the Mujahedeen and enjoyed the support of the National Front as well as Bazargan and Ghotbzadeh. Worse still, Bani-Sadr openly courted the three Grand Ayatollahs of Qom as well as Ayatollah Qomi and Ayatollah Abdullah Shirazi in Mashhad. The latter two responded by strongly supporting Bani-Sadr and condemning the principle of the Regency of the Theologian, the cornerstone of the Imam's system. Beheshti was now convinced that Bani-Sadr with the help of the army was preparing a coup d'état aimed at ousting the mullahs from power.

In March 1981 Khomeini called Bani-Sadr, Beheshti and a few other key leaders to a reconciliation meeting. Sayyed Ahmad, who supported Bani-Sadr, was also present. The angry Imam told everyone present to stop quarrelling and concentrate on defeating Iraq. He told Bani-Sadr to stop 'acting like a child'. 'I could have you arrested and kept in the cellar of this house for the rest of your life,' the Imam warned his 'spiritual son'. 'And don't think I shall allow you to escape and join our enemies abroad.'[9] He ordered all those present to stop attacking each other. Everyone emerged with smiles and assurances of friendly relations. But within a few days Bani-Sadr resumed his attacks on his rivals, and by June he was at the centre of what looked like a burgeoning insurrection. In violent articles and speeches he indirectly attacked Khomeini for his 'personality cult', and called for the dissolution of Parliament, the dismissal of Raja'i as Premier and of Beheshti as Chief Justice, and the abrogation of the Council of Guardians. Imitating some of Khomeini's own tactics against the Shah, Bani-Sadr also called on the Tehran bazaar to close down for a day of protest. The bazaar did not close, however, as an angry Imam threatened to 'cut off the hands of anybody' involved in such a move.[10]

Some members of Khomeini's own family supported Bani-Sadr. Sayyed Ahmad remained loyal to the President until the very last. Morteza, the Imam's elder brother, and his son, Reza, also backed Bani-Sadr, as did Hussein, Khomeini's grandson. Hussein made a speech in Mashhad in June in which he warned the nation of 'the establishment of religious Fascism which is the worst kind of Fascism'.[11] The Imam had the erring grandson brought to him in Jamaran and kept him a prisoner there for six months, by which time Bani-Sadr was already in exile in France. Several attempts by the National Front and the Mujahedeen to organize rallies in support of the President failed. On 10 June a Party of Allah mob, led by Ghaffari, attacked and routed a Mujahedeen rally, and demonstrated its ability to control the streets of Tehran. At a time when most major political issues were settled in the streets, such control proved decisive in the power struggle. Khomeini dismissed Bani-Sadr as Commander-in-Chief and the army reacted with total indifference. Two weeks later the Majlis approved a motion calling for the President's removal. And the Imam hammered the last nail in Bani-Sadr's political coffin by signing a nine-word decree dismissing him as President. The Mujahedeen failed to deliver on their promise of a nationwide armed insurrection but offered Bani-Sadr protection in one of their safe houses, and a few days later arranged for his flight out of Iran aboard a hijacked air force Boeing 707. Accompanying Bani-Sadr on the flight was the Mujahedeen leader, Massoud Rajavi, who was later to become the ousted President's son-in-law and, for a while, his political ally, before he abandoned him in his turn.

The alliance between Bani-Sadr and the Mujahedeen had been based on each party's overestimation of the other side's strength. Bani-Sadr had been led to believe that Rajavi's guerrillas would be able to defeat the Party of Allah militants in the streets of Tehran. Rajavi, for his part, had half believed Bani-Sadr's claims of enjoying the support of the army and thought that the army would neutralize the Revolutionary Guards and allow the Mujahedeen guerrillas to seize control of Tehran. Unknown to Bani-Sadr, at least before he had fled to France, the Mujahedeen had also worked out a plan for the physical elimination of Beheshti and most of the other key figures in the Imam's administration. Both fugitives were confident that their exile would not last more than a few weeks. They were to be proved wrong.[12]

On 28 June a powerful bomb destroyed the headquarters of the Islamic Republic Party in south Tehran, killing Beheshti and more than seventy other leaders, including Mohammad Montazeri ('Ayatollah Ringo') and ten ministers and under-secretaries. Hashemi-Rafsanjani, the Speaker of the Majlis, and Raja'i had escaped certain death by leaving the meeting of the party leadership minutes before the explosion. The death of strongman Beheshti and of so many key figures threw Tehran into confusion, and for a few hours the Islamic regime seemed on the verge of collapse. Once again, however, the Imam responded with an appeal for firmness and greater sacrifice. He called on the Party of Allah not to abandon the revolution which would never abandon them. He compared the death of Beheshti and his colleagues to the martyrdom of Hussein and his companions and urged the nation to avenge 'the fallen heroes'. The performance, on television, revealed Khomeini at his best as a *rowzeh-khan*. The regime was able to creep back from the edge of the precipice. The revolution was safe once again.

The terrorist campaign, however, did not cease. Assassinations of mullahs and officials continued throughout the country as the Mujahedeen threw in all they had in the hope of bringing down a confused enemy. On 30 August the campaign of terror claimed still more victims. A powerful explosion destroyed part of the building housing the Prime Minister's office. Raja'i, who had in the meantime been elected President, was killed instantly, together with Bahonar, the new Prime Minister, and two police and security officials. Mahdavi-Kani, the Interior Minister who immediately took over as Premier, would have been among the victims had he not been late for the meeting, which was to discuss a new security plan aimed at curbing terrorism.

The revolutionary regime once again proved itself capable of rallying and replacing its 'martyrs' with new officials. Khameneh'i was elected President and quickly appointed Mir-Hussein Mussavi Premier. The two men were said to be half-brothers. Thus, Khameneh'i, who had in his turn narrowly escaped assassination and now enjoyed the title of *shahid-zendeh* (the living martyr), became the first mullah to head the Iranian state. Khomeini, who had frustrated Beheshti's presidential ambitions by insisting that mullahs should not seek the presidency, had at first been reluctant to change his mind for Khameneh'i. But the Imam was by now thoroughly disappointed in politicians and believed that only mullahs were truly trust-worthy. In a speech he gave vent to his anger with the politicians and admitted that he had been wrong to expect them to serve the revolution with dignity. The Imam's low opinion of politicians, including those who had served him before and after the revolution, was prompted by a number of factors. Bazargan had proved to be weak and vacillating. Bani-Sadr had betrayed his 'spiritual father'. The Mujahedeen who had killed in his name were now turning their guns against him. Documents seized from the occupied US embassy building showed that almost all 'nationalist' leaders had been in touch with the Americans in one way or another. Finally, raids by Revolutionary Guards on the homes of a number of 'liberal' politicians who had at first cooperated with Khomeini revealed a series of 'horrors'. These houses turned out to be modern versions of Ali Baba's cave, with stocks of alcohol, caviar (which was forbidden under Islam), collections of objects that turned out to be 'sex aids' and piles of copies of *Playboy* and erotic literature. Khameneh'i and his supporters succeeded in persuading Khomeini that all non-mullah politicians were corrupt, devious and in the pay of foreign powers.

The Mujahedeen's campaign of terror hardened the regime's attitude towards dissent. A triumvirate of exceptionally brutal men consisting of two mullahs, Mohammad Mohammadi-Gilani and Hussein Mussavi-Tabrizi, together with Assadollah Lajevardi, one of the closest friends of the assassinated Raja'i, was formed to quell the Mujahedeen revolt. A wave of executions began and continued unabated for a whole year. On a single day (19 September) 149 people, mostly aged between sixteen and twenty-five, and including thirty-two women, were shot in Tehran's Evin Prison. Tabrizi and Lajevardi acted as prosecutors and Gilani worked as the sole judge. The number of executions was to reach six thousand before the end of the year. Among those shot or hanged in public were injured guerrillas who had been dispatched to Evin rather than to hospital. Gilani, citing the Imam's theological authority, announced that there was no age limit for executions and, in fact, there was none. 'A nine-year-old girl is considered an adult in Islam,' the Hojat al-Islam announced. 'So such a girl is responsible for her acts and can be executed if she tries to war on Allah.'[13] The youngest prisoners to be executed were Zahra Maqsadi, a ten-year-old girl, and the two Mesbah sisters aged thirteen and fifteen. The regime responded to violence with even greater violence. Many prisoners who had been sentenced to various terms of imprisonment were taken out of their cells and shot. Sa'id Soltanpour, a Communist poet, was abducted at his wedding and executed at Evin. The Imam approved the repression as 'a necessary surgery' and called on the people, especially children, to keep an eye on the activities of everyone around them. They were to form 'an espionage network of 38 million people' and would be rewarded in the hereafter as the spies of Allah. The argument was that no act was evil so long as it was performed in the service of Allah, whereas acts normally considered noble would be nothing but crimes if directed against the Almighty's will.[14] Revolutionary Guards supported by members of the Party of Allah raided the hideouts of the guerrillas and killed hundreds of them in gun battles. Among those gunned down was Moussa Khiabani who had operated as the Mujahedeen's Supreme Commander during the revolt. He was barely thirty and his supporters mourned him as 'the Great General of the People'. Throughout the repression the Tudeh Party worked closely with the Islamic authorities and was indirectly responsible for the deaths of hundreds of guerrillas.

Apart from convincing Khomeini that he could not trust anyone but those totally committed to him, the campaign of violence had two other immediate effects. It radicalized the mood of the mullahs, who could now claim to have invested their own blood in the revolution. Thanks to Khomeini's tactics, the mullahs had suffered virtually no casualties during the campaign against the Shah, having cleverly hidden behind middle-class politicians and Leftist guerrillas. This was one of the reasons why the mullahs were considered as usurpers of the revolution. But the Mujahedeen changed that by killing some two thousand mullahs, including at least a dozen very prominent religious leaders in provincial centres throughout the country. The mullahs could now claim the revolution as truly their own; they had not only designed, started and led it but had also given their blood for it. No other social group had offered so many martyrs to the revolution. The second result of the campaign of terror and counter-terror was to block all avenues of possible political challenge to the regime. The Mujahedeen raised the stakes high above the reach of ordinary mortals. There was no longer any question of exerting pressure on the regime through propaganda, strikes, rallies and other peaceful means. Politics in Iran was reduced to the art of killing and getting killed. That meant that the vast majority of the people could only act as spectators watching a gladiatorial duel. The proverbial 'fish-in-water' guerrilla was isolated in the aquarium of his own illusions and quickly netted by the regime. The rule of the Imam emerged from the confrontation with added strength and a ready excuse for greater repression.

The third effect of the confrontation was the emergence of the Hojatieh as a powerful force. This ultra-conservative religious group had all along been worried about the revolution's Leftist rhetoric, which had been mainly imposed by the Mujahedeen, the Fedayeen and Tudeh. Hojatieh could now work their way up the state structure, benefiting from the rout of the Islamic Left. Being the only religious group with a solid nationwide organization, Hojatieh helped its members capture key positions in the Cabinet and local administration. Its leader, Ayatollah Shaikh Mahmoud Halabi, was neither seen nor heard in public but exercised great influence from his semi-derelict two-storey mud-brick home in south Tehran. Hojatieh rejected Khomeini's claim to be either an Imam or even the sole 'regent' of the Hidden Imam. Halabi was reported to have described Khomeini as 'a child who plays with fire'. An attempt by Morteza, Khomeini's elder brother, to arrange a reconciliation in 1982 failed. Halabi would not call on the Imam unless first called upon – a suggestion which was out of the question. Khomeini described Halabi as 'a fart in a storm'.[15] A year later, he ordered Hojatieh to disband. Halabi obliged by calling on his supporters to go underground.

The Mujahedeen revolt at times included fullscale battles involving up to two hundred armed guerrillas. It enhanced the powers of the Revolutionary Guards, now commanded by Mohsen Reza'i, who had been trained in a PLO camp near Beirut. The army's professional soldiers seized the opportunity offered by the Guards' preoccupation with crushing the guerrillas to reassert their authority and regain control of the war with Iraq. The new Chief of Staff, Brigadier General Qassem-Ali Zahir-Nezhad, emerged as a competent military leader capable of turning the tide of the war. Under his leadership Iran liberated almost all the territory it had lost to Iraq, including twelve towns and more than a thousand villages. And in July 1982 Iranian forces launched their first invasion of Iraq itself. For a few exciting weeks the Iraqi regime appeared on the verge of collapse, and the Imam was speaking of an early liberation of Jerusalem as the natural sequel to victory in Mesopotamia. However, victory was to prove far more elusive, and the war continued into 1985, adding to its horrors the use of chemical weapons by Iraq. The Imam recognized the war's potential attraction for Iran's children and young people, who formed a majority of the population, and issued an edict allowing male children aged above twelve to volunteer for the front without the permission of their parents or guardians if that proved unobtainable. They were to become wards of the Imam and could be sure of a place in paradise if they died on the battleground.

Tens of thousands of children and adolescents, wearing crimson headbands with the slogan 'Hail to Khomeini', poured into the war zone. Many received plastic 'Keys to Paradise', manufactured in Taiwan. These young 'wards of the Imam' cleaned minefields by simply running through them, often getting blown to pieces. They attacked and destroyed Iraqi tanks in kamikaze style. Before entering battle they all wrote their wills, with the help of scribes especially dispatched to the front for the purpose. Most wills came in the form of letters addressed either to the Imam or to 'my kind mother'.

One such testament read, in part: 'How poor, how miserable, how ignorant was I in all the fourteen years of my wretched life that was passed in the ignorance of Allah. The Imam gave light to my eyes. . . . How sweet, sweet, sweet is death − this blessing of Allah to those who are favoured.'[16] The child soldiers felt safe and comfortable in one another's company. They were about to become heroes instead of facing the prospect of a hard life of poverty and need. One poem, inspired by the battle of Chezabeh Pass in which at least three thousand child soldiers died, read in part:

> What a joy to fight
> alongside friends
> and to die
> alongside friends
> on the road to paradise.[17]

The child soldiers' devotion to the Imam contrasted with the treachery of the older generations. Khomeini was particularly grieved by the discovery of a plot to murder him involving Ghotbzadeh in 1982. Of the dozen or so 'student' revolutionaries who had rallied to Khomeini soon after his exile in 1964, Ghotbzadeh was, without doubt, the favourite of the Imam. He was allowed to address the Imam in the familiar appellation of 'Haj Agha' and had the courage to oppose Khomeini's views in his presence. One day, when he was still Foreign Minister, he even took his French girlfriend, suitably shrouded in a *chador*, on a visit to the Imam. The Minister's 'best friend' was allowed a glimpse of the holy man before withdrawing to an outer room where she waited for her escort to emerge from a meeting with the Imam.

Ghotbzadeh was charged with having plotted a coup d'état with the help of monarchist officers and the blessing of Shariatmadari. Among those arrested were Shariatmadari's son-in-law and Hojat al-Islam Abdul-Karim Hejazi, another favourite of the Imam. Ghotbzadeh and Hejazi confessed to having plotted to seize power but denied charges of conspiracy to assassinate the Imam. But the prosecutor was able to demonstrate that plans for destroying the Imam's residence by rocket had been prepared by the conspirators. Twenty men were sentenced to death and Ghotbzadeh and Hejazi were among them. Ghotbzadeh was offered the chance to recant on television but refused. Bazargan, an old friend of Ghotbzadeh, managed to obtain an audience with the Imam to intercede on behalf of the fallen Minister. Khomeini listened in silence and then rose suddenly and left the room, murmuring, 'It is time for my prayers.' A few minutes later he told Sayyed Ahmad to give the go-ahead for Ghotbzadeh's execution. Hejazi, however, was reprieved and later released. Khomeini was remaining faithful to his dictum that a mullah does not kill a mullah.

Shariatmadari's case was far more difficult. Lajevardi wanted the octogenarian Grand Ayatollah to be sent to Evin, tried and shot as a 'corrupter of the earth'. Had the plotters succeeded, Shariatmadari, using his religious authority, would have been able to mobilize popular support for a new regime headed by Ghotbzadeh. He had to be eliminated. A concerted campaign to discredit Shariatmadari was launched in which the Grand Ayatollah was described as an agent of the CIA and not a religious man at all. Shariatmadari was also threatened with the instant execution of his son-in-law. The old ayatollah decided to have recourse to the traditional technique of 'telling lies to save oneself from the tyranny of ignorant brutes'. He appeared on television admitting his guilt and asking for pardon. He was the first Grand Ayatollah in the history of Shi'ism to be defrocked and was forced to wear a European suit. He had on countless occasions helped Khomeini and had played a crucial role in the early stages of the revolt against the Shah. Now Khomeini repaid him by sparing his life. The Imam also allowed Shariatmadari to continue to wear his beard, although his turban was not to be restored to him. Shariatmadari, anxious to avoid bloodshed, accepted the humiliation and refused to call his supporters to revolt. No action of the regime could divest him of his theological position as one of the six Grand Ayatollahs forming the highest echelon of Shi'ite leadership. He refused offers by his fellow Grand Ayatollahs in Qom − Golpayegani and Mara'ashi-Najafi − to intercede on his behalf with

Khomeini, and agreed to become a virtual prisoner in his own home. He had remained faithful to his life-long belief that bloodshed and violence would not advance the cause of Islam. 'Power is like a hungry dragon demanding more and more flesh,' he had said years earlier in another context.[18] There was no sign that he had changed that belief.

By allowing such a high-ranking religious dignitary to suffer public humiliation, Khomeini alienated himself from the mass of traditionalist mullahs who had hitherto given him their reluctant support. The Imam was now more of a political than a religious leader in the eyes of many mullahs and *talabehs*. He never once spoke about Shariatmadari directly and later ordered that the defrocked Grand Ayatollah be provided with all his needs.

By April 1985 it had become clear that Shariatmadari was still considered a potential threat. President Khameneh'i claimed, in a speech, that disgruntled mullahs and *talabehs* were converging on Qom from all over the country in the hope of reviving the defrocked Grand Ayatollah's prestige, presenting him as a 'martyr' and the true custodian of 'Islamic purity'. But it was equally clear that Shariatmadari would remain silent as long as Khomeini was alive and in power.

The defeat of Shariatmadari enabled the Imam to devote most of his attention to exporting his revolution. He was now sure that no one could threaten his authority at home. He began referring to Islamic countries by their Qur'anic or historic names. Saudi Arabia became Hejaz and Najd, while Iraq was Bayn al-Nahrayn or Mesopotamia. Syria and Lebanon were grouped together as Shamat. This indicated that the Imam did not recognize the existence of separate Muslim states and wanted to unite the Muslim world under his own command. The idea of exporting the Islamic Revolution had originally been advanced by Bani-Sadr. But now it was Montazeri who was put in charge of a massive propaganda drive which was soon to include the training of thousands of Enteharis or volunteers for suicide attacks on the enemies of Islam. Several camps were set up in Tehran and Qom for the purpose, including one for women near Tehran itself.[19] It is probable that Syria, a close ally of the Imam in the war against Iraq, helped with the training and organization of terrorist groups which came to be known under a variety of names.[20] Some of the Enteharis may have been involved in terrorist attacks that cost the lives of some three hundred American and French soldiers in Beirut in 1983. Montazeri himself was, by all accounts, not involved in the terrorist side of the operation, which was led by lesser mullahs in cooperation with the Revolutionary Guards.

In August 1983 an international Islamic seminar financed by the Islamic Republic in London called on Muslims throughout the world to follow Khomeini as their sole leader, but stopped short of declaring him Caliph as some delegates had apparently demanded. The caliphate, abolished by Atatürk in 1921 and briefly restored by T. E. Lawrence, who persuaded his friend Sharif Hussein to assume the title, was not to be revived.

# 16

# *The Prisoner of Jamaran*

I pray for your father; for I understand him. He is a prisoner in Jamaran just as he has made me a prisoner here in my own house.

Grand Ayatollah Sayyed Kazem Shariatmadari to Sayyed Ahmad, Imam Khomeini's son[1]

*J* amaran, in the foothills of northeast Tehran, is a featureless village long overshadowed by its prestigious neighbour, Niavaran, where the Shah had his winter palace. The village, the name of which means 'the abode of the snakes', was shunned by the Tehrani aristocracy and the *nouveaux riches* who dotted the slopes of snow-capped Towchal with sumptuous villas and palatial mansions. Jamaran was notorious for its poisonous adders which were reputed to launch a general attack on human beings once every seven years. It was, probably, to escape such an ordeal that most owners of land in Jamaran decided to make a present of their property to the Religious Endowments Office. Because the sayyeds claim one fifth of all wealth in the country, at least 20 per cent of the endowed land went to them almost instantly. A local ayatollah, issuing an edict, announced that Jamaran's adders would be powerless against the sayyeds. So the village, which enjoys an excellent climate, came to have an unusually high percentage of sayyeds. It was perhaps for this reason that Khomeini's son Sayyed Ahmad chose Jamaran as a suitable place for his father to live. The Imam moved into a house donated to him, as *sahm-e-Imam* (the Imam's share), by a faithful follower in 1980. He moved there in February 1980 and never left it. Within a few weeks other faithful followers were encouraged to make donations of their homes which bordered the one occupied by the Imam. The new possessions were quickly allocated to the Imam's close relatives and personal bodyguard. Eventually the entire village was sealed off, and by 1985 most of its original inhabitants had left, enabling the Revolutionary Guards to turn Jamaran into a fortress. Khomeini could walk the eight-metre-long alley that separates his residence from Jamaran's *hosseinieh* without fear of assassination. The fortified village became something of a prison for the Imam, who, for the first time in his life, was unable to pray at a holy shrine for more than four years.[2] Warned by his security advisers not to venture out of his home and thus unable to go to the people, the Imam now has people brought to him. Every day he receives several groups of officials, militants, relatives of the martyrs and foreign visitors. Television cameras record these audiences, which follow a set pattern.

The group of houses which constitute the Imam's residence and offices is protected by an electronic security system installed by Siemens for £4 million. A battery of anti-aircraft guns provides a shield against bombardment from the air, which had been the central part of two different plots against the Imam: one in which Ghotbzadeh was involved and another led by an air force Brigadier, Ayat Mohaqeqi, and the nationalist Neqab (the Mask) organization in 1980. Some 1200 handpicked Revolutionary Guards are on full alert at Jamaran. In 1982 Khomeini was informed by Syrian intelligence that Saddam Hussein, the Iraqi President, was offering more than £100 million to professional killers for the murder of the Imam.[3] A year before that the Mujahedeen had planned to attack Jamaran and hold Khomeini hostage.[4]

From 1981 onwards, the safety of the Imam became synonymous with the preservation of the republic. He had personally to intervene to mobilize popular support both for the continuation of the war against Iraq and for repairing the damage done by the armed insurrection organized by the Mujahedeen. From then on all major decisions were taken at Jamaran, often by Khomeini alone. The 175-point constitution gave him unlimited powers and he began to use them. Bani-Sadr's defection, followed by Ghotbzadeh's 'treason', had already persuaded Khomeini that politicians were motivated only by personal ambition. A number of incidents in 1981 and 1982 began to affect his attitude to the mullahs as well. His old pupil Khalkhali was accused of having received bribes totalling £14 million, and was unable to offer an adequate defence. He was dismissed from his position as the sole judge of the anti-narcotics court, a post given to him by Bani-Sadr. Another favourite of the Imam, Hojat al-Islam Ma'adikhah, had to be dismissed as Minister of Islamic Orientation following rumours of scandal linking his name with that of a former TV newscaster. In 1983 the Imam was so angered by the 'loose conduct' of some mullahs in the provinces that he ordered the dismissal of fifty out of 157 prayer leaders throughout the country. He also became bitter about the endless wranglings of the mullahs in the Majlis and the Council of Guardians, which prevented any major piece of legislation from being completed. Addressing the mullahs both in the Majlis and in the Council he warned that he would 'box your ears'. He said: 'Your quarrels [together] are not for Allah. You are quarrelling for your own ends. You cannot fool me by saying that your quarrels are about the interests of Islam. You are fighting for power and I know it. Each of you is saying: more, give me more power. Your quarrels occur because none of you is content to sit on his own carpet and wants to stretch his legs on someone else's carpet as well.'[5]

These remarks reflected only part of the truth and illustrated Khomeini's belief that individuals are motivated to do good or evil not because of their social and economic status and interests or class affiliations but as a result of their success or failure in curbing 'the devil inside' (*Nafs-e-ammarah*). The 'quarrels', as the Imam called them, were, however, not over personal ambitions alone. They reflected deep class divisions among the mullahs themselves. Broadly speaking, the mullahs, who had established an almost complete monopoly of political power in Iran from 1982 onwards, were divided in three groups. One group, consisting of well-to-do mullahs, interpreted Islam to mean a set of moral rules that could be observed independently of the society's economic infrastructure. The late Beheshti was a leading figure in that group. His mantle was inherited by Mahdavi-Kani and Hashemi-Rafsanjani who, despite their own differences, support a mixed economy and a gradual improvement in relations with the West. As far as this group is concerned, the revolution has achieved most of its objectives inside Iran and should now devote its attention to the imposition of Islamic rule elsewhere, notably in the Persian Gulf and the Middle East. The veil is back and strict rules of dress are applied for both men and women. Music and most other 'satanic arts' have been suppressed or eliminated. Islam, or at least the version of it presented by Khomeini, has become the dominant ideology in Iran for the first time in nearly 150 years. Alcohol cannot be obtained legally, while prostitution and pornography have been driven underground. The Baha'is have been forced out of the civil service and are under growing pressure to recant. As far as the economy is concerned, the Qur'anic rule which says 'people have control over their persons and their possessions' is construed to mean respect for private property and free enterprise. To be sure, the government must be on guard against excessive profiteering, usury and other immoral practices. Apart from that, however, *laissez faire* should be the rule. This group, enjoying a majority in the Council of Guardians, has been able to veto a series of proposed bills designed to 'socialize' the economy. These included two separate attempts at legislating for the distribution of agricultural land among the peasants. The mullahs had never promised to give anyone any land, but after the revolution they had to advocate land reform as part of their tactics for divesting the Left of its potentially popular slogans. The peasants, often led by radical mullahs, seized some 850,000 hectares of land – one tenth of the area actually under cultivation. But deeds for only 30,000 hectares had been issued by March 1985 when the High Council of the State, the republic's highest court, ruled that all land seizures during the revolution were illegal. Farmers working 'confiscated' fields were ordered to pay rent to 'legitimate owners' on the basis of 'free consent'. Another important bill that was stopped by the council envisaged the nationalization of all foreign trade. This would have dealt a serious blow to the bazaar, one of the early supporters of the revolution. A third bill designed to replace the labour code which existed under the Shah was also stopped by the group of mullahs in question. The group succeeded in imposing the system of Qissass as the law of the land, declaring all laws passed by Parliament before the revolution to be null and void. The Imam lent his authority to this measure by issuing an edict. In practice, however, the move failed and by 1985 most of the laws passed under the Shah were back in force – including, surprisingly enough, the Family Protection Act which had been denounced by Khomeini himself as 'a law to turn our women into whores'.[6] The Act makes the taking of a second wife without the consent of the first illegal, in direct contravention of *shari'a* law. A dual legal system was tacitly accepted from 1984 onwards. Thus the same offence could be punished in two entirely different ways. A man found guilty of stealing can have his arm chopped off, by a new electrical machine which was set in operation in January

1985, in accordance with the Qissass system or, if he is lucky, he may be sentenced to a term of imprisonment under laws enacted by the *ancien régime*.

The second group of mullahs within the coalition consists mostly of individuals with a lower-middle-class background. These people are strongly attracted to radical and socialist ideas and for them Islam represents the earliest form of 'socialism'. The community of faith ought to be completed by the collective owner-ship of the means of production, distribution and exchange. The state, representing the interests of the *ummah*, should run the economy. This group opposes attempts at exporting the Islamic Revolution and insists that the most urgent task at the moment is the complete destruction of the Iranian bourgeoisie which is a potential fifth column for 'the Great Satan'. Khameneh'i, the President, Mussavi, the Prime Minister, and Khoiniha, the 'Prince of the Pilgrims', are among the key figures of this group, which also advocates a more liberal policy on rules of dress, social conduct and the arts. It is, for example, not opposed to women swimming in the sea, or in swimming pools for that matter, provided they are covered from head to toe. It was also under the influence of this group that Khomeini agreed to the lifting of the ban on broadcasting the female voice in any form. Now women's voices can be broadcast under certain conditions.[7] So far as foreign policy is concerned, the group advocates closer ties with the non-aligned and socialist countries.

The third group in the coalition consists of those mullahs who have no particular views on either the economy or the political future of the country so long as their newly won position of financial and social power is maintained. Forming the vast majority of the mullahs cooperating with the regime, the group does not have recognizable national leaders. But such personalities as Ayatollah Ehsan Bakhsh, the Prayer Leader of Rasht, and Hojat al-Islam Abbas Va'ez-Tabassi, the Dean of the Holy Shrine at Mashhad, have achieved national notoriety and influence. In the continuing power struggle between the first two groups, members of the third alternately side with one or the other in accordance with their own interests.

Each group is, in turn, divided into several subgroups, and all are represented in the Majlis. In some cases it was only thanks to the Imam's intervention that the coalition succeeded in post-poning its inevitable disintegration.

Not all the mullahs are involved in the government or support

Khomeini's vision of an Islamic state. The highest ranking ayatollahs are, at least in private, unhappy about the course of events in the Islamic Republic. Some mullahs have even actively opposed the rule of the Imam. An estimated two thousand mullahs and *talabehs* were in prison on political charges in 1982.[8] The rule that mullahs should not kill mullahs was observed all along, but by 1987 the number of mullahs and talabehs in prison because of their opposition to the regime's policies was put at more than 3,000 by unofficial sources. Almost as many mullahs were estimated to have been 'defrocked' between 1979 and 1987 on Khomeini's orders.

The Imam himself stood above the factions and combined in his person the radical aspirations of each group. A cnservative in economic matters, Khomeini remained in the vanguard of radicalism in the imposition of Islamic rules and the 'exporting' of the revolution. His resolute opposition to any settlement of the Iran–Iraq war prior to the overthrow of President Hussein's regime was the key factor in the prolongation of the conflict. In 1984 he relieved General Qassem-Ali Zahir-Nezhad, the popular army Chief of Staff, of his position, because of a remark by the general that the 'normal military objectives of the war' had been achieved.[9] Years of experience taught the Imam that leading a revolution is like riding a bicycle: any hesitation in pedalling forward could mean a nasty fall. In 1982, the Imam, under pressure from Montazeri and others, promulgated an eight-point edict aimed at softening the process of 'Islamicization' and limiting the powers of the revolutionary *komitehs*. The edict created a sensation for a while, but was quietly abandoned after it became clear that its implementation would only please middle-class elements who would in no circumstances accept Khomeini's rule willingly. That was the only time Khomeini had allowed himself to be forced into a position where he would seem less radical than the most radical elements in the movement. The gaffe was quickly corrected and the revolutionary *komitehs*, helped by a new brigade for 'Enjoining the Good and Preventing the Evil', were allowed to make sure that Islam was not being violated even in the privacy of people's homes. The campaign, however, later lost its momentum as people in each neighbourhood worked out their own arrangements with the enforcers of the Good.

The preservation of the Islamic state and the maintenance of its security remained the overriding objective of the Imam. From 1981 onwards loyalty to the regime was advanced as the supreme quality of every individual. The Imam tried to ensure the loyalty of people in key positions in two different ways. First, he promoted to positions of responsibility people sharing common roots with himself. Of the thousand key posts in the government at all levels, no fewer than six hundred were held by sayyeds, with the Mussavis forming the vast majority among them. Apart from Khomeini himself, who is a Mussavi sayyed, the President, the Prime Minister, the Chief Justice and twelve out of the twenty-two members of the Cabinet belong to the same branch of the Prophet's descendants. The Mussavi sayyeds also occupy fifty-three seats in the 271-seat Parliament. Seven out of twenty-three provincial governors-general are Mussavi sayyeds, while their blood brethren head seventy-five out of the top 120 public enterprises in the country. Men directly related to Khomeini himself hold some fifty key positions, including those of Deputy Prime Minister and the director of the Imam Fund, which is worth £10,000 million. The system of extended families in Iran means that literally hundreds of people who are related to each other either by blood or through marriage know each other and remain in contact. The Imam made use of the system as a means of re-ensuring his rule (see Appendix 4, p. 333). Sayyed Ahmad acts as the godfather of the extended family. He refused the post of Prime Minister when it was offered to him by Bani-Sadr in 1981 but by 1982 had emerged as the second most powerful man in the republic after Hashemi-Rafsanjani.

The inner circle of people related to Khomeini is, as we have seen, strengthened by the two outer circles of the Mussavi sayyeds in particular and the sayyeds in general. The sayyeds, as descendants of the Prophet, consider it their birthright to rule over all Muslims. A fourth circle encompassing the three already mentioned is provided by the clergy in general. The sayyeds form no more than 30 per cent of all mullahs. A fifth circle is provided by Shi'its mainly from three provinces of Isfahan, Fars and Yazd. Almost 70 per cent of all key posts are held by people from these three provinces, which nevertheless represent only 10 per cent of the country's total population. A sixth circle belongs to the Shi'ites in general who occupy every single key post in the administration plus 95 per cent of the seats in Parliament. Sunni Muslims, who claim to number 6 million in Iran, have virtually no role in the government. And the country's estimated 1.5 million religious minorities are by definition excluded from any position of responsibility in the administration.[10]

The security of the regime is further maintained through a number of coercive organs acting alongside the police and the paramilitary forces inherited from the Shah. The Revolutionary Guards, with an estimated strength of 120,000 men in 1985, duplicates the regular army and also deals with armed insurrections and tribal revolts against the government. Baseej Mustadh'afeen (the Mobilization of the Downtrodden) counterbalances the Revolutionary Guards and recruits children and teenagers for a variety of tasks ranging from the war with Iraq to assisting the Ministry of Information and Security. The Ministry itself was believed to employ some 25,000 full-time or part-time informers and agents in 1985 and included a special 'Department of Islamic Informing' with agents in schools, offices, factories and the bazaars. The *komitehs*, due to be put under the Ministry's supervision by 1987, had an effective membership of 35,000 in 1985 and were present in twenty-six major cities. Smaller groups such as Jond-Allah (the Army of Allah), Thar-Allah (the Blood of Allah) and Gasht-e-Zaynab (Zaynab's Patrols)[11] specialize in enforcing religious rules of conduct in private and public life. The four hundred or so leading mullahs in Tehran and the provinces have independent bodyguards of their own. In 1984 the regime spent something like £3000 million, or 15 per cent of the oil revenue, on internal security alone.[12]

The coercive apparatus of the state is complemented by a number of organizations designed to distribute favours and advantages among the supporters of the revolution. These include Bonyad-e-Shahid (the Martyrs' Foundation), Bonyad-e-Mustadh'afeen (the Foundation for the Downtrodden), Komiteh-e-Imam (the Imam's Committee), Helal Ahmar (the Red Crescent) and Jahad-e-Sazandehgi (Holy War for Construction). In addition all the leading mullahs, such as prayer leaders and members of the Majlis and the Council of Guardians, have special allocations of their own, which they distribute among supporters of the regime. An estimated 1.2 million people, supposed to be totally committed to the revolution, enjoy direct and indirect favours and advantages estimated to represent some 10 per cent of the gross national product. The government protects the poor further through a system of rationing all basic necessities. The sale of ration coupons to the well-to-do had by 1982 developed into an important source of income for the poor. Supporters of the regime enjoy a number of other benefits as well. They are given priority for going on pilgrimage to Mecca or Damascus.[13] They also receive such rare luxuries as refrigerators, colour television sets and cars at subsidized prices. By selling them on the black market, they make profits of between 400 and 600 per cent. Perhaps the most important function of the Middle Eastern state has always been the distribution of favours and advantages. Under the Shah most of these went to a few thousand people, with members of the royal family and those related to them receiving the lion's share. Under Khomeini the distribution of favours and advantages has been 'democratized' in the sense that now more than 2 to 3 million receive at least a few crumbs. The same 2 or 3 million people now feel that for the first time in history they have a real share in power. Unaffected by the catastrophic economic results of the revolution thanks to rationing and the direct distribution of cash by the mullahs, the 'downtrodden' feel that Khomeini has restored their dignity in this world while ensuring their place in the coming paradise. The government finances this belief with some £60 million in oil revenues every day. Having abandoned the Shah's ambitious industrial and military projects, the Islamic regime can spend almost all of the oil income on current expenditure to keep its supporters happy and the rest of the people quiet.

Those who receive most of the favours and advantages distributed by the state also provide most of the sacrifices. More than 80 per cent of those killed in the war against Iraq belonged to poor families and more than half of them came from the three provinces of Isfahan, Fars and Yazd – the heartland of support for the Imam. There are families who have had up to six sons killed in this war. The urban bourgeoisie, however, has remained largely unaffected by the war. It has dispatched many of its sons to Europe and North America via the illegal escape routes operating through Pakistan and Turkey, and it opposes the rule of the mullahs through a mixture of passive resistance and psychological warfare. The regime is also opposed by the bulk of the urgan working class which, threatened by unemployment and unhappy about the bigotry of some mullahs, began to flex its muscles with a series of strikes and work-to-rule exercises throughout 1984 and in the early months of 1985. The peasantry, still forming almost half the population, remained apolitical as ever. The partial reopening of the universities between 1983 and 1985 quickly showed that the Islamic regime could not count on the automatic support of students. An attempt at a 'Cultural Revolution' failed disastrously in 1982–84 and in many cases books and syllabuses belonging to the past were gradually restored.

The attempts of the Imam, between 1981 and 1985, to change his charismatic rule into an ideological one capable of surviving him produced mixed results. There is no doubt that some of the newly created institutions may be able to continue without the presence of the Imam. The revolution has also attracted or trained thousands of young men and women who are committed to it not because of blood links or pecuniary advantages but on strictly ideological grounds. It is perhaps ironic that many of the people devoted to the revolution as a way of life[14] are the products of various American universities and colleges. The vast majority returned to Iran during or soon after the revolution. They see in Islam an alternative to 'American materialism' and 'Soviet barbarism'.[15] They genuinely believe that Islam can and must make its own distinct contribution to the discussion and solution of the main problems facing contemporary man. Khomeini tells them: Neither East nor West can save mankind. This is because both sides lack an adequate number of people who are ready to die for their convictions. Islam, however, can 'make people beg to die for it'.[16] Those ideologically committed to the revolution will not disappear with the Imam's physical demise, but the effect of Khomeini's absence on the popular masses, however, is certain to be different. No one can replace the Imam or come close in any way. The Imam's own preference was always for Ayatollah Hussein-Ali Montazeri to succeed him as the all-powerful Faqih. And in February 1985 a closed session of the Assembly of Experts, which must pick the Imam's successor, seemed to have reached agreement on Montazeri's nomination.[17] But Montazeri, wearing a white turban rather than a black one as worn by the Imam, is of a moderate temperament and is thus rejected by the most radical supporters of the revolution. He is also a junior ayatollah and would not be accepted as *primus inter pares* by the others.[18] What is more, he lacks Khomeini's forceful character and brutal determination. He is polite where the Imam can be extremely rude. In 1981

Montazeri received the Soviet Ambassador Vladimiri Vinogradov at his residence in Qom. After a two-hour meeting he accompanied the ambassador to the door. Informed of the incident, Khomeini telephoned his favourite heir and told him off. 'The ambassador of a pagan power deserves no show of respect from a Regent of Islam,' he told Montazeri.[19] The same Vinogradov received a stern lecture when he met the Imam and was repeatedly cut short in the middle of his sentences. The meeting was suddenly terminated when the Imam rose and left the room without saying goodbye. The Imam had found out that the Kremlin's envoy would not abandon his atheistic convictions.

The difference between Khomeini and Montazeri is, however, not solely one of style. Khomeini genuinely believes that the establishment of Islamic government in Iran is an end in itself. Montazeri sees the capture of political power by the clergy only as a means which ought to be used in order to improve the material and spiritual conditions of life of the people. Khomeini believes that, if need be, people should be forced to behave in an Islamic way. Montazeri, for his part, argues in favour of persuasion through the setting of examples. Both men advocate a return to the simple life and have helped popularize such notions as frugality, a reduction in one's expectations from life, a cut in consumption and a distaste for luxuries. Both want the Iranians to sleep on the ground, sit on the floor, eat only one or two simple meals a day, make do with very few clothes and be content with living in one or two rooms. The difference is that Montazeri believes that human nature itself tends towards the good if given the chance. Khomeini, however, pinpoints the little devil he sees hiding within every man, and thinks nothing of enforcing the good at bayonet point if necessary. Between 1981 and 1985 the two leaders adopted basically contradictory positions on almost every major issue, with Montazeri playing the liberal and Khomeini remaining true to his image of the uncompromising radical. Opponents of the regime accuse the two men of offering an Islamic version of the soft-cop–tough-cop interplay in order to confuse the people. But this is almost certainly unfair. The difference of approach between the two men is genuine. The two complement each other, representing different shades of opinion within the revolutionary coalition. The difference of approach between Khomeini and Montazeri extends to the important issue of exporting the revolution as well. Montazeri emphasizes proselytization and propaganda;

Khomeini is inclined to see an effective answer only in the use of force. In 1981 the Imam ordered the creation of an 'Army of Twenty Million' which, when and if fully ready, would fight to hoist the flag of Allah in every capital of the world.

The gap between expectations and achievements – or in Khomeini's words: the difference between Truth and Fact – continued to widen through 1985 with reality adamantly refusing to reflect the Imam's slogans. The war with Iraq reached new heights of brutality with what came to be known as 'the war of the cities' as the two belligerents, frustrated on the actual battlefields, began attacking civilian targets. Iran was bound to suffer more since, with its air force virtually grounded for lack of spare parts and new equipment, it had virtually no means of defending its urban centres against raids by Iraq's ultra-modern fighter-bombers supplied by France and the Soviet Union. Between March and June 1985 the Iraqis carried out no fewer than 300 air raids against Tehran and more than a dozen other major Iranian cities. The Islamic authorities, reversing their policy in the early phases of the war when they had deliberately exaggerated the number of Iranian casualties in deference to the cult of the martyr, now went out of their way to play down the effect of the Iraqi raids and at times divided the number of the victims by ten. The myth that a mere prayer by the Imam would turn the Iraqi bombers into 'falling leaves' had been propagated by mullahs in mosques throughout the country. But when the prediction did not materialize the mullahs began working on yet another myth – this time one suggested by the Imam himself. It was claimed that the war was being waged on behalf of Allah and that its outcome would reflect only His Will. 'Even our total defeat in this war shall be a blessing from the Almighty and a sign of His Wisdom which we cannot fully understand,' the Imam said in a nationwide address shortly before going into 'holy seclusion' for the duration of the fasting month of Ramadan in May 1985.

The Iraqi bombing raids, which probably claimed no fewer than 6000 lives in just over three months, brought home the horrors of a war that had often been conveniently forgotten by pulpit militants whose slogan, 'War, War, Until Victory', now rang hollow. During the bombing raids the Imam himself was compelled to change his place of residence on several occasions. Using underground tunnels connecting his Jamaran home to neighbouring 'safe houses', Khomeini, accompanied by Batul,

Ahmad and other members of the family, had to spend the night in houses whose exact location was communicated to them only at the last moment. The nearest the Iraqi bombers came to Jamaran was in late May when they bombed Lavizan, only two kilometres from the Imam's hide-out. But the Iraqis knew that Jamaran was strongly defended by anti-aircraft guns and that they would risk heavy losses in attacking it.

The air raids, plunging the capital and other major cities into darkness for hours on end, strengthened the feeling of gloom. Khomeini had said there was no joy in Islam and that Shi'ism was a religion of suffering and pain. The war hammered this message home in a direct way. The Revolutionary Guards, who lost at least 20,000 men in an ill-prepared attack across the River Tigris in March 1985, continued to support the Imam in his policy of continuing the war until an Islamic Republic was established in Baghdad. But the army high command and an increasing number of Majlis members began to doubt more and more openly the wisdom of such a stance. Khomeini was prepared neither to amend Iran's foreign policy so that the Islamic Republic could secure the arms it needed for defending itself, nor to negotiate a cease-fire with the Iraqis. His advice was: Take courage, write your wills and be prepared for death! Many people took his advice and notaries-public in urban areas reported a boom in the business of preparing and attesting wills. Khomeini, Batul, Ahmad and other adult members of the family wrote and sealed their wills in accordance with Shi'ite Tradition in March 1985. The Imam's personal, private will 'was different from his political testament' which addressed not members of his immediate family but Muslims throughout the world.

In February 1983 the Imam signed and sealed what was described as his last testament. The thirty-page document was presented to the Assembly of Experts by Sayyed Ahmad with instructions that it should be opened and read only after the death of the Imam. In his testament the Imam is said to have indicated his full trust in Montazeri without, however, going so far as to urge the 'experts' to vote for him. The Imam began preparing for his own eventual absence by ordering Hashemi-Rafsanjani to prepare a complete plan for coping with any dangers that might face the republic as soon as the sad news is released. During the general election of 1981, when the Imam was unwell, he authorized the government to keep news of his death a secret for as long as necessary if that were deemed essential for the safety of the state. Under Islamic law a man should be buried within twenty-four hours of his death. Khomeini was apparently using his authority as Imam to suspend that rule in his own case.[20] In February 1985 the emergency plan that is to be put into effect on the death of the Imam was given a trial run in Tehran. This included the closure of the international airport for eight hours and the positioning of the Zulfiqar Brigade on all land approaches to the capital.[21] Members of the Party of Allah were also mobilized to occupy all major streets of the capital in numbers sufficiently large to discourage any demonstrations by the opposition.

The advent of the Islamic Revolution in Iran, at first looked upon as a strange aberration, was by 1981 treated as a direct menace to almost every Islamic state from Indonesia to Morocco. In the almost unbroken chain of riots in more than a dozen Muslim countries, from Bangladesh to Egypt, Tunisia and Morocco, portraits of Khomeini and translations of his thoughts in local languages were essential parts of the revolutionary arsenal. The assassins of Egypt's President Anwar Sadat invoked Khomeini's name during their trial and King Hassan of Morocco went on television to single out the Imam as the man behind the North African kingdom's nation-wide revolts in 1983. It became evident that Khomeini's appeal was not limited to Shi'ites. Sunni radicals also adopted his slogans in their efforts to mobilize popular support. Fear of Khomeini was in part responsible for the sudden and almost concerted reintroduction of strict Islamic laws in Malaysia, Bangladesh, Pakistan, Abu Dhabi, Jordan, Yemen, Iraq, Egypt, Sudan, Somalia, Tunisia, Morocco and Mauritania. Even secular Turkey had to move some steps away from Kemalism in order to accommodate the new mood of Islamic militancy exported by Iran. One reason for the initial success of Khomeini's brand of radicalism was that all the three repositories of radical politics in the Middle East had become discredited by the end of 1970s. Arab nationalism, and more particularly Nasserism, never recovered from the June 1967 defeat at the hands of Israel. Communism, a potent force in the 1950s and early 1960s in the region, had been unmasked as an instrument of Soviet policy and, finally, emerged as an enemy of Islam with the Soviet invasion of Afghanistan. The third kind of radicalism, represented by the Palestinian resistance movement, was also fading by the time the 1970s were drawing to a close, with Yasser Arafat speaking of negotiations and an eventual peace settlement with Israel. The Muslim Middle East, where some 50 per cent of the population is aged below twenty and where, despite its recent oil wealth the poor masses still form a majority, has an inevitable radical energy which is bound to seek expression as long as its causes are not removed. Khomeini's Islamic Revolution is the latest such expression, but certainly not the last. The young love the Imam's almost anarchistic invitation to disobedience and rebellion against authority. They hear him curse the United States which, from the Atlantic to the Indian Ocean, is considered to be the real power behind all existing governments. They also admire the old man of Jamaran for the fact that his has been the only revolution in the Middle East in which a monarchy has been overthrown without a military coup d'état followed by army rule. The Imam also offers the faithful protection against the modern world which, after being ardently desired from the middle of the nineteenth century through the oil boom of the 1970s, is now feared or loathed by many Muslims. Modernization has become synonymous with Westernization which, in turn, is taken to mean 'greed, prostitution and satanic corruption'.[22] Furthermore, Khomeini has succeeded in appropriating a cause abandoned by almost every other political leader in the region but still enjoying genuine support in some sections of society: the cause of physically destroying the Israeli state and forcing its inhabitants out of the Middle East. Other leaders, whether Left or Right, pro-American or supposedly socialist, no longer dare speak in such terms even though they may dream of Israel's death in private. Khoemini has no inhibitions about branding the Jews as responsible for almost all the ills of this world and calling on Muslims to prepare for holy war and *qital* (killing in the name of Allah) against the Jewish state.

The Imam's militant talk, coming after over a decade of moderate discourse in the region, was bound to attract some support. On 4 February 1985 the Imam told a number of visiting Muslim radical leaders from some thirty countries to take the offensive against 'satanic rule'.

Brothers, do not sit at home so that they [the enemy] attack. Move onto the offensive and be sure that they shall retreat. . . . This was what happened in Iran and Iran's power was far greater than most of the other countries. . . . Do not content yourself with teaching the people the rules of prayer and fasting. The rules of Islam are not limited to these. . . . Why don't you recite the sura of *qital?* Why should you always recite the suras of mercy? Don't forget that killing is also a form of mercy. . . . There are ills that cannot be cured except through burning. The corrupt in every society should be liquidated. . . . The Qur'an teaches us to treat as brothers only those who are Muslims and believe in Allah. [It] teaches us to treat those who are not thus differently; teaches us to hit them, throw them in gaol and kill them. . . .[23]

His constant emphasis on the prime role of the *ulama* has given him a standing unique in recent times. Today, there are Sunni preachers and doctors of theology who consider the Imam's militant version of Islam as the only means of protecting youth against both communism and Western-style materialism. Like Khomeini, they describe the ideal society of Marx and Lenin as 'a concentration camp' while the West can only create 'a brothel on a universal scale'.[24]

Despite its exceptional potency, which is likely to ensure it a lasting following in the region, the appeal of the Imam began to show signs of fading from 1985 onwards. Iran's failure to win the war against Iraq, the success of Shi'ite moderates, led by Nabih Berri, in Lebanon, the failure of the Iraqi Shi'ites to stage an uprising and the systematic exposure of the excesses of the revolutionary regime in Tehran began to turn the Islamic Revolution for many Muslims into a warning rather than an example. The Muslim middle class, which in Iran had enthusiastically supported the Imam in the early stages of the revolution, was dismayed by the rule of Hezb-Allah or the tyranny of the underdog. The cult of personality built under Khomeini began to damage his image as a simple, pious, unassuming preacher of the truth. The pouring of Iranian money into vast programmes of propaganda, designed and carried out by an army of professionals mainly recruited among Indian and Pakistani Muslims, also put the Islamic Republic on a par with other regional states fighting each other for influence. The payment of Iranian money to Muslim women to wear the prescribed headgear in Lebanon and Jordan angered many people. And in Casamance, southern Senegal, the Imam's emissaries became objects of ridicule when they proposed stipends to women who would agree to cover their bare breasts and wear the veil. In Pakistan the Islamic Embassy was found to have served as a cover for gun-running and the financing of anti-state sabotage. And in Indonesia a poster showing Khomeini holding the Qur'an in the position traditionally reserved for the Prophet Muhammed in religious portraits created much bitterness against Tehran.

The mullahs, however, know that Khomeini's charisma remains their chief asset – at least as long as the Imam lives. Thus the Imam is presented as a chosen instrument of Allah's will. On March 29, 1987, for example, Tehran Radio broadcast a sermon entitled 'The Chosen of the Chosen'. It said in part:

'Allah chose Abraham above all men and then He chose Ismael from among Abraham's sons. And it was Kanana who was chosen by Allah from among the sons of Ismael. The Quraysh tribe issued from Kanana and was Allah's Chosen Tribe. And within the Quraysh it was the Bani-Hashem clan that was chosen above all by the Almighty. The Chosen of Allah among the Bani-Hashem was our Prophet Muhammad. And today it is a descendant of our Prophet who is chosen by Allah to lead Islam on to victory over the Idols of the modern times: It is our Imam who must and will unite all Muslims under one banner and show them the path to world domination.'

Khomeini's leadership proved to be of crucial importance in the difficult period of 1985–87, which saw the republic's oil revenues drop by nearly two thirds while the cost of the war against Iraq continued to grow. The Imam appeared on television on a number of occasions to remind the people that his revolution had never promised them a good material life and that the Prophet of Islam himself often went to bed hungry and cold.

The Imam also acted to cement the unity of a badly divided leadership. It was his personal intervention that prevented the Islamic Majlis from voting Premier Mussavi out of office on at least two occasions in 1986 and 1987. And it was also Khomeini's prestige that finally ensured the election of Montazeri as his future heir in February 1986. Montazeri's opponents, led by Rafsanjani, would have preferred the formation of a 'Council of Theologians', consisting of five ayatollahs, to perform Khomeini's constitutional functions as 'Supreme Guide'.

The nation's growing financial problems from 1985 onwards persuaded a majority of the ruling mullahs to seek ways and means of bringing the war against Iraq to an end. The Imam, however, remained adamant: the war should continue until the fall of the Iraqi President Saddam Hussein and his Ba'athist regime in Baghdad. In 1985 Iranian troops succeeded in dislodging the Iraqis from almost all Iranian territory still occupied by Saddam's forces. And in 1986 Iran won its most impressive victory in the war by capturing the strategic Fao Peninsula, thus cutting off Iraq from the Persian Gulf. The Fao victory was followed with further Iranian advances that brought the armies of the Imam to the gates of Basra, Iraq's second most populous city. Through much of 1986 and part of 1987 the Iraqis responded to Iran's victories on the ground by launching air raids against Tehran and more than 50 other Iranian cities. On at least two occasions the Iraqis tried to bomb Khomeini's residence in Jamaran but failed. On one occasion, in January 1987, an Iraqi MiG dropped its bombs on a housing complex less than two miles from the Imam's 'earthly abode'. This led to rumours, invented and spread by the mullahs, that the bombs had been pushed away from the Imam's house by 'angels sent from Heaven' to frustrate the Iraqi plan to kill Khomeini. The Imam himself remained indifferent to Iraqi bombing raids and refused to leave Jamaran. He did not even break his habit of sleeping on the terrace of his residence when Tehran's weather began to get warmer. To him the Iraqis, representing Satan on earth, were simply doing their job by bombing civilian targets in cities, and using chemical weapons against soldiers on the front. This was part of the game, so to speak, and in no way changed Iran's resolve to pursue the war.

By 1986 the war seemed virtually out of control and proceeded according to its own independent, infernal logic. It was, therefore, only natural that the Imam should look for new partners who could supply him with the arms necessary to pursue the conflict. Israel, which had stopped supplying Iran with arms and spare parts in 1984, partly under pressure from the United States, was approached in 1985 and responded positively to suggestions that it should help meet some of the Islamic Republic's military needs. This Israeli connection was, from 1986 onwards, also used by Tehran for establishing contact with the United States. Supplies of arms and equipment from the US, in exchange for the release of three American hostages in Beirut, played a major role in Iran's victory in the Fao Peninsula. More importantly, the US also supplied Tehran with valuable information concerning Iraq's military plans and intentions. At the same time Washington misled the Iraqi leadership by persuading them that the next Iranian attack will come not in Fao, but in the central sector of the front. The exposure of the Tehran–Tel Aviv–Washington axis as a result of revelations that led to the so-called Iran–Contra scandal, deprived the Imam, at least temporarily, of an important source of material and psychological support.

Khomeini, apparently anxious to reply in advance to objections from his supporters who would not understand the logic of dealing with 'The Great Satan', recalled in speeches that the 'Prophet Muhammad himself had also formed tactical alliances, even with Jews' whenever these suited his plans. The scandal of secret negotiations with the US nevertheless did some damage to the regime's position as a militant anti-Imperialist force in the realm of Islam.

Differences of opinion concerning relations with the United States and Israel, however, was only one of four areas of conflict within the leadership in Tehran. The most important of these remained the dispute over whether or not revolutionary power should be used for the purpose of transforming the Iranian society by destroying the potentially pro-West middle classes. Khomeini's own preference was clearly for such a policy to be put into immediate effect. But the war against Iraq and the fact that the mullahs could not run the country without help from the middle classes, prevented him from giving the green light necessary for what could become a Cambodian-style massacre of 'all those who have been corrupted by the temptations of this world.' A third area of conflict within the clerical leadership concerned which institutions should exercise which powers within the state. The bureaucracy, inherited from the Shah, remained powerful and effectively present in many domains, while institutions created by the revolution often only duplicated the state apparatus already in place. Finally, the leadership remained split as a result of the different backgrounds of its members. In many cases the only point that the leaders had in common was their more or less sincere devotion to the person of

Khomeini and their belief that Islamic rules, such as the veil for women, must be strictly observed.

Fear of a military coup d'etat either by the Revolutionary Guards or the regular army remains a constant preoccupation of the ruling clerics, although Khomeini himself seemed to be certain that no such move could be made during his life-time. Frequent government purges of high-ranking officers of both the army and the Revolutionary Guards showed the military would never become genuinely loyal to a government dominated by the clerics. In 1986 the Revolutionary Guards were split into five independent commands with each commander directly reporting to the Imam's Representative. More than 200 guards officers were put on an early retirement list without adequate explanation. Also in 1986 the Commander of the Ground Forces, Colonel Ali Sayyad-Shirazi, who had led the Iranian forces in their victory in Fao, was replaced on Khomeini's orders. The idea behind the move seemed to be that no army officer would attain a status above his peers. Another sign of the Imam's suspicion of the military's real sentiments was his refusal to approve plans under which some 700 officers would have been promoted to the rank of full colonel in 1987. The Iranian army in 1987 did not include a single officer ranking above brigadier-general. The same army under the Shah boasted more than 1,500 generals.

The Imam retained the last word not only in the conduct of the war but also in shaping economic policy. In 1986 he vetoed a plan for a $1,000 million loan arranged by the Central Bank through a number of Japanese finance houses. Ignoring government advice, the Imam insisted that the Islamic Republic should live without foreign debts. The Governor of the Central Bank was fired and in 1987 Iran remained the only Third World country without foreign debts. The price for Khomeini's financial puritanism was the scrapping of a few development projects that the government had planned to complete. Civil servants and workers employed in the public sector were also asked to accept pay cuts of between five and fifty per cent as part of an austerity plan put into effect from March 1987. The government was able to alleviate further the effects of a drop in oil revenues by reducing its subsidies for Syria whilst also securing the return to Iran of hundreds of millions of Iranian money 'frozen' in French and American banks since the fall of the Shah. But the main burden of the austerity plan was still borne by the 'downtrodden of the Earth' who saw their daily rations of food and other necessities of life reduced, and their real wages cut by inflation.

Disaffection among the urban poor led to major anti-regime demonstrations in August 1986 and January 1987. Counter-revolutionary groups, ranging from the Marxist–Leninists to the Monarchists, and supporters of the Iraqi-sponsored Mujahedeen Khalq Organisation, tried to exploit largely spontaneous demonstrations, but did not succeed. Although a few portraits of the Imam were burned in south Tehran's poor districts, the anger of the demonstrators was chiefly directed against the prime minister and other officials. Rumours regarding the Imam's ill-health brought the demonstrators into mosques to pray to Allah to grant him 'eternal life'. The Tehran poor who had sacrificed their children to the cause of Khomeini were not, even in 1987, quite prepared to stand against him because of material hardship. Nevertheless, there was little doubt that the revolution was losing its grip on some of its most steadfast supporters.

The Imam himself has been conscious of the fragility of his achievement. In 1983 he warned his supporters that their 'victories' could prove as transitory as 'the triumphs of Hitler'. 'I have the fear that, like Hitler, we may enter history as people who achieved quick victories followed by defeat.'[25] It is possible to argue that the Imam has mobilized tremendous social forces only in order to render them ineffective in achieving any meaningful and lasting transformation of society. He has brought millions of people onto the streets of Tehran, or into the mosques for Friday's communal prayers, and has taught them to wave their clenched fists and shout 'Death to America' as soon as they spot a television camera. He has told them that America, dominated by 'evil Jews', is Islam's arch-enemy, but he has not told them why. More importantly, he has not told them how to combat this arch-enemy except by killing American soldiers in their sleep or holding American diplomats hostage. Far from beating a retreat, the United States has reinforced its political, economic and military presence in the region and is for the first time the dominant foreign military power in the Persian Gulf itself. Iranian ships sailing to and from the Gulf have to steer clear of the US naval task force. Most Arab states, including even Algeria, have drawn closer to the United States since the Islamic Revolution in Iran. Iranian pilgrims gathering at Mecca during the Haj season often stage special demonstrations designed for television programmes back home. They shout 'Death to America and death to Russia', but are never told anything of consequence about the actual role of the two superpowers in the contemporary world. The Imam's anti-imperialism does not transcend the limits of ceremonial gatherings and almost ritualistic slogans. Iran's own economic dependence on both East and West is today far greater than at any time since the nineteenth century. Unable to provide a serious analysis of the economic and political realities of a world he invites the Muslims to blow up, the Imam seems content with processions, chants and cries of 'Allah is the Greatest'.

At home, the whole of society remains in a state of flux: Iran could move in almost any direction after Khomeini is gone. Such basic issues as the ownership of property, the distribution of land, the control of foreign trade, the penal code, the labour code, the rights of women under Islam and the role of the government and its relationship with the numerous revolutionary institutions that rival it in authority, remain unsolved, and in some cases, are not even discussed for fear of exposing the split in the leadership. Some of the old rich have left the country or have fallen a few rungs down the economic ladder. But the gap between the rich and the poor has widened.[26] Unprecedented profits are being made on the black market and from the miseries of a nation hit by war and revolutionary dislocation. In the summer of 1984 Premier Mussavi exposed a swindle that had robbed the state of some £180 million in an agri-business project in East Azerbaijan. The 'new profiteers', as Mussavi calls them, are making fortunes undreamed of anywhere else in the region. They, of course, pay the share due to the Imam in accordance with religious rules and observe regulations concerning individual dress and behaviour to the letter. They attend the communal prayers on Fridays, sitting in the first row and staring into the television cameras. They grow respectable, carefully trimmed beards and pay generously to the poor. And their fortune continues to grow. Under the Shah they used to pray in the privacy of their homes and have fun in public. The revolution has reversed that process. These *nouveaux riches* of the revolution finance the conservative mullahs, from the Combatant Clergy of Tehran to the secret Hojatieh society, and they are sure that once the Imam has gone their undoubted economic power will be translated into political power as well.

They will still have the 'children' of the Imam to contend with: a whole generation of child soldiers who, in the words of Khomeini, have known no school except the trenches of the Iran–Iraq war and who have learned to kill and to die before they were taught to read and write. Many of these children will be long buried by the time the Imam responds to the call of Allah. Many more will be injured and disabled for life with tens of thousands committed to wheelchairs for the rest of their days. But a sufficient number will remain to recall the teachings of Khomeini and be prepared to kill for their realization. In the absence of an equally powerful alternative ideology, the teachings of Khomeini might well dominate the Iranian political scene for many more years to come. The rich, the conservative mullahs and the middle class would have no alternative but to put up with military rule at least for a while. The army, depoliticized under the Shah, has been repoliticized along with the rest of society during the first six years of the revolution. It may form a broad alliance with the Revolutionary Guards, the police, the gendarmerie and the paramilitary forces in order to emerge as the only institution around which the broken Iranian nation-state can be re-created. Whether or not the Islamic Republic will survive Khomeini has been a moot point for the past six and a half years. What is certain, however, is that the Imam's words will continue to resonate long after he is gone:

> The heritage of Satan is none other than egoism. All the corruption the world has suffered from results from this: every corruption caused by individuals or governments in every society. . . . Satan is everywhere, even alongside those who sit at home and pray. . . . Every path can lead to Hell: Science could lead Man to Hell; at times even Monotheism can lead Man to Hell; Mysticism can lead Man to Hell; Theology can lead Man to Hell; Ethics can lead Man to Hell. . . .[27]

Peace be unto all those who follow the Right Path.

# Notes

## Introduction

1. The voice was that of Hojat al-Islam Mahmoud Doa'i who broadcast anti-Shah programmes on Baghdad Radio in the early 1970s.
2. Sadr and his militant sister Bent al-Hoda were shot by Barzan Takriti, the Iraqi security chief. Their murder was followed by the execution of some thousand other mullahs and their relatives, almost all of them related to Khomeini by blood or through marriage.
3. The words of Sa'id Raja'i-Khorassani, the Imam's Permanent Delegate to the United Nations in a debate on Human Rights in January 1985.
4. Meaning former US President Jimmy Carter, the assassinated Egyptian President Anwar Sadat and Israel's former Prime Minister Menachem Begin.

## Chapter 1

1. The question was first asked by *Le Monde*'s Paul Balta during the trip from Paris to Tehran. The Ayatollah's reply was so surprising that Mansur Taraji, an Iranian journalist also accompanying the Ayatollah on the journey home, asked it again in front of a television camera. Khomeini gave the same reply.

## Chapter 2

1. For an exciting account of the Constitutional Revolution, see Ahmad Kasravi's *Tarikh Mashrutiyat* (*History of the Constitution*).
2. A series of books on Nuri have appeared since the Islamic Revolution, all of them laudatory. The most balanced one is *Shaikh Shaheed* (*The Martyred Shaikh*) published in Qom in 1984.

## Chapter 3

1. In Persian the word does not end in an 'h' and is pronounced 'mol'la'.
2. Khomeini describes the Saudi clergy, for example, as *akhund darbari* (courtesan akhunds) and *wo'az as-salateen* (preachers of the sultans).
3. Morteza Motahari, *Ijtihad*, Qom, 1979.
4. *Shenakht Ijtihad* (*Knowing Ijtihad*), a collection of papers, Qom, 1980.
5. This means getting to know the ancestry of the men who relate traditions from the Prophet or the Imams.
6. Khomeini, in *Kashf al-Asrar* (*Key to the Secrets*), Qom, 1961.
7. See A. R. Nurizadeh in *Kayhan*, London, 22 February 1985.

8. The term was possibly coined by Imam Shamel in the 1920s and later adopted by anti-Communist Iranian mullahs.

9. *Kashf al-Asrar*, p. 39.

## Chapter 4

1. *Kashf al-Asrar*, p. 132.

2. *Tarikh Mobarezat Imam* (*History of the Imam's Struggles*), Tehran, 1980, p. 72. (Henceforth, *Tarikh*.)

3. Kuchak Khan was presented as a mullah after the Islamic Revolution and declared to be a 'Hero of Islam'. He was, in fact, a clan leader with a keen taste for vodka and very young women.

4. *Kashf al-Asrar*, p. 69.

5. *Tarikh*, p. 55.

6. ibid., p. 71.

7. *Khianat Pahlavi-ha* (*The Treason of the Pahlavis*), Qom, 1980, p. 11.

8. *Gozideh Payam-ha Imam Khomeini* (*Selection of Imam Khomeini's Messages*), Tehran, 1979, p. 78. (Henceforth, *Gozideh*.)

9. Khomeini, *Towzih al-Masayel* (*Explication of Problems*), Qom, 1962, p. 392. (Henceforth, *Towzih*.)

## Chapter 5

1. Mrs Batul Khomeini in an interview with the Beirut magazine *Shater al-Shoara*, April 1980. Also quoted in *Bamdad*, Tehran, 21 November 1979. She also says that her father had already met Ruhollah in Qom.

2. Mrs Farideh Mostafavi, Khomeini's daughter, in an interview with the Tehran magazine *Zan-e-Ruz*, 6 February 1982, vol. 966.

3. Related by Ayatollah Sayyed Mehdi Ruhani in a private interview in Paris in October 1983.

4. *Kashf al-Asra*, p. 71.

5. In a speech in Qom, 4 September 1980.

6. Electricity had come to Qom in the autumn of 1938.

7. Interview with *Iran Post*, London, 8 January 1980.

8. Hamid Ruhani in notes to *Dastani Keh Nagofteh Mand* (*A Tale That Remained Untold*), Tehran, 1980.

## Chapter 6

1. *Navab va Yaranash* (*Navab and his Comrades*), Qom, 1981, p. 24.

2. Mohammad Massoud developed this theme in his editorials in *Mard Emruz* (*Man of the Day*). He was assassinated by a Tudeh gunman in 1945.

3. Ayatollah Shaikh Ali Tehrani quoted in *Erchad*, Paris, November 1984. Tehrani was one of Khomeini's favourite pupils and, later, a close associate. He broke with the Ayatollah and joined the opposition in 1983. Tehrani's wife is a sister of Ali Mussavi-Khameneh'i, the third President of the Islamic Republic. She defected to Iraq in April 1985.

4. Hussein Emami was later executed, together with other members of the Fedayeen of Islam in 1949.

5. *Yadnameh Ayatollah Borujerdi* (*In Memory of Ayatollah Borujerdi*), Tehran,

1978, p. 14. Ayatollah Ruhani confirms the animosity between Borujerdi and Khomeini. Since the revolution, suggestions for honouring Borujerdi have been vetoed by Khomeini.

6. The theme of the Shah having abandoned Islam became a favourite of Khomeini and was used in countless speeches and leaflets. See *Gozideh*.
7. Related by Ehsan Naraqi who was, at the time, Kashani's secretary. (In a private interview, Tehran 1978.)
8. Related by Ali Nayyeri and Abbas Hori who taught in Qom at the same time and knew Beheshti. In separate interviews in Paris (1980) and New York (1982).
9. Shaikh Ali Tehrani, quoted in *Erchad*, Paris, January 1985.
10. Ayatollah Ruhani in a private interview.

## Chapter 7

1. Fakhreddin Hejazi in a speech in Tehran on 10 February 1983.
2. Nader Naderpour in a private conversation in Paris, January 1982.
3. ibid.
4. *Towzih*, Introduction, p. 19.
5. *Gozideh*, p. 75.
6. Ruhani related the story in a private conversation in Tehran in 1977.
7. *Gozideh*, p. 81.
8. ibid.
9. ibid.
10. Ali Davani, *Nehzat Ruhaniyat dar Iran* (*The Clergy's Movement in Iran*), Tehran, 1980, vol. VI, p. 31. (Henceforth, *Nehzat*.)

## Chapter 8

1. The theological term used is *ja'er*, which means 'he who makes people suffer'.
2. *Nehzat*, vol. VI, p. 53.
3. In a speech broadcast by Tehran Radio on 14 February 1979.
4. Tearing the Qur'an is a grave sin, punishable by death in Shi'ite tradition.
5. *Nehzat*, vol. VI, p. 70.
6. ibid., p. 83.
7. ibid., p. 84.
8. The episode was related by Colonel Ali Taqavi, who headed the section of SAVAK at the time, in a private conversation in Los Angeles in April 1981.
9. Private conversation with Shariatmadari in Qom in September 1978. The Grand Ayatollah continued to defend that position at the cost of much suffering to himself and his family.
10. Disagreement between the authorities and the revolutionary mullahs as to the exact number of victims was one of the main features of the psychological war being waged in 1978.
11. Assadollah 'Alam related the episode in a series of interviews in January 1973. These interviews appeared in *Kayhan* in the same month.
12. General Pakravan in private conversation in September 1978.

13. 'Alam in the interviews cited in 11 above.
14. *Nehzat*, vol. VII, p. 57.
15. Pakravan in the conversation cited in 12 above.
16. Pakravan's tragic fate was reported by mutual friends in Tehran.
17. Shariatmadari, quoted in *Nehzat*, vol. VII, p. 92.
18. Grand Ayatollah Tabataba'i-Qomi's declaration in Mashhad in March 1980. Tabataba'i-Qomi continued to oppose all major aspects of Khomeini's policies to 1985.
19. *Zendegi-Nameh Imam Khomeini*, Tehran, 1980, p. 91.
20. ibid., p. 102.
21. The Shah's speech was delivered on 22 June 1973. But policy aims had been set as early as 1964.
22. *Nehzat*, vol. VII, p. 122.
23. ibid., p. 123.
24. *Gozideh*, p. 70.
25. ibid., p. 71.
26. ibid., p. 72.
27. ibid., p. 74.
28. *Nehzat*, vol. IX, p. 34.
29. Sayyed Ahmad Khomeini in an interview for *Maktab Islam* magazine, Qom, vol. 152. Also briefly quoted in *Bamdad*, 22 November 1979.

## Chapter 9

1. *Donyaye Fada'yan Islam* (*The World of the Fedayeen of Islam*), Tehran, 1980, pp. 19 and 20.
2. *Ettelaat Hafategi* magazine, Tehran, 22 October 1984.
3. Mrs Mostafavi's interview mentioned in note 2 of chapter 5.
4. See Orion's *U.N. Ambassadeur Extraordinaire*, Paris, 1983.
5. *E'lamieh hay Imam Khomeini* (*Imam Khomeini's Declarations*), Tehran, Ministry of Islamic Orientation, 1983, vol. IV, p. 20. (Henceforth, *E'lamieh*.)
6. ibid., p. 22.
7. Amir Abbas Hoveyda related this in private conversation in 1973.
8. Related in private conversation by Shaikh Mohammad Osman Naqshabandi in Paris, October 1983.
9. *E'lamieh*, vol. V, p. 11.
10. Speech by Khomeini broadcast by Tehran Radio on 2 January 1984.
11. The Imam does not know Plato directly and learned about the Greek philosopher's ideas from commentaries by Islamic thinkers of the tenth century.
12. *Hokumat-e-Eslami* (*Islamic Government*), Tehran, 1980, p. 11.
13. The Shi'ite theologians are divided on the 'true' meaning of the term. Grand Ayatollah Khonsari, for example, believed that only the mentally or physically handicapped could be described as *mustadh'af*.
14. Details were given in *Bultan Maharamaneh* (*The Confidential Bulletin*), January 1970, which was jointly produced by SAVAK and the Ministry of Information and available to about a hundred officials. Copies, however, were often leaked to the press.

15. ibid.
16. ibid.
17. *E'lamieh*, p. 68. The Ayatollah's 'declaration' was circulated as photocopies in October 1970.
18. ibid.
19. Sir Denis related this in a conversation in London in December 1982.
20. Olivier Warin, *Le Lion et le Soleil*, Paris, 1975, p. 60.

## Chapter 10

1. Related by Hoveyda in private conversation in October 1978.
2. The new calendar was based on the date of the foundation of the Persian Empire rather than Prophet Muhammed's hegira from Mecca to Medina.

## Chapter 11

1. *Tarikh*, p. 145.
2. SAVAK gave several reports on the subject, claiming 'special agents' among the clergy would help the regime. Motahari was considered a 'border-line' case from 1977 onwards.
3. All five quickly disappeared from the scene. Motahari and Beheshti were assassinated. Golzadeh-Ghafouri was forced into house arrest from July 1981 onwards, while Anvari and Mowla'i preferred to retreat into a quiet life of prayer. The last three saw the role of the clergy as one of guidance and supervision and not of exercising political power.
4. Related by Haj Ebrahim Dardashti, who visited Khomeini a few days after Mostafa's death, in conversation in Tehran, 1978.
5. *Nehzat*, vol. X, p. 33.
6. ibid., p. 40.
7. ibid., p. 45.
8. ibid., p. 48.
9. *E'lamieh*, vol. VII, p. 26.
10. Claim made by Attar Pour, a SAVAK functionary, in September 1978 and reported by Mahmoud Ja'afarian in private conversation in the same month.
11. Hezb Melall Eslami (Islamic Nations Party) leaflet published in Qom, October 1980.
12. ibid.
13. The insignia consisted of two sickles, one spanner, two machine guns and the sign of Allah in a crescent.
14. *E'lamieh*, vol. VII, p. 57.
15. The declaration was issued on behalf of Mara'ashi-Najafi at about the same time.
16. *Nehzat*, vol. VIII, p. 42.
17. Halabi was later to become a powerful enemy of Khomeini.
18. The estimate was made by the Endowments Office in 1978 and reported by Ali-Naqi Kani, then Minister of State in charge of Religious Affairs, in private conversation in September of the same year.
19. Khoiniha was later to become Emir al-Haj (Prince of the Mecca Pilgrims) on

Khomeini's orders.

20. *Tarikh*, p. 201.

21. ibid., p. 203.

22. ibid., p. 230.

23. ibid., p. 243.

24. A new edition of the book became available in a 'clandestine' edition in August 1978 and sold thousands of copies.

25. A copy of the confidential report was made available to me by Hoveyda to help in an inquiry I was making about the disturbances. The result of the inquiry appeared on 6 March 1978 in the Persian edition of *Kayhan* under the heading 'The Renovation of Iran's Politics Has Become Inevitable'.

26. Both were quickly released.

27. Sharif-Emami in private conversation in September 1978.

28. Foruhar in private conversation in October 1978.

29. I was intimately involved in the abortive attempt at fostering a dialogue.

30. There were also several rude slogans about the Shah's twin sister, Princess Ashraf.

31. Names of members cannot be mentioned since most are still in Iran.

32. I did not allow the letter to be printed in *Kayhan*.

33. Homayun had not even read the letters and passed them on through an aide.

34. The name of the writer cannot be mentioned since he is still in Tehran. Another man, Parviz Nik-khah, was erroneously executed as the author of the insulting letter. Nik-khah had not even read the letter when he faced the firing squad in February 1979 in Tehran.

35. Shariatmadari sent the message through his son-in-law Abbasi.

36. Contrary to subsequent claims by the clergy, there had been no order from Tehran to fire on demonstrators.

37. The Shah made the speech at a meeting of the Iranian Women's Association on 11 January 1978.

## Chapter 12

1. The *talabeh* killed was seeking sanctuary (*bast* in Persian) which is a right recognized by tradition. The residence of a Grand Ayatollah who is a *marja-e-taqleed* (source of imitation) is inviolate under the tradition. The Shah's troops had broken this tradition by forcibly entering Khomeini's home in 1964 and were now repeating the act by breaking into Shariatmadari's residence.

2. An exception was made when the Shah granted me two extended interviews in October 1976 and October 1977.

3. In an interview in October 1976.

4. During a private audience in September 1978 in Tehran.

5. Schmidt later became Federal Chancellor and the Shah believed him to have been the only Western leader to have urged strong support for the Iranian Government during the Western summit at Guadeloupe in 1978.

6. Strauss, however, did not join the group in the end.

7. The phrase was that of the Minister of State for Political Affairs, Holaku

Rambod, in a speech in the Majlis in February 1978.

8. The title of the book in Persian is *Akharin Talsh-ha dar Akharin Ruz-ha*, Tehran, November 1984.
9. Yazdi, op. cit., pp. 17 and 19.
10. The title of Bazargan's book in Persian is *Enqelab Iran dar do Harekat*.
11. The meeting with Foruhar was in Isfahan and with Moqadam in Tehran.
12. Foruhar said this in our conversation in Isfahan.
13. SAVAK accused the Tudeh Party and the Soviet Embassy in Tehran.
14. Zahedi said this in a private conversation in Tehran in December 1977.
15. The Shah's comment was reported by Hoveyda. Princess Ashraf also refers to it in her book *Faces in a Mirror*, New York, 1981.
16. Subsequent events showed that Carter had no policy vis-à-vis Iran at the time although members of his entourage may have been opposed to the Shah.
17. Reported by Haj Mohsen Torabi who attended several sessions in Najaf. The speech was also widely published in cassette form.
18. *Gozideh*, p. 193.
19. Reported by several businessmen who attended the meeting.
20. The Shah in a private audience in September 1978.
21. I had weekly meetings with Emami at the house of a mutual friend from August to October 1978. During those meetings he spoke cynically of the mullahs.
22. For a fuller list of the revolution's slogans, see Appendix 3.
23. In the early stages of the movement the mullahs accompanied demonstrators but remained on the pavements.
24. *E'lamieh*, p. 203.
25. ibid.
26. ibid., p. 205.
27. *Nehzat*, vol. X, p. 31.
28. *Navid*, Tehran, no. 24.
29. Sharif-Emami in private conversation on 20 September 1978 in Tehran.
30. *E'lamieh*, p. 217.
31. I raised the matter with Shariatmadari during a private conversation in Qom in October 1978. He estimated the number of dead to have been around seven hundred. When asked why he did not say so to correct the much more exaggerated figures, he replied that the Shah had exaggerated everything for years and that he should now have a taste of what that meant.

## Chapter 13

1. Published in *Jonbesh*, edited by Ali-Asghar Haj-Sayyed Javadi, in Tehran, January 1979.
2. Related by Mohammad Baheri who was Minister of Justice at the time and prevented the organization of a show trial.
3. Reported by Hoveyda after conversation with the Shah.
4. Hoveyda arranged for the Dino de Laurentis film to be screened for the Shah and the Empress.
5. Yazdi in *Last Efforts in Last Days*, pp. 23 and 74.

6. Bazargan in *Enqelab Iran dar do Harekat*, p. 23.

7. ibid.

8. Shah said this at a meeting at Nowshahr on 24 August 1978. Jamshid Amuzegar, then Prime Minister, and Hoveyda were also present, together with Empress Farah.

9. Oveissi related this in Paris in 1980.

10. Emami at a meeting at the residence of Javad Sa'id, the Speaker of Parliament in October 1978.

11. Related by Kani himself, in private conversations in Tehran in 1978 and in Paris in 1982.

12. Central Bank of Iran estimate in February 1979.

13. The scheme had the support of Generals Khosrowdad and Amin Afshar and was discussed at meetings at Zahedi's Hessarak residence in October 1978.

14. Related by Oveissi in Paris in November 1982.

15. The Shah's historic speech was not printed anywhere at the time since the press was on strike. Its full text has been published by Bazargan as an appendix to his book (see note 6 above).

16. ibid.

17. The massacre at Mashhad claimed more than two hundred victims and only made matters worse as Ayatollah Qomi, until then well disposed towards a compromise with the regime, was forced to interrupt all dialogue.

18. The subsequent claim that the Israelis were the first to realize that the Shah was about to fall cannot be supported by facts but is used by subscribers to the 'conspiracy theory' as a means of 'proving' the involvement of the Jewish state in the overthrow of the Shah.

19. *Navid*, no. 28.

20. Related by Sadeq Qomi, the son of the ayatollah, in a conversation in Mashhad in November 1978.

21. SAVAK mobilized its network to help spread the rumour.

22. At an audience with the Shah on 17 November 1978. Manuchehr Ganji, a former Education Minister, and Reza Ghotbi, the former head of radio and television, were also present.

23. *Gozideh*, p. 245.

24. Quoted in *Zendegi Reza Shah* (*The Life of Reza Shah*) by Ali Adibi, Tehran, 1976.

25. Motahari related this to a mutual friend in Tehran in February 1979.

## Chapter 14

1. Bakhtiar's supporters believe that Huyser, then deputy commander of NATO, was dispatched to Tehran to encourage the generals to stage a coup. Huyser himself, however, says he had the mission of preventing such a move. The debate continues but is largely irrelevant since, with hindsight, we now know that no coup would have been possible or could have stopped the tide of revolution.

2. A. R. Nurizadeh, then a close friend of Ghotbzadeh, was present and relates the unusual intermission in the Ayatollah's hectic schedule at the time.

3. ibid.
4. Related by Bakhtiar himself. See, for example, his *Yek-rangi*, Paris, 1983.
5. Related by Hassan Nazih who was close to Bazargan at the time, in conversation in Paris in January 1983.
6. Related by Nurizadeh in private conversation in London, in 1984.
7. Arafat did eventually visit Tehran once but was allowed no publicity. He had to wear European clothes and was whisked to the Shah's palace from the airport for a two-hour audience in January 1971 before being whisked back to catch the first plane out.
8. Hani al-Hassan, interviewed by Tehran Radio on 20 February 1979.
9. Related by a mutual friend who met Qara-nay regularly shortly before the general was gunned down.
10. Forqan, reconstituted as a political group with headquarters in Paris, was responsible in 1985 for the murder of many close Khomeini aides and was accused of cooperation with former SAVAK operatives.
11. Related by Madani in private conversations in Paris in 1983 and 1984. Madani later ran for President but was eventually forced to flee the country.
12. The slogan was that of the Mujahedeen but was often used by Marxist groups as well.
13. Khalkhali in an interview with *Sobh Azadegan*, September 1984.
14. Khomeini in a speech at Qom on 9 April 1979, broadcast by Tehran Radio.
15. Khalkhali in an interview with the magazine *Ferdowsi* in Tehran, 19 April 1978.
16. Haj-Sayyed Javadi in an interview with the daily *Khalq Mossalman*, Tehran, 3 November 1979.
17. ibid.
18. Broadcast by Tehran Radio from Qom on 11 July 1979.
19. ibid.
20. Broadcast by Radio Iran from Qom on 20 August 1979.
21. Address at Qobad mosque in Tehran on 20 July 1981.
22. Ayatollah 'Alameh Tabataba'i in *Qur'an dar Islam*, Qom, 1980.
23. This was one of the Imam's favourite phrases.

## Chapter 15

1. *Asnad Laneh Jassussi (Documents from the Nest of Spies)*, sixty-one volumes of documents seized at the US Embassy in Tehran.
2. The tragic incident in which eight members of a rescue mission died in the collision between two helicopters and a transport aircraft near the Iranian desert town of Tabas, persuaded Khomeini that the USA was still hostile to his regime.
3. For an account of the secret negotiations, see Hamilton Jordan's *Crisis*, New York, 1983. Jordan, however, does not reveal the identity of Beheshti's envoy at the secret talks.
4. In statements broadcast by Tehran Radio on 27 January.

5. Hamid Ruhani in notes to the Persian translation of Muhammad Haykal's *The Return of the Ayatollah* (in Persian, *Dastani keh nagofteh mand*), Tehran, 1982.
6. *Sobh Azadegan*, 28 October 1981.
7. Bazargan relates this in his book, p. 178.
8. On 4 October 1980.
9. *Sobh Azadegan*, 8 July 1981.
10. ibid.
11. Hussein Khomeini's speech was reproduced as a leaflet by Bani-Sadr's supporters in June 1981.
12. Bani-Sadr and Rajavi later separated and became political enemies.
13. *Sobh Azadegan*, 20 June 1981. Also the *Guardian*, London, 24 June 1981.
14. Khomeini develops this in his *Kashf al-Asrar*.
15. Related by Haj Nasser Tahami, who was, in part, involved in the mediation (private interview, Paris, September 1984).
16. The magazine *Shaheed* (*Martyr*), June 1983.
17. Poem by Mim Atash.
18. Private interview with Shariatmadari in 1968. He was criticizing the Shah at the time.
19. See, for example, Senator Jesse Helms in testimony to the Senate, *Congressional Record*, 7 February 1985.
20. The names often used by the groups include Jahad Islami (Islamic Holy War) and Martyr Hussein's Squad.

## Chapter 16

1. Quoted in *Enqelab Eslami*, Paris, February 1985.
2. He was unable to visit Mashhad or even the shrine of Abdul-Azim south of Tehran.
3. *Al-Majallah*, London, 26 February 1985.
4. *Sobh Azadegan*, Tehran, 3 March 1983.
5. *Sokahnrani Imam beh monasebat payan Majlis Khebregan* (*The speech of the Imam on the occasion of the conclusion of the work of the Assembly of Experts*), published by Pishva, Tehran, 1984.
6. ibid.
7. A woman's voice is allowed if she reads from a text in an ordinary way 'not causing lust or stirring sexual desires'. The singing female voice is allowed only if more than two women sing together provided their song is in praise of Allah or supportive of the revolution. The style of singing should not be conducive to 'lust or sexual desires'. Full conditions are listed in the magazine *Pasdar Islam*, Qom, October 1984. In March 1985 two other edicts seemed to 'liberalize' rules concerning women. Public laundries were allowed to accept women's clothing for dry-cleaning, and the development and printing of photos of women by professionals was also declared 'halal' (permitted). Nevertheless ambiguities continued and the daily newspaper *Kayhan* ran into trouble for publishing a crowd photo that showed several Lebanese women without the 'Islamic' headgear.

8. *Neda*, Paris, June 1982.

9. In an interview with the magazine *Saf*, Tehran, August 1984.

10. The religious minorities are the Armenians, the Assyrians, the Jews, the Zoroastrians, the Sabeans, the Baha'is and the Yazidis. The last three, however, are not considered as religious communities but as 'political entities'.

11. This group is charged with the task of forcing women to obey the rules of Islam.

12. The oil revenue for 1985 was projected to be at least 15 per cent lower than that of 1984.

13. The shrine of Zaynab, the sister of Imam Hussein, is situated at the Zaynabiah suburb of Damascus.

14. They are known as the *maktabis*, or those who follow the revolution from an ideological point of view rather than for emotional reasons.

15. A term borrowed from the French *nouveaux philosophes*.

16. *Kayhan*, airmail edition, 13 February 1985.

17. ibid.

18. See Appendix 4.

19. Quoted in the *Gahnameh Enqelab* (*Calendar of the Revolution*), Tehran, March 1983.

20. Related by Rafsajani in a Tehran Radio interview on 10 February 1983.

21. This handpicked brigade is charged with the task of protecting the capital against a possible military coup d'état.

22. *Kayhan*, airmail edition, 13 February 1985.

23. ibid.

24. *Ahle-Maktab* (*The People of the School*), Tehran, June 1984.

25. *Neda*, Paris, July 1983.

26. Report by Budget and Planning Ministry, Tehran, October 1984.

27. *Kayhan*, airmail edition, 13 February 1985.

# Appendix 1

# *Two Poems by Ayatollah Khomeini*

### The Almond Tree

This *ghazal* or sonnet is taken from Khomeini's *Gozideh Ash'ar* (*A Selection of Poems*) published in Qom in 1979. The poem itself bears no date but was probably written in the 1930s.

> It's spring and there is blossom on the almond tree.
> The bride of the garden is, verily, the almond tree.
> A sight that gives comfort to all tired eyes,
> Filling with joy the hearts of widows and orphans.
> To the sick man, to the dying it gives hope of cure
> A message from the Creator is this almond tree.
> It tells you that: beauty and life are created
> From the ugly earth that wore the death mask of winter.
> Carefree and joyful flock to the garden young and old
> Foolishly taking as eternal the blossoms of the tree.
> And yet suddenly the sky darkens with a thunderous cloud.
> Rain shakes the almond tree, scattering its blossoms.
> The bride of the garden stands naked and trembling
> Like an old beggar woman chased off a street.
> A moment's oblivion, the ingratitude of one moment
> Leads to a terrible lesson for those who forget God.
> 'Hindi', knowing all this, remembers at every breath
> Not the beauty of the blossoms but He who made them so.

### Tamerlane

The following poem, also taken from *Gozideh Ash'ar*, may have been written in the 1940s.

I know not in which book I read
The story of Tamerlane's exploits.
He who put young and old to the sword,
He who ignored the commands of the Lord.
At night he was struck by insomnia
Crying aloud and writhing with pain.
Doctors who came to offer him a cure
Saw the wound of a sword around his neck
Strangling him. That's the revenge of God.
So as the Tatar pierced the roof with his cries,
The Angel of Revenge chuckled noiselessly.
There is One who lays the mighty low.
There is He who chops the guilty into pieces
To him is devoted 'Hindi' and to no other one.

# Appendix 2

# *Some Key Words in Khomeini's Political Vocabulary*

| | |
|---|---|
| *A'alam* | He who knows more than others. The title of the leading personality among Grand Ayatollahs at any given time. |
| *'Adl* | Justice. The concept of Allah as just and the belief that divine Justice must be realized in this world too. |
| *Ahl-e-Kitab* | The People of the Book. Christians, Jews and Zoroastrians. They can retain their faith within a Muslim community but have to pay a head tax. |
| *Amr bel-ma'aruf* | Enjoining the Good. Making sure that everyone in the community is on the Right Path. |
| *Ayatollah* | The symbol of Allah. The title of mullahs who have attained the degree of authority to rule on matters of theology. |
| *Ayatollah al-Odhma* | Grand Ayatollah. The highest title in the Shi'ite theological hierarchy. |
| *Faqih* | The theologian. A doctor of theology. |
| *Feqh* | Theology. |

| | |
|---|---|
| *Hadith* | Tradition. The sayings of the Prophet and the twelve Imams which have the authority of common law. |
| *Hojat al-Islam va al-Moslemeen* | The Vicar of Islam and of the Muslims. The title of high-ranking mullahs just one grade below ayatollah. |
| *Hosseinieh* | The House of Hussein. A place where believers gather to mourn the martyred Imam Hussein. |
| *Imam* | Community leader. Khomeini has altered the meaning of the word which now denotes a person who rules over Muslims in the name of Allah. |
| *Iman* | Faith. The firm belief that every word in the Qur'an is divine, eternally true and unalterable. |
| *Ja'er* | Evil-doing. Illegitimate. The term used to describe all governments of Islamic countries except that of Iran under Khomeini. |
| *Jihad* | Holy war. Originally a war waged by Muslims against hostile non-Muslims or for conquest of territory for Islam. Khomeini has extended it to mean fighting unacceptable Muslim governments as well. |
| *Kaffir* | Pagan. All mankind except the Muslims and the *ahl-e-kitab*. |
| *Kufr* | Paganism. Belief in any religion except Islam and those of *ahl-e-kitab*. |
| *Mahdur ad-damm* | He whose blood must be shed. A term reserved for almost anyone who opposes the rule of the Imam as well as heretics from Islam. |
| *Mufsed fel-Ardh* | Corrupter of the earth. He who |

spreads corruption in the community. In practice those who oppose the Imam.

*Muharib an al-Allah*  
He who wages war on Allah. In practice those who rebel against the rule of the Imam.

*Munafiq*  
Hypocrites. In practice it designates members of the Mujahedeen guerrilla organization.

*Murtad*  
Heretic. He who has abandoned Islam. In practice it designates members of the Baha'i community.

*Mustadh'afeen*  
The Dispossessed or the Downtrodden. As a theological term it designated orphans, mentally deranged persons, widows and other vulnerable individuals. Khomeini takes it to mean the vast majority of Muslims who, because they are poor and illiterate, are vulnerable and need the protection of the Imam.

*Mustakbareen*  
The mighty. In practice, those of the rich and the powerful who do not support the rule of the Imam and who should, therefore, be eliminated through revolution.

*Nabi*  
Emissary of Allah. Term designating those of the Prophets who also had the right to exercise political and military power on behalf of the Almighty.

*Nahy an al-Munkar*  
Preventing the doing of Evil.

*Qital*  
Killing in the course of fulfilling the will of Allah. In practice, to realize the objectives of the Imam through the physical elimination of his opponents.

*Rowzeh-khan*  
Literally, he who reads from the book of the garden. Designates mullahs who relate the story of Karbala.

| | |
|---|---|
| *Sayyed* | A descendant of the Prophet and as such entitled to special honours and pecuniary advantages. (Literally, mister.) |
| *Shahadah* | Martyrdom. A Muslim's most noble achievement according to Khomeini. |
| *Shari'a* | Qur'anic law. |
| *Shaytan* | Satan. 'Shaytan Bozorg', the 'Great Satan', designates the United States and, to a lesser extent, the USSR. |
| *Sherk* | Polytheism. Khomeini has extended the meaning of the term to cover all excessive attention to anything except obedience to Allah and the rule of the Imam. |
| *Taghut* | The Rebel. One of the many appellations of Satan in the Qur'an. Khomeini used the term to designate the Shah and, later, all those opposed to his rule. |
| *Takieh* | The back-up unit for the mosque. A place where believers gather to mourn Imam Hussein and to organize processions during Muharram and Safar. |
| *Taqieh* | Dissimulation. Hiding one's true faith and beliefs when in a position of weakness. |
| *Taqleed* | Imitation or emulation. Acting in accordance with rules set by the theological hierarchy. |
| *Taqwa* | Piety. To Khomeini this is but an individual quest for merit and not enough. |
| *Tasdeeq* | Realization of the Divine Intention as revealed in the Qur'an. In practice, the establishment of Islamic government on a universal scale. |

| | |
|---|---|
| *Tazkieh* | Self-purification. To emancipate oneself from the little devil inside; to be modest, self-deprecating. |
| *Towheed* | Monotheism. |
| *Ummah* | The Muslim community throughout the world. |

# Appendix 3

# *The 'Sources of Imitation'*

Six men form the highest echelon of Shi'ite religious leadership. Known as the maraj-e-taqleed (sources of imitation), they have the authority to promulgate laws on every aspect of life. They are, in order of seniority:

Grand Ayatollah Hojat al-Islam va al-Moslemeen Haj Sayyed Abol-Qassem Mussavi-Kho'i (aged ninety-eight, lives in Najaf, Iraq)

Grand Ayatollah Hojat al-Islam va al-Moslemeen Haj Sayyed Shahabeddin Husseini-Mara'ashi-Najafi (aged ninety-six, lives in Qom)

Grand Ayatollah Hojat al-Islam va al-Moslemeen Haj Sayyed Ruhollah Mussavi-Khomeini (aged eighty-five, lives in Tehran)

Grand Ayatollah Hojat al-Islam va al-Moslemeen Haj Sayyed Mohammad-Reza Mussavi-Golpayegani (aged eighty-four, lives in Qom)

Grand Ayatollah Hojat al-Islam va al-Moslemeen Haj Sayyed Hassan Tabataba'i-Qomi (aged eighty-three, lives in Mashhad)

Grand Ayatollah Hojat al-Islam va al-Moslemeen Haj Shaikh Mohammad-Taqi Qomi (aged seventy-two, lives in Paris)

**The 'sources of imitation' can be succeeded, on their death, by a member of the second group of ayatollahs. This second group consisted, in 1987, of the following personalities who are listed in order of seniority:

Ayatollah Haj Sayyed Mohammad Sadeq Ruhani (lives in Qom)

Ayatollah Haj Shaikh Hussein-Ali Montazeri (lives in Qom)

Ayatollah Haj Sayyed Mohammad-Reza Alemi (lives in Tehran)

Ayatollah Haj Shaikh Ali-Akbar Meshkini (lives in Qom)

Ayatollah Haj Shaikh Mohammad-Hussein Javadi-Amoli (lives in Tehran)

Ayatollah Haj Shaikh Mohammad Vahidi (lives in Qom)

# Appendix 4

# *Who rules the Islamic Republic? The social structure of political power in the Islamic Republic*

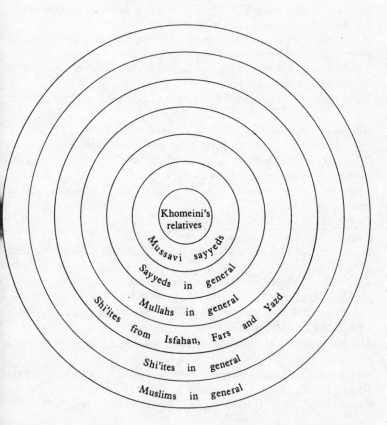

Khomeini's relatives

Mussavi sayyeds

Sayyeds in general

Mullahs in general

Shi'ites from Isfahan, Fars and Yazd

Shi'ites in general

Muslims in general

# Selected Bibliography

Ali 'Abiri, *Yeksad Mosahebeh Imam Khomeini* (*One Hundred Interviews of Imam Khomeini*), Tehran, 1979.

Karim Abolhoda, *Ahl-e-Bayt* (*Members of the Household*), Qom, 1974.

Ervand Abrahamian, *Iran Between Two Revolutions*, Princeton, New Jersey, 1982.

Taher Ahmadzadeh, *Hokumat Eslami va Monafeqeen* (*Islamic Government and the Hypocrites*), Rome, 1984.

Firuz Akbari, *Tariq-e-Shohada* (*The Way of the Martyrs*), Tehran, 1979.

Shahrough Akhavi, *Religion and Politics in Contemporary Iran: The Clergy–state relationship in the Pahlavi era*, Albany, New York, 1980.

Hamid Algar, *Religion and State in Iran, 1785–1906: The Role of the Ulama in the Qajar Period*. Berkeley and Los Angeles, 1969.

Jalal Al-Ahmad, *Khedmat va Khianat Roshanfekran* (*Service and Treason of the Intellectuals*), Tehran, 1979.

Shams Al-Ahmad, *Hadith Enqelab* (*Narrative of the Revolution*), 2 vol., Tehran, 1981.

Hussein Amir-Sadeqi, *Twentieth-Century Iran*, London, 1977.

Abbas Amirie (ed.), *Iran in the 1980s*, Tehran and Washington, 1978.

Gilles Anquetil, *La Terre a Bougé en Iran*, Paris, 1980.

Hassan 'Arfa, *Under Five Shahs*, London, 1964.

Farah Azari (ed.), *Women of Iran: The Conflict with Fundamentalist Islam*, London, 1983.

Taqi 'Azimi-Far, *Ijtihad dar Islam* (*Ijtihad in Islam*), Qom, 1972.

Philippe 'Aziz, *Les Sectes Secrets de l'Islam*, Paris, 1983.

Imadeddin Badr, *Nahdhat al-Islamiyah fel Iran* (Religious Movement in Iran), Qom, 1984.

Shaul Bakhash, *The Reign of the Ayatollahs*, London, 1984.

Shapour Bakhtiar, *Ma Fidélité*, Paris, 1983.

Abol-Hassan Bani-Sadr, *Eqtesad Towhidi* (Unitarian Economics), Paris, 1977.

Abol-Hassan Bani-Sadr, *L'Espoir trahi*, Paris, 1983.

Abol-Hassan Bani-Sadr, *Osul Payeh va Zavabet Hokumat Eslami* (*The Principles and Yardsticks of Islamic Government*), Tehran, 1979.

Mohammad-Hussein Bani-Yaqub, *Khomeini Cheh Amukht?* (*What Did Khomeini Teach?*), Tehran, 1981.

Siavash Bashiri, *Divar Allah-Akbar* (*The Allah-Akbar Wall*), Paris, 1981.

Mangol Bayat, *Mysticism and Dissent: Socioreligious Thought in Qajar Iran*. Syracuse, New York, 1982.

E. A. Bayne, *Persian Kingship in Transition*, New York, 1968.

Mehdi Bazargan, *Enqelab Iran dar do Harekat (Iran's Revolution in Two Moves)*, Tehran, 1984.

Mehdi Bazargan, *Showraye Enqelab va Hokumat Movaqat (The Revolutionary Council and the Provisional Government)*, Tehran, 1982.

Leonard Binder, *Iran: Political Development in a Changing Society*, Berkeley and Los Angeles, 1962.

Zbigniew Brzezinsky, *Power and Principle: Memoirs of the National Security Adviser 1977–1981*, New York, 1983.

Olivier Carre and Gerard Michaud, *Les Frères Musulmans (1928–1982)*, Paris, 1983.

Jimmy Carter, *Keeping Faith*, New York, 1982.

Bahram Chubineh, *Ta'shayu va Sisasat (Shi'ism and Politics)*, 2 vol., Düsseldorf, West Germany, 1983.

Henry Corbin, *En Islam Iranien: Aspects spirituels et philosophiques*, 4 vol., Paris, 1971–73.

Henry Corbin, *Face de Dieu, Face de l'Homme: Herméneutique et Soufisme*, Paris, 1983.

Ali-Mohammad Damghani, *Zendegi Imam (Life of the Imam)*, Qom, 1979.

Yahya Danesh, *Naqshe Imam dar Enqelab (The Role of the Imam in the Revolution)*, Tehran, 1982.

Ali Davani, *Nehzat Ruhaniyat dar Iran (The Clergy's Movement in Iran)*, 11 vol., Tehran, 1980–83.

Fat'hollah Derakhshan, *Rah Imam (The Path of the Imam)*, Qom, 1984.

Mohammad, Derakhshesh, *Haftad sal Besouye Sarab (Seventy Years Towards a Mirage)*, Washington, DC, 1984.

William Eagleton Jr, *The Kurdish Republic of 1946*, New York, 1963.

Laurence P. Elwell-Sutton, *Persian Oil: A Study in Power Politics*, Westport, Connecticut, 1976.

John L. Esposito (ed.), *Voices of Resurgent Islam*, Oxford University Press, 1983.

Mohammad-Javad Fazel-Harandi, *Shahadat dar Isalm (Martyrdom in Islam)*, Tehran, 1984.

Prince M. Firouz, *L'Iran Face à l'Imposture de l'Histoire*, Paris, 1971.

Michael M.F. Fischer, *Iran: From Religious Dispute to Revolution*, Cambridge, Massachusetts, 1982.

William H. Forbis, *Fall of the Peacock Throne*, New York, 1981.

Richard Frye, *Iran*, London, 1960.

Yahya Ganjavi, *Jonbesh Towhidi Saff (The Unitarian Saff Movement)*, Qom, 1979.

Roger Garaudy, *Promesses de l'Islam*, Paris, 1983.

Abbas-Karim Gharabaghi, *Haqayeq darbareh bohran Iran (Facts about the crisis in Iran)*, Paris, 1984.

Robert Graham, *Iran: The Illusion of Power*, London, 1980.

Fred Halliday, *Iran: Dictatorship and Development*, London, 1978.

Nasser Hariri, *Mosahebeh ba Tarikh-Sazan Iran (Interview with the Makers of*

*Iran's History*), Tehran, 1979.

Mohammad Haykal, *The Return of the Ayatollah*, London, 1982.

Mehdi Heravi, *Iranian–American Diplomacy*, Brooklyn, New York, 1969.

Dilip Hiro, *Iran under the Ayatollahs*, London, 1985.

Fereydoun Hoveyda, *The Fall of the Shah*, London, 1979.

Asaf Hussein, *Political Perspectives on the Muslim World*, New York, 1985.

Sornsh Irfani, *Revolutionary Islam in Iran*, London, 1982.

Charles Issawi, *The Economic History of Iran (1800–1914)*, Chicago, 1971.

Ali-Mohammad Izadi, *Nejat (Salvation)*, Toronto, Canada, 1984.

Christian Jambert, *La Logique des Orientaux*, Paris, 1983.

Mohsen Javadi, *Sayri dar Andisheh Imam. (A Journey Through the Thoughts of the Imam)*, Qom, 1982.

Bizhan Jazani, *Capitalism and Revolution in Iran*, London, 1980.

Hamilton Jordan, *Crisis*, New York, 1983.

Benjamin Z. Kadar, *Crusade and Mission: European Approaches Towards the Muslims*, Princeton, New Jersey, 1984.

Morteza Kamali, *Zendegi Ostad Motahari* (Life of Master Motahari), Qom, 1981.

Ryszard Kapuściński, *Shah of the Shahs*, London, 1985.

Ahmad Kasravi, *Shiagari (Shi'ism)*, West Germany, 1984. (Originally published in Tehran in 1946.)

Mohammad Khajeh-Nasiri, *Varess Molk Kiyan (Heir to the Realm of Kings)*, Los Angeles, 1980.

Nikki R. Keddie (ed.), *Religion and Politics in Iran*, New Haven and London, 1983.

Nikki R. Keddie, *Roots of Revolution*, London, 1981.

Mehdi Khaze'i, *Shahid Mehrab (Martyred for the Faith)*, Shiraz, 1984.

Ruhollah Khomeini, *Gozideh Ash'ar (A Selection of poems)*, Tehran, 1979.

Ruhollah Khomeini, *Gozideh Paym-ha va Mosahebeh-ha (A Selection of Messages and Interviews)*, Tehran, 1981.

Ruhollah Khomeini, *Hokumat-e-Eslami (Islamic Government)*, Tehran, 1979.

Ruhollah Khomeini, *Kashf al-Asrar (Key to the Secrets)*, Tehran, 1980.

Ruhollah Khomeini, *Tafsir Sureh Hamd (Comment on the Hamd Sura)*, Tehran, 1980.

Ruhollah Khomeini, *Tahrir al-Wassilah (Noting down the Means)*, Tehran, 1984.

Ruhollah Khomeini, *Towzih al-Masayel (Explication of Problems)*, Qom, 1964.

Ruhollah Khomeini, *Valayat-e-Faqih (The Regency of the Theologian)*, Tehran, 1980.

Marc Kravetz, *Irano Nox*, Paris, 1982.

Chris Kutchera, *Le Mouvement National Kurde*, Paris, 1979.

Hassan Kuzeh-Kanani, *Ta'azieh (Shi'ite Passion Plays)*, Tehran, 1984.

Anne Katherine Swynford Lambton, *Landlord and Peasant in Persia: A Study in Land Tenure and Revenue Administration*, London, 1953.

Anne Katherine Swynford Lambton, *Theory and Practice in Medieval Persian Government*, London, 1980.

John Laffin, *The Dagger of Islam*, London, 1981.

H. Laoust, *Les Schismes dans l'Islam*, Paris, 1965.

Mohmmad-Hussein, Larijani, *Shari'at Islam* (*Islamic Jurisprudence*), Qom, 1960.

George Lenczowski, *Iran under the Pahlavis*, Stanford, California, 1978.

Bernard Lewis (ed.), *L'Islam d'Hier et d'Aujourd'hui*, Paris, 1981.

Abtin Livani, *Nehzat Ruhaniyat dar Qafqaz* (*The Religious Movement in the Caucasus*), Tabriz, 1980.

Marie-Agnes Malfray, *L'Islam*, Paris, 1980.

G. S. Hodgson Marshall, *The Venture of Islam*, 3 vol., Chicago, 1974.

Louis Massignon, *La Passion d'Hallaj*, 2 vol., Paris, 1922.

Ali Mir-Fetros, *Hallaj*, West Germany, 1982.

Richard Mitchell, *The Society of Muslim Brothers*, London, 1969.

Hussein-Ali Montazeri, *Towzih al-Masayel* (*Explication of Problems*), Tehran, 1984.

Edward Mortimer, *Faith and Power: The Politics of Islam*, London, 1982.

Morteza Motahari (Ayatollah), *Maqam zan dar Islam* (*Women's Status in Islam*), Tehran, 1980.

Kazem Nabavai, *Zendegi Imam Jaafar Sadeq* (*Life of Imam Jaafar Sadeq*), Qom, 1961.

Nader Naderpour, *Sobh Dorugheen* (*False Dawn*), Paris, 1981.

Hushang Nahvandi, *L'Anatomie d'une Révolution*, Paris, 1982.

V. S. Naipaul, *Among the Believers, an Islamic Journey*, London, 1981.

Gholam-Hussein Omrani, *Tarikhcheh Mobarezat Ruhaniyat dar Iran* (*A Brief History of the Struggle of the Clergy in Iran*), Mashhad, 1979.

Orion, *L'Ambassadeur Extraordinaire*, Paris, 1983.

Ashraf Pahlavi (Princess), *Faces in a Mirror*, New York, 1981.

Ashraf Pahlavi (Princess), *Jamais Résignée*, Paris, 1983.

Mohammad-Reza Pahlavi (Shah), *Mission for My Country*, New York, 1961.

Mohammad-Reza Pahlavi (Shah), *Réponse à l'Histoire*, Paris, 1979.

Mohammad-Reza Pahlavi (Shah), *Tamadon Bozorg* (*The Great Civilization*), Tehran, 1977.

Anthony Parsons, *The Pride and the Fall*, London, 1984.

J. P. Peroncel-Hugoz, *Le Radeau de Mahomet*, Paris, 1983.

J. Piscatori (ed.), *Islam in the Political Process*, Cambridge, 1983.

Mohammad-Taqi Qomi, *Taqrib Eslami* (*Islamic Convergence*), Paris, 1984.

Jamaleddin Qorbani, *Khomeini Bedoun Neqab* (*Khomeini Without the Mask*), Düsseldorf, West Germany, 1979.

Fazlur Rahman, *Islam*, Chicago, 1979.

Valiollah Rahmani, *Ruz-hay khunin Enqelab* (*Bloody Days of the Revolution*), Mashhad, 1979.

Zaynolabedin Rahnema, *Piambar* (*The Messenger*), Tehran, 1967.

Massoud Rajavi, *Tabyin Jahan* (*Making Sense of the World*), 2 vol., Paris, 1982.

Maxime Rodinson, *Mohammad*, London, 1973.

Maxime Rodinson, *Islam and Capitalism*, London, 1977.

Barry Rubin, *Paved with Good Intentions: The American Experience and Iran*, Oxford University Press, 1980.

Hamid Ruhani, *Shariatmadari dar Dadgah Tarikh* (*Shariatmadari Tried by History*), Tehran, 1985.

Malise Ruthven, *Islam in the World*, London, 1984.

Mohammad-Baqer Sadr (Ayatollah) *Eqtesadena (Our Economics)*, Tehran, 1982.

Edward Said, *Covering Islam*, London, 1981.

Amin Saikal, *The Rise and Fall of the Shah*, Princeton, New Jersey, 1980.

Shojaeddin Shafa, *Dar Paykar ba Ahriman (Fighting the Satan)*, Paris, 1984.

Shojaeddin Shafa, *Towzih al-Masayel (Explication of Problems)*, Paris, 1983.

Ali Shariati, *Fatemeh Fatemeh Ast (Fatima is Fatima)*, Tehran, 1970.

Ali Shariati, *Haj*, Tehran, 1975.

Ali Shariati, *Shia Alavi va Shia Safavi (Alawite Shi'ism, Safavid Shi'ism)*, Tehran, 1972.

Charles-Ismail Shemkus, *The Fall of Iran, 1978–1979: A Historical Anthology*, New York, 1979.

Kalim Siddiqi, *Al-Harakah al-Islamiah: Qadaya wa Ahdaf (The Islamic Movement: Issues and Goals)*, London, 1985.

John D. Stempel, *Inside the Iranian Revolution*, Bloomington. (USA), 1981.

William Sullivan, *Mission to Iran*, New York, 1981.

Sayyed Mohammad-Hussein Tabataba'i, *Qur'an dar Islam (Qur'an in Islam)*, Qom, 1980.

Amir Taheri, *Mara Cheh Mishavad? (What Is Wrong with Us?)*, compiled by Pari Sekandari, Paris, 1982.

Sayyed Mahmoud Taleqani, *Islam va Malekiyat (Islam and Ownership)*, Tehran, 1980.

John Upton, *History of Modern Iran: An Interpretation*, Cambridge, Massachusetts, 1961.

Cyrus Vance, *Hard Choices: Critical Years in America's Foreign Policy*, New York, 1983.

Montgomery Watt, *Islam and the Integration of Society*, London, 1970.

Donald N. Wilber, *Reza Shah*, Hicksville, New York, 1975.

Denis Wright, *The Persian Amongst the English*, London, 1985.

Ibrahim Yazdi, *Akharin Talash-ha dar Akharin Ruz-ha (Last Efforts in Last Days)*, Tehran, 1984.

Abraham Yeselson, *United States–Persian Diplomatic Relations 1883–1921*, New Brunswick, New Jersey, 1956.

Sepehr Zabih, *The Communist Movement in Iran*, Berkeley, California, 1966.

Rahim-Ali Zarbaf, *Payam Qom (The Message of Qom)*, Qom, 1984.

Marvin Zonis, *The Political Elite of Iran*, Princeton, New Jersey, 1971.

Abdul-Karim Zubin, *Labayk ya Khomeini (Hail to Khomeini)*, Tehran, 1984.

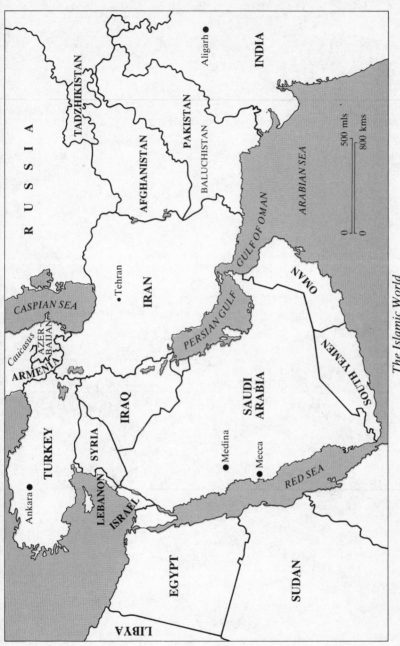

The Islamic World

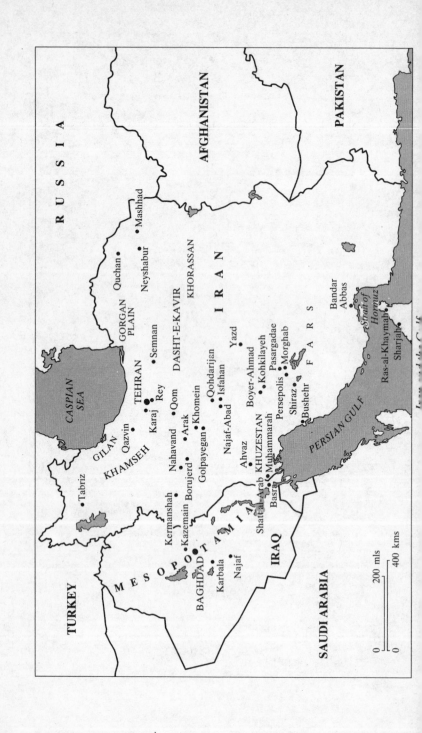

*Iran and the Gulf*

# Index

Athens, 55
Australia, 208
Austro-Hungarian Empire, 180
Ayat, Hassan, 280
Azerbaijan, 65, 67, 107, 178, 210, 221, 256, 269, 306–7
Azerbaijan Democratic Sect, 165
Azhari, Gholam-Reza, 238–9, 241
Azmun, Manuchehr, 224, 225

Ba'athist Party (Iraq), 165, 170
Babylon, 167
Badreh'i, General Abdul-Ali, 244, 250
Baghdad, 165, 169, 177, 229, 276, 277
Baghdad Radio, 158
Baha'i, Shaikh, 179
Baha'i faith, 83, 113–14, 115–16, 131, 148, 190, 192, 197, 198, 251, 262, 293
Bahar, Mohammad-Taqi, 59
Bahonar, Hojat al-Islam Mohammad Javad, 113, 128, 183, 192, 282
Bakhsh, Ayatollah Ehsan, 294
Bakhtiar, Shapour, 124, 273; becomes Prime Minister, 241, 243, and Khomeini's return to Iran, 243, 245, 246, 248–9; cancels American contracts, 268; flees Iran, 250
Bakhtiar, Major General Teymour, 114, 124, 165–6, 169
Bakhtiari tribes, 56, 72
Baku, 221
Baluchistan, 56, 254
al-Bana, Shaikh Hassan, 98
Bandar Abbas, 153
Bangladesh, 303
Bani-Hashem clan, 138
Bani-Ka'ab tribe, 72
Bani-Sadr, Abol-Hassan, 199, 230, 292; and the 'second revolution', 271; Americans want to use as agent, 273; elected as President, 274, 275; and the war with Iraq, 276, 278, 279; proposes export of Islamic Revolution, 288; fall from power, 279–81, 283, 291
Bani-Sadr, Azra, 199–200
Banu-Turuf tribe, 72
Barzan Takriti, 228, 229
Barzani, Mullah Mostafa, 165
Baseej Mustadh'afeen (Mobilization of the Dispossessed), 279, 297
Basr, 39
Batmanqelech, Lieutenant General, 114
Bavaria, 209
Bazargan, Mehdi, 122, 201, 231, 232, 251, 252, 254, 273, 283; and the preparations for revolution, 212, 218; visits Khomeini in France, 231; chosen as head of provisional government, 234, 248–9, 272; hides Bakhtiar, 250; and the executions, 253, 261, 262; rejects idea of

Islamic republic, 255; as Prime Minister, 257–8; wants to return to normality, 259; tries to contain mullahs, 260; relations with America, 268; and the American embassy occupation, 271; in the Majlis, 275; supports Bani-Sadr, 280; tries to prevent Ghotbzadeh's execution, 287
Behbehani, Ayatollah, 39, 41
Behesht-e-Zahra, Tehran, 245, 252
Beheshti, Ayatollah Mohammad-Hussein, 192, 292; as follower of Khomeini, 113; preparations for revolution, 122, 123, 183; and the hayats, 149; and Mansur's assassination, 156; accuses Shah of being a Jew, 197; visits Khomeini in France, 231; tactics, 233; spreads the longing for Khomeini, 242; emerges as strong man, 260; and the American embassy occupation, 271, 273; political ambitions, 274, 275, 280, 282; and the war with Iraq, 276; and the Chief of Staff's air crash, 278; assassination, 281–2
Behshahr, 263
Beirut, 165, 166, 259, 285, 288
Bengal, 52
Berlin Radio, 98, 99
Berri, Nabih, 305
Bohlul, 93
Bojnurdi, Sayyed Kazem, 189
Bokhara'i, Mohammad, 156
Bolshevik Revolution, 65–6
Bolsheviks (Fedayeen Khalq), 259–60
Bolsheviks (Russia), 56, 65, 68, 71
Bonyad-e-Mustadh'afeen (the Foundation for the Downtrodden), 297
Bonyad-e-Shahid (the Martyrs' Foundation), 297
Borhan, Karim, 127
Borujerd, 103
Borujerdi, Grand Ayatollah Mohammad-Hussein, 103–4, 105–11, 114, 115–17, 122, 125, 135, 146
Boyer, Ahmad, 129
Brandt, Willy, 208
Brigade of Cossacks, 69
Britain, 152, 167–8, 209, 215, 224, 277; First World War, 38–9, 56; military presence in Iran, 40; influence in Iran, 64–5, 66, 174; and the 1921 putsch, 70, 72; anti-British feeling in Mesopotamia, 97–8; Second World War, 99–100, 169; and the Fedayeen of Islam, 102; and the downfall of Mossadeq, 110; Khomeini movement seeks support from, 123–4; loans to Iran, 150; Iranians in, 168, 195, 231; Shah blames for his problems, 173, 174; advises Shah to leave Iran, 234
British Broadcasting Corporation (BBC), 16, 98, 99, 158, 219, 223
Brzezinski, Zbigniew, 235

MOSSAD (Israeli Intelligence), 138, 143
Mossadeq, Dr Mohammad, 109, 110, 123, 136, 143, 200, 202, 241
Mossadeqists, 122–3, 129, 185, 186, 200, 201, 238, 241
Mostafa, Sayyed (Khomeini's father), 29, 30–3, 47, 81, 92
Motahari, Ayatollah Morteza, 107, 112, 121, 155, 165, 225, 230, 231, 234; and proposal of direct rule by mullahs, 122, 123; preparations for revolution, 128, 198, 200, 201, 202, 203, 219; and the *hayats*, 149, 168–9; and Mansur's assassination, 156–7; and Khomeini's exile, 159, 163; Khomeini's message to, 182–4, 186–7; nationwide organization, 188–9, 190, 192–3, 195, 197, 217; and the anti-Shah riots, 210; crowd demonstrations, 218; Islamic committees, 222–3; tactics, 233; final phase of revolution, 243; and Khomeini's return to Iran, 245; fears Khomeini may be assassinated, 247; and the trials, 251; assassination, 258, 260
Motorihay-e-Allah (Allah's Motorized Ones), 222, 226
Mowla'i, Ayatollah Ahmad, 183
Mozaffareddin Shah, 40–1
Muawyyah, Caliph, 26
Muhammarah, 72, 277
Muhammed, Prophet, 25, 26, 29, 32–3, 35, 56, 57, 61, 77, 80, 85, 92, 119, 138, 147–8, 162, 176, 178, 241, 245, 305
Muharram, 128, 132, 133, 136, 142, 188, 194
Mujahedeen-e-Khalq-e-Iran (People's Combatants of Iran), 199, 220, 225, 259, 269, 279–85, 291
*mujtahid*, 55, 63–4
mullahs, 51–4, 62–5, 174–5; opposition to Reza Shah, 75–6, 80–1, 94; pilgrimage to Mashhad, 82–7; Reza Shah's hatred of, 88–9; opposition to Tudeh Party, 102, 110; and the Fedayeen of Islam, 106; Mossadeq and, 109; simplicity of life-style, 119; Khomeini proposes direct rule by, 122, 123, 181; opposition to the 'White Revolution', 124–5; the Shah antagonizes, 134–5; under the Safavids, 178–9; *khums*, 31–2, 43, 179–80; the Shah's operations against, 191; Khomeini's support amongst, 192–3; anti-Shah riots, 210; lose secret donations from Prime Minister, 217; Khomeini's treatment of, 256; after the revolution, 260; and the American embassy occupation, 273; and the parliamentary elections, 275; and the war with Iraq, 277; assassinations of, 282, 284; and the defrocking of Shariatmadari, 288; factionalism, 291–5

Muscat, 255
Muslim Brotherhood, 97, 98, 102
Muslim Students' Association of North America, 214
'Muslim Students Following the Imam's Line', 272
Mussa Ibn Jaafar, 7th Imam, 27, 92
Mussavi, Mir-Hussein, 191, 282, 294, 305–6
Mussavi-Ardabili, Ayatollah Abdul-Karim, 234
Mussavi sayyeds, 26–7, 296
Mussavi-Tabrizi, Hussein, 283

Nabavi-Nuri, Ali-Akbar, 191
Nader Shah Afshar, 28
Naderpour, Nader, 120
Nahavand, 189
al-Nahiyan, Shaikh Zayed Ibn Sultan, Emir of Abu Dhabi, 236
Najaf, 17, 25, 27, 38, 80, 96–8, 102–5, 116, 135, 142, 144, 153–4, 155–66, 170, 180, 214–16, 229
Najaf-Abad, 132, 263
Najafi, Grand Ayatollah, 257, 264
Naji, General Reza, 221, 253
Nasiri, Shaikh Mohammad (Yahya Nuri), 226
Nasiri, General Nematollah, 139, 143, 144, 145, 153, 155, 159, 169–70, 187, 252, 253
Nasser, Gamal Abdel, 143
Nassereddin Shah, 29, 181
Nasserism, 303
National Front, 122–3, 124, 202, 231, 280, 281
National Iranian Oil Company (NIOC), 211, 235
National Police, 240
nationalism, Arab, 168, 303; Persian, 72–4, 177, 278
NATO, 244
*Navid (Good News)*, 223, 242
Nawab, 114
Nawab-Safavi, Mohammad, 97, 101–2, 106, 161
Nazih, Hassan, 232
Nazism, 42, 97–8, 106, 131
Neauphle-le-Château, 230–2, 242, 251
Nejati, Hassan, 127
Neqab (the Mask), 291
Neshat, General Ali, 250
New York, 269–70
Neyshabur, 28
Neyshaburi, Sayyed Mohammad-Hussein, 28–9
Niavaran Palace, 228, 290
Niknezhad, Morteza, 156
Nixon, Richard M., 167, 208, 209, 212, 213, 272
Nixon Doctrine, 208